The Acts
of the Apostles
Through the Centuries

Wiley Blackwell Bible Commentaries

Series Editors: John Sawyer, Christopher Rowland, Judith Kovacs, David M. Gunn

The Acts of the Apostles Through the Centuries

Heidi J. Hornik
and
Mikeal C. Parsons

WILEY Blackwell

Registered Office
John Wiley & Sons, Ltd, The Atrium, Southern Gate, Chichester, West Sussex, PO19 8SQ, UK

Editorial Offices
350 Main Street, Malden, MA 021485020, USA
9600 Garsington Road, Oxford, OX4 2DQ, UK
The Atrium, Southern Gate, Chichester, West Sussex, PO19 8SQ, UK

For details of our global editorial offices, for customer services, and for information about how to apply for permission to reuse the copyright material in this book please see our website at www.wiley.com/wileyblackwell.

Library of Congress Cataloging-in-Publication Data

Names: Hornik, Heidi J., 1962– author. | Parsons, Mikeal Carl, 1957– author.
Title: The Acts of the Apostles through the centuries / Heidi J. Hornik and Mikeal C. Parsons.
Description: Chichester, West Sussex ; Malden, MA : John Wiley & Sons Inc., 2016. |
  Includes bibliographical references and index.
Identifiers: LCCN 2016024933| ISBN 9781405176354 (cloth) | ISBN 9781118597897 (epub)
Subjects: LCSH: Bible. Acts–Criticism, interpretation, etc.–History.
Classification: LCC BS2625.52 .H66 2016 | DDC 226.6/0609–dc23
LC record available at https://lccn.loc.gov/2016024933

A catalogue record for this book is available from the British Library.

Cover image: St Michael fighting the dragon (Revelation 12:7-9), woodcut by Albrecht Dürer, 1498, from The Revelation of St John
Cover design: Cyan design

Set in 10/12.5pt Minion by SPi Global, Pondicherry, India
Printed and bound in Malaysia by Vivar Printing Sdn Bhd

10 9 8 7 6 5 4 3 2 1

Contents

List of Figures

The Wiley Blackwell Bible Commentaries series, the first to be devoted primarily to the reception history of the Bible, is based on the premise that how people have interpreted, and been influenced by, a sacred text like the Bible is often as interesting and historically important as what it originally meant. The series emphasizes the influence of the Bible on literature, art, music, and film, its role in the evolution of religious beliefs and practices, and its impact on social and political developments. Drawing on work in a variety of disciplines, it is designed to provide a convenient and scholarly means of access to material until now hard to find, and a much needed resource for all those interested in the influence of the Bible on Western culture.

Until quite recently this whole dimension was for the most part neglected by biblical scholars. The goal of a commentary was primarily if not exclusively to get behind the centuries of accumulated Christian and Jewish tradition to one single meaning, normally identified with the author's original intention.

The most important and distinctive feature of the Wiley Blackwell Commentaries is that they will present readers with many different interpretations of each text, in such a way as to heighten their awareness of what a text, especially a sacred text, can mean and what it can do, what it has meant and what it has done, in the many contexts in which it operates.

The Wiley Blackwell Bible Commentaries will consider patristic, rabbinic (where relevant), and medieval exegesis as well as insights from various types of modern criticism, acquainting readers with a wide variety of interpretative techniques. As part of the history of interpretation, questions of source, date, authorship, and other historical critical and archaeological issues will be discussed, but since these are covered extensively in existing commentaries, such references will be brief, serving to point readers in the direction of readily accessible literature where they can be followed up.

Original to this series is the consideration of the reception history of specific biblical books arranged in commentary format. The chapter by chapter arrangement ensures that the biblical text is always central to the discussion. Given the wide influence of the Bible and the richly varied appropriation of each biblical book, it is a difficult question which interpretations to include. While each volume will have its own distinctive point of view, the guiding principle for the series as a whole is that readers should be given a representative sampling of material from different ages, with emphasis on interpretations that have been especially influential or historically significant. Though commentators will have their preferences among the different interpretations, the material will be presented in such a way that readers can make up their own minds on the value, morality, and validity of particular interpretations.

The series encourages readers to consider how the biblical text has been interpreted down the ages and seeks to open their eyes to different uses of the Bible in contemporary culture. The aim is to write a series of scholarly commentaries that draw on all the insights of modern research to illustrate the rich interpretative potential of each biblical book.

John Sawyer
Christopher Rowland
Judith Kovacs
David M. Gunn

Preface

Acts Through the Centuries is the fourth book we have coauthored together. The first three comprised the trilogy *Illuminating Luke*, which considered Renaissance and Baroque depictions of scenes unique to the Gospel of Luke as examples of "visual exegesis". In some important ways, those books prepared us for this assignment; in some other ways, however, they did not. As part of the context for the paintings, we researched the reception history of the selected passage in the exegetical tradition. This exercise proved extremely useful since it introduced us to a variety of ancient and early modern authors to whom we return for this project. But the *Illuminating Luke* trilogy was very focused and limited: one major painting from a circumscribed historical period (Italian Renaissance/Baroque) that portrayed a specific Lukan scene.

With *Acts through the Centuries* we were charged with covering the entire interpretive history from the composition of the document in the late first/early second century to the twentieth/twenty first century. That was a daunting task that proved, predictably, an impossible undertaking. We have done the best we could to choose verbal and visual interpretations that are either representative of the interpretive traditions or that, in some respect, represent interpretations that depart from the conventional wisdom in distinct and interesting ways. We did not know when we began the project whether we would encounter an embarrassment of exegetical riches or just an embarrassment. We found both!

There are many persons to thank for a project such as this. The University Research Leave Committee at Baylor University granted each of us, at different times, a semester release from our normal duties to undertake this assignment. Our department chairs, Mark Anderson (Art) and Bill Bellinger (Religion) have been unrelenting in their support of our work on this and other projects. Lee Nordt, Dean of the College of Arts and Science and Divisonal Dean for Humanities and Social Sciences Robyn Driskell have supported us in various ways over the course of the project. Allbritton Grants for Faculty Scholarship in the Department of Art provided the resources for research travel as well as for copyright permissions and color illustrations. Mikeal's research assistants over the years, particularly in the final stages, Greg Barnhill, John Duncan, Michael Barnard, and Ryan Harker have rendered enormous help with good cheer. New Testament Series Editors, Judith Kovacs and Christopher Rowlands, gave remarkably detailed and perceptive feedback on various drafts of the manuscript, expanding its scope and enriching its quality. Remaining flaws, of course, are ours.

Over the decade during which we have worked, off and on, on this book, our sons, Mikeal Joseph and Matthew Quincy, have grown from pre adolescent children to young men, both are now in college. They continue to amaze and humble us with their accomplishments! We have learned so much from this project. We hope you too, dear reader, benefit from this catalogue of what others have thought and understood about the Acts of the Apostles through the centuries.

Heidi J. Hornik
Mikeal C. Parsons
Baylor University

Acknowledgements

1. The following materials were used with permission.
    Heidi J. Hornik and Mikeal C. Parsons. "Philological and Performative
    Perspectives on Pentecost." Pp. 137–153 in *Reading Acts Today*. Steve
    Walton, Scott Spencer, Tom Phillips, and Barry Matlock, editors.
    New York: T & T Clark, 2011. By kind permission of Continuum
    International Publishing Group.

    Mikeal C. Parsons and Peter Reynolds. "Early Pentecostals on
    Pentecost." *Perspectives in Religious Studies* 42 (2015): 205–15. Used by
    Permission of the editors.

2. Citations from the following materials were gathered from online databases and websites.

Early modern interpreters were taken from Early English Books Online (writings are indicated in Bibliography).

Martin Luther, Thomas Aquinas, and G. K. Chesterton were taken from the Past Masters Online.

John Chrysostom's *Homilies on Acts*, John Wesley's *Notes on the New Testament*, and John Calvin's *Commentary on Acts* were taken from the online Christian Classics Ethereal Library, with permission.

List of Abbreviations

1 Apol.	Justin, *First Apology*
ACCS	Ancient Christian Commentary on Scripture
Acts Paul	Acts of Paul and Thecla
Adv. Jud.	Tertullian, *Adversus Judaeos*
ANF	*Ante-Nicene Fathers*
Ant.	Josephus, *Jewish Antiquities*
Apol. Rel.	Aquinas, *An Apology for the Religious Orders*
Bapt.	Tertullian, *De baptismo*
Barn.	Barnabas
BW	Bonhoeffer, *Dietrich Bonhoeffers Works*. 17 volumes. Philadelphia: Fortress, 1996–2014.
CCEL	*Christian Classics Ethereal Library* (www.ccel.org)

CCF	*Creeds and Confessions of Faith in the Christian Tradition.* Edited by Jaroslav Pelikan and Valerie Hotchkiss. 3 volumes. New Haven: Yale University Press, 2003.
CCSL	Corpus Christianorum: Series Latina
CD	Karl Barth, *Church Dogmatics*
Cels.	Origen, *Contra Celsum*
CGPNT	J. A. Cramer, ed. Catenae Graecorum partum in Novum Testamentum. 8 vols. Oxford: Clarendon Press, 1840.
Civ.	Augustine, *De civitate Dei*
Clem. Rec.	*Recognitions of Clement*
Coll.	Cassian, *Collationes*
Coll. Max. Ar.	Augustine, *Collatio cum Maximino Arianorum episcopo*
Comm. Acta	Cornelius á Lapide, *Commentaria in Acta Apostolorum*
Comm. Acts	Bede, *Commentary on the Acts of the Apostles: Translated, with an Introduction and Notes.* Translated by Lawrence T. Martin. Kalamazoo, MI: Cistercian Publications, 1989.
Comm. Dan.	Hippolytus, *Commentarium in Danielem*
Comm. Gal.	Aquinas, *Commentary on St. Pauls Epistle to the Galatians*
Comm. Jo.	Origen, *Commentarii in evangelium Joannis*
Comm. Rom.	Aquinas, *Commentary on the Letter of Saint Paul to the Romans*
Comm. Rom.	Origen, *Commentarii in Romanos*
Conf.	Augustine, *Confessions*
c. Symm.	Prudentius, *Liber contra Symmachum*
Cyp. Epist.	Cyprian, *Epistulae*
Cyp. Pat.	Cyprian, *De bono patientiae*
Dem. ev.	Eusebius, *Demonstratio evangelica*
De or.	Cicero, *De oratore*
Dial.	Justin, *Dialogue with Trypho*
Dom. or.	Cyprian, *De dominica oratione*
Ecc. Hist.	Socrates Scholiasticus, *Ecclesiastical History*
Eleem.	Cyprian, *De opera et eleemosynis*
ENNT	John Wesley, *Explanatory Notes on the New Testament*
Etym.	Isidore of Seville, *Etymologies*
Faust.	Augustine, *Contra Faustum Manichaeum*
Fid.	Ambrose, *De fide*
GARBC	General Association of Regular Baptist Churches
Gen. litt.	Augustine, *De Genesi ad litteram*
Geogr.	Strabo, *Geographica*
Gos. Bir. Mary	Gospel of the Birth of Mary
Haer.	Irenaeus, *Adversus haeresus*

Hist. eccl.	Eusebius, *Historia ecclesiastica*
Hom. 1 Cor.	Chrysostom, *Homiliae in epistulam i ad Corinthios*
Hom. Act.	Chrysostom, *Homiliae in Acta apostolorum*
Hom. Lev.	Origen, *Homiliae in Leviticum*
In Matt.	Theophylact, *Explanation of the Gospel of Matthew*
Inf.	Dante, *Inferno*
Inf. Gos. Thom.	Infancy Gospel of Thomas
In Joann.	Augustine, *In Evangelium Iohannis tractatus*
In Ps.	Augustine, *Ennarationes in Psalmos*
Inst.	Quintilian, *Institutio oratoria*
Instit.	Calvin, *Institutes of the Christian Religion*
Jer. *Epist.*	Jerome, *Epistulae*
Jov.	Jerome, *Adversus Jovinianum libri II*
JP	*Søren Kierkegaards Journals and Papers.* 7 volumes. Bloomington: Indiana University Press, 1967–1978.
J.W.	Josephus, *Jewish War*
KJN	*Kierkegaards Journals and Papers.* 11 volumes. Princeton, NJ: Princeton University Press, 2007.
KW	*Kierkegaards Writings.* Princeton, NJ: Princeton University Press, 1978–2000.
LB	Erasmus, *Opera omnia*, ed. J. Clericus. Lugduno Batauorum 1703–1706, 10 vols.
LCL	Loeb Classical Library
LXX	Septuagint
LW	Luther, *Luthers Works.* 55 volumes. Philadelphia: Fortress Press; Saint Louis: Concordia Publishing House, 1955–1986.
Marc.	Tertullian, *Adversus Marcionem*
m. Hag.	m. Hagiga
NIV	New International Version
NPNF	*Nicene and Post-Nicene Fathers*
NRSV	New Revised Standard Version
OAA	*Arator's On the Acts of the Apostles.* Edited and translated by Richard J. Schrader. Translated by Joseph L. Roberts III and John F. Makowski. The American Academy of Religion Classics in Religious Studies 6. Atlanta: Scholars Press, 1987.
Or.	Origen, *De oratione (Peri proseuches)*
Or. Bas.	Gregory of Nazianzus, *Oratio im laudem Basilii*
Per.	Plutarch, *Pericles*
PL	Patrologia Latina [= Patrologiae Cursus Completus: Series Latina]. Edited by JacquesPaul Migne. 217 volumes. Paris, 1844–1864.

Pud.	Tertullian, *De pudicitia*
Pol. *Phil.*	Polycarp, *To the Philippians*
Prax.	Tertullian, *Adversus Praxean*
Prog.	Theon, *Progymnasmata*
Ps.Mt.	Gospel of Pseudo-Matthew
Purg.	Dante, *Purgatorio*
RCS	Reformation Commentary on Scripture
Reg.	Augustine, *Regula ad servos Dei*
Res.	Tertullian, *De resurrectione carnis*
Rhet. Her.	*Rhetorica ad Herennium*
SBC-Lifeway	Southern Baptist Convention – Lifeway Publishing
Scorp.	Tertullian, *Scorpiace*
SKS	*Søren Kierkegaards Skrifter.* 55 volumes. Copenhagen: Gad, 1997.
ST	Aquinas, *Summa Theologiae*
Tert. *Pat.*	Tertullian, *De patientia*
Trin.	Augustine, *De Trinitate*
UCSB	University of California, Santa Barbara
Unit. eccl.	Cyprian, *De catholicae ecclesiae unitate*
Virg.	Tertullian, *De virginibus velandis*
Vit. Ant.	Athanasius, *Vita Antonii*
WA	Augustine, *The Works of Saint Augustine.* Edited by Boniface Ramsey. 50 volumes. Hyde Park, NY: New City Press, 1990.

Introduction

Orienting the Reading

References to Sabbath observance are relatively infrequent in the Scriptures of Israel (cf. e.g., Exod 20:8, 31:14; Lev 23:3; Deut 5:12), and yet the interpretations of Sabbath observance that developed in later Judaism are myriad. The rabbis of old observed this phenomenon and concluded that the many "laws of Shabbat are like mountains hanging from a strand" (m. Hagiga 1:8). The image is arresting: mounds of interpretation hanging from a few strands of Scripture!

The New Testament has generated an equally massive amount of interpretation. The interpretation of the New Testament has been described as a discipline that is "an inch wide but a mile deep" (Epp 1989, xxi). For others, "the

The Acts of the Apostles Through the Centuries, First Edition. Heidi J. Hornik and Mikeal C. Parsons.

New Testament appears like a tiny treasure buried under a mountain of scholarly debris" (Baird 1992, xiii).

What is true of Shabbat regulations or the New Testament generally is no less true of the history of interpretation of the Acts of the Apostles. One need only consider the recently-published, four-volume, 4,500+ page commentary on Acts by Craig Keener (Keener 2012–15); it is a mountain of interpretation by itself! But Acts has not always drawn that kind of attention. In one of his Easter homilies on Acts delivered in 401 C.E., John Chrysostom, Bishop of Constantinople, called Acts a "strange and new dish" and complained that "there are many to whom this book is not even known, and many again think it so plain that they slight it. Thus to some their ignorance, to others their knowledge is the cause of the neglect" (*Hom. Act.* 1). By the twentieth century, however, W.C. van Unnik could famously refer to the Lukan writings as "a storm center in contemporary scholarship" (van Unnik 1980, 15–32). This attention has not come without a price. The theology of Acts has often been labeled as "early Catholic" by modern critical scholarship and, in comparison with Paul's theological vision, found lacking (Vielhauer 1980, 33–50). This reception history commentary on Acts aims to chart the reception of the book of Acts from its relative obscurity in the early church to its recent focus of attention.

The Acts of the Apostles Through the Centuries attempts to fill in the gap created by critical biblical scholarship, which has sought to explicate what Acts "meant" in its original context, and what it now "means" in contemporary terms (cf. Stendahl 1962, 1:418–32). Unfortunately, this construal has operated from the assumption that we need only understand the context of the first century in which most NT texts were produced and the twenty-first century in which these texts are read. In this view, the intervening period (of nearly two thousand years!) is mostly an obstacle to be avoided. Between the original communication, "what it meant," and the contemporary interpretive context, "what it means," however, lies a largely neglected element, "what it *has* meant" at critical moments in its interpretive history. The Blackwell Bible Commentary on Acts joins other efforts in this series, along with scholars such as Brevard Childs (1977), David Steinmetz (1986), Ulrich Luz (2001–2008), and François Bovon (2001–2013), *inter alia*, who have written of the importance of patristic, medieval and reformation hermeneutics. The intent is to scour the "scholarly debris" of interpretation of Acts. After all, one person's trash is another person's treasure!

In this commentary, we examine not only the formal exegetical tradition, but also the influence of Acts on art, literature, music, liturgy, theology, Christian creeds, and film, as part of the *Nachleben*, the afterlife of these stories as they are reconfigured for a different place and time. Sources were chosen because they typify the most common rendering of the text OR, conversely, because they represent some kind of innovation in the tradition. In short, we propose to adopt a "Noah's Ark Principle," in which we include as many species of interpretations from as wide a chronological span, geographical distribution, and theological spectrum as possible (Pelikan and Hotchkiss 2003, henceforth *CCF*).

Certain passages in Acts have drawn more attention than others. For example (with some notable exceptions), the first half of Acts (chapters 1–12)—with the colorful and compelling stories of the Ascension, Pentecost, the Stoning of Stephen, the "Conversion" of Paul, and the liberation of Peter from prison—has generally been the object of more sustained attention than the second half (chapters 13–28), which focuses more on the movements of Paul. And even within each chapter, certain verses have proven to be "magnet texts" for interpreters—especially patristic through early modern—who were interested in finding in Acts scriptural warrant for particular practices or doctrines.

Our textual excavation has revealed that not every verse of Acts has interpretive traditions that run a mile deep. Because of the particular contours of Acts' reception, we have adopted a "sail and dip" method in which we have focused on those magnet texts that either for a particular period or across the span of reception have proven irresistible to subsequent interpreters. This has sometimes resulted in lingering (perhaps overly long) over the interpretive history of a particular text, or even word. Sometimes the focus has resulted in longish quotations from sources that might be unfamiliar to the modern reader. With the visual interpretations, especially, we have labored to provide a sense of how the artwork under consideration fits within the oeuvre of the artist, the theological and cultural context of the artist (and/or patron), as well as the interplay between the style and iconography of the art and interpretation of the text. Our assumption is that the visual tradition, and how to understand it, may be less familiar to readers of Wiley Blackwell's Commentary Series.

Conversely, this focus on the "purple passages" of reception history has resulted in the relative neglect of other passages; readers may be disappointed to find brief or no treatment of certain favorite passages. Our hope is that this disappointment is at least partially compensated for by the rich theological and cultural fare that the commentary does provide. Given our strict word limit and the fact that Acts is the longest document in the New Testament, this is the best we could do!

The plot to the interpretive history of Acts, if there is one to be recovered, has been moved along by a series of conflicts in interpretation, whether between "Petrine" and "Pauline" forms of Christianity (Bauer and the Tübingen

School), or between an apocryphal (e.g., Apocryphal Acts) or canonical reception (e.g., Eusebius) of its historiography/hagiography, or between the tension in reading "history in Acts" (William Ramsay 1897; Gerd Lüdemann 1987/1989) or "Acts in history" (Henry Cadbury 1955). One might be tempted to construe the plot of Acts' interpretation to emulate the Tübingen School's Hegelian reading of Acts (indeed of all early Christian history) as thesis/antithesis/synthesis. We have resisted that construal because (1) the history of interpretation of Acts is not evolutionary (in the sense of making "progress" in a straight line), and (2) the conflict has not frequently resolved in any kind of synthesis. Nonetheless, we will attempt to tell a coherent story of Acts interpretation, while at the same time embracing as much of its interpretive reception as possible. In this regard, we are more interested in the *history* of reception and "on the ways in which readings have developed, interacted, become embodied in the lives of communities, opened up perspectives on, that is, the history of the meanings which the text has generated" than in reception *exegesis*, that is, the "focus on *the text itself* and the *authors' engagement with it*" (Riches 2014, 383–87, esp. 386). Below we briefly sketch the resources available for such an enterprise.

Acts in its Ancient Literary Context(s)

The material in this commentary has been organized into rhetorical units that reflect the relevant attention given to it in the history of interpretation. In some cases, several chapters have been grouped together in units of roughly the same length (see outline below). Acts 2, however, which is the focus of so much attention across the centuries, has been given a double portion. A brief description of the contents of each unit, "Overview," highlights the specific texts that have received the most attention in subsequent reception. This section is followed by "Reception and Interpretation" which deals with sub-units of the text or important themes as they appear sequentially in the text. The interpretations are arranged more or less in chronological order. This chronicle of interpretations constitutes the bulk of the commentary. At times, however, chronology gives way to a thematic grouping of interpretations that, even though from different time periods, address similar issues. By occasionally placing ideas from disparate time periods in conversation with each other, distinct and contrasting interpretations of the text are placed in bolder relief. While we attempt to show the limits and contours of the various receptions, for the most part we refrain from judging their efficacy in reflecting the *intentio operis* or intention of the work.

An Outline of Acts

Acts 1	Jesus' Ascension and the Beginning of the Church
Acts 2	Pentecost
Acts 3–5	Healings and Tensions
Acts 6–8	Stephen and Philip
Acts 9	Paul: Conversion and Call
Acts 10–12	Peter, Cornelius, James, and Herod
Acts 13–14	Paul's Initial Missionary Campaign
Acts 15	The Jerusalem Council
Acts 16–17	Paul in Macedonia and Achaia
Acts 18–19	Paul in and around Ephesus
Acts 20–23	Paul and Jerusalem
Acts 24–26	Paul before the Authorities
Acts 27–28	Paul's Voyage to and Time in Rome

The first half of Acts (chs. 1–12) focuses on events (Ascension, Pentecost) and personalities (Peter, Barnabas, Stephen, Philip) in the earliest church; the second half tends to focus on Paul in different places (Macedonia, Achaia, Ephesus, Jerusalem) and in various predicaments (on trial, on a sea voyage). One of the earliest images of the Apostle Paul comes from a mosaic in Ravenna, Italy and dates to the fifth-sixth century (**Figure 1**). As in later renditions and in keeping with early literary descriptions (see Acts Paul 2.3), Paul is balding; he is also bearded and depicted wearing Roman garb, indicative of his Roman citizenship.

Acts in the Exegetical Tradition(s) of Commentary and Homily

Paul Steuhrenberg (Stuehrenberg 1987, 100–131, has conveniently compiled a list of 148 pre-Reformation authors who have written commentaries or homilies or made extended comments on Acts. Many of these remain unpublished and largely inaccessible.

Pre-modern interpretations of Acts: Patristic through Reformation

Before commenting on individual pre-modern interpreters of Acts, it is important to note some unusual features of the text of Acts. First, the text of Acts has come to us in two forms, commonly known as the "Western" and "Alexandrian" versions

FIGURE 1   *St. Paul*. 5th–6th century. Detail of the vault mosaics. Archbishop's Palace, Ravenna, Italy. Photo: Scala/Art Resource, NY

(Metzger 1994, 222). While arguments have been offered that the Western tradition holds priority over, or at least equal footing with, the Alexandrian version (e.g., Blass 1895; Clark 1933; Boismard and Lamouille 1984; Strange 1992; Ruis-Camps and Read-Heimerdinger 2004–2009), the general consensus is that the Western tradition, which is roughly 8.5–10% longer, is a later and secondary expansion of the Alexandrian text. As such, it represents an early stage in the reception history of canonical Acts (amongst others, cf. Haenchen 1971; Metzger 1975, 272).

Codex D (Cantabrigiensis), a fifth-century bilingual Greek and Latin manuscript, is considered the chief (but not sole) witness to the Western text of Acts. Often the variants in the Western tradition of Acts reflect an intentional effort on the part of ancient readers to clarify certain ambiguities in the text. For example, in Acts 16:6, early users added referents to specify whose "word" (*logos*) was in focus: the word becomes "the word of God" (http://larryhurtado. wordpress.com/2013/10/30/textual-ambiguity-and-textual-variants-in-acts/).

Other variants in Codex D suggest certain kinds of theological tendencies on the part of the scribe(s). These tendencies may include an anti-Jewish bias (cf. Acts 14:2; Epp 1966, 136–7, 169), or a bias against women (1:14; 17:4, 12; Malick 2007, 171–75), or a proto-papacy inclination to elevate the role of Peter among the apostles (Acts 1:23; CroweTipton 1999).

Contemporary readers of Acts are most likely to encounter the impact of the Western version on the interpretation and reception of Acts in those four places in which verses are completely omitted from their translation (or in some versions, such as the NRSV, printed in a footnote):

Acts 8:37: And Philip said, "If you believe with all your heart, you may." And he replied, "I believe that Jesus Christ is the Son of God."
Acts 15:34: But it seemed good to Silas that they remain, and Judas journeyed alone (Codex D; cf. the Majority text, which reads: "But it seemed good to Silas to remain there").
Acts 24:6b–8a: And we would have judged him according to our law. But the chief captain Lysias came and with great violence took him out of our hands, commanding his accusers to come before you.
Acts 28:29: And when he had said these words, the Jews departed, holding much dispute among themselves.

All four additions are in Western witnesses (though Codex D is not extant in three of those instances). In each case, these additions attempt to expand upon or clarify the immediate context. In all four verses, the Western tradition was taken up into the Byzantine or Majority text, which was the basis for the first editions of the Greek text and also the earliest English translations with versification, including the Authorized King James Version. Once it was determined that the verses in question were not part of the "base" text, the editors and translators of the various Greek editions and English translations, rather than renumbering the verses from that point forward, opted rather to omit the verses and the numbers they had been given altogether (as they did in other places in the NT). These variants illustrate the ways in which early readers inscribed their responses into the text itself.

Another interesting issue regards the relationship of Acts to the Gospel of Luke. Common authorship has been assumed since the second century (with some notable exceptions). The two writings, however, have distinct textual histories; there is no Western version of Luke comparable to the Western version of Acts. Furthermore, Luke and Acts were typically treated as separate documents in the early church (see Gregory 2003), a point underscored by the fact that there is no evidence that the two ever circulated together in any pre-canonical form, nor did the two texts ever stand side-by-side in any canonical arrangement of the New Testament (Parsons and Pervo 1993). This early reception of Acts apart from Luke raises questions regarding the best way to read Acts: as "Luke-Acts," that is, as a single, continuous narrative with a single preface (Luke 1:1–4) and intentional parallelisms between the characterization of Jesus in the Gospel and Peter and Paul in Acts? As a sequel to Luke, recognizing certain common literary devices and theological themes, while still respecting differences in emphases and perhaps genre? Or as a sequel to an emerging multi-fold Gospel (that finds later expression in the Tetraevangelium, the Four-Fold Gospel), the chief of which is the Gospel of Luke? (on these and other options, see e.g., Gregory and Rowe 2010).

Irenaeus (c. 125–200), Bishop of Lyon, is the first author to draw extensively on Acts. He cites Acts repeatedly in the early part of Book Three of *Against Heresies*, but also refers to, quotes from or alludes to it in all five books of this work. Tertullian (c. 155–240) also knows and appreciates the book of Acts (see *Bapt.* 4, 10, 13, 18; *Res.* 55; *Prax.* 30; Tert. *Pat.* 14; esp. *Marc.* 5). Likewise, Cyprian, in the middle of the third century, repeatedly uses the expression "in the Acts of the Apostles" (Cyp. *Epist.* 7.3; *Unit. eccl.* 25; *Dom. or.* 32; *Eleem.* 6.25; Cyp. *Pat.* 16; cf. Bovon 2006). Clement of Alexandria (ca.150– ca. 215) and Origen (c.185–235) also make use of Acts.

A list of fourth-century sources containing references to Acts is illustrative of the material available: Apollinaris of Laodicea (310–390), Athanasius (295–373), Basil the Great (329–379), Didymus the Blind (ca. 313–98), Eusebius (260–339), Ephrem the Syrian (c. 306–373), "Commentary on Acts"; John Chrysostom (347–407), *Homilies on the Acts of the Apostles*; among others. Later authors include Arator (sixth century) *On the Acts of the Apostles*.

The Venerable Bede (672/3–735) was a British monastic leader and author of the first extant British commentary on Acts, *Commentary on the Acts of the Apostles*; Humanist Erasmus (1466–1536) also wrote a commentary, *Paraphrase on Acts*. In addition, Augustine (354–430) and Aquinas (1225–1274) made frequent reference to Acts, even though neither produced a commentary per se (on ancient commentary, see Martin 2006).

Much of the material in this early period draws on Acts for theological and Christological reflection. For example, presumably the Apostles' Creed (second century) and later the Nicene Creed (fourth century) both draw on Acts 1 to depict the Ascension as the visible manifestation of Christ's exaltation. Irenaeus found Acts useful in his debates against certain groups regarding the "bodily resurrection and ascension" of Jesus (cf. *Haer.* 1.10.1).

Acts continued to draw the attention of medieval and reformation commentators (cf. Chung-Kim and Hains 2014). John Calvin (1509–64) had a two-volume commentary on Acts. Neither Thomas Aquinas (c.1225–74) nor Martin Luther (1483–1546) wrote full-blown commentaries on Acts, but both made numerous references to the work in their writings. Acts was a favorite text also among those engaged in Radical Reformation, since their views of ecclesiology were profoundly shaped by the witness of Acts. Debates of who should hold church offices and what those offices should be were often underpinned by references to the Acts of the Apostles (especially chapters 6 and 13).

The "invention" of Paul's "three missionary journey"—never referred to by Luke as such—is an example of the use of Acts as scriptural warrant for certain endeavors in the early modern period. The missionary journeys of Paul were part of the propaganda developed by the Society for Promotion of Christian Knowledge (founded 1698) and the Society for the Propagation of the Gospel in Foreign Parts (founded 1701) to provide a biblical pattern for missionaries going out from a central location to the "ends of the earth" and then returning periodically for spiritual renewal, administrative guidance, and financial support (Townsend 1985/1986, 99–104).

The Interpretation of Acts in the Modern Period

It is during the "modern" period (which we will designate as covering the eighteenth century forward) that the questions typically associated with the historical-critical study of Acts emerged. Among the pre-modern assumptions that were critically re-examined was a cluster of assertions surrounding the identity of the author of (Luke and) Acts: (1) the same person wrote both the Third Gospel and Acts; (2) that person was Luke the Physician; (3) Luke was a companion of Paul; (4) and Luke was a Gentile who wrote for a Gentile audience. What one thinks about the identity of Luke rests in large part on one's assessment of early traditions. Either those in the early church had independent access to traditions about the identity of the author of Luke and Acts no longer available to us, or someone deduced the author's identity from the NT evidence and secured a place for Luke very early on. In favor of the first option is the stability of the tradition in identifying Luke as the author. Strictly speaking, Acts, like the other canonical narratives, is an anonymous document making no claims itself about authorship, unlike the disputed Petrine and Pastoral epistles, which, if inauthentic, are pseudonymous, written in the name of someone else. When compared, for example, with the debate that raged in the early church about the authorship of Hebrews, another anonymous document, that all testimony agrees on Luke's identity is no trivial matter. Added to that fact is the relative obscurity of Luke, known only through three passing references in the NT (Philemon 24; Colossians 4:14; 2 Timothy 4:11).

On the other hand, it is possible that someone looking to identify the otherwise anonymous author might have deduced Luke's identity from the text of the NT itself. Presumably the Prologue (Luke 1:1–4), where the author seems to identify himself as a second-generation Christian who was relying on other eyewitness testimony, excludes identifying the author as an Apostle (and thus making the choice of a "lesser" figure almost inevitable). The "we-sections" in Acts (16:10–17; 20:5–15; 21:1–18; 27:1; 28:16) demand someone who was a companion of Paul, and Luke emerges as a likely (though, importantly, not the only) candidate. If, as some now think, the name of Luke was attached to the document shortly after its publication to distinguish it from other Christian Gospels, already known to the general Christian public, then this very early attribution might account for the uniformity of the identification. Many modern interpreters today are agnostic about, or at least less interested in, the issue of authorship, perhaps because of the view that Luke and Acts can be adequately interpreted, despite our limited knowledge about their author. Others, despairing of traditional questions about authorship, have set their eyes on other aspects of the author. Some, using the language of "social location," have tried to position the author (implied or real) in terms of rank, education, relationship to technology, etc. (e.g., Robbins 1991, 305–332).

Another issue that emerged in full force in the modern period revolved around the historical (un)reliability of Acts. Nineteenth-century German historian F.C. Baur famously saw Acts as part of a larger *Tendenz* to reconcile Gentile and Jewish forms of Christianity, represented by Paul and Peter, respectively, and thus questioned the historical reliability of the account (Baur 1887, 1:135; cited in Baird 1992, 1:267). Sir William Ramsey, on the other hand, moved from a skeptic regarding Luke's historical reliability to the position that Luke was a careful and reliable historian. He pointed, for example, to the use by Luke of the correct local titles for local political authorities (Ramsay 1915, 95–97). In *The Book of Acts in History*, Henry Cadbury (1955) proposes to turn the focus from history *in* Acts, that is, questions of historicity, to Acts *in* history, that is to the Greek, Roman, Jewish, and Christian settings in which the book was produced. Others have persisted in their attempts to defend the historical reliability of Acts (Hengel 1980; Hemer 1989). When it comes to the "life of Paul," the modern scholarly consensus is that Paul's letters are to be given priority over Acts in any historical reconstruction (cf. J. Knox 1950; though see also Moessner et al 2014). With the critically acclaimed film, *A Polite Bride*, by author and director Robert Orlando, the views that Acts is secondary to Paul's letters as a historical source and that Acts must be carefully sifted and mined for historical information have now made their way into cinematic culture.

Recent feminist studies and post-colonial studies also have contending views regarding the ideological perspective reflected in the text. These are taken up at relevant points in the commentary (Anderson 2004; Aymer 2012; Gaventa 2004; O'Day 1998).

Conclusion: Key Interpreters

While the voices of a large number of interpreters, spanning many centuries, will be heard in this book, the voices of the following interpreters will be heard especially frequently:

John Chrysostom (347–407) preached an important collection of sermons on Acts, *Homilies on the Acts of the Apostles.*

St. Augustine (354–430) was Bishop of Hippo and an influential theologian in Western Christianity. His interpretations of Acts frequently reflected past interpretation or shaped subsequent reception.

Arator (490–550), wrote an influential commentary on Acts in poetic form, *On the Acts of the Apostles.*

Venerable Bede (673–735) wrote one of the first commentaries on Acts.

Aquinas (c.1225–74) was a medieval Christian theologian who made many references to Acts in his writings.

Erasmus (1469–1536) was a renowned Dutch Humanist theologian who wrote a commentary on Acts, *Paraphrases on Acts.*

Martin Luther (1483–1546) was leader of the Protestant Reformation in Germany. He made many influential references to Acts but did not publish a commentary on it.

John Calvin (1509–64) was a Magisterial Reformer who wrote an important two-volume commentary on Acts.

Søren Kierkegaard (1813–55) was a Danish philosopher and theologian who made significant use of Acts in his writings.

Karl Barth (1886–1968) was a Swiss Reformed theologian and leader of the "neo-Orthodox" movement, who made significant use of Acts in his highly influential *Church Dogmatics.*

Dietrich Bonhoeffer (1906–45) was a German Lutheran theologian and martyr. Acts figured prominently in his writings.

The interpretations of these core authors provide a touchstone throughout the commentary; we have consulted them for every section of Acts. When the comments of each of these authors are read together (with the aid of the index), they reveal interpretive threads that at times reflect the dominant exegetical traditions and, at times, resist them. A list of brief biographies of interpreters, along with a glossary of selected terms, is located at the back of the volume to assist the reader.

Acts in the Liturgical Tradition of Calendar, Lectionary and Creeds

Although Acts is not part of the regular readings in the various lectionary traditions, it does appear with some frequency (though curiously with nothing beyond chapter 19; http://www.textweek.com/acts.htm. Accessed 9 November 2006). Two of the four principle feasts of the Christian calendar—the Feast of the Ascension and the Feast of Pentecost—are based on the book of Acts (these are also holy days of obligation in the Roman church). In addition, the Feast Days of Saint Stephen and Saint Paul use readings from Acts in their liturgy.

	RCL	Roman	Episcopal	Lutheran	United Methodist
Acts 1:1–11	Ascension ABC	Ascension ABC	Ascension ABC Easter 7A	Ascension ABC	Ascension ABC
Acts 1:6–14	Easter 7A	Easter 7A	Easter 7A	Easter 7A	Easter 7A
Acts 1:15–26	Easter 7B	Easter 7B	Easter 7B	Easter 7B	Easter 7B
Acts 2:1–21	Pentecost A Pentecost B Pentecost C	Pentecost A Pentecost B Pentecost C	Pentecost A Pentecost B Pentecost C	Pentecost A Pentecost B Pentecost C	Pentecost A Pentecost B Pentecost C
Acts 2:14–41	Easter 2A Easter 3A	Easter 3A Easter 4A	Easter 2A Easter 3A	Easter 2A Easter 3A	Easter 2A Easter 3A
Acts 2:42–47	Easter 4A	Easter 2A	Easter 3A	Easter 4A	Easter 4A
Acts 3:1–7					
Acts 3:12–26	Easter 3B	Easter 3B	Easter 2B	Easter 3B	Easter 3B
Acts 4:5–12	Easter 4B	Easter 4B	Easter 3B	Easter 4B	Easter 4B
Acts 4:23–37	Easter 2B	Easter 2B	Easter 4B	Easter 2B	Easter 2B
Acts 5:12–29		Easter 2C	Easter 2C		
Acts 5:27–41	Easter 2C	Easter 3C	Easter Evening A Easter Evening B Easter Evening C Easter 2C	Easter 2C	Easter 2C
Acts 6:1–9		Easter 5A	Easter 4A		
Acts 7:1–60	Easter 5A	Easter 7C	Easter 4A	Easter 5A	Easter 5A
Acts 8:5–8		Easter 6A			
Acts 8:14–17	Baptism C	Easter 6A		Baptism C	Baptism C

	RCL	Roman	Episcopal	Lutheran	United Methodist
Acts 8:26–40	Easter 5B		Easter 5B	Easter 5B	Easter 5B
Acts 9:1–20	Easter 3C		Easter 3C	Easter 3C	Easter 3C
Acts 9:26–31		Easter 5B			
Acts 9:36–43	Easter 4C			Easter 4C	Easter 4C
Acts 10:25–34		Easter 6B			
Acts 10:34–43	Baptism A Easter Day A Easter Day B Easter Day C	Baptism A Easter Day A Baptism B Easter Day B Baptism C Easter Day C	Baptism A Easter Day A Baptism B Easter Day B Baptism C Easter Day C	Baptism A Easter Day A Easter Day B Easter Day C	Baptism A Easter Day A Easter Day B Easter Day C
Acts 10:44–48	Easter 6B	Easter 6B		Easter 6B	Easter 6B
Acts 11:1–18	Easter 5C			Easter 5C	Easter 5C
Acts 11:19–30			Easter 6B		
Acts 13:14–52		Easter 4C Proper 7C/Ordinary 12C	Easter 4C Easter 5C		
Acts 14:8–18			Easter 6C		
Acts 14:21–27		Easter 5C			
Acts 15:1–29		Easter 6C			
Acts 16:9–15	Easter 6C			Easter 6C	Easter 6C
Acts 16:16–34	Easter 7C		Easter 7C	Easter 7C	Easter 7C
Acts 17:1–15			Easter 5A		
Acts 17:22–31	Easter 6A		Easter 6A	Easter 6A	Easter 6A
Acts 19:1–7	Baptism B			Baptism B	Baptism B

Acts has also played an important role in the various confessions and creeds produced over the two thousand-year history of the Christian church. Fortunately, Jaroslav Pelikan and Valerie Hotchkiss have collected nearly three hundred creeds and statements of faith from a wide variety of confessional communities and published them in a magisterial three-volume work, *Creeds and Confessions of Faith in the Christian Tradition* (2003). Since creeds often reflect the theological conflicts and tensions of the age in which they were produced, we drew upon these resources to gain a deeper understanding into the role of Acts in these hermeneutical and theological debates. In particular, we have made use of creeds and confessions formulated in sixteenth- and seventeenth-century England by dissenters, Baptists, and nonconformists, and have referred to important individuals from this period (John Smyth, John Gill, Hanserd Knollys, and others). This period represents a complicated and "rough and tumble" period of religious history in which dissenters were engaged in debates with establishment Anglicans as well as each other. Religious leaders moved in and out of various groups, which were themselves quite fluid. Political issues mingled with doctrinal controversies to produce a period of tumultuous upheaval. The confessions produced by Baptists and Separatists during this period provide a window into these debates in which the interpretation of Acts figured prominently (on issues such as the separation of church and state, the validity of infant baptism, church polity and governance, etc.), and we make ample use of them.

- 1611 Declaration of Faith
- 1612–1614 Propositions and Conclusions Concerning True Christian Religion
- 1644 First London Baptist Confession
- 1651 The Faith and Practice of Thirty Congregations
- 1654 The True Gospel-Faith Declared According to the Scriptures
- 1656 The Somerset Confession of Faith
- 1655 Midland Confession of Faith
- 1660 The Standard Confession
- 1678 The Orthodox Creed
- 1689 Second London Baptist Confession

We do not mean to imply that Acts does not play a significant role in creeds produced by other denominations. Pelikan and Hotchkiss list over 1200 references to Acts in some 300 creeds over the history of the Christian tradition. In Appendix 1, we have produced a scriptural index to those creeds for readers interested in learning how Acts has figured in other Christian traditions.

In conclusion, by gaining some sense of how Acts "has been prayed and sung in its liturgy, confessed in its creeds and confessions of faith, [and] defended by its seven ecumenical councils" (Pelikan 2005, 26) we may come to a better understanding of the liturgical function of the book within worshipping communities over the ages.

Acts in Literature and the Arts

The influence of the book of Acts on the "aesthetic" tradition has not been inconsequential. Certain figures (Stephen, Judas) and events (Pentecost, Paul's Damascus Road experience) have entered into the cultural thesaurus of popular religious imagination (cf. Jeffrey 1992). Likewise, at least since the medieval hymn, *Veni Sancte Spiritus* (the "Golden Sequence" sung during the Mass of Pentecost), various themes in Acts have been pursued in music, especially (but not exclusively) in the Christian hymn tradition. For example, echoes of Acts appear in the hymns by the Wesley brothers, John and Charles. In *A Collection of Hymns, for the Use of the People Called Methodists* (London, 1780), Wesley sometimes prefaces a hymn with a scriptural reference or (less frequently) a citation, as is the case with Hymn 860:
> "Peter and John went up into the temple at the hour of prayer" –

> Acts iii, 1.
> WHO Jesus our example know,
> And his Apostles' footsteps trace,
> We gladly to the temple go,
> Frequent the consecrated place
> At every solemn hour of prayer,
> And meet the God of mercy there.

One of the distinctive features of this volume is the sustained attention paid to the reception of the text in the visual arts. Visual depictions of the biblical text, until recently, represent understudied examples of the reception history of the biblical text. Connoiseurship, stylistic analysis, and especially iconography can illuminate our understanding of the text by a particular artist (and/or patron).

Luke as Painter

The focus on Acts in art may also be justified, in part, by appealing to an ancient legend attributed to Theodorus Lector (c. 530) that Luke was himself an artist, most famous for painting an icon of the Virgin Mary (see Hornik and Parsons 2003). The origins of the legend about Luke the painter are not clear. One fascinating theory has emerged that the motif of the painting evangelist had a long pre-history (Klein 1933). The image of the reading philosopher in the classical period became, in the Augustan period, that of a writer, which served as a model for the writing evangelist. Later a painting board was substituted for the codex, transforming the figure into the painter saint. What this view fails to account for is why it is Luke and not one of the other Evangelists around whom this legend grows. Two possibilities commend themselves.

First, note that all the paintings attributed to Luke are paintings of Mary and, in fact, countless Byzantine images of the Madonna have been attributed to Luke. Augustine, fourth–fifth century Bishop of Hippo, had commented that no one knew what the Virgin looked like (*Trin.* 8.5.7), but at some point there arose the need is to have a *"vera ikon"* (a true image) of the Madonna. Logically, the image had to have been painted by someone who lived in Mary's time. Who better than Luke, who writes more about Mary and the infancy of Christ than all the other canonical Gospel writers combined, fits the bill? Thus, the desire for an "authentic" likeness of the Madonna may have spurred the transformation of Luke into a painter.

Second, in addition to Luke's apparent knowledge of Mary, his literary artistry as a writer may also have contributed to his depiction as a painter. Jerome (c.340–420) comments several times on the quality of Luke's writing style. In his *Commentary on Isaiah*, he asserts that Luke's "language in the Gospel, as well as in the Acts of the Apostles, that is, in both volumes is more elegant, and smacks of secular eloquence" (3.6). Elsewhere, he notes that Luke "was the most learned in the Greek language among all the evangelists" (*Jer. Epist.* 20.4). Evidence of the high regard for Luke's literary prowess, while sporadic, continued right through the Medieval and Renaissance Periods. In *The Golden Legend*, for example, Jacobus de Voragine (1229–1298) praises Luke's writing as clear, pleasing, and touching.

Clarity is combined with vividness as virtues extolled in the ancient rhetorical handbook tradition from the Hellenistic period (see Quintilian, *Inst.* 8.3.62; *Rhet. Her.* 4.39.51). The authors of the so-called *progymnasmata* (rhetorical exercises for schoolboys) also commended the vividness, clarity, and style of both the accomplished speaker and writer. The first-century C.E. author, Aelius Theon, combines clarity and vividness when he asserts that the "desirable qualities of a description are these; above all, clarity and vividness, in order that what is being reported is virtually visible" (*Prog.* 7.53–55). Since "clarity" was so often linked to "vividness" (i.e., appealing to the eye and not the ear), it was a simple move to characterize Luke the rhetorical artist as the painting evangelist. Thus, Luke's attention to Mary combined with his rhetorical artistry commended him as the one obvious choice to be credited with painting an authentic likeness of Mary.

These traditions of Luke as physician and painter coalesced in a most remarkable way around an image of the Virgin and Child in S. Maria Maggiore.

The *Golden Legend* reports that St. Gregory the Great (c. 540–604) carried the portrait of the Virgin, attributed to Luke, through the city streets in an effort to stop the plague. Thus, just as Luke's literary work was believed to be an example of his expertise in the "art of curing souls" (Eusebius, *Hist. eccl.* 3.4), so here Luke's work of art also becomes a vehicle of healing.

The image of Luke painting the Virgin becomes itself a popular subject in the regions north and south of the Swiss Alps during the Renaissance period (e.g., Rogier van der Weyden, *St. Luke Drawing the Virgin and Child*, c. 1435; Guercino, *Saint Luke Displaying a Painting of the Virgin*, 1652–53). Eventually, this tradition of Luke the Painter gave rise to another, Luke as patron saint of artists. Thus, late medieval Florentine painters belonged to the Guild of Doctors and Pharmacists not only because they ground their colors as pharmacists ground materials for medicines, but also because painters and doctors enjoyed the protection of the same patron saint, St. Luke, physician and painter (Howe 1996, 19:787–789). Thus artists may have been drawn to subjects found in Acts (and Luke) because of the affinity they felt to Luke the painting evangelist!

In any case, the visual tradition of depicting Acts in art is an important, if often neglected, aspect of the history of interpretation. In this volume, we will discuss in detail more than forty images from across the centuries so as to remind readers (most of whom are more accustomed to dealing with texts than images) of the importance of examining these works of art within their historical context(s). Our assumption is that most readers are better prepared to provide the larger context for the various textual intepretations than they may be for the visual arts.

In this volume, then, we utilize an art-historical methodology of interpretation on the works of art. Each object is placed in its historical context and informed by the political, social and religious cultures in which it was created. The object's meaning or iconography is discussed alongside its formal stylistic characteristics (color, line, shape, composition, medium). The patron and original program (if known) complete the iconological interpretation. Many of the objects have been shaped by the concerns of the patrons who often introduce visual elements drawn from extra canonical sources (written and visual) where needed. So, against popular imagination, rarely do we ever have the artist as individual genius interpreting the text as *Scriptura Nuda* (the bare text), but always informed by theological advisors and shaped by various traditions of which the text is first among equals. To leap into iconography prematurely and to avoid a discussion of the artist, the patron, the style and the iconology does a disservice to the object and gives an incomplete interpretation. We hope the reader will enjoy this brief glimpse into art history in a truly trans-disciplinary study of Acts through the centuries.

Conclusion

The Acts of the Apostles has exerted an enormous influence on subsequent Christian theology, liturgy, and practice, and obviously we have not in this survey been able to deal adequately with all the issues surrounding its interpretation across the centuries. Various observations about the ways in which the text's reception history illuminate its originating meaning(s) are scattered throughout the commentary. But the use and influence of sacred texts has value more than simply clarifying or reinforcing textual meaning. One scarlet thread running through much of this material is an explicit interest in using the Scripture to articulate (or sometimes to justify) doctrine or to shape (or sometimes to justify) ecclesial practices. The interpretation of Acts has not only been shaped by its reception; the world receiving Acts has been profoundly shaped by the text. As Luke Timothy Johnson has observed:

> At the beginning of the 21st century, precisely when the limitations of the historical-critical approach to the Bible have become clear to nearly everyone, there has simultaneously arisen the corresponding realization that the examination of the world that produced the Bible is not nearly so satisfying or important as appreciating the world that the Bible produced (Johnson 2004, 41).

It is "the world that the Bible produced" and the specific ways in which Acts contributed to that world that demands our attention in the pages that follow. The differences in interpretation, however, cannot only, or always, be explained on the basis of the social location or vested theological interests of the interpreter; rather, they may reflect to some degree the wonderful and mystical polyvalence and ambiguity of the language of Scripture (or indeed any language) that continues to baffle its readers and their attempts to explain the ineffable.

Acts 1

Overview

The first chapter of the Acts of the Apostles narrates two events: Jesus' final instructions to and departure from the disciples who then return to Jerusalem (1:1–14), and the death of Judas and his replacement in the circle of the Twelve with Matthias (1:13–26). In the first section, it is the nature and significance of Jesus' ascension that occupy the attention of subsequent interpreters, both modern and premodern, especially in the creedal tradition.

The Acts of the Apostles Through the Centuries, First Edition. Heidi J. Hornik and Mikeal C. Parsons.
© 2017 Heidi J. Hornik and Mikeal C. Parsons. Published 2017 by John Wiley & Sons, Ltd.

In the New Testament, the ascension is alluded to in John 20:17, Ephesians 4:8–10, and 1 Timothy 3:16, but the departure of the resurrected Jesus is narrated only in Luke 24:50–52 (although see the textual problem in 24:51), Acts 1:1–11, and Mark 16:19 (the Markan account is generally accepted to be dependent on Luke/Acts, see Kelhoeffer 2000). Whether or not Jesus ascended bodily was of concern to patristic interpreters (cfr. Irenaeus below), and while Augustine could boast that the whole world accepted the bodily resurrection, that view would be severely challenged with the rise of historical skepticism in the Enlightenment (see Strauss 1835). The Ascension scene was a favorite in various media, from bas relief sculpture to book illumination to oil on panel. Who witnessed the ascension (only the apostles? Mary? others?) and where the event took place are also items of concern to some intepreters.

In the second unit (1:15–26), attempts to harmonize Acts' account of Judas' death with Matthew's (and sometimes also Papias) resulted in a variety of solutions (cf., among others, Ephrem the Syrian and the Vulgate translation). Further, the details of the selection process for Judas' replacement intrigued readers: did the whole community participate, or was it just the Apostles, or even Peter alone? Less popular than the death of Judas in the visual arts, but not entirely overlooked, was the election of Matthias to replace Judas (see Rockefeller-McCormick manuscript illumination). Over the centuries, most of the interpretations, in general, have focused on the christological and ecclesiological issues that arise from these two passages.

Reception and Interpretation

Jesus' Ascension (1:1–14)

Before Jesus ascends, Luke notes that he appeared to the disciples over the course of forty days (1:3). The Venerable Bede, eighth-century British monk and exegete, draws a typological comparison: "Now this number [forty] designates this temporal earthly life, either on account of the four seasons of the year, or on account of the four winds of the heavens. For after we have been buried in death with Christ through baptism, as though having passed over the path through the Red Sea, it is necessary for us, in this wilderness, to have the Lord's guidance" (*Comm. Acts* 10).

Karl Barth focuses on the command that the Christian bears witness (Acts 1:8) to the mighty deeds of Christ:

> "Ye shall be witnesses unto me" (Ac. 1[8]) – this is enough for the one to whom Christ speaks and who has heard Him. Whether strong or weak, willing or unwilling, successful or unsuccessful, the Christian is a witness, irrespective of

whether the miracle occurs, or whether it occurs visibly or invisibly. In all circumstances and with his whole existence he is a responsible witness of the Word of God. He is called to be this (*CD* 4.3.609).

Following Christ's commission to the disciples, he departs from them. Luke is the only New Testament writer to narrate Jesus' ascension (Acts 1:9–11, Luke 24:50–53; but the event is alluded to in John 20:17 and found in the longer ending of Mark [16:19]; see also Eph 4:7–10). The Ascension was viewed as a visible manifestation of Christ's exaltation to the right hand of the Father. Early Christian creedal formulations ("He ascended into heaven, and sits at the right hand of God the Father Almighty"), such as is found in the second-century Apostles' Creed and the fourth-century Nicene Creed, reflect language of Christ's ascension and exaltation that borrows directly, if only partially, from Acts (the depiction of Christ's exaltation in terms of being seated "on the right hand" derives from early Christian interpretation of Ps 110:1; echoed also in, e.g., Mark 16:19; Rom 8:24; Heb 1:3, 8:1, 10:12; Eph 1:20; Col 3:1). The significance of Jesus' ascension for the creeds and confessions of the Church has been captured in the "Syndogmaticon" ("an index of the doctrines of the Christian tradition as they appear in the various creeds and confessions of faith") by Pelikan and Hotchkiss, who catalogue nearly thirty representative creeds and confessions that echo the claim of the Niceno-Constantinopolitan Creed that Christ "went up into the heavens" (*CCF*, 1:915).

Early Christians drew out theological implications from what they believed was the reality of Christ's bodily ascension into heaven. Pseudo-Justin appealed to Acts 1 in defense of the view that not only could flesh be resurrected, it could also rise: "And when he had thus shown them that there is truly a resurrection of the flesh, he also wished to show them that it is not impossible for flesh to ascend into heaven (as he had said that our dwelling place is in heaven), so 'he was taken up into heaven while they beheld,' just as he was in the flesh" (*Fragments of the Lost Work of Justin on the Resurrection* 9; *ANF* 1:298; ACCS, 11).

This emphasis on the "bodily resurrection" was also useful to Irenaeus (c. 125–200), in his polemic against Gnostic epistemological, cosmological, and anthropological dualism, which viewed ascension as "a strictly vertical affair" meant to disassociate the spiritual from the "corrupt realm of material existence" (Farrow 1999, 46). Near the beginning of *Adversus omnes haereses*, Irenaeus asserts that God's Spirit had "proclaimed through the prophets and the dispensations of God, and the advents, and the birth from a virgin, and the passion and resurrection from the dead, and *the ascension into heaven in the flesh* [*et in carne in caelos ascensionem*] of the beloved Christ Jesus, our Lord" (*Haer.* 1.10.1; a theme he returns to at the end, cf. 5.36.3). It is crucial for

Irenaeus that Christ descended and ascended "in the flesh" in order to redeem the flesh (see *Haer.* 1.9.3; 3.6.2; 3.16.5ff; etc.).

Origen, on the other hand, recommends "thinking of the ascension of the Son to the Father in a manner more befitting his divinity, with sanctified perspicuity, *as an ascension of the mind rather than of the body*" (*Or.* 23.2; emphasis added). Origen, in agreement with certain Gnostics, separates the exalted Christ from the human Jesus, precisely at the point of the ascension, though his affirmation of the historicity of the incarnation and resurrection caused him to occupy a space somewhere between Irenaeus and the Gnostics on the issue (Farrow 1999, 99–100).

In *The City of God*, Augustine asserts the triumph of the "bodily ascension" with what would be viewed as hyperbole today, if not then as well: "Even if we should grant the resurrection of the earthly body was once beyond belief, the fact is that the *whole world* now believes that the earthly body of Christ has been taken up to heaven. Learned and unlearned alike no longer doubt the resurrection of his flesh and his ascension into heaven, while there is but a handful of those who continue to be puzzled" (*Civ.* 22.5; emphasis added). Despite his physical absence, Christ continues to be present in the Eucharist: "he ascended into heaven, and is no longer here. He is there indeed, sitting at the right hand of the Father; and he is here also, never having withdrawn the presence of his glory" (*In Joann.* 50.13).

The Disciples' Response and the Role of Mary

The fourth-century Munich ivory (**Figure 2**) is a Hellenistic or Western type (defined as a realistic rendering typical of the Greco-Roman style) (Dalton 1909, 191). The ivory is one of the earliest visual depictions of the Ascension and reflects a meditative aspect of the journey of both Christ and pilgrim (Hansen 2011). While later depictions will often couple the ascension with the Second Coming and/or Last Judgment, the artist here has combined it with the resurrection account. By collapsing the two events into one scene, the point is made that without the resurrection there can be no ascension (Hansen 2011). The artist borrows details from Matthew 28 to depict two soldiers at the tomb, one of whom has apparently fainted (Matt 28:4). The focus of the scene, however, is on the ascension and the meditation of three Marys on that event. Their gaze is directed by the angel to Christ's ascension. Luke's description of the Mount of Olives as a "sabbath's day journey from Jerusalem" (Acts 1:12) highlights the scene of the ascension as a distinct location, the only narrative setting dignified as a "mountain" in Acts (Alexander 2001, 1031). The ivory picks up this detail, depicting a beardless Christ ascending a mountain, while

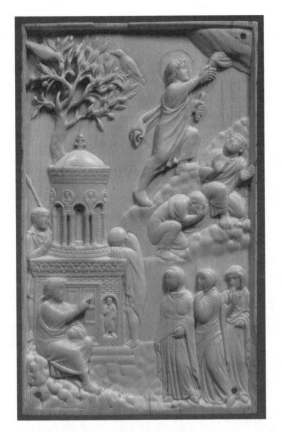

FIGURE 2   *Ascension and the Three Marys.* 4th century. Ivory plaque. Bayerischers Nationalmuseum, Munich. Photo: Bayerischers Nationalmuseum, Munich. Inv.-No. MA 157, Photo No. D27841

one disciple gazes upward in astonishment and the other kneels in prayer. On the ivory, the hand of God reaches towards Christ and helps him make his final ascent into heaven. Through the disciple's example of contemplative prayer, the viewer of the ivory is encouraged "to experience the events surrounding the Resurrection first-hand" (Hansen 2011). Christ climbs up a hill rather than being levitated to Heaven (for a more "ephemeral" ascension, see William Blake's Ascension, 1803–05, Fitzwilliam Museum, Cambridge; Butlin 1981, vol. 2, plate 574). The artist may have been aware of extra-biblical traditions such as the apocryphal *Gospel of Peter* that stated Christ ascended directly from the tomb (Kessler 1979, 110).

   The Oriental or Eastern type of the Ascension is depicted in the Rabbula Syriac Gospels (**Figure 3**), written in Zagba, Mesopotamia by the monk Rabbula

FIGURE 3   *Ascension.* Miniature depicted on folio l3v. of the Syriac Evangeliary of Rabbula (Ms. Plut. I 56). 586. Parchment codex. Bibliotcca Laurenziana, Florence, Italy. Photo: Alinari/Art Resource, NY

in the year 586 C.E. (Wright 1973, 197, 199–208). These two depictions of the Ascension not only offer two of the earliest depictions in ivory and on parchment, respectively, but also set the iconography for centuries to come. The ascending Christ and the earthly–heavenly realms, as well as the focus on the Virgin Mary who is mentioned in Acts 1:14 though not in the account of the ascension (and especially prominent in the Rabbula Gospels' depiction), will remain the two primary compositional arrangements. The other women mentioned in Acts 1:14 did not fare so well among early Christian interpreters as did Mary. In Acts 1:14, Codex D adds the words "and children" to the word "women," which has the effect of changing the phrase's meaning from the "women" (presumably who followed Jesus since Galilee; see Luke 8:3) to the "wives and children" of the apostles.

The beginning of the Rabbula manuscript includes nineteen pages of canon tables, with illustrations of the life of Christ (fols. 3v–12v). A colophon near the end of this Syriac codex dates the completion of the book by a monk named Rabbula to 586 C.E., and although there is disagreement on whether the twenty-six pages of illustrations preceding the Gospel text were part of the original manuscript or inserted at the time of the colophon's composition, there is general agreement that the illustrations date no later than the completion of the manuscript late in the sixth century C.E. Full-page illustrations include the rarely depicted election of Matthias (fol. 1r, depicting Acts 1:15–26) and Virgin and Child (fol. 1v). The last two pages depict the crucifixion and empty tomb (fol. 13r), the ascension (fol. 13v), Christ enthroned (fol. 14r), and Pentecost (fol. 14v). The addition of two scenes from Acts to a Gospels manuscript is rare, but not unprecedented: P45, in the Chester Beatty Library, is the earliest, extant collection of the four Gospels (third century C.E.) and also contains Acts.

The figure of Christ is positioned in a mandorla (almond-shaped frame) with his right hand in a blessing gesture and his left holding a scroll. The background of the mandorla is an aquamarine blue. Christ, flanked by two angels, is bearded and wears a golden nimbus (a special type of halo reserved for Christ that reveals the arms of the cross). Two additional angels on either side of Christ, clothed in pale blue gowns with rose-colored mantles, offer crowns to Christ. Below the mandorla are four orange wings filled with eyes, and from the wings project the heads of an angel, an ox, an eagle, and a lion (Dewald 1915, 282). These are the iconographic symbols of the four Gospel writers: Matthew, Luke, John, and Mark, respectively, a tradition that goes back to Revelation 4:6–8, as interpreted by Irenaeus (*Haer.* 3.1.8). The hand of God is also visible below the wings. There is a clear distinction between this heavenly realm and those figures who remain on earth.

Two angels appear on either side of Mary, and each addresses a group of six apostles. Peter, carrying a cross, is present on the right-hand side of the group. Paul, holding a book in his hand, leads the group on the left. Although Paul was not present in Luke's account of the Ascension, his presence in Rabbula's depiction here reminds the viewer of the central role these two figures, Peter and Paul, hold in the organization of Acts. In fact, the parallelism between Peter and Paul in Acts is largely responsible for the pairing of these two key figures in subsequent Christian art; see, for example, El Greco's portrait with Peter (with his

FIGURE 4   El Greco (1541–1614). *Saints Peter and Paul.* 1587–92. Oil. Hermitage, St. Petersburg, Russia. Photo: Scala/Art Resource, NY

iconographic symbol, the kingdom's keys) on the viewer's left, and the balding Paul (with a book to indicate that he is a scholar-writer) on the right (**Figure 4**).

In the Rabbula Ascension depiction, however, center stage on the "earthly realm" belongs to Mary, who stands directly beneath the mandorla of Christ. Her hands are open in exaltation and direct the viewer to each of the angels standing beside her. While Mary is not explicitly mentioned by Luke as being present at the ascension, she is introduced immediately thereafter at 1:14, and her prominence at the ascension grows in both the literary and visual presentations of the event (see also Fra Angelico's version of this scene below). Mary's growing importance in the theological tradition had been signaled by her affirmation as *Theotokos,* "Mother of God," at the Synod of Ephesus in 431 (Wood 2012, 32). Combined with her symbolic representations as the "Second Eve" and the "church," Mary's role as the "one who gave birth to the one who is God" (Pelikan 1996) formed the basis of Marian piety in the Middle Ages. While the text of Acts does not explicitly state that Mary (and other women and disciples) were present at Pentecost, neither does it preclude such an interpretation.

A depiction from the workshop of the Italian Renaissance artist, Fra Angelico, offers another example of the prominence of Mary at Christ's ascension, in which Christ is now only partially visible as he ascends to heaven (**Figure 5**). The fifteenth-century monk of San Marco was in the employ of both father and son, Cosimo and Piero de' Medici, at the time that this panel was painted (Hood 1993, 239). This was a commission by Piero, but Fra Angelico was also completing the last stages of work in the monastery fresco decorations of the monks' cells. Piero de' Medici commissioned the artist to decorate the doors of a silver treasury for the new oratory to be constructed near the chapel of the Santissima Annunziata in the church of the same name (Spike 1997). This is the last commission received by Fra Angelico, and he was not able to complete it before he was called back to Rome, where he died in 1455. Santissima Annunziata was the mother church to the Servite order, which was founded in Florence (the only order originating in the city) by St. Filippo Benizzi (c. 1233–1285). The church had just been renovated by the architect Michelozzo at the request of Piero de' Medici, and the *armadio degli argenti* (Silver Chest) was to hold the silver offerings to the Annuciation. By the early fifteenth century, the church had become the center of a major cult of the Annunciation and received donations of precious silver.

The chest was wooden, and the two movable shutters containing forty small scenes were to be painted by Fra Angelico and his assistants. Thirty-two of these scenes have survived on three large panels containing nine, twelve, and eleven scenes. The *Ascension* is part of the panel (123 × 160 cm) containing Scenes from the Life of Christ. The scenes on this panel are Christ Carrying the Cross, Derobing of Christ, Crucifixion, Deposition, Descent into Limbo, Women at the Tomb, Ascension, Pentecost, Last Judgment, Coronation of the Virgin, and "Lex Amoris" (the "law of Love"). The subjects are found in biblical and extra-biblical writings.

The *Ascension* by Fra Angelico uses the heavenly–earthly composition also found in the Rabbula manuscript. The eleven apostles, two angels and Mary are united in a circle in the lower half of the painting. Peter, with his keys, is identifiable to the right of Mary. He is the only apostle with an attribute. Only the lower portion of Christ's drapery can be seen in a yellow circle in the heavens. The top and bottom borders of the square composition contain legible inscriptions on scrolls. The upper register quotes from the Old Testament (as was typical in these scenes), in this case Psalm 17:11:

SCHEDIT SVP CELOS TYOLAVIT SVP PENAS VENTORVM P S XVIIC

(which can be reconstructed as: [Et a]chendit sup[er] celos, [e]t volavit sup[er] pen[n]as ventorum; Ps 17[:11] = "And he ascended upon the cloud, and he flew upon the wings of the winds").

The lower scroll quotes a New Testament passage, in this case, Mark 16:19:

DHS YHS POSTQLOCVTVS E ASSVTVS E ICELVM M VLTIMO

(which can be reconstructed as: Dhs [= Dominus] Ihs [= Iesus] post q[uam] locutus e[st] assu[m]tus e[st] i[n] celum. M[r] ultimo = "The Lord Jesus, after he had spoken, was taken up into heaven. The ending of Mark").

Although the banners focus on the ascending Christ, visually Mary once again occupies center stage. In Fra Angelico's version she does not even have to share it with Christ!

The poem on Acts by Arator (sixth-century Latin poet and orator) also included a focus on Mary, drawing the familiar contrast between Mary and Eve (first made by Justin Martyr, *Dial.* 100) while defending the nature of woman in the process: "Mary, the gateway of God, the virgin mother of her Creator, formed by her own son, was sitting at a religious gathering. The second virgin put to flight the woes of Eve's crime; there is no harm done to the sex; she restored what the first took away. ... The person, not the nature [of woman] caused ruin; in those days [of Eve] a pregnant woman [brought forth] peril. In these [of Mary] one grew great to bring forth God, the one begetting mortal things and the other bearing divine—she through whom the Mediator came forth into the world and carried actual flesh to the heavens" (*OAA*).

Likewise, the York Mystery Plays, which were performed by the various craft guilds in the city of York, England, from the middle of the fourteenth century until the middle of the sixteenth century, emphasized Mary and reflected again the rise of Marian piety in the Middle Ages. The Tailors' guild was responsible for performing the play celebrating the Ascension. Christ's long discourse ends with these words:

> Fulfilled, my father's will now be.
> Therefore, farewell to each one here.
> I'll go prepare a place for thee [John 14:2],
> To dwell in endless joy up there.
> Father, send down a cloud for me [Acts 1:9] –
> I come to you my father dear.
> The father's blessing, most mighty
> I give to all whom I leave here.

Following his speech, the angels sing, "Ascendo ad Patrem Meum" (I ascend to my Father). Mary then speaks:

> Almighty God, the most in might,
> This is a wondrous sight to see:
> My son who thus is ravished right,
> Wending in a cloud from me.
> My heart is both heavy and light:
> Heavy that this twinning must be,

And light, that he keeps his word aright,
And in great power ascends from me
(http://www.reed.utoronto.ca/yorkplays/York42.html).

Literal or Figurative Ascension?

John Calvin continued the trend of understanding that the significance of Jesus' ascension depended on its being a concrete event:

> Because it is one of the chiefest points of our faith, therefore does Luke endeavor more diligently to prove the same; yea, rather, the Lord himself meant to put the same out of all doubt, when as he ascended so manifestly, and hath confirmed the certainty of the same by other circumstances. For, if so be it he had vanished away secretly, then might the disciples have doubted what was become of him; but now, saith that they, being in so plain a place, saw him taken up with whom they had been conversant, whom also they heard speak even now, whom they beheld with their eyes, whom also they see taken out of their sight by a cloud, there is no cause why they should doubt whither he was gone (*Commentary on Acts*, 1:9–11).

Despite conceding that the biblical authors seem to presume that Jesus "ascended to some place above the clouds, where God has his peculiar residence," the Welsh Unitarian minister, Timothy Kenrick (1759–1804), balked at readings like Calvin's, arguing that such episodes "ought no more to be understood literally, than when they speak of the Deity as having hands, and eyes, and other organs of a man, or as moving from place to place." He further opines: "In regard to the place which is designed to be the residence of good men after resurrection, it is probably this earth, after it has undergone certain important revolutions which may be necessary to prepare it for this purpose" (Kenrick 1828, 3:10).

German theologian D. F. Strauss (1808–1874) also severely challenged these literalistic interpretations in *The Life of Jesus Critically Examined* (1835). Strauss muses:

> "How can a palpable body, which has *still flesh and bones*, and eats material food, be qualified for a celestial abode? how can it so far liberate itself from the laws of gravity, as to be capable of an ascent through the air? and how can it be conceived that God gave so preternatural a capability to Jesus by a miracle ... As an attempt to set us free from such difficulties and absurdities, the natural explanation of this narrative must needs be welcome. ... the Rationalists tell us that we are not to understand επηρθη as signifying an elevation above the earth, but only that Jesus,

in order to bless the disciples, drew up his form and thus appeared more elevated to them. They then bring forward the word διεστη, *he was parted from them*, in the conclusion of Luke's gospel [Luke 24:52], and interpret it to mean that Jesus in taking leave of his disciples removed himself farther from them. Hereupon, they continue, in the same way as on the mount of Transfiguration, a cloud was interposed between Jesus and the disciples, and together with the numerous olive-trees on the mount, concealed him from their sight; a result which, on the assurance ot two unknown men, they regarded as a reception of Jesus into heaven (Strauss 1835, 859–60).

Strauss, like Calvin, then claimed a place of priority for the ascension, albeit in a mythological sense. This skepticism regarding the historicity of Jesus' ascension into heaven persisted among many twentieth-century scholars. In 1942, Oxford University biblical scholar H. Wheeler Robinson queried whether the reference to the ascension in Acts 1 should be taken as "spatial in the literal sense" (1942, 201). In these comments Robinson himself anticipates the writing of another British Robinson (John A.T.) who began his theological bombshell, *Honest to God* (1963), by asserting the impossibility of taking the ascension account literally. Dale Allison concludes that "whatever tradition may lie behind Acts 1:9–11, it is not likely to be very old" (2005, 260). Karl Barth has also commented on the difficulty in gleaning a "nucleus of genuine history" from Acts 1. About the symbolism of the forty days of Jesus' post-resurrection appearances (Acts 1:3), he writes:

The statement in Ac. 1³ to the effect that the appearances extended over forty days is obviously connected with the forty days of the flood (Gen. 7⁴; cf. also Ez. 4⁶; Jonah 3⁴), and with the forty days of the temptation at the beginning of Jesus' ministry (Mt. 4²; Lk. 4²). And they may also have some positive connexion with the forty days spent in Canaan by the spies when they went on ahead of the children of Israel (Num. 13²⁵), and with the forty days and nights it took Elijah to get to Horeb, during which he went in the strength of the meat provided by the angel. These parallels are sufficient to show that the forty days are not to be taken literally but typically. They do not offer precise chronological information as to the duration of the appearances (*CD* 3.2.452; see also Bede's earlier comment).

About the Ascension itself, Barth writes:

There is no sense in trying to visualise the ascension as a literal event, like going up in a balloon. The achievements of Christian art in this field are amongst its worst perpetrations [!]. But of course this is no reason why they should be used to make the whole thing ridiculous. The point of the story is not that when Jesus left His disciples He visibly embarked upon a wonderful journey into space, but that when He left them He entered the side of the created world which was provisionally inaccessible and incomprehensible, that before their eyes He ceased to be before their eyes. This does not mean, however, that He ceased to be a creature, man. What it does mean is that He showed Himself quite unequivocally to be *the* creature, *the* man, who in provisional distinction from all other men lives on the God-ward side of the universe, sharing His throne (*CD* 3.2.453–54).

N.T. Wright has also balked at reading Acts 1:9–11 as a straightforward, historical narrative:

> We may remind ourselves at this point of two basic rules for modern readers reading ancient Jewish texts. First, two-decker language about a "heaven" in the sky above the earth almost certainly did not betoken a two-decker, let alone a three-decker, cosmology. Just as we speak of the sun "rising", even though we know that the earth is turning in relation to the sun, so ancient Jews were comfortable with the language of heavenly ascent without supposing that their god, and those who shared his habitation, were physically situated a few thousand feet above the surface of the earth. Second, and related to this, the language of "heaven" and "earth" … was regularly employed in a sophisticated theological manner, to denote the parallel and interlocking universes inhabited by the creator god on the one hand and humans on the other (2003, 655).

This view leads Wright to tease out the political implications of the ascension for Christians: "the ascension demands that we think differently about how the whole cosmos is, so to speak, put together … heaven and earth in biblical cosmology are not two different locations within the same continuum of space or matter. They are two different dimensions of God's good creation … the one who is in heaven can be present simultaneously anywhere and everywhere on earth: the ascension therefore means that Jesus is available, accessible, without people having to travel to a particular spot on the earth to find him … [Jesus is] in charge not only in heaven but also on earth, not only in some ultimate future but also in the present (Wright 2008, 110–111).

Other modern scholars who have wished to preserve the historical character of the account and, at the same time, acknowledge modern questioning of a three-tiered universe in which Jesus ascended "up" into heaven are often forced into the kind of exegetical logic offered by Bruce Metzger:

> Though Jesus did not need to ascend in order to return to that sphere which we call heaven, yet in fact he did ascend a certain distance into the sky, until a cloud took him out of sight. By such a miraculous sign he impressed upon his followers the conviction that this was now the last time he would appear to them, and that

henceforth they should not expect another manifestation, but should realize that the transitional period had ended (Metzger 1968, 86).

Edinburgh theologian Oliver O'Donovan (1945–) has taken a different tack, reminiscent of Barth, in exploring the historical dimensions of the ascension as well as teasing out its theological implications. He does not think that the ascension can be understood only as a way to explain Jesus' final departure *from* the disciples (see Metzger above). He attempts to move beyond the modernist dichotomy which speaks either of the ascension as a literal movement through space (typical of premodern interpretations) and the "idealist solution" which assigns the ascension to "a realm of noumenal or mental reality" (30):

> Insofar as these transitions have one foot in our space and time, they are seen there as events—events which, however, have another end to them beyond the historical sequence of which, at this end, they form a part. … There is more to be said about the event than that it was the cessation of the resurrection appearances. It is not only a 'taking from', it is a 'taking up.' It is a material event which involves the material body of Jesus; it leaves the spatio-temporal order to enter the immediate presence of the Creator. … The transition from the earth to Heaven is more than a reversal of the incarnation, at which God 'came down'; it is the elevation of man, physical, spatio-temporal man, into an order that is greater than the physical and the spatio-temporal, and which is not his native habitat. … there is a beaten path that lies before us, linking our physical existence to an existence in the presence of God which lies beyond its conditions. We cannot see the path … but we know that the path has been taken, and that we are to take it too (O'Donovan 1986, 36–37).

That we, too, are to follow in Jesus' path is a point English cleric and poet John Donne (1572–1631) made in his poetry:

> Salute the last and everlasting day,
> Joy at the uprising of this Sun and Son …
> Behold the highest, parting hence away,
> Lightens the dark clouds,
> Which he treads upon,
> Nor doth he by ascending, show alone,
> But first he, and he first enters the way,
> O strong Ram, which hast batter'd heaven for me
> (Donne 3321; RCS, 10).

And the Book of Common Prayer offers this petition that God "exalt us to the same place where our Savior Christ has already gone" ("Collect for the Sunday After the Ascension," 1549, 58).

A Sabbath Day's Journey

Some early interpreters puzzled over the distance between Jerusalem and the Mount of Olives, the site of the ascension. According to Ammonius, a "Sabbath day's journey" (1:12) was literally the distance "allowed for the Jews to walk ... on the Sabbath for the purpose of meditation" (CGPNT 10.14–16; see also 10.17–21 in which Ammonius cites Origen for the same view). Bede allegorized the distance to refer to "anyone who becomes worthy of an interior vision of the glory of the Lord as he ascends to the father, and of enrichment by the promise of the Holy Spirit, here enters the city of everlasting peace by a Sabbath journey" (*Comm. Acts* 1.12b).

Replacement of Judas (1:15–26)

The Death of Judas

There are three early Christian traditions regarding the death of Judas. These portrayals of Judas' death fit with distinct themes found within each respective account (Robertson 2012). In Acts, Judas "falling headlong, burst open in the middle and all his bowels gushed out" (1:18). For Luke, Judas' death was the result of a divine punitive miracle, whose punishment fit the crime (for other eviscerations, see the accounts of Jehoram in 2 Chr 21:12–19 and Josephus, *Ant.* 9.99–104; and Catullus in Josephus, *J.W.* 7.453; cf. Robertson 2012, 101–108). In Matthew, Judas hangs himself after his attempt to return the thirty pieces of silver is rejected by the religious authorities (Matt 27:3–8). Papias (c. 70–163) reports a second variation of Luke's account:

> Judas went about in this world as a great model of impiety. He became so bloated in the flesh (*prēstheis*) that he could not pass through a place that was easily wide enough for a wagon ... he died on his own land ... no one can pass by that place without holding his nose. This was how great an outpouring he made from his flesh on the ground (Papias, frag. 4.2–3; LCL trans. Ehrman; a similar tradition is preserved in the Armenian and Old Gregorian versions, which read *prēstheis* [swollen] instead of *prēnēs* [headlong]; Metzger 2002, 247).

Post-Enlightenment interpreters saw these variations as incompatible. Timothy Kenrick, for example, argued that the contradictions between Matthew and Acts are so stark that the verses in Acts must be an interpolation from a later hand (Kenrick 1828, 3:15). In earlier interpretations, the canonical accounts were often harmonized into one (including the Vulgate's translation of

Acts 1:18, "he fell headlong," *prēnēs genomenos*, with *suspensus crepuit mediu*, "after being hanged, he burst in the middle" and followed later by Luther in his translation of the same phrase in Acts as "erhängt") as in this rather vivid description attributed to Chrysostom:

> But that he fell on the earth and burst and his bowels gushed out, is like this. For he shut the doors against himself before he strangled himself, and he remained there on the gibbet the Friday and the Saturday. When he had swollen up and grown heavy, the cord was cut by which he hung: he fell, burst asunder, and was poured out. But the stench of the putrifying heap and of his guts brought together the children of Jerusalem to come and view his infamous end, which was for him the precursor of hell-fire (cited by Conybeare 1926, 150).

The thirteenth-century *Golden Legend* compiled by Jacobus de Voragine both harmonizes and moralizes Judas' death: "It was fitting that the bowels which had conceived the betrayer should burst and spill out, and that the throat from which had emerged the voice of the traitor should be strangled by a rope" (*Golden Legend*, "45. Saint Matthias, Apostle"; cf. Theophylact, *In Matt.* 27).

Judas' hanging is perhaps the one most frequently repeated of the three traditions in the early church, but Acts' version of Judas bursting in the middle is not missing altogether. Judas' death is echoed in the description of the death of Arius (256–336) by Socrates Scholiasticus (c. 380–439):

> Soon after a faintness came over him [Arius], and together with the evacuations his bowels protruded, followed by a copious hemorrhage, and the descent of the smaller intestines: moreover portions of his spleen and liver were brought off in the effusion of blood, so that he almost immediately died. The scene of this catastrophe still is shown at Constantinople, as I have said, behind the shambles in the colonnade: and by persons going by pointing the finger at the place, there is a perpetual remembrance preserved of this extraordinary kind of death (*Ecc. Hist.* 37).

Athanasius, fourth-century anti-Arian Bishop of Alexandria, in his letter to Serapion, also cites Acts 1:18 as a way of describing Arius' death (*Letter* 54; NPNF 2.4).

It was commonly accepted in the medieval church that Judas' name, Iscariot, derived from "Issachar," which means "money, to denote the traitor's price, because he sold the Lord" (Isidore of Seville, *Etym.* 8.9; cf. also Jerome, *Tractatus in Librum Psalmorum* 108). Treason motivated by greed would have been most offensive to the simple lifestyle of the Franciscans who were committed to a life of poverty and who had commissioned the fresco cycle (Robson 2004, 41). If Judas' despair is symbolized by the hanging, the divine punishment for his avarice is marked by the spilled intestines disclosed by his torn tunic. In his *Divine Comedy*, Dante assigns Judas to the ninth and final circle of hell. Judas is joined by others who had committed great acts of betrayal (*Inf.* 34.10–15).

The Election of Matthias

The fact that the decision to replace Judas was made by all the disciples (1:23) did not escape the notice of early interpreters. The involvement of the congregation was noted, albeit disapprovingly, by the scribe of the fifth-century, Codex D (Cantabrigiensis), who changed the text in Acts 1:23 from "they put

FIGURE 6   *Election of Matthias.* 1269. Manuscript illumination. MS 965 fol. 106v (Rockefeller-McCormick New Testament). Photo: Special Collections Research Center, University of Chicago Library

forward two" to "he [Peter] put forward two," perhaps in an effort to highlight and enhance the role of Peter in the oversight of this first instance of "apostolic succession."

The role of Peter in the selection of Matthias (described in Acts 1:15–20) is also highlighted in the thirteenth-century illuminated Rockefeller-McCormick manuscript (Codex 2400, **Figure 6**), which was discovered by Edgar J. Goodspeed in 1929 and acquired by Mrs. Edith Rockefeller-McCormick for the Collection of the University of Chicago (Riddle 1929). The manuscript is typically Byzantine and contains nearly one hundred illuminations (Willoughby 1933, 3–74). While gazing at two of the apostles, the apostle Peter gestures with his left hand and introduces the newly-appointed Matthias. For John Wesley (1703–91), the fact that the apostles could only reduce the number of candidates to two suggests the need for divine guidance: "So far the faithful could go by consulting together, but no further [than choosing two]. Therefore here commenced the proper use of the lot [Acts 1:26], whereby a matter of importance, which cannot be determined by any ordinary method, is committed to the Divine decision" (*ENNT*, Acts 1:23).

Overview

Acts 2 records the events associated with Pentecost and is comprised of three segments: the miracle of Pentecost (2:1–13); Peter's Pentecost sermon (2:14–40); and a narrative summary describing the practices of the early Christian community (2:41–47). Interpreters are divided regarding the most appropriate background against which to understand the Pentecost event (2:1–13). Does the gift of the Spirit parallel the gift of the law at Sinai (so Augustine, Cyprian,

The Acts of the Apostles Through the Centuries, First Edition. Heidi J. Hornik and Mikeal C. Parsons.
© 2017 Heidi J. Hornik and Mikeal C. Parsons. Published 2017 by John Wiley & Sons, Ltd.

Luther, and Wesley)? Or is it a reversal of Babel (Gen 11; so Ambrose, Calvin, Lightfoot)? The pro-Apartheid Dutch Reformed Church in South Africa saw Pentecost as a confirmation, not a reversal, of the effects of separate language (and ethnic) groups. Some (e.g., Luther) associated Pentecost with Creation, while others (e.g., Chrysostom) related it to the Endtime events of Consummation. There is also debate as to whether Pentecost was a "miracle of speech" or a "miracle of hearing." Pentecost has been a favorite scene in the visual tradition, with pre-modern renditions giving Mary a prominent place in the scene as representative of the Church. Finally, biblical Pentecost is the scriptural basis for the beginnings of the Pentecostal movement in the early twentieth century, even though the claim that xenolalia (speaking in a known, but unstudied tongue) gave way to glossolalia (ecstatic speech as presented especially in Paul's first letter to the Corinthians, 12–14) as a necessary manifestation of Spirit baptism.

Within Peter's speech, two passages served as "magnet texts" for interpreters. Acts 2:18, a quotation of Joel 2:28 ("your sons and your daughters shall prophesy"), has been the basis for including women in positions of church leadership from the diaries of the 16th-century mystic, Katherine Sutton, to the sermons of the twentieth-century African American preacher, Ella Mitchell. Acts 2:38 was the basis of a denominational dispute between Baptists and Church of Christ Disciples over the necessity of water baptism, a debate which spilled over into the scholarly pages of the *Journal of Biblical Literature*!

The summary statement in Acts 2:41–47, along with the summary in Acts 4, were used by Pachomius (292–348) and other proto-monastics as scriptural warrant for ascetic community life. Others saw the passage as a touchstone text for developing a theology of possessions (see Chrysostom, Pachomius, Peter Olivi, Winstanley [on Ch. 4], Rauschenbusch, and the Creedal tradition).

Reception and Interpretation

The Miracle of Pentecost (Acts 2:1–13)

Sinai or Babel? Creation or Consummation? Connecting Pentecost with the giving of the law at Sinai was a common strategy among patristic writers. St. Augustine observed:

> The Pentecost, too, we observe, that is, the fiftieth day from the passion and resurrection of the Lord, for on that day He sent to us the Holy Paraclete whom He had promised; as was prefigured in the Jewish passover, for on the fiftieth day after the slaying of the lamb, Moses on the mount received the law written with the finger of God [Exodus 19–31]. If you read the Gospel, you will see that the

Spirit is there called the finger of God [Luke 11:8]. Remarkable events which happened on certain days are annually commemorated in the Church, that the recurrence of this festival may preserve the recollection of things so important and salutary (*Faust.* 32.12; cf. *Oration 31*, "On Pentecost"; Jer. *Epist.* 78.12; St. Leo the Great, *Sermo de Pentecoste* 1).

St. Cyprian, third-century Bishop of Carthage (*Treatises*, 101.555), further connected the Pentecostal tongues of fire with the smoke and fire of Sinai and the burning bush (Exod 3:2–3; cf. Jeffrey 1992, 597; cf. also Severus of Antioch in CGPNT 20.4–32; 21.7–14).

Others, such as fourth-century Bishop of Milan St. Ambrose (*Sermo* 36.2), read the Pentecost event as a typological reversal of the story of Babel (Gen 11): "if pride caused the division of tongues at Babel, humility was the condition necessary for the coming of the Spirit at Pentecost" (see also St. Maximus of Tours, *De Solemnitate Sanctae Pentecostes*; PL 17.371–80, 629–42). John Calvin sides with those who read Acts 2 as a reversal of Babel:

> For whence came the diversity of tongues, save only that the wicked and ungodly counsels of men might be brought to nought? [Gen. 11.7]. But God doth furnish the apostles with the diversity of tongues now, that he may bring and call home, into a blessed unity, men which wander here and there. These cloven tongues made all men to speak the language of Canaan, as Isaiah foretold [Isa. 19.18] (*Commentary on Acts*, 2).

In his commentary on Acts, British cleric and Vice-Chancellor of Cambridge University John Lightfoot (1602–1675) makes a similar argument (1645, 41). Luther, on the other hand, reads the Pentecost scene in parallel with the giving of the law at Sinai: "The law of the letter was given from Mt. Sinai to those to whom temporal blessings were promised; but the Law of the Spirit was given, not from Jerusalem but rather from heaven on the day of Pentecost" (*LW* 27:319). John Wesley (1703–91) also favored the interpretation connecting Pentecost to Sinai: "At the Pentecost of Sinai in the Old Testament, and the Pentecost of Jerusalem in the New, were the two grand manifestations of God, the legal and the evangelical; the one from the mountain, and the other from heaven, the terrible and the merciful one" (*ENNT*; cf. J.G. Herder [1744–1803] 1967, 4–59).

In sharp contrast to these inclusivistic interpretations that appeal to the echoes of the Babel story behind Acts 2 stands the interpretation of the Dutch Reformed Church (*Nederduitse Gereformeerde Kerk*) during the Apartheid era in South Africa. In 1975, the DRC published a highly influential report commissioned by its General Synod under the title, *Human Relations and the South African Scene in Light of Scripture*. The report stated that the language miracle of Pentecost "confirms that it is the will of God that each man should learn of the great deeds of God in his own language" (86). In this interpretation, Acts 2 (and other OT and NT texts) provided the biblical underpinnings to the apartheid practice of insisting that each language group (e.g., race in the South African context) must form its own separate, racial churches and that transfer of membership from one church to another was prohibited. After all, Acts 2 (echoing Genesis 11 according to the report) affirms the "cultural identities, linguistic barriers and the psychological distinctiveness of each people" (86). In an ironic twist on the Babel/Pentecost typology, this pro-Apartheid interpretation understood that the effects of Babel were not reversed by Pentecost (so Chrysostom, Calvin, etc.) but rather were carried over to and sustained by the Pentecostal Church (and later confirmed by Paul; cf. comments on Acts 17:26)! Among the early critical responses to the report was that by Douglas Bax, a South African Presbyterian minister, who wrote in 1983 that the gift of Pentecostal tongues removed the curse of Babel and that "though these different languages remain, the barrier of communication which they have set up between those who speak them is dramatically broken down" (Bax 1983, 129; cited by Burridge 2007, 341).

Cuban American Methodist historian Justo González also notes the diversity of languages in a direction radically different from that proposed by the pro-Apartheid Dutch Reformed Church:

> Had the Spirit made all the listeners understand the language of the apostles, we would be justified in a centripetal understanding of mission, one in which all who come in are expected to be like those who invite them. However, because what the Spirit did was exactly the opposite, this leads us to a centrifugal understanding of mission, one in which as the gospel moves toward new languages and new cultures, it is ready to take forms that are understandable within those languages and cultures. In other words, had there been an "Aramaic only" movement in first-century Palestine, Pentecost was a resounding no! to that movement. And it is still a resounding no! to any movement within the Church that seeks to make all Christians think alike, speak alike, and behave alike (González 2001, 39).

Other interpreters were interested in connecting Pentecost with creation and consummation. Luther connected the imagery of the wind with the assertion that "Christ is Lord over all creation":

> At Pentecost, to be sure, the sound of the wind was stronger than it usually is; there the wind roared and blew in a different way, although it was the same wind as before. It proclaimed that the Christ is Lord over all creation, Creator of heaven and earth, seated at the right hand of the Father, Lord of the angels and of the celestial and earthly creatures as well as those who dwell in hell and superior to all the powers of the earth (*LW* 22:318).

At the other end of the spectrum, some early Christian writers connected Pentecost with the Last Judgment. Chrysostom observes: "Do you perceive the type? What is this Pentecost? The time when the sickle was to be put to the harvest [Revelation 14], and the ingathering made" (*Hom. Act.* 4; cf. Jeffrey 1992, 598). The radical Anabaptist, Hans Hut, also predicted that the end of the world would occur on Pentecost in 1528 and set about to "ingather'" the 144,000 faithful (Klaassen 1986, 16).

Not everyone in the story, however, understands the meaning of the glossolalia (Acts 2:12–13). St. Cyril of Jerusalem (ca. 315–86) comments that those who heard but did not comprehend experienced "a second confusion, replacing that first evil one at Babylon [sic] ... For in that confusion of tongues there was division of purpose, because their hearts were at enmity with God. Here minds were restored and united, because the object on which they focused was of God. The means of falling were the means of recovery" (*Catechetical Lectures* 17.15, 17). Cyril also observed that those mocking the apostles by saying, "They are full of new wine," actually "spoke truly though in mockery. For in truth the wine was new, even the grace of the New Testament; but this new wine was from a spiritual Vine which had often-times ere this borne fruit in the Prophets, and had now blossomed in the New Testament" (*Catechetical Lectures* 18–19).

The Venerable Bede, eighth-century British monk and exegete, bears witness to a "miracle of hearing" interpretation of Acts 2: "Was the marvel rather the fact that the discourses of those who were speaking were understood by every-one of the hearers in his own language? ... each of them would perceive what they heard in terms of his own language and would grasp the meaning" (*Comm. Acts* 2; cf. also Gregory of Nazianzus, *Or. Bas.* 41, who considers this view but ultimately rejects it). Some modern commentators have also noticed the aural dimension of the text. Harvard Divinity Professor Kirsopp Lake (1872–1946), for example, suggested about Acts 2 that "there was a miracle of hearing as well as a miracle of speaking," although his assessment of the event would differ radically from that of Bede (Jackson and Lake 1933, 5.12, 5.120). Lake suggests that Luke has redacted an earlier source in which Pauline ecstatic speech was interpreted by those within the community (1 Cor 14:5, 27–28). For Lake, the account as it stands in Acts is largely implausible:

> Just as it is extremely likely that the Day of Pentecost was marked by the first instance of glossolalia in the Christian community, it is extremely unlikely that this took the form of speaking in foreign languages. The tradition of the foreign languages is the attempt to explain the glossolalia by a friendly author, separated by time from the actual event, just as the charge of drunkenness was the attempt of unfriendly observers, separated by lack of sympathy (Lake 1933, 5.120).

Acts 2:1–11 raises questions (Sinai or Babel? Creation or Consummation? Speaking or Hearing?) that resist any facile answer!

Symbolic Imagery and "Visual Exegesis" of Pentecost

John Chrysostom commented on the use of similes in the Lukan account and cautions against having "gross sensible notions of the Spirit":

> Nor is this all; but what is more awful still, 'And there appeared unto them', it says, 'cloven tongues like as of fire' [v. 3]. Observe how it is always, 'like as'; and rightly: that you may have no gross sensible notions of the Spirit. Also, 'as it were of a blast': therefore it was not a wind. 'Like as of fire'. For when the Spirit was to be made known to John, then it came upon the head of Christ as in the form of a dove: but now, when a whole multitude was to be converted, it is 'like as of fire. And it sat upon each of them'. This means, that it remained and 'rested upon them'. For the sitting is significant of settledness and continuance (*Hom. Act.* 2).

Severian of Gabala (fl. c. 400) asked why the tongues of fire fell on the apostles' heads rather than on their mouths. Drawing an analogy with the way water runs down a mountain from top to bottom, he argued: "The grace of the Spirit invaded first the head and then the mouth and the heart, and it filled the entire person from the head down" (*Catena on Acts* 22.15–17). As in the patristic period, several modern commentators note that the images of fire and wind are particularly poignant: "The thing about a flame is that the more you divide it, the more there is to go round: split a flame in half and you get more, not less. So the coming of the Spirit is a gift of new life to the community, which brings out the individual gifts of each member, a gift that brings God's living word to articulate expression in a host of individual tongues" (Alexander 2006, 29).

Not all appropriations of Pentecostal imagery and symbolism occurred within ecclesiastical contexts. The Transcendentalist, Ralph Waldo Emerson (1803–1882), equated the "tongue of flame" (Acts 2:3) with the language of Nature, which knits all of the world together through its "music." In "Woodnotes 2," he records the following conversation between the pine tree and the poet:

> The least breath my boughs which tossed
> Brings again the Pentecost;
> To every soul resounding clear
> In a voice of solemn cheer, –
> 'Am I not thine? Are not these thine?'
> And they reply, 'Forever mine!'
> My branches speak Italian,
> English, German, Basque, Castilian …
> (133–55; cited in Jeffrey 1992, 600).

Nor were all 'performances' of the Pentecostal signs necessarily edifying. One need only consider the parody of the flatulent friar's 'mighty wind' in Chaucer's *Summoner's Tale* (Levitan 1971, 236–46)!

Pentecost has a long and varied history in the visual reception of the text. Despite Chrysostom's caveats, artists faced a particularly difficult problem in visualizing the signs of Pentecost. The concretization of the "tongues of fire" in the visual tradition should not lead automatically to the assumption that the artists or their audience disagreed with Chrysostom's assessment. Loveday Alexander has astutely observed that Luke's "vision was one that lent itself to liturgical performance: it became embedded in the daily and yearly cycles of Catholic and Orthodox devotion. And these cycles in turn form the underwater reef which gives their distinctive shape to the iconographic traditions of Eastern and Western religious art" (Alexander 2000, 170). Pentecost falls fifty days after Easter Sunday. In Orthodox traditions, Pentecost (also called Trinity Sunday) is celebrated over a three-day period, the Scripture lessons include Joel 2 and Acts 2, and its liturgical color is green. In the West, Pentecost is also known as "Whitsunday," the lectionary texts include Genesis 11 and Acts 2, and its dominant liturgical color is red.

Perhaps the earliest visual depiction of Pentecost is that found in the Rabbula Gospels (**Figure 7**; see comments on Acts 1:1–14). David Wright has argued that the original arrangement of illustrations (found in the canon tables) was a

FIGURE 7   *The Descent of the Holy Spirit.* 586. Manuscript illumination from the Syriac Evangeliary of Rabbula. Biblioteca Laurenziana, Florence, Italy. Photo: Alinari/Art Resource, NY

"full Christological cycle in logical order" (Wright 1973, 204). If this is the case, then it is striking that this life of Christ cycle concludes, not with the ascension of Jesus, but rather with the scene of Pentecost and the birth of the Church. The image visually anticipates C.K. Barrett's aphorism: "In Luke's thought, the end of the story of Jesus is the Church" (Barrett 1961, 57).

One striking feature of the Rabbula depiction of Pentecost is the prominent place that Mary holds in the scene (see comments on Acts 1:1–14). Some have an even more expansive view of those present at Pentecost. The reading that "all those gathered" included the 120 mentioned in Acts 1:15 goes back at least to Chrysostom (*Hom. Act.* 4). Chrysostom's view that the entire troupe of 120 were included in the Pentecost scene has gained traction among recent commentators. Loveday Alexander, for example, comments: "Luke uses several words to stress the togetherness of Jesus' followers on this occasion (v. 1), which makes it look as if he means to include all the 120 believers of 1:14–15 (including Jesus' family and the women) not just the Twelve" (Alexander 2006, 28). The fact that several mss (e.g., 326, 2495, etc.) insert "the apostles" after "all" (*pantes*) is indirect evidence that such an interpretation was acknowledged (and rejected) from early on.

The illustrator of the Rabbula Gospels, however, does not intend to stress Lukan inclusivity, but rather to highlight the prominence and significance of the Virgin Mary at Pentecost. Mary holds a similar position of importance in the Rabbula Gospels' depiction of the Ascension (fol. 13v). There, Mary is also in the center of the illustration; her dark blue robe stands in contrast to the paler blue of the Apostles, and her halo is golden in comparison with the understated violet of the Apostles. Why does she hold such an important position? Herbert Kessler argues that it is the result of an ecclesiological focus that runs parallel to the Christological emphasis of the Rabbula cycle (and is found in both the Ascension and Pentecost scenes):

> Mary's dominant presence is even more important; not mentioned in scriptural accounts of the Ascension, she stands for the Church, left behind as the custodian of Christ's law until the Second Coming. The last folio in the codex depicts Pentecost, the foundational moment of the Church; the Virgin is pictured again amid the apostles, there inspired by the Holy Spirit (Kessler 2007, 166).

Both aspects of the Rabbula Gospels' illustration of Pentecost (that Pentecost is the logical end to the life of Christ and the importance of Mary's representative role in symbolizing the Church) are brought together by the Holy Spirit in the form of a dove, hovering just above Mary in the Rabbula Pentecost. The dove echoes Jesus' baptism, illustrated earlier in the canon tables (fol. 4v).

The themes reflected in the Rabbula Gospels' depiction of Pentecost are found in later art; Giotto's *Pentecost* and Botticelli's *Descent of the Holy Ghost* are exemplary in this regard. The first point illustrated by the Rabbula Gospels' Pentecost (that Pentecost is viewed as a logical conclusion to the life of Christ) is seen again in the 1304–06 work of Giotto di Bondone in the Scrovegni Chapel at Padua (**Figure 8**). This series of frescoes is considered to be the most complete series by Giotto done in his mature style. The chapel in Padua, a university town not far from Venice, is usually called the "Arena Chapel" because it is constructed above an ancient Roman arena. A wealthy merchant and influential Paduan citizen, Enrico Scrovegni, acquired the original chapel, dedicated to the Virgin Annunciate in 1300. He rebuilt it with the likely intention of atoning for his sins, and those of his father, Reginaldo, for usury. In *The Divine Comedy*, Dante banished Reginaldo Scrovegni to the seventh circle of hell, the part reserved for usurers. The church was dedicated to Saint Mary of Charity on March 16, 1305.

The chapel is very simple architecturally. It has a rectangular form with a starry sky in the barrel vault, a gothic triple lancet window on the façade and

Figure 8   Giotto di Bondone (1266–1336). *Pentecost*. c. 1305. Fresco. Scrovegni, Chapel, Padua, Italy. Photo: Alfredo Dagli Orti/Art Resource, NY

narrow windows on the southern wall. The apse is in the east and the main entrance in the west. The iconographic program is intellectually complex. Theological advisers, who were in consultation with the patron, directed Giotto. The frescoes follow three main themes: scenes in the lives of Mary's parents, Joachim and Anna; scenes from the life of the Virgin; and scenes from the life and death of Christ. A large number of the representations are from the *Legenda Aurea,* or *Golden Legend,* by Jacobus da Voragine in 1264.

The magnitude of the project required Giotto to obtain assistance from his workshop although he executed the principal figures in each scene and devised each spatial composition. Giotto and his assistants painted from top to bottom. Moist plaster had to be applied only to as much surface as could be painted in a day. This area, known as a *giornata,* prevented a premature drying of the wall and assured a true *fresco* composition. Calculated by the *giornate* seams, scholars have determined the frescoes were painted in 852 days (Richards 2001).

Giotto was probably commissioned to decorate this chapel by Enrico Scrovegni because of the artist's contemporary reputation. The *Chronicle* of Giovanni Villani, written just a few years after Giotto's death, described the artist as among the great personalities of the day. The Trecento humanist Boccaccio claimed that Giotto had "brought back to light" the art of painting "that for many centuries had been buried under the errors of some who painted more to delight the eyes of the ignorant than to please the intellect of the wise" (*Decameron* VI, 5). Dante also predicted Giotto's fame and influence on contemporary culture in the *Divine Comedy* (*Purg.* 11.94). The Byzantine style of Giotto's teacher, Cimabue, would soon be discarded by Tuscan artists in favor of the style derived from nature painted by Giotto.

Pentecost is the final scene of the life of Christ cycle and is located on the lowest level of the three bands of narratives on the northern wall. It is also the scene closest to the eastern altar. The arrangement around a table is organized in a similar manner to the *Last Supper* that is directly opposite it on the south wall. This balance is typical of Giotto. The artist placed the figures inside an architectural space that is clearly defined by a succession of four pointed arches (that illusionistically create a vaulted ceiling under which the apostles are seated) and a right side that is half the length of the front with a two-arched colonnade. This created the illusion that the event occurred within a small church. Basil De Selincourt suggested that the Gothic arch is used for the first time to symbolize the Christian church (De Selincourt 1905, 149).

Visual sources that came before Giotto are rare, but it can be argued that this is the first time a visual depiction of Pentecost was painted in a prominent location. Giotto will repeat the subject in the Florentine church of Santa Croce in 1306–12. There he extended the visual depiction of the story to include verses up to Acts 2:1–13, rather than stopping at Acts 2:1–4. This allowed him to include three figures outside the house. The Santa Croce cycle also included the tongues of fire over the apostles' heads and added the Holy Spirit, represented as a dove (missing in the Scrovegni depiction). In the Scrovegni chapel speech is portrayed through the hand that is gesturing or "the speaking hand" (Barasch 1987, 15–17). This allows the critical message of the biblical story, that the twelve all start speaking in different languages, to be conveyed in a silent picture. Giotto chooses the hand because it is able to communicate so many different meanings and emotions. Precedents of this speaking hand are the orators of Greek and Roman art, whose gesturing hand indicates they are in the act of speaking. The Holy Spirit is represented through rays of light emanating out of the painted ceiling. Giotto does not depict Mary among the twelve. Instead, the church itself is inscribed in the architecture, in the "church-like structure" encompassing, containing and protecting the event from the world outside.

Two centuries later in 1495–1505, Sandro Botticelli executed *The Descent of the Holy Ghost* (**Figure 9**). Botticelli, a student of Fra Filippo Lippi, is one

FIGURE 9   Botticelli (1447–1510). *Descent of the Holy Ghost*. 1495–1505. Oil. Birmingham City Museum, Great Britain. Photo: Birmingham Museums Picture Library

of the best-known Florentine Renaissance masters due to his famous works, the *Birth of Venus* and the *Primavera*, painted for the Medici c. 1483. Botticelli received both secular and religious commissions throughout his artistic career as an independent master that began in 1472 when he joined the Compagnia di San Luca in Florence. Botticelli was the master of a successful workshop and was included in major projects throughout the Italian peninsula including three frescoes (*Temptations of Christ*, *Moses and the Daughters of Jethro* and the *Punishment of the Korah*) on the walls of the Sistine Chapel in 1481 for Pope Sixtus IV della Rovere. Botticelli was in the personal and professional company not only of the Popes and the Medici but also with Michelangelo, Giorgio Vasari, Domenico Ghirlandaio and Pietro Perugino. His works and opinions had major influence on the city of Florence. In 1491, Botticelli helped select the façade for the Santa Maria del Fiore with twenty-five artists and the church board. Botticelli's importance in Florentine society was again documented when he served on the board that decided the location of Michelangelo's *David* in 1505 along with Giuliano da Sangallo, Cosimo Rosselli, Leonardo da Vinci, Filippino Lippi and others.

Botticelli painted the *Descent of the Holy Ghost* or *Pentecost* scene between 1495 and 1505, when he was most influential in the Florentine Renaissance. It is considered a mature work as Botticelli died on May 17, 1510. Although Botticelli's early influences were Verrochio and Fra Filippo Lippi, he was also influenced by Girolamo Savonarola (1452–1498). In 1491, during Lent, Savonarola, a friar at San Marco, preached a message of radical reform against secular culture and art in Florence. In 1497, Botticelli may have provided drawings for Savonarola's *Triumphant Crucis* (Levy 1967, 97). Savonarola was excommunicated for insubordination in 1497 and executed by Pope Alexander VI in 1498 in Florence.

Pentecost is currently located in the City Museum and Art Gallery in Birmingham, England. The work is oil on poplar panel. The painting has sustained damage and about twenty percent has been completely lost and another twenty percent has been over painted. A dove above the Virgin was added in the nineteenth century but has now been removed from the painting. The panel on the right hand side was also replaced at that time. There remain connoisseurship issues related to the painting. Some scholars believe it to be a workshop piece, while others maintain an attribution to Botticelli (Cannon-Brookes 1968, 274–77). Botticelli may have prepared the design and began the painting but allowed his workshop to complete it. This was typical at this time in major workshops.

The Virgin Mary and the twelve apostles are depicted in the painting looking up toward the heavens. The Holy Spirit descends, and the moment illustrated is Acts 2:3. The disciples have not yet begun to speak as is stated in verse four.

Botticelli's *Pentecost* focuses on the reaction of the disciples to the event. Their expressions reveal awe and contemplation (especially on the part of the figure on Mary's immediate left). The gold tongues of fire rest on the forehead of each person. Each individual has a halo with his or her name inscribed on it. Many of the inscriptions are no longer legible, but the Birmingham Museum and Gallery staff have attempted an identification starting from the lower left and moving clockwise: Matthew, James, Andrew, Jude, Simon, John, Mary, James of Zebedee, Peter, Bartholomew, Barnabas, Matthias and Philip.

The depiction of Mary probably reflects Savonarola's influence. Botticelli's earlier depictions of Mary were more regal. Here she is painted with a modest air that is well suited to the chaste Virgin invoked by Savonarola (Kroegel 2003, 53–67). An image of the Virgin as depicted in the earlier works by Botticelli prompted the address Savonarola gave to painters in 1496: "Do you believe the Virgin Mary went dressed this way, as you paint her? I tell you she went dressed as a poor woman, simply, and so covered that her face could hardly be seen [...]. You make the Virgin Mary seem dressed like a whore. Now it really can be said that the worship of God is corrupt!" (cited in Kroegel 2003, 67). In response, this Mary in this depiction is a woman of monumental dimensions and dressed in poor garments, of an ashen and rather tarnished beauty: less and less a woman and more and more Ecclesia, perhaps even here the Mother of the Church. Mary represents the renewed Church, authentically Christian and the bearer of hope, the Mary that Botticelli learned to cherish listening to the word of Savonarola and, earlier still, reading those of Dante (Kroegel 2003, 67). This formulates an important connection between the new visualization of Mary and her role as representing the Church, a symbol particularly rich within the Pentecost iconography; this scene is appropriately referred to as the birth of the Church.

Pentecostalism

Few, if any, biblical events have lent their name to describe a religious movement; yet this is exactly the case for Pentecost. Even before the rise of Pentecostalism, Pentecost was a significant date on the Christian calendar. The Book of Common Prayer was first used on Pentecost Sunday, 9 June 1549, and the occasion is now commemorated "on the first convenient day following Pentecost." Pentecost was the setting for a variety of festivals and tournaments in medieval literature. Mallory notes that it was also the Feast of Pentecost when "all manner of men assayed to pulle at the swerde that would assay, but none myghte prevaille," and it was also the day when the quest for the Holy Grail commenced (*Le Morte D'Arthur* 1.7; 13.7; cited by Jeffrey 1992, 598).

There is a general (but not universal) consensus among Pentecostal historians that the defining belief of Pentecostalism, namely "that in apostolic times, the speaking in tongues was considered to be the initial physical evidence of persons having received the baptism in the Holy Spirit," was first established by Charles Parham at his Bethel Bible School at the end of 1900 in Topeka, Kansas (Dunn 1970, 2). Parham's account of the Topeka experience is one of the best known in Pentecostal history:

In December of [1900] we had had our examination upon the subject of repentance, conversion, consecration, sanctification, healing and the soon coming of the Lord. We had reached in our studies a problem. What about the 2nd Chapter of Acts? ... I set the students at work studying out diligently what was the Bible evidence of the Baptism of the Holy Ghost ...

Leaving the school for three days at this task, I went to Kansas City for three days' services [and returned] to the school on the morning preceding Watch night services [i.e., on New Year's Eve] ... to get their report on the matter in hand. To my astonishment they all had the same story, that while there were different things [which] occurred when the Pentecostal blessing fell, that the indisputable proof on each occasion was, that they spake with other tongues. About 75 people beside the school which consisted of 40 students had gathered for the watch night service. A mighty spiritual power filled the entire school. At 10:30 p.m. sister Agnes N. Ozman [now La Berge] asked that hands might be laid upon her to receive the Holy Spirit as she hoped to go to foreign fields. At first I refused, not having the experience myself. I laid my hands upon her head and prayed. I had scarcely repeated three dozen sentences when a glory fell upon her, a halo seemed to surround her head and face, and she began speaking in the Chinese language, and was unable to speak English for three days.

On January 3 Parham reports the following incident when he entered the second floor "Upper Room" of Stone's Folly, the site of the Bible School:

The door was slightly ajar, the room was lit with only coal oil lamps. As I pushed open the door I found the room was filled with a sheen of white light above the brightness of the lamps.

Twelve ministers, who were in the school of different denominations, were filled with the Holy Spirit and spoke with other tongues. Some were sitting, some still kneeling, others standing with hands upraised. There was no violent physical manifestation, though some trembled under the power of the glory that filled them.

Sister Stanley, an elderly lady, came across the room as I entered, telling me that just before I entered tongues of fire were sitting above their heads. ...

After praising God for some time, I asked Him for the same blessing. He distinctly made it clear to me that He raised me up and trained me to declare this mighty truth to the world, and if I was willing to stand for it, with all the persecutions, hardships, trials, slander, scandal that it would entail, He would give me the blessing. And I said "Lord I will, if you will just give me this blessing." Right then there came a slight twist in my throat, a glory fell over me and I began to worship God in the Sweedish tongue [sic], which later changed to other languages and continued so until the morning (*Apostolic Faith*, 2–3).

There are verbal echoes between Parham's account and the Pentecost narrative in Acts 2. In addition to the gift of tongues, the twelve ministers recall the twelve apostles, both gathered in upper rooms. Sister Stanley's report of "tongues of fire" sitting over the ministers' heads, of course, also recalls Acts 2:3. Less obvious, but intriguing nonetheless, is the total number of people gathered on the first night, 115 (75 observers plus 40 students) which, of course, roughly corresponds to the 120 who are gathered in Acts (1:15; 2:1) (Anderson 1979, 56–57). The scene setting of a room lit by oil coal lamps recalls another passage about a nocturnal, lamp-lit Christian meeting in Acts (20:7–12).

About using xenolalia, speaking in known languages, on the mission field, Parham said:

Any missionary going to the foreign field should preach in the language of the natives. That if God had ever equipped His ministers in that way He could do it today. That if Balaam's mule could stop in the middle of the road and give the first preacher that went out for money a bawling out in Arabic [!] that anyone today ought to be able to speak in any language of the world if they had horse sense enough to let God use their tongue and throat (Parham, 1930, 51–52).

Parham's teaching on baptism in the Holy Spirit consisted of three interrelated points: (1) tongue-speaking was the required initial evidence of Holy Spirit reception; (2) those who received this Pentecostal power were "sealed" for the impending rapture and would play a key role as the "Bride of Christ" in the eschaton; and (3) tongues would always be in the form of xenolalia (known human languages) and thus would signal the "dawn of a missionary explosion," serving a utilitarian purpose of global, end-time evangelism (Goff 1988, 14–15, 132). This last emphasis is not new. The Jesuit scholar, Cornelius á Lapide (1567–1637), who provided much of the exegetical underpinnings of the Catholic reformation, argued that Pentecostal glossolalia involved actual working languages of Europe, the Middle East, and Africa and allowed for the spread of the gospel (*Comm. Acta* 2.80–81; cited by Jeffrey 1992, 599). The archangel in Milton's *Paradise Lost*, Michael, "predicted" an expansive Pentecostal evangelistic mission to Adam:

> The Spirit
> Pour'd first on his Apostles, whom he sends
> to evangelize the Nations, then on all

> Baptiz'd, shall them with wondrous gifts endue
> To speak all Tongues, and do all Miracles
> As did the Lord before them
> (*Paradise Lost* 12.497–5020).

Only the first of Parham's three points (tongues as the initial evidence of Holy Spirit reception) survived in any robust way in post-Azusa Street expressions of Pentecostalism (the Azusa Street revival in Los Angeles, CA, beginning in 1906, is generally acknowledged as the origin of Pentecostalism). The loss of Parham's influence was due in part to sodomy charges brought against him in San Antonio, TX in 1907 (and later dropped), in part because Parham's racism became increasingly evident in his reaction to the prominent roles African-Americans held in the Azusa Street movement (which he expected to take over when arriving), and in part because xenolalia, so important to Parham's view of global end-time evangelism, never materialized in quite the way he had hoped (Goff 1988, 136–44). Grant Wacker did list Sophie Hansen as "one first-generation pentecostal who claimed a permanent gift of missionary tongues" (Wacker 2001, 46–47).

Opposition to Pentecostalism and Cessationism

Well before the rise of the Pentecostal movement there was aversion to ministerial "enthusiastic utterance." Jonathan Swift (1667–1745) accused some Puritans of creating a "fellowship of Christ with Belial," for "such is the analogy they make between 'cloven Tongues' [e.g., divided tongues, Acts 2:3] and 'cloven Feet'" (*Mechanical Operation of the Spirit* 2.1). Later, in the *Scarlet Letter*, Nathaniel Hawthorne (1804–1864) depicted this animus among some Puritan clergy:

> All that they lacked was the gift that descended upon the chosen disciples, at Pentecost, in 'tongues of flame', symbolizing, it would seem not the power of speech in foreign and unknown languages, but that of addressing the whole human brotherhood in the heart's native language. These fathers, otherwise so apostolic, lacked Heaven's last and rarest attestation of their office, the Tongue of Flame (chap. 11; cited in Jeffrey 1992, 600).

In response to emerging Pentecostalism, Princeton theologian B.B. Warfield (1851–1921) developed the "classic" non-Pentecostal view of cessationism:

> Everywhere the Apostolic Church was marked out as itself a gift from God, by showing forth the possession of the Spirit in appropriate works of the

Spirit—miracles of healing and miracles of power, miracles of knowledge, whether in the form of prophecy or of the discerning of spirits, miracles of speech, whether of the gift of tongues or of their interpretation. ... (Warfield 1918, 5)

These gifts [miracles, prophecies, tongues, etc.] were not the possession of the primitive Christian as such; nor, for that matter, of the Apostolic Church or the Apostolic age for themselves; they were distinctively the authentication of the Apostles. They were part of the credentials of the Apostles as the authoritative agents of God in founding the church. Their function thus confined them to distinctively the Apostolic Church, and they necessarily passed away with it (Warfield 1918, 5-6).

Incidentally, Parham's view that tongues as known languages served a utilitarian purpose of end-time evangelism actually anticipated and was apparently immune to Warfield's criticism. The reason speaking in tongues so rarely if ever manifested itself across the history of the Church, Parham reasoned, was because they were reserved for end-time evangelism. The "Early Rain" in which God's Spirit was poured out, as Joel promised, at the beginning of the church had its corresponding bookend in End-time Pentecostal "Latter Rain" evangelism.

It is important to point out that for "the first five or six years most [Pentecostals] saints likely shared his [Parham's] view. ... most soon gave up the notion that *all* tongues consisted of actual languages, yet almost all continued to believe that *some* did" (Wacker 2001, 45). A letter published in 1908 in the British Pentecostal paper *Confidence* illustrates this shift beautifully. In the letter, A.G. Garr (1874-1944), who had gone to India after having received what he believed to be several Indian languages and expecting to preach to the indigenous peoples, confessed: "I supposed He would let us talk to the natives of India in their own language, but he did not, and as far as I can see, will not use that means to convert the heathen" (Garr 1908, 22). He later adds: "So far I have not seen any one who is able to preach to the natives in their own tongue with the languages given with the Holy Ghost" (Garr 1908, 22). In spite of this disappointment, Garr validates his Pentecostal experience saying that when he speaks in tongues he can "feel the power of God in most every instance when I speak at length, and can truly bear witness to the scripture that 'speaking in tongues edifies the one speaking'" (1 Cor. 14:4; cf. *Confidence* 2 [1908]: 22).

In this way, Garr's experience mirrored that of the larger movement; when the hope of "missionary tongues" was abandoned he took refuge in Paul. For all practical purposes, then, thus ends the first chapter of Pentecostal interpretation of Pentecost in which the Lukan paradigm of Acts 2 took priority over the Pauline version, especially with regard to missionary tongues, or xenolalia. In other words, during the first several years of the spread of Pentecostalism, the Pentecostal experience recorded in Acts 2 provided both the Scriptural warrant and paradigm for Pentecostal experience, and while the book of Acts continued to hold a singular place of importance in subsequent Pentecostal theology, for many the interpretive paradigm shifted from Acts to Paul (specifically 1 Cor 12–14), so that Pentecostal experience was viewed from the Pauline perspective of heavenly or ecstatic utterance. Glossalalia as xenolalia was still possible, but no longer normative (for the view that Pentecostalism was never completely bound to tongues as "initial evidence," see Richmann 2014).

We note one very minor but fascinating stream within the early Pentecostal movement, namely the view that Acts 2 provided warrant for the gift of *aurolalia,* that is, "the ability to understand (though not to speak) an unstudied foreign language" (Wacker 2001, 287 n. 71). Dr. Finis Yoakum (1851–1920), a medical doctor who gave up his lucrative career following a personal healing and started the Pisgah Home movement for the indigent in Los Angeles (Burgess and McGee 1988, 907–08), gave an account concerning evangelistic meetings at the Kona Orphanage in Hailua, Hawaii, that he had led in July, 1908:

> Now the wonderful part of the meetings is to be told. We four, which included Sister Cornelia Muzum, whom I brought with me, found the Lord withheld the gift of tongues from us. Here most of the people were Japanese, Portugese, Chinese, and natives, who could not speak nor understand English tongues. We asked the Father in Jesus' name to give them (the people) interpretation of our tongue. Glory, He did! Nearly one hundred have been converted. Often we see the four nationalities kneeling at the altar and seeking my Lord at the same time. Arising with shining faces they tell that for the first time they have heard the Bible read, or, some would say, the first time they ever were in church, and they understood what was read and said. And glory to God! He gave me the interpretation of their testimonies. Oh, how I praise Him! No need of an interpreter now! (*The Pentecost* 1:4 [December 1908]: 14; cf. *Latter Rain Evangel* [February 1909]: 13)

Clearly here Yoakum understands "interpretation of tongues" mentioned by Paul in 1 Cor 12:10 as a "spiritual gift" to mean "translation," and both he and his audience share in this gift. While a distinctive, perhaps unique, perspective among Pentecostals, his view has deep roots in the Christian exegetical tradition (see Venerable Bede above).

Finally, here is a short quotation from Caleb Oladipo, a Nigerian (Yorubaland) Christian, about the role of the Holy Spirit:

> The spiritual destiny of the Yoruba people is fully guaranteed by the outpouring of this Holy Spirit. In this way, the effloresecence of the Holy Spirit enables the Yoruba people to see the Holy Spirit as the "Grand-Ancestor." ... most Christians in Yorubaland understand that when someone is filled with the Holy Spirit, he is

a passive instrument of a power coming from without. ... ecstatic utterances are common and these utterances are believed to be the manifestation of the Holy Spirit (Oladipo 1996, 108, 112–113).

Oladipo's comments are a reminder of the way in which Christian theology is indigenized in other cultures and that the growth of Christianity in Africa and the Global South so often is accompanied by Pentecostal and Charismatic renewal (Jenkins 2002, 2006).

Acts 2 in Hymns and Music

In the Roman Catholic hymnal, *Gather Hymnal* (1994), the following hymns have Acts 2 as their scriptural basis:

A Hymn of Glory Let Us Sing	453	Venerable Bede
Come Down, O Love Divine	465	Bianco da Siena
Come, Holy Ghost	469	Rabanus Maurus
O Holy Spirit, by Whose Breath	461	Rabanus Maurus
Veni Creator Spiritus	460	Rabanus Maurus
Hail the Day That Sees Him Rise	457	Charles Wesley

There is also a rich musical tradition associated with Pentecost from the ninth-century *Veni Creator Spiritus* to the "Pentecost Songs," a twenty-five cut album (including a rendition of *Veni Creator Spiritus*) released by Cardiphonia in June, 2012.

Peter's Pentecost Sermon (2:14–40)

Peter's interpretation of the Pentecost experience is nearly three times longer than the narrative account detailing the event itself. Different aspects of Peter's Pentecost sermon (2:14–41) were emphasized by various interpreters (see Martin 2006, 27–36).

Radical inclusivity (2:17–18). As one might anticipate in our pluralistic context, the note about "your daughters shall prophesy" (2:17) has been a favorite among those who favor gender inclusiveness in ministry. What might surprise is that as early as 1655, Katherine Sutton (1630–1663), an early English mystic and hymn-writer, found scriptural warrant in Acts 2:17–18 for her "gift of singing":

And often in prayer I did cry unto God, saying, speak Lord, for thy servant desires to hear; and was very desirous to know, what the Lord would have me to understand by this word; and when I had considered I found some thing in my imployment sinful, and a hinderance unto my spiritual injoyments, to convince mee of which, the Lord was pleased to withhold his blessing upon that imployment, which before I had found therein; to the convincing and converting of some to himself, so finding something in it contrary to his will, I was constrained to leave it off, and after much seeking of the Lord for councel, these Scriptures were much with mee, [after citing Math. 7:7, 11].

And on my servants, and on my hand maidens will I pour out of my spirit, and they shall prophesy. Acts 2:18.

These promises did dwell with mee for a long season, so that I was much stirred up to pray to the Lord, that he would please to accomplish them upon mee, and pour out of his blessed Spirit upon mee. And after long seeking (especially one day) being very earnest and importunate with the Lord, after which I went out to walk, and on a sudden I was indued with the gift of singing, in such a way and manner as I had not been acquainted with before; and immediately this following song came in (as fast I could sing) as followeth: it was in the year 1655 in the Month of February (Sutton 1663).

In the latter part of the twentieth and beginning of the twenty-first centuries, the Pentecost narrative served as a starting point for discussion of inclusiveness. The comments by Ella Mitchell (1917–2008), an African-American Baptist preacher and professor and first female Dean of Sisters Chapel at Spelman College, typify this line of argument:

Acts 2:17 has long been a powerful proof text for female liberation in the church. Recently, I have been moved to look at it harder than ever, and certainly much more fruitfully. Today, let this text be a powerful reminder of our standing as persons, a standing that is based on the very word of God. …

All flesh—not just men but women, not just male but also female, not just freeborn persons but slaves as well. And if you have any other distinctions, they go out the window also: not only the rich but the poor, not only the educated but the uneducated, not only the sage and wise ones but those who are limited in their intellectual capabilities (Mitchell 1998, 51).

Elsewhere, she reads the text autobiographically:

God said that he would pour out his Spirit on all flesh, and he has dumped the bucket on a whole lot of women a whole lot of times. He poured it out on me many times before I rose up and came forward, before I made it known that as far back as my teen years I had been called by God, called to preach and as well as to teach. This is in the mind and will of God, and God who changeth not has never willed it otherwise. It's we faltering humans who have the hangups (Mitchell 1985, 1.13–14).

Amos Yong, a Pentecostal professor of theology, has used Acts 2 to speak about a "pneumatological imagination" as a "framework for thinking about the one and its relationship to the many." He writes:

> I suggest that the tongues of Pentecost can be understood to include ... the post-colonial voices of women and persons of color from outside the Euro-American West, as well as those of people with disabilities (e.g., Deaf culture or disability culture). Again the pneumatological imagination provides a theological rationale for engaging the (auto)biographies of people with Down Syndrome and other disabilities and invites us to pay attention to these experiences so as to discern how the Holy Spirit is present and active beyond our assumptions (Yong 2007, 12–13; see also Mitchell 1999, 52).

In contrast to the view of the Dutch Reformed Church in South Africa (discussed above), Pope John Paul II (1920–2005) also understood the power of Pentecost in overcoming divisions according to ethnic groups. On June 3, 1979, upon his first visit to his homeland of Poland after his election as Pope, Pope John Paul II addressed the faithful in his Pentecostal homily, describing the importance of Cyril (826–869) and Methodius (815–885) in bringing Christianity to Greater Moravia in the ninth century:

> After so many centuries the Jerusalem church upper room was again opened up and amazement fell no longer on the peoples of Mesopotamia and Judea, Egypt, and Asia, and visitors from Rome, but also on the Slav peoples and the other peoples living in this part of Europe, as they heard the apostles of Jesus Christ speaking in their tongue and telling in their language "the mighty works of God." ... These languages cannot fail to be heard especially by the first Slav Pope in the history of the Church. Perhaps that is why Christ has chosen him, perhaps that is why the Holy Spirit has led him—in order that he might introduce into the communion of the Church the understanding of the words and of the languages that still sound strange to the ear accustomed to the Romance, Germanic, English and Celtic tongues (Pope John Paul II 1982, 1.3–4, alluding to Acts 2:7).

Billy Graham places Pentecost into the larger Christian narrative of Protestant evangelicalism:

> Unquestionably the coming of the Holy Spirit on the day of Pentecost marked a crucial turning point in the history of God's dealings with the human race. It is one of five past events, all of which are essential components of the Christian gospel: the Incarnation, the Atonement, the Resurrection, the Ascension, and Pentecost. A sixth component is still future: the Second Coming of Jesus.

… Pentecost, the fifth, assures us that the Spirit of God has come to achieve His certain purposes in the world, in the Church, and in the individual believer! (Graham 1978, 21–22).

Across denominational boundaries and theological lines, Pentecost continues to hold a prominent place in Christian thought and practice.

Saved and Ensnared (2:21, 24)

Didymus the Blind (ca. 313–398) distinguishes between those who merely utter the name of Jesus and those "who call on the name of the Lord" (2:21); only the latter "will be saved": "It is not the same to call upon the name of the Lord and to just say it. For indeed the one who prays, and some who desire out of goodness, to receive will call upon the name of the Lord, after which salvation comes. But the one who pretends to be a servant says, 'Lord, Lord' to Jesus, even though he does not do the things of a servant. … He is Lord when one serves him by deed and by disposition, but not when he calls Jesus 'Lord' with only a mere utterance" (*Catena on Acts* 2:21; 38.6–16).

In Acts 2:24, Peter claims that "it was not possible for him [Christ] to be held." Luther connects this with the image of sinners ensnared in the net of the devil and death:

> In Christ God overthrows death and devil similarly; they also had the power to catch and entangle sinners in their net. However, when they tried to use their net also for Christ, thinking: "I have devoured so many of them. I shall also devour Him," they were brought up short and burned their fingers. For he was not the quarry that fit their net. They were warned against going after him. And that is why He stormed through the net and tore it so that it can no longer hold a Christian (*LW* 28:129–30).

Baptismal Regeneration (Acts 2:38)

At the conclusion of Peter's sermon, he urges his hearers: "Repent and be baptized, every one of you, in the name of Jesus Christ, for the remission of your sins …" (2:38a). This verse became a linchpin in the conversion theology of the Stone-Campbell movement, a nineteenth-century restorationist movement that began on the American frontier. Although the non-creedal and congregational nature of Stone-Campbell Movement (SCM) churches has fostered significant doctrinal diversity, a majority of thinkers in the SCM have agreed that baptism is a command one must obey to receive the promises of God. Citing Acts 2:38, most SCM thinkers have concluded that when one confesses (that Christ is Lord), repents, and is baptized, then God forgives that person's sins and gives them the Holy Spirit during the act of baptism. Therefore, many SCM thinkers implicitly and sometimes explicitly have promoted a sacramental view of baptism. M. Eugene Boring has made the case that "Acts 2:38 first attains prominence in Disciples' theology in the preaching and writing of Walter Scott" (1997, 50 n. 45; the Disciples of Christ are an offshoot of the Stone-Campbell Restoration Movement). On the other hand, Barton Stone, another of the founders, credits Alexander Campbell, one of the movement's architects, with bringing his attention to Acts 2:38:

> The subject of baptism now engaged the attention of the people very generally, and some, with myself, began to conclude that it was ordained for the remission of sins, and ought to be administered in the name of Jesus to all believing penitents. I remember once about this time we had a great meeting at Concord. Mourners were invited every day to collect before the stand, in order for prayers (this being the custom of the times). The brethren were praying daily for the same people, and none seemed to be comforted. I was considering in my mind what could be the cause. The words of Peter at Pentecost rolled through my mind: "Repent, and be baptized for the remission of sins, and you shall receive the gift of the Holy Ghost." I thought, were Peter here, he would thus address these mourners. I quickly arose and addressed them in the same language, and urged them to comply. Into the spirit of the doctrine I was never fully led, until it was revived by Brother Alexander Campbell some years after (Rogers, Stone, and Rogers 1910, 182–84).

Alexander Campbell (1788–1866) interprets Acts 2:38 as follows:

> This is what the apostle proposed to his inquiring audience when he said, "Be immersed every one of you into the name of the Lord Jesus for the remission of your sins; and you shall receive the gift of the Holy Spirit; for the promise of this gift is to you and to your children," &c … when we understand the gift of the Holy Spirit promised on Pentecost and that bestowed on the first converts from among the Gentiles, as the words import in the New Testament usage, we are perfectly exempted from every difficulty and from any reasonable objection, in proposing to mankind indiscriminately the remission of sins and the Holy Spirit through faith *and* immersion (Campbell 1828, 453–54; emphasis added).

In his commentary on Acts, Frank Stagg, a Baptist seminary professor (1911–2001), sought, on the basis of grammatical and hermeneutical grounds, to "correct" the view that water baptism was *necessary* for the forgiveness of sins:

> A much disputed verse (38) appears in this paragraph. [Acts 2:37–40] Is baptism represented as a condition for forgiveness of sins? This is a favorite "proof text" for those who believe in baptismal regeneration. … The clear teaching of the New Testament as a whole would rule out baptismal regeneration … (Stagg 1955, 62–64).

A possible translation, permitted by the Greek, is as follows: "Repent, and let each of you be baptized in the name of Jesus Christ *on the basis of* the forgiveness of your sins, and you shall receive the free gift of the Holy Spirit." This translation depends upon the possibility of the causal use of the Greek preposition *eis* followed by the accusative case. Though this construction in the Greek New Testament usually denotes result, there can be no doubt that it is used for grounds or reason (causal) a few times in the New Testament:

> Probably the phrase in question, "for the forgiveness of your sins," is to be taken primarily with "repent" rather than with "be baptized." Forgiveness followed repentance, not baptism. Baptism was a means of portraying the repentance, a public confession of faith in Jesus (Stagg 1955, 62–64).

In an interesting spillover of ecclesiastical debates into academic circles, a series of articles published in the *Journal of Biblical Literature* in the 1950s discussed whether or not the Greek preposition *eis* could have a causal sense and whether it did so in Acts 2:38 (be baptized because of the remission of sins). J.R. Mantey made the ultimately unconvincing case for a causal sense. Although Mantey was a Baptist and, like Stagg, had some denominational interests in promoting causal *eis*, we should note that Mantey's *JBL* interlocutor was not from the Stone-Campbell movement, but was none other than renowned Jewish scholar, Ralph Marcus, of the University of Chicago (Mantey 1951, 45–48; Marcus 1951, 45–48; Marcus 1952, 43-44), who rejected Mantey's arguments. Furthermore, the doctrinal debate cannot be decided purely on grammatical grounds, since there are many grammarians who reject the causal *eis* interpretation and yet do not advocate a baptismal regeneration interpretation for Acts 2:38. Daniel Wallace, for example, sees in Acts 2:38 a combination of a "spiritual reality" and a "physical symbol" (Wallace 1996, 370).

For Oneness Pentecostals, such as founder Frank Ewart (1876–1947), the baptismal formula, "in the name of Jesus," became a foundational text in their non-Trinitarian theology. One last interesting note, Acts 2:38 (with forty citations) is the most quoted *verse* in Acts in the 292 creeds and confessions indexed by Pelikan and Hotchkiss (2003).

Visual Interpretation of Acts 2:38

Donald Jackson brings us to the contemporary age with his illustration of Acts 2:38 in *The Saint John's Bible* (**Figure 10**, color plate). The Order of Saint Benedict in Collegeville, Minnesota created a Bible with handwritten text and illumination to allow a medieval tradition to live on in an ecumenical and contemporary way. Peter's statement, "Do penance, and be baptized every one of you in the name of Jesus Christ," is written on the opening page of the Acts of the Apostles.

This work is not a new endeavor for the Benedictines, whose communities of monks have been the calligraphers and illuminators of Bibles for over fifteen hundred years. On the occasion of the second millennium of Christ's birth, *The Saint John's Bible* has been created "to inspire a renewed love of Scripture intertwined with art" (http://www.saintjohnsbible.org/Products/9056/psalms.aspx).

As the first handwritten and illuminated Bible commissioned since the invention of the printing press in the late fifteenth century, *The St. John's Bible* is "the one thing we'll probably be remembered for 500 years from now," writes Eric Hollas, OSB, a monk at Saint John's Abbey and Associate Director of Arts and Culture at Saint John's University who has been instrumental throughout the project.

The Saint John's Bible grew out of a meeting between the distinguished calligraphic artist Donald Jackson and Fr. Hollas in 1995. Jackson, a native of Lancashire, England, decided at a young age that he wanted to do two things with his talent—to become the "Queen's Scribe" and to inscribe and illuminate the Bible. He achieved the first goal when he became scribe to Her Majesty Queen Elizabeth's Crown Office at the House of Lords at age twenty-six, and he achieved the second with the completion of *The Saint John's Bible*. The patron raised four million dollars over eight years from individuals, groups, and corporations. On Ash Wednesday in the year 2000, Jackson penned the first words of *The Saint John's Bible*; they were the opening verses of the Gospel of John: "In the beginning was the Word, and the Word was with God, the Word was God" (http://www.saintjohnsbible.org/).

Jackson called this project his "Sistine Chapel." In the medieval workshop tradition, he oversaw the work of ten designers, illustrators, and illuminators at a scriptorium in Wales. Some of the artists return to their own studios with the pages after receiving direction from Jackson.

The original manuscript of *The Saint John's Bible* is bound in seven volumes (15¾ in wide by 23½ in tall when closed) with a total of 1150 pages and 160 illuminations. The lettering was devised by Jackson and then replicated by the scribes. The *Bible* was inscribed on vellum (calf skin or parchment) using swan, goose, and turkey quills, natural handmade inks, handground pigments, and gold leaf. Over 250 skins have been rubbed and sanded; on thinner pages, lines were drawn for writing, and thicker skins were prepared for the illuminations. The volumes of the original manuscript will be a source for religious, artistic, educational, and scholarly programming and exhibitions. Reproductions of the *Bible* are being produced at sixty-two percent of actual size (9¾ in × 15 in) for purchase by congregations and individuals.

The text is carefully arranged on each spacious page to encourage readers to notice the lettering and ponder its meaning. In contemporary artistic jargon, this is truly a project of "mark-making." The illuminators use egg yolk to bind the colors together and give the images great luminosity, a beautiful technique borrowed from the tempera panel paintings in the Renaissance. In another ancient practice, thin slices of gold leaf are placed on gesso (sugar, fish glue, whole lead powder, and slate plaster) and then on to the vellum. *The Saint John's Bible* also incorporates modern themes, contemporary illustrations, and production technology of the twenty-first century.

In a significant departure from medieval practice, the words of Scripture are presented in English rather than Latin. The use of the New Revised Standard Version translation shows the influence of the project's Protestant and Jewish advisors. Its predecessor, the Revised Standard Version of the Bible, had the distinction of being officially authorized for use by all major Christian churches—Protestant, Anglican, Roman Catholic, and Eastern Orthodox. The NRSV is a modern English translation that maintains traditional references to God but uses gender-inclusive language for humanity in an unobtrusive manner.

The illumination of Acts 2:38 combines the words, "Repent and Be Baptized Every One of You in the Name of Jesus Christ" with the images of St. John's Abbey and University Church emerging from the wall of the golden Jerusalem. The crowd stems from a Saint John's University football game. The checkered flags fly at the Saint John's campus on graduation day. *The St. John's Bible* unites symbols from the campus church community (the abbey and University Church) with the church of Jerusalem. The crowd that Peter addresses becomes the St. John's football fans. The graduation flags mark the beginning of the lives of those students who move beyond the campus boundaries and, as baptized Christians, will continue the ministry of Christ on Earth. The juxtaposition of blue and gold reminds the viewer of not only medieval illumination but also of mosaics and stained glass. The fragmented quality found in the lower half of the painting also recalls the passing of light through a colored window.

Community Possessions (Acts 2:41–47)

Patristic writers were attentive to the ways in which the early Church responded to issues of wealth and possessions (Acts 2:42–47). John Chrysostom, for example, commented about the example of the early Church recorded in Acts 2: "Neither did they consider their brethren's property foreign to themselves; it was the property of a Master; nor again deemed they aught their own, all was the brethren's. The poor man knew no shame, the rich no haughtiness. This is gladness. The latter deemed himself the obliged and fortunate party; the others felt themselves as honored herein, and closely were they bound together" (*Hom. Act. 7*).

In addition, the monastics who preferred ascetic life that consisted of living in community (cenobitic) rather than in solitary isolation (eremitic) based much of their way of living on the summaries in Acts chapter 2 and especially chapter 4 (for more, see comments on 4.32–35). For example, the monastic Coptic community established by Pachomius (c. 292–346) referred to itself as the *koinonia*, a term featured prominently in Acts, and especially Acts 2:42. "We should love another and show that we are truly servants of the Lord Jesus Christ and sons of Pachomius and disciples of the *koinonia*" (*Liber Orsiesii* 23).

Peter Olivi (1248–98) was a radical theologian and leader of the Spirituals, the "rigorist wing" of the Franciscan Order (Garnsey 2012, 35). Their distinctive interpretation of the Bible (especially Acts 2 and 4) led them to renounce both individual and communal ownership of property (thus challenging the very foundations of the monastic movement). In his pamphlet, *Tractatus*, Olivi argued that the vow of poverty taken by members of the Franciscan Order meant they should use things only to the degree that necessity demanded (*usus pauper*). Further, Olivi argued that the Apostles were "proto-Franciscans" who "renounced all rights over property, both as individuals and as a community" (Garnsey 2012, 38). Thus, Olivi interprets Acts 2:44 ("they held all things in common") to refer only to those things necessary for use by the evangelical poor such as daily bread and basic clothing. Everything else was sold that would violate the practice of evangelical poverty (Garnsey 2012, 40; Garnsey 2007; see also comments on Acts 4:32–37).

Walter Rauschenbusch (1861–1918), father of the Social Gospel movement, was careful to distinguish between the Early Christian practice of sharing goods and communism: "But whatever the extent of this generosity may have been, it was always generosity and not communism in any proper sense of the word. No one was required to turn his property into the common fund of admission" (1907, 122; cf. Walton 2008, 99–111).

Acts 2:41–47 is also an important text in the creedal tradition. According to the index to *Creeds and Confessions of Faith in the Christian Tradition*, Acts 2:42–47, with forty-six citations, is the most oft-cited *passage* (with references to the entire passage as well as individual verses) in Acts. Often these verses are referenced in articles dealing with the nature and/or practices of the Christian Church (see, e.g., Westminster Confession of Faith, 1646, Article XXV "Of the Church").

Acts 3–5

Overview

Acts 3–5 is composed of two episodes: the healing of a lame man (3:1–4:31) and reports of the internal and external tensions and conflicts experienced by the first Christian community (4:32–5:42). The first episode, the healing of the lame man, divides into four scenes: the first two (3:1–10; 3:11–4:4) take place in the vicinity of the Jewish Temple. The healing (3:1–10) is a favorite among artists; Raphael and Poussin are treated here. Within Peter's speech (3:11–26) and the story of his arrest (4:1–4), Acts 3:20–21 is the focus of

The Acts of the Apostles Through the Centuries, First Edition. Heidi J. Hornik and Mikeal C. Parsons.
© 2017 Heidi J. Hornik and Mikeal C. Parsons. Published 2017 by John Wiley & Sons, Ltd.

Christology: Cambridge University biblical scholar John A.T. Robinson (1919–1983) sees in it the most "primitive Christology" in the New Testament, and Søren Kierkegaard notes an ambiguity of theological significance in the Greek. Does Christ take his place in heaven? Or does heaven take Christ up? The third and fourth scenes take place more generally in Jerusalem, in the council chambers of the Sanhedrin (4:5–22) and the house in which the Jerusalem believers were meeting (4:23–31). Acts 4:12, with its assertion that there is "no other name ... by which we must be saved," is the center of exegetical attention in these sections, from Venerable Bede (eighth century), who related it to the fate of Old Testament figures, to the 1974 Lausanne Covenant adopted by participants in the International Congress of World Evangelization who cite it in their soteriological claims regarding the exclusivity and universality of Christ.

The second episode, 4:32–5:41, also consists of two units: 4:32–5:11, which addresses issues of conflict within the community, and 5:12–41, which considers issues of conflict with those outside the community. Commenting on the first unit, interpreters explore the implications of the shared life of the early community (4:32–37). The passage provided scriptural warrant for the cenobitic ascetic lifestyle advocated by Pachomius, the radical views of Peter Olivi, the restribution of wealth by Gerrard Winstanley, and the call to Christian benefaction by John Wesley. The story of Sapphira and Ananias (5:1–11) captured the imagination of artists like Massacio, Raphael, Poussin, and their patrons. In the second unit, Acts 5:12–41, Acts 5:29 ("we must obey God rather than any human authority") was utilized in a number of conflicts, whether theological debates between Reformers and the Catholic Church or between Radical Dissenters and the civil authorities over the relationship between Church and State.

Reception and Interpretation

Healing a Lame Man (Acts 3:1–4:31)

The Healing (3:1–10). John Chrysostom commented on the remarkable response to the lame man by Peter, who performed the miracle expecting nothing in return (3:4–6):

> What then does Peter do? He did not despise him; he did not look about for some rich subject; he not say, 'If the miracle is not done to some great one, nothing great is done.' He did not expect any payment from him, nor was it in the presence of others that he healed him. For the man was at the entrance, not inside, where

the crowd was. Peter did not look for any of these things, nor did he enter and preach; no, it was his bearing that drew the lame man to ask. And the wonder is that he believed so readily (*Hom. Act.* 8).

Eusebius of Caesarea (260–339) comments on Peter's response that he has no silver or gold to share (Acts 3:6): "And who would not be astonished at their indifference to money, certified by their not turning from but welcoming a Master who forbade the possession of silver and gold?" (*Dem. ev.* 3.5; ACCS, 41).

Ammonius compares the healing of the lame man with the Gospel stories of the healing of the paralytic (Matt 9:2) and the woman with the hemorrhage (Matt 9:22); in all three, a commensurable faith between supplicant and healer is highlighted: "Therefore, it is necessary for the faith of both to agree, that is the faith of the one who is made well and the faith of the one who prays earnestly, just like in the time of the paralytic and the woman suffering from a hemorrhage" (*Catena on Acts* 3:16; 64.14–16).

With the rise of historical criticism came skepticism regarding the historicity of many of the events in the Gospels and Acts. Gerd Lüdemann's comments about the lack of historicity in the healing account of Acts 3, while blunter than usual, are not atypical: "There is no historical nucleus to the tradition of the miracle story in vv. 1–10. Those who are lame from their childhood are (unfortunately) not made whole again" (Lüdemann 1987, 54).

Peter's Speech (3:11–26). This address of Peter speaks of the sending of Jesus by the "God of Abraham," his suffering "according to the prophets," death, resurrection, exaltation to heaven and future return in the "time of universal restoration." Cassiodorus, sixth-century monk, highlights the reference in Peter's sermon to the power of God: "His might was also made known when Peter and John made the lame man from birth walk, and they said, 'Men of Israel, why marvel at this, as if by our own strength or devotion we had made this man to walk?' And a little later they say that he was made whole in the name of Christ Jesus" (*Exposition of the Psalms* 144.12; ACCS, 42).

The consensus of modern critical scholarship has been that the speeches in Acts (mostly) reflect the theological perspective of the author (Dibelius 1951). One notable exception to this *opinio communis* was the provocative proposal of John A.T. Robinson who argued that Acts 3:12–26 preserved what he called the "earliest Christology of all." Robinson clarified that in Peter's speech in Acts 3, Jesus would not become the "Messiah/Christ" until his Parousia, or as the author of Acts put it, God will "send the Messiah appointed for you, that is, Jesus, who must remain in heaven until the time of universal restoration" (3:20–21). This "primitive view" asserts that Jesus is "still only the Christ-elect and is to be fully installed as Messiah when God sends him again for the salvation of Israel." According to Robinson, this position is "embedded in the book of Acts like a fossil of a by-gone age" (Robinson 1956, 177). This is not, of course, the way the verse is used in the creedal traditions, which tend to deploy the passage in straightforward support of the Second Coming or Parousia of Christ, who was already Messiah during his earthly life: The First Confession of Basel (1534), Article 6.d; Westminster Confession of Faith (1647), Chapter 29.6.m; New Hampshire Confession (1833/1853), Article 1.a; United Presbyterian Church *Confessional Statement* (1925), Article 40; Westminster Confession of Faith (1647), Chapter 32.1.c; Cumberland Presbyterian Church, *Confession of Faith* (1814/1883), Article 105.c; United Presbyterian Church *Confessional Statement* (1925), Article 2; True Confession (1596), Article 35; Catechesis and Confession of Faith of Polish Brethren (1574), [C].6 Question 7; *Second Helvetic Confession* (1566), Chapter 11.[12]; United Presbyterian Church *Confessional Statement* (1925), Article 12; French Confession (1559/1571), Article 36.a; Bohemian Confession (1535), Article 6.[2]; New Hampshire Confession (1833/1853), Article 18.o; The Transylvanian Confession of Faith (1579), Article 1; Second Vatican Council (1962-65), §5.1, Chapter 7.48.

Between 1833 and 1836, Søren Kierkegaard translated Acts 1–4 from Greek into Latin "as part of his participation in the instruction at the University of Copenhagen" (Bruun and Jensen 2010, 224). In a marginal note on Acts 3:20–21, he comments on the intentional ambiguity of his translation:

> I have taken pains to include an ambiguity in my translation. One can say either: "whom it behoves to take [his place in] heaven" or "whom it behoves heaven to take," which seems to have more of a meaning for dogmatics, since the work of Christ was not completed before his return, and to that extent heaven takes him up, i.e., he returned to where he was before, in order subsequently to take dominion over heaven (*SKS* 17:149; cited in Bruun and Jensen 2010, 227).

No Other Name (Acts 4:12). In Acts 4:12, Peter claims that "there is no other name under heaven given to people, whereby we must be saved." The Venerable Bede employs this passage to comment on the fate of figures from the OT: "If the salvation of the world is in no other but in Christ alone, then the fathers of the Old Testament were saved by the incarnation and passion of the same Redeemer, by which we also believe and hope to be saved" (*Comm. Acts* 4:12; cf. Aquinas, *ST*; *CCEL* 2657). Chrysostom comments on the same passage:

> "For there is no other name under heaven given among persons by which we must be saved." These words belong to a soul that has renounced the present life. His great outspokenness demonstrates this. Here he makes it clear that even when he speaks in lowly terms of Christ, he does it not because he is afraid but of condescension. Now that the time has come, he speaks in lofty terms to amaze all his listeners by the very change. Behold another miracle no less great than the earlier one (*Hom. Act.* 10; NPNF 11.67).

Medieval French philosopher and theologian Peter Abelard alludes to Acts 4:12 in his *Confession of Faith to Hèloïse* (1139–42): "I do not wish to be a philosopher if it means conflicting with Paul, nor to be an Aristotle if it cuts me off from Christ. For there is no other name under heaven whereby I must be saved" (cited in *CCF*, 1:737).

Zwingli (1530) alludes to Acts 4:12 to criticize certain practices of medieval Catholicism: "I know that there is no other victim for expiating crimes than Christ; for not even was Paul crucified for us; that there is no other name under the sun in which we must be saved than that of Jesus Christ. Here, therefore, not only the justification and satisfaction of our works are denied, but also the expiation or intercession of all saints" (*A Reckoning of the Faith*; cited in *CCF*, 2:253; cf. e.g., *Second Helvetic Confession* [1566] 5.4 and Church of England *Thirty-Nine Articles* [1571], Article 18; cited in *CCF*, 2:466, 533). At the Council of Trent, the Catholic Church used Acts 4:12 to re-assert the efficacy of baptism, properly administered: "If anyone denies the actual merit of Christ Jesus is applied to both adults and infants through the sacrament of baptism duly administered in the form of the church: let him be anathema; for there is no other name under heaven given among people by which we must be saved" (*Dogmatic Decrees of Council of Trent* [1546], "Decree on Original Sin"; cited in *CCF*, 2:825). In its argument against membership in "secret societies," the (old) Mennonite church alluded to Acts 4:12: "We are opposed to membership in secret societies and loges, because such membership would involve an unequal yoke with unbelievers, and because these organizations employ hierarchical titles, require oaths, stand for organized secrecy, and may offer salvation on grounds other than faith in the Lord Jesus Christ" (*Mennonite Confession* [1963], Article 17 "Christian Integrity"; cited in *CCF*, 3:684). Appealing to Acts 4:12, more than 2,700 participants in the international Congress on World Evangelization, self-identified "evangelicals" from 135 denominations and 150 countries, voted to oppose what was thought to be global relativization of the historic Christian claim about the soteriological "uniqueness and universality of Christ" (*The Lausanne Covenant* [1974]; cited in *CCF*, 3:755).

Symbolism of Forty Years? (Acts 4:22). The Venerable Bede, using the symbolism of forty (the age of the lame man according to Peter) to draw a comparison to Israel, stated: "According to the historical sense, this shows that the man's mature age [made him] invincible to detractors. Allegorically, however, [the passage signifies that] the people of Israel ... in the land of promise continued always to limp along [*claudicabat*] with the rites of idols together with those of the Lord" (*Comm. Acts* 4.22). Fifth-century bishop Severus of Antioch, on the other hand, sees the lame man as a type of the church, "[how it] is lame to the knowledge of God from ancient times, and having been in sin from her [the church's] mother's womb, because of the transgression of Adam and Eve" (*Catena on Acts* 3:6–7; 59.21–25). Modern commentator, Scott Spencer, agrees with Bede on the symbolism of forty, though he infers a different significance for the number: "As God's saving purpose for ancient Israel was finally realized after forty years of stumbling and meandering throught the wilderness, so the moment of fresh renewal—signalled by the dance of a forty-year-old cripple—has dawned upon the present Israel" (Spencer 1997, 52; contra Johnson 1992, 97).

Community Prayer (4:25–31). The prayer of the church in Acts 4:25–31, in which believers ask God the creator to grant them boldness in speaking, has been viewed as a model for subsequent Christians. Irenaeus (c. 125–200) observed: "These [are the] voices of the church from which every church had its origin; these are the voices of the metropolis of the citizens of the new covenant; these are the voices of the apostles; these are the voices of the disciples of the Lord, the truly perfect, who, after the assumption of the Lord, were perfected by the Spirit, and called on the God who made the heaven and earth and the sea—who was announced by the prophets—and Jesus Christ his Son whom God anointed and who knew no other [God]" (*Haer.* 3.12.5; ACCS, 53). Alexandrian theologian and biblical exegete Didymus the Blind (ca. 313–398) appeals to the prayer to combat those with "heretical views" who attempted to separate the "Father of Jesus Christ" from the "demiurge" God of the OT:

> In accordance with their blasphemous view, they say that these gods are in opposition to each other; and their scriptures as well; that those who seek refuge in the Lord are enemies of the demiurge and better people obtain the latter … The present Scripture passage exposes their impiety by bringing in the apostles. After their release from the plot of the high priests and elders, they went to their friends, that is, they who share their faith. Together with them they sent up a hymn of thanks to the Creator of heaven and earth, mentioning that he spoke through the mouth of David (in the Holy Spirit, naturally) … After all this it is clear that the demiurge and the Father of the Savior is the same God and that both covenants are given by him (*Catena on Acts* 4.25; ACCS, 53–54).

Arator comments briefly on Luke's notice that the place where the believers "were gathered was shaken" (4:31): "The power of the apostles' words, which made those created from earth have faith, altered and set in motion the ground … the joyful earth was moved under the tread of them [the apostles] to whom peace was given by the word of the Holy Master" (*OAA*, 1).

Visual Exegesis of the Healing of the Lame Man (Acts 3:1–4:31). The story of the healing of the lame man captured the imagination of artists over the centuries. We consider two depictions by Renaissance Old Masters, Raphael (**Figure 11**) and Poussin. The painting style of Raphael (1483–1520) is the reason he was chosen in 1513 by the newly-elected Giovanni de'Medici as Pope Leo X (1513–1521) to design tapestries for the walls of his private

FIGURE 11   Raphael (1483–1520). *The Healing of the Lame Man.* 1515–16. Watercolor
on paper mounted onto canvas (tapestry cartoon), 3.4 × 5.4m. Victoria and
Albert Museum, London, Great Britain. Photo: V&A Images, London/Art Resource, NY

chapel, the Sistine (Evans and Browne 2010; cf. White and Shearman 1958,
193–221, 229–323; Shearman 1992, 216–18, 223, 238–39, 252–53; Fermor
1996; Fermor 1998, 236–50). The ten tapestries, woven in Brussels from cartoons made by Raphael, were to hang beneath the frescoes commissioned by
Pope Sixtus IV della Rovere (1471–84) in the early 1480s (Gilbert 1987, 533–
50). Very few visitors today realize that the Sistine Chapel decoration is
incomplete without the tapestries. The iconographic importance of the tapestries to the Sistine Chapel program rivaled Michelangelo's ceiling (1508–12),
commissioned by Pope Julius II (1503–13), in fame and beauty during the
sixteenth century.

The narrative scenes of the original tapestry program were tailored to continue the iconography of the *Capella papalis.* The proper titles for the Sistine are
Capella palatina and *Capella magna* (or *maior*) in the Vatican. Together with
the Basilica of St. Peter's, the chapel was the primary location for the liturgical
feasts of the pope and his court. St. Peter's was the premier church of
Christendom, and the chapel represented Christ's vicar on earth, the pope. The
manifestation of the *Maiestas Papalis* occurred not only in the magnificence of
these structures and the money spent on the gold and silver threads used to
weave the tapestries but also in the narratives painted on the walls under Sixtus,
the ceiling under Julius, and the tapestries under Leo.

The theme of papal authority is continued through the placement of the life of Peter tapestries beneath the scenes from the life of Christ frescoes on the north wall. The narratives of Paul's life woven into tapestries are located beneath the painted life of Moses on the opposite wall. Sharon Fermor explains the selection of these tapestry narratives: "Peter and Paul are portrayed as the twin founders of the Christian church, with special missions to convert the Jews and Gentiles respectively. They are also presented as the joint sources of the Pope's own authority and the tapestries were certainly intended to have a personal and political dimension for Leo in his role as Pope" (Fermor 1996, 10). Each tapestry series parallels the 1480s frescoes: Peter and Christ, Moses and Paul. The tapestries were not permanently on display but were put up on special occasions.

As one faces the altar, the Peter scenes are placed below the Christ frescoes and begin on the right side of the altar and move clockwise onto the side wall in the following order: *Miraculous Draught of Fishes* (Luke 5:3–10), *Christ's Charge to Peter* (Matt 16:18–19; John 21:15–17), *Healing of the Lame Man* (Acts 3:1–11), *Death of Ananias* (Acts 5:1–6). The scene on the left side of the altar is the *Stoning of Stephen* (Acts 6,7). The Paul scenes continue along the side wall, in a counter-clockwise direction, below the Moses frescoes. The Paul compositions are: *Conversion of Saul* (Acts 9:1–9), *Blinding of Elymas* (Acts 13:6–12), *Sacrifice at Lystra* (Acts 14:8–18), *Paul in Prison* (Acts 16:23–6), *Paul Preaching at Athens* (Acts 17:15–34). The cartoons are lost for the *Conversion of Saul, Paul in Prison* and *Stoning of Stephen*.

The tripartite division of the scene in the *Healing of the Lame Man* derives from Early Christian sarcophagi. The twisted columns are based upon the twelve antique spiral columns that created the screen in St. Peter's basilica and were believed to have come from Solomon's Temple in Jerusalem (Evans and Browne 2010, 83). Probable sources used by Raphael for the composition include the relief of *The Healing of the Lame Man* from the ciborium of Sixtus IV, and Albrecht Durer's engraving of the same subject, dated 1513 (Evans and Browne 2010, 83).

The crowd has gathered at the Beautiful Gate, the *Porta speciosa*, between the second and third of the peripheral courts around the Temple of Jerusalem. Peter stands in the center with John looking towards the lame man. Peter is healing the man through a blessing gesture. In the cartoon Peter raises his left hand but the tapestry will be woven in reverse. This act is symbolic of Peter's spiritual healing and the conversion of the Jews (Evans and Browne 2010, 83).

Painters throughout time have interpreted biblical stories by incorporating narrative details with technical characteristics of the contemporary artistic style. Such is the case with Nicholas Poussin's *Saints Peter and John Healing the Lame Man* (**Figure 12**). By this later point in his career, Poussin was an established Baroque painter who preferred the revival of classicism in art rather than

FIGURE 12   Nicolas Poussin (1594–1665). *Saints Peter and John Healing the Lame Man*. 1655. Oil on canvas, 49 1/2 × 65 in. Marquand Fund, 1924 (24.45.2).
The Metropolitan Museum of Art, New York, NY, U.S.A. Image copyright © The Metropolitan Museum of Art. Image source: Art Resource, NY

the realism of his contemporary, Caravaggio. He painted this work in 1655 for a merchant and treasurer from Lyons named Mercier. It has been called Poussin's swansong to the Renaissance tradition of rhetorical history painting (Verdi 1995, 300–301).

Poussin's style blends the Baroque and Classical movements that were in high debate in Rome during the 1630s. This story is not told through the expected Baroque methods of dramatic gesture or illusionistic effects. Poussin organized narratives using small stages with wax figures and arranged draperies. The mind of the viewer was Poussin's focus as he painted.

This is the third and last of Poussin's great cityscapes of the mid-1650s. Both Raphael's own cartoon rendition of the same story for the tapestries of the Sistine Chapel discussed above and his *School of Athens*, a 1509 fresco painted in the Stanza della Segnatura for Pope Julius II, served as compositional sources. Poussin applied Michelangelo's gesture between God and Adam in the *Creation of Adam* from the Sistine ceiling (1508–1512) to that of Peter and the lame man. John the Beloved is a supporting character in the story and, literally, in the painting as he holds the elevated arm of the lame man.

The event, as in the Raphael cartoon, occurs on the steps of the Temple in Jerusalem. Poussin's depiction of the Beautiful Gate uses classical architectural columns. The lame man, reclining in a typically classical pose, has a malnourished body but it is not obvious that he cannot walk. No deformity or disability is evident in this classical figure. Poussin manipulated the conventions of classical art: the heavily-draped figures in highly-saturated colors recently found in Roman wall paintings and rhetorical, animated gestures. It is a stage set in a most simplistic and effective manner. The gestures are exaggerated whether the figures sit, stand, turn from or face us (Sprinson 2003; http://www. metmuseum.org/toah/works-of-art/24.45.2/ [accessed 21 July 2016]). In addition to Raphael, another possible source is Philips Galle's engraving of 1558 after Maerten van Heemskerck's composition (Kurita 1998, 747–48). Theodore Gericault (1791–1824) later drew Poussin's painting in reverse, probably for an engraving (Thompson 1992, 46).

In the Acts account, the healing is not a popular event with the religious authorities who command the Apostles "not to speak at all nor teach in the name of Jesus" (Acts 4:27). Almsgiving is a central aspect of both this painting and the works of the Apostles. A wealthy nobleman is giving alms to the man at the left of the composition where the observer's eyes begin to view the picture. The triangular design brings the eye upward to the central scene and then back down to the right to an elderly man who actually points toward the nobleman and the reclined figure on the right where the viewer began. Part of the teachings of the Apostles emphasized that God's mercy would be shown to those performing acts of charity. The theme of the rich selling their possessions and distributing their wealth to the poor is also reflected in another painting by Poussin from the Acts narratives, *The Death of Sapphira* (see below).

Tensions Within and Without (Acts 4:32–5:42)

Community Possessions (Acts 4:32–37). Cyprian Bishop of Carthage (c. 200–258) sees in Acts 4:32–37 the scriptural basis for almsgiving as a central activity of the Church (*Eleem.* 25; cited by Garnsey 2007, 68–69). Soon after, Acts 4:32–37 (along with Acts 2:41–47) provided a kind of "blueprint" for later Christian ascetics, particularly those who preferred cenobitic life (living in community) to the eremitic life (living in isolation). In his account of the ascetic Anthony's conversion, fourth-century Bishop of Alexandria, Athanasius, alludes to Acts 4: "As he was walking along he collected his thoughts and reflected how the Apostles left everything and followed the Savior, also how the people in Acts sold what they had and laid it at the feet of the Apostles for distribution among the needy, and what great hope is laid up in heaven for such as these" (*Vit. Ant.* C2; cited by

Martin 1972, 31–32). Likewise, Acts 4 figured prominently in this description of Pachomius, one of the early and chief proponents of cenobitic ascetism: "This arrangement which he had established with them could be adjusted in keeping with their weakness as the apostle says: 'I became weak with the weak in order to gain the weak' (1 Cor 9:22) ... he proceeded in this way because he saw that they were not ready yet to bind themselves together in that perfect community as it is described in the Acts in regard to the believers; 'they were of one heart and one soul and all goods were in common and no one said of the things that belonged to him 'this is mine'" (*Les Views coptes de Saint Pachôme*, Lefort ed. S [1] 3, 12–32; cited by Martin 1972, 32). One of the early rulebooks of Pachomian spirituality features the language and concepts of Acts 4:

> We read in the Acts of the Apostles: 'The multitude of believers was of one heart and soul, and no one called anything his own; rather they held everything in common. The apostles gave witness to the Resurrection of the Lord Jesus with great power' (Acts 4:32–33). ... So those of us who live in coenobia and are joined to one another by mutual love, should be zealous for discovering how, in this life, we may have fellowship with the holy fathers so that in the future life we may share in their lot; knowing that the Cross is the source of our doctrine, and that we must suffer along with Christ (Rom 8:17) ... (*Liber Orsiesii* 50).

John Cassian, fourth/fifth-century monk, provided further scriptural warrant for this proto-monastic lifestyle by aligning Acts 4:32–35 with Acts 15 and arguing that, after the Apostolic Council, some of the early community set off for the desert where they practiced community of goods and celibacy: "This was the only kind of monk and the oldest; first not only in time but also in grace, and which preserved itself inviolate to the time of the Abbas Paul and Anthony, and whose traces we can see today in fervent coenobia" (*Coll.* 18:5; cited by Martin 1972, 38).

Similarly, Augustine used Acts 4 (and 2) as the scriptural foundation for a statement of principle, the *Praeceptum*, for the shared monastic life that he began in Hippo: "The chief motivation for your sharing your life together is to live harmoniously in the [one] house and to have one heart and one soul seeking God—*in deum*. Do not call anything your own. Possess everything in common (*Praeceptum* 2; cited by Brown 2012, 171). In fact, Acts 4:32–35 is theologically operative in no less than fifty places in the writing of Augustine (Martin 1972, 36)! He was particularly drawn to the description of the primitive community as being of "one heart and soul" (4:32): "... the souls of many men, after they had received the Holy Spirit and in a certain way had been welded together by the fire of love, made up but one soul ... so many hearts, so many thousands of hearts, the love of the Holy Spirit calls one soul because he had made them but one soul" (*Coll. Max. Ar.,* 12; PL 42:715; cited by Martin

1972, 36; cf. *In Ps.* 131; PL 37:1718; *In Joann.* 39.5; CCSL 36:347 f.; *Reg.*; PL 32:13–37). The sharing of possessions was a material expression of this spiritual unity so important to Augustine (Brown 2012, 168).

The "Spiritual" Franciscan, Peter Olivi, had an interesting interpretation of Acts 4:32b ("no one claimed private ownership of any possessions, but everything they owned was held in common"), making Luke, as it were, an "honorary Franciscan." Olivi claimed "the simple use of the possession of some things, for example, clothing or food or books or houses, can be held without any legal right or dominion or proprietary right" (Garnsey 2012, 40, 41). Further, Olivi argued, the Apostles had authority over the proceeds laid at their feet (4:35, 37), but it belonged to no one. Thus, the community could consume food and use clothing without possessing it, and the apostles could dispense bread and goods, like cooks and waiters, or rather oversee their distribution, again without possessing them. This is one of the most radical readings of Acts 4 found in the interpretive tradition (see Garnsey 2012, 42; cf. also comments on Olivi at Acts 2:41–47).

In 1649, in the immediate aftermath of the execution of Charles I and the establishment of a commonwealth in Britain, erstwhile merchant, Gerrard Winstanley (1609–1676), published a pamphlet entitled, "The New Law of Righteousnes," in which he argued that all lands were to be shared communal property rather than held by individuals. Acts 4:32 (and other texts) provided scriptural warrant:

> Leave of this buying and selling of Land, or of the fruits of the earth, and as it was in the light of Reason first made, so let it be in action, amongst all a common Treasurie; none inclosing or hedging in any part of earth, saying, this is mine; which is rebellion and high treason against the King of Righteousnesse: And let this word of the Lord be acted amongst all; work together, eat bread together. Acts 4.32. (Winstanley 1649, in Corns et al. 2009, 523; cf. Gurney 2007, 100).

Shortly after publication of the pamphlet, Winstanley and his followers, known as the "Diggers," took over some common land in Surrey, raised crops, and distributed the produce freely among commoners; other Digger communities soon dotted the English countryside. As a result of action by local landowners, the Diggers' houses and crops were destroyed. Within a year the Digger communities had been disbanded. Winstanley later died as a Quaker in 1676 (cf. Gurney 2013).

John Wesley (1703–91) preached a sermon entitled "Scriptural Christianity" based on Acts 4:31 at St. Mary's, Oxford on August 24, 1744. In his application of the scripture to his university audience, he queried:

> And, first, I would ask, Where does this Christianity now exist? Where, I pray, do the Christians live? Which is the country, the inhabitants whereof are all thus filled with the Holy Ghost? – are all of one heart and of one soul? Cannot suffer one among them to lack anything, but continually give to every man as

he hath need; who, one and all, have the love of God filling their hearts, and constraining them to love their neighbour as themselves; who have all "put on bowels of mercy, humbleness of mind, gentleness, long-suffering?" [Col. 3:12] Who offend not in any kind, either by word or deed, against justice, mercy, or truth; but in every point do unto all men; as they would these should do unto them? With what propriety can we term any a Christian country, which does not answer this description? Why then, let us confess we have never yet seen a Christian country upon earth(http://www.umcmission.org/Find-Resources/John-Wesley-Sermons/Sermon-4-Scriptural-Christianity#sthash.kTrTOe7H.dpuf).

We return to *The St. John's Bible* for a visually interesting interpretation of Acts 4:32–37 (for an introduction to the *St. John's Bible* project, see our discussion of Acts 2:1–47). The community page illumination is depicted in a medieval, almost Byzantine style (**Figure 13**, color plate). The perspective is both splayed and hierarchical. The emphasis of the uppermost register is on the risen Christ. Christ is positioned in a *mandorla* or almond shape that is found throughout the Romanesque and Gothic periods above church portals or doors on tympana. He maintains the traditional blessing gesture with his right hand raised but, instead of the expected Alpha and Omega Greek characters on the open book, the words "I AM" are revealed. Two angels flank Christ. A modern church is placed on the left side of the next level while the bell banner of the Abbey church situated on the campus of Saint John's Abbey is on the right. This illumination acknowledges the Saint John's Abbey community as the manuscript's patron. An inverted "U-shape" aligns both the seated group and the table at which they are to dine. An altar table is in the foreground with candle, Gospel book, bread and chalice holding red wine all present. There is the usual medieval use of gold leaf behind the figures and forming their halos. The flatness of the composition is understood as one begins to think about how the feet seem to just be sliding down towards the table and what would happen if the figures were to stand.

The words of Acts 4:32–34 are written in the four corners or quadrants of the circular figural area. The triangular shape of these corners is reminiscent of pendentives used in Byzantine churches to structurally support the weight of a massive circular dome. Pendentives were unifiers of the most basic geometric shapes, the circle and the square. Here, too, the words unify the figural illumination with God. The words tell a story visually depicted in the illumination and inspired by God.

The beginning of catechism with a meal is another theme presented in this illumination. The Virgin Mary sits at the center of the table and is surrounded by six Apostles on her right and six on her left. They are joined by women, a child, a monk, a nun, and another man, all seated at the table. There are a variety of ages present. Some figures raise their hands about to speak while others listen attentively. Luke's reading of the community in Acts 4 and in Acts 2 shows not a "perfect" community but a community that discusses and maybe even debates. An ideal community is one that exchanges ideas and comes to a point of agreement. The website statement, "For the better part of a year, the Saint John's Board of Regents and the monastic community engaged in a spirited debate (yes, monks do debate) about the wisdom and value of embarking on this journey," describes the actions of an "ideal community" that ultimately would decide, "Yes, we want to embark on this monumental project. We want Donald Jackson to bring the Word of God to life on vellum for the next 500 years" (http://saintjohnsbible.org).

Occasionally, an illuminator will be identified for his illustration in the online pages of the Bible. Aidan Hart is the creator of this image. Hart was born in England and was raised in New Zealand. He completed a degree in English literature and zoology but began painting and carving icons after becoming a member of the Orthodox Church at the age of 25. He studied Greek for two years in Mount Athos, Greece as part of a twelve-year period of testing a vocation to the monastic life (http://saintjohnsbible.org/). Hart's blend of spiritual calling and artistic training is visible in the blending of eastern and western church imagery.

Ananias and Sapphira (Acts 5:1–11). The story of Ananias and Sapphira (Acts 5:1–11) was the focus of many early interpreters who concentrated on the nature of their sin as well as the role of Satan in their misdeed, "Why has Satan filled your heart?" (Acts 5:3; see Martin 2006, 58–61; see also Ammonius, *Catena on Acts* 5.3; 85.6–23). Jerome, for example, notes: "For having made a vow they offered their money to God as if it were their own and not his to whom they had vowed it; and keeping back for their own use a part of that which belonged to another, through fear of famine which true faith never fears, they drew down on themselves suddenly the avenging stroke, which was meant not in cruelty toward them but as a warning to others" (Jer. *Epist.* 130.14; ACCS, 60). Ammonius uses the story of Ananias to convict those in his audience who are guilty of half-hearted conversion:

> If he dies because he has appropriated a part of the silver for his own uses and because he has not placed all at the feet of the Apostles, what, then, shall we also say concerning those who do not bring themselves completely to God but only partly do the things of God if by chance it turns out that way, and partly are subject to their own desires? A much greater punishment will meet them, since God is able to destroy both life and body in hell; but these things I say, for the sake of those faithful ones who do not hastily steal in order to live (*Catena on Acts* 5.1–2; 84.24–31).

An anonymous author of a catena on Acts 5:5 defends Peter against charges that he was himself responsible for the deaths of Ananias and Sapphira:

> For Peter did nothing other than expose the lie. Now the Holy Spirit, *who* knows all things, not only the secrets of humans, but also the depths of God [1 Cor 2:10], like one who has authority even over life and death, destroys those who sin against Him. "Yes," he says, "You think that you made this defense plausible; but what do you have to say about Sapphira? Didn't Peter kill her?" Stop this absurdity! Stop it! For the two of them did/committed the offense, and even you yourself will concede this! So the Judge condemned both of them equally (*Catena on Acts* 5.5; 86.21–27).

Aquinas, on the other hand, appeals to Acts 5 as scriptural warrant that "even clerics may kill evil-doers" (*ST*; *CCEL* 3328)!

Masaccio depicts St. Peter distributing the alms to the poor. This scene occurs immediately before the death of Ananias (Acts 5:5), yet he is seen dead at Peter's feet in this fresco (**Figure 14**). This scene is part of the Peter cycle in the Brancacci chapel in the church of Santa Maria del Carmine in Florence. Masaccio is sometimes called the founder of Renaissance painting, for during his short life of only twenty-seven years his innovative art moved the entire city of Florence into a rebirth of classical culture. He used one-point linear perspective to depict a realistic sense of depth on a two-dimensional wall or panel. His figures were three-dimensional with individual personalities evident through their facial features, gestures, and emotions.

Masaccio worked on the Brancacci family chapel alongside Masolino (c. 1383–1447), who may have been his teacher. Pietro Brancacci (d. 1366/7) had founded the chapel, but it was owned by his nephew, Felice Brancacci, when the two artists began painting a cycle of biblical stories about Peter on its walls. This iconographic program of the chapel frescos may be in honor of the founding father's patron saint.

Masaccio and Masolino worked separately on the fresco scenes but attribution issues remain. Both artists did major rectangular scenes on the side walls and smaller, vertical panels on the center wall of the chapel. Because Masolino was called to work in Hungary and Masaccio to Pisa before the decorations were completed, Filippino Lippi finished the fresco cycle decades later, in the early 1480s.

When the chapel was restored in the 1980s and the grime was removed from its frescos, colors reminiscent of Giotto (d. 1337) were revealed. Masaccio and Masolino respected the fourteenth-century master and his ability to produce beautiful fresco cycles in Padua and Assisi. Renaissance artists felt tradition and

FIGURE 14   Tommaso Masaccio (1401–28). *Saint Peter Distributing the Common Goods and Punishment of Ananias.* 1425. Fresco. Brancacci Chapel, Sta Maria del Carmine, Florence. Photo: Alfredo Dagli Orti/The Art Archive at Art Resource, NY

method were very important, so they respected and admired the work of their predecessors. Thus it was that Michelangelo came to the Brancacci chapel to study the manner in which Masaccio painted gesture, drapery, and lifelike figures in motion.

Although sources for Peter cycles occur in Early Christian art (St. Peter's, for example), the distribution of alms is a relatively rare subject. In the Brancacci chapel Peter healing with his shadow (Acts 5:15), the distribution of goods, and the death of Ananias are complementary in an original way. They are constructed with a shared vanishing point which coincides with the upper part of the altarpiece (Joannides 1993, 336). Peter's healing flanks the left side of the altarpiece while the distribution of alms with the death of Ananias is on the right side. The reward for faithfulness becomes a subsidiary theme when the viewer realizes the corpse of Ananias is also in the painting. The lack of visual precedents may have caused Masaccio to look for effects in everyday Florentine life. The mother carries a chubby child whose buttocks flatten against her forearm and whose attire is contemporary Florentine (Joannides 1993, 336). There is also a balding man who walks with a crutch and an older, veiled woman to his left. John (recognizable by his relative youth) stands at Peter's side. The architecture is not proportional or perspectivally accurate. Masaccio does not paint every scene with believable architecture but places the emphasis on the narrative instead.

We turn back to Raphael's cartoons for the tapestries of the Sistine Chapel walls for a very fine and often copied rendition of *The Death of Ananias* (**Figure 15**; cf. Acts 5:1–11). *The Death of Ananias*, the fourth tapestry, is presented in a very straightforward manner. Peter and the apostles have persuaded wealthy men to sell off land and property and distribute the proceeds to the poor. One of them, Ananias, kept back some money and Peter rebukes him. Ananias falls dead before the entire crowd in the front right foreground of the composition. The shock is seen in the faces of a group of men delivering sacks on the right. Two figures on the left, a man and a woman, also react in horror

Figure 15   Raphael (1483–1520). *The Death of Ananias.* 1515–16. Watercolor on paper mounted on canvas (tapestry cartoon), 3.4 × 5.3m. V&A Images/The Royal Collection, on loan from HM The Queen. Victoria and Albert Museum, London, Great Britain. Photo: V&A Images, London/Art Resource, NY

to the sudden death before them but the alms distribution by the other apostles on the far left continues without anyone seeing what has happened.

Even though the main event occurs in the center of the composition, two later stories are referred to on the left and right sides of the cartoon. The distribution of alms is not only a way to show the action of the apostles as an exemplary act but also refers to the distribution of the common good of the church, for which purpose the office of deacon was instituted. Stephen was one of those deacons appointed after the death of Ananias (Acts 6:1–6; Shearman 1972, 57). On the viewer's far right, Sapphira is shown counting her coins as she, too, kept back some of the wealth. She will be struck dead within a few short hours because of her greed and deceit (5:10).

Nicholas Poussin paints *The Death of Sapphira* (**Figure 16**) one hundred and forty years later, set not in Jerusalem but in the architecture of sixteenth-century Rome. The identifiable buildings include Michelangelo's Palazzo dei Conservatori, Baldassarre Peruzzi's Villa Farnesina, Palladio's Palazzo Thiene, and the Palazzo Alberini by Raphael and Guildo Romano (Cavina 2008: 45). The setting is an homage to Raphael's primary cultural project – the renovation of Rome to restore it to its past grandeur. This appealed to the Baroque classicism so often favored by Poussin. As in *Saints Peter and John Healing of the Lame Man*, Poussin used not only Raphael's work but also Northern engravings

FIGURE 16   Nicolas Poussin (1594–1665). *The Death of Sapphira*. c. 1652. Oil. Musée du Louvre, Paris. Photo: Gianni Dagli Orti/The Art Archive at Art Resource, NY

by Maerten van Heemskerck as sources for *The Death of Sapphira* (Kurita 1998, 747–48).

Peter is punishing Ananias and Sapphira for their disobedience. It has also been interpreted as punishment arising from the embezzlement of church funds. This is somewhat ironic as Pope Leo X himself was accused of diverting funds for the payment of the tapestries (Evans and Browne 2010, 89). Sources for this composition are not from other depictions of the Death of Ananias but instead are classical sculptures such as the *Oratio Augusti* from the *Arch of Constantine* and the *Dying Gaul*. Michelangelo's *Death of Haman* from the Sistine ceiling may also be a source for the pose of the woman with upraised hands looking back at the dying Sapphira (Evans and Browne 2010, 89).

Obeying God rather than People (Acts 5:29)

After the death of Sapphira, Acts describes the persecution of the apostles (5:17–42). Peter, giving a defense before the Sanhedrin, declares, "We must obey God rather than any human authority" (Acts 5:29). In the midst of the "Quartodecimanian" controversy (regarding the date of Christian observance of Passover), Polycrates, Bishop of Ephesus (c. 196), appealed to Acts 5:29 in his defense of the local practice of following the Jewish calendar to establish the date of the "Savior's Passover":

> Moreover I also, Polycrates, who am the least of you all, in accordance with the tradition of my relatives, some of whom I have succeeded—seven of my relatives were bishops, and I am the eighth, and my relatives always observed the day when the people put away the leaven—I myself, brethren, I say, who am sixty-five years old in the Lord, and have fallen in with the brethren in all parts of the world, and have read through all Holy Scripture, am not frightened at the things which are said to terrify us. For those who are greater than I have said, "We ought to obey God rather than men" (cited in Eusebius, *Hist. eccl.* 5.24).

Many of the references to Acts 5:29 among patristic writers had to deal with the contested relationship of church and state (Rahner 1992). Acts 5:29 ("We must obey God rather than people") was among a cluster of scripture passages (e.g., Matt 22:17/Luke 20:25; Luke 22:38; Rom 13:1; 1 Pet 2:17; 1 Cor 2:6) that figured prominently in those discussions. Hippolytus of Rome (d. 235) writes:

> One who has faith in God ought not dissemble or fear the powerful, especially those who use power for evil. If they are compelled to do something opposed to

their belief, their better choice is death rather than submission. ...The apostles, forbidden by the rulers and scribes from preaching the word, did not cease to "obey God rather than man" [Acts 5:29], and for this reason the rulers, despising them, threw them into prison (*Comm. Dan.* 20–25).

Origen (185–235) draws a contrast between Paul's comments in Romans 13 about not opposing civil authorities and Acts 5: "Here the question is not of those in authority who persecute the Faith; of those it is said, 'It is better to obey God than men' (Acts 5:29). But Paul is speaking here of just authority" (*Comm. Rom.* 9.26–30).

In the fifth century, amidst intense conflict between Church and Empire, Pope Felix II (reigned 483–492) issued a brief but blistering letter to the Emperor Zeno. Although he does not quote Acts 5 explicitly, its message is close beneath the surface of Felix's epistle: "I leave the choice to you—Do you prefer communion with the Blessed Apostle Peter or Peter of Alexandria [a Miaphysite supporter and opponent of the Chalcedonians]? I think that it would be well for you, who prefer to have your laws obeyed rather than violated, to obey God's decrees, and though you have been given command of human affairs, let there be no doubt about the fact that the things of God should be received from those persons whom God has designated to dispense them" ("Letter to Emperor Zeno"; cited in Rahner 1992, 171). The struggle for political power in the fourth and fifth centuries was entangled in the Christological debates of the so-called "Arian controversy." By denying the full deity of Christ, the "Arians" were able to argue that "while Christ is the head of man, God is the head of Christ and that in consequence the God-enthroned ruler is superior to the bishops instituted by Christ." The "orthodox," on the other hand, argued for the full deity of Christ, Head of the Church, and thus procured the "immunity of his ecclesiastical Body to infiltrations of any improper influence from the imperial *pontifex maximus*, however Christian his professions" (Williams 1993, 317). Acts 5:29 did not provide a compelling scriptural warrant for either position. It was potentially too subversive for the Arians, pitting claims of God against temporal powers; it lacked sufficient Christological focus to serve well the "Catholic" position.

With some exceptions (see below), during the medieval period the church–state issue often revolved around the personalities of pope and emperor, and other texts that were interpreted as underpinning the authority of one or the other (1 Pet 2:17; Matt 16:19 *inter alia* suggested a coexisting role for both sacral and temporal powers). Eventually, Luke 22:38 took precedence in the debate over Acts 5:29 as scriptural warrant. The words of Pope Gelasius (492–96) in a letter to the emperor Anastasius shaped the debate for the next millennium and clearly echo the "two swords" logion of Jesus, as interpreted by ecclesiastical authorities: "Two there are, august emperor, by which this world is chiefly ruled, the sacred authority of the priesthood and the royal power. Of these the responsibility of the priests is more weighty in so far as they will answer for the kings of men themselves at the divine judgment" (cited in Tierney 1964, 13, document 3). That would change in the aftermath of the Reformation, especially among those who identified with various parts of the Radical Reformation (see below).

In his *Summa Theologica*, Aquinas appealed to Acts 5:29 in answer to the query "Whether human law binds a man in conscience": "laws may be unjust through being opposed to the Divine good: such are the laws of tyrants inducing to idolatry, or to anything else contrary to the Divine law: and laws of this kind must nowise be observed, because, as stated in Acts 5:29, 'we ought to obey God rather than man'" (*ST*, "Of the Power of Human Laws," Article 4; *CCEL* 2325).

Martin Luther employed Acts 5:29 in his arguments against the papacy. In a sharp retort that pitted obedience to God against allegiance to the Pope, he wrote:

> Whatever ideas you may have about obedience, the keeping of vows is obedience to God and God's commandment; in this we may not obey anyone else, not even an angel, as St. Paul says in Galatians 1[:8] and Peter in Acts 5[:29]: "We must obey God rather than men." If they have departed from obedience to God for the sake of obedience to the pope, they have departed from heaven and have gone to hell. No, you cannot treat God's commandments and obedience to him in such an off-handed way ("The Gospel for the Festival of the Epiphany," *LW* 52:267; cf. Zwingli, *Acta Disputationis Primae*, 618).

Many other early modern interpreters employed Acts 5:29 to address the vexing relationship of Church and State. The verse is routinely cited in articles dealing with the connection between churches and civil powers in various confessions of faith (see, for example, Augsburg Confession (1530), Article 28; Bohemian Confession (1535), Article 16.[6]; First Helvetic Confession (1536), Article 26.b; Treatise on Power and Primacy (1537), Article 38.b; Heidelberg Catechism (1563), Question 94.m; True Confession (1596), Article 42; Eastern Confession of the Christian Faith (1629 [1633]), Chapter 18; Westminster Confession of Faith (1647), Chapter 20.2.l, 23.3.29; Cumberland Presbyterian Church, *Confession of Faith* (1814/1883), Article 72.f; Lutheran General Synod, *Definite Platform* (1855), Article 16; New Hampshire Confession (1833/1853), Article 16.h; Protestant Christian Batak Church, *Confession of Faith* (1951), Article 10; Second Vatican Council (1962–65), §9.11.

John Calvin argued:

> But in the obedience which we have shown to be due to the authority of
> governors, it is always necessary to make one exception, and that is entitled
> to our first attention,—that it do not seduce us from obedience to him, to
> whose will the desires of all kings ought to be subject, to whose decrees all
> their commands ought to yield, to whose majesty all their sceptres ought to
> submit. ...
>   I know what great and present danger awaits this constancy, for kings cannot
> bear to be disregarded without the greatest indignation. ... But since this edict
> has been proclaimed by that celestial herald, Peter, "We ought to obey God
> rather than men,"—let us console ourselves with this thought, that we truly per-
> form the obedience which is required of us, when we suffer not any thing rather
> than deviate from piety (*Instit.* 4.32; cf. Zwingli, *Brevis In Evangelicam Doctrinam
> Isagoge*, 273).

Radical reformers such as William Jeffrey, a seventeenth-century British
Baptist incarcerated for his beliefs, acknowledged that the Scriptures (such as
Rom 13) mandated that Christians were to be subject to the Magistrates in
political and legal matters, but this obedience did not extend to matters of the
"worship of God." Jeffrey used 5:29 (and others) to resist civil interference in
matters of religious practice and to protest the imprisonment of fellow Baptists
in the county of Kent:

> Because the Apostles themselves (that gave forth those commandements that are
> written in Scripture, to be obedient to Magistrates) refused to be obedient to
> their Rulers, when they were commanded to forbear, that which they judge part
> of the Worship of God, and said, *Whether it be right in the sight of God, to harken
> unto you more than unto God, judge ye.* [Acts chap. 4. 19. 5. 29.] ... And now O
> King, that no man as he is a Christian, hath power to be a Lord over anothers
> Faith, or by outward force to impose any thing in the Worship of God, is as clear
> (Jeffrey 1660, 8).

Reformer Thomas Müntzer also appealed to Acts 5:29 to challenge any
tyrannical usurpation of God's authority: "A prince and territorial ruler is
placed in authority over temporal goods, and his power extends no further. ...
He shall by no means rule our souls, for in these matters it is necessary to obey
God rather than men" (*Müntzer Schriften*, 283–84; cited by Stayer 1976, 96).
"The greater the confidence in the Christian sanctity of the Sword from Luther
to Müntzer, the greater was the belief in the justice of political resistance against
'tyrants'" (Stayer 1976, 330).

Søren Kierkegaard utilized Acts 5:29 in support of his view of individual conscience, or "Christianity within 'Christendom.'" He writes:

In Acts we read: We ought to obey God rather than men. There are situations, therefore, in which an established order can be of such a nature that the Christian ought not put up with it. … But let us see how the apostles did not act, for everyone pretty well knows how those venerable ones did act.

The apostles did not go around talking among themselves, saying: "It is intolerable that the Sanhedrin makes preaching the Word punishable … What should we do about it? Should we not form a group and send an appeal to the Sanhedrin—or should we take it up at a synodical meeting? …

On the contrary how did they act? … Essentially, "the apostle" is a solitary man. … one apostle does not look at another apostle to see what he should do; each one is personally bound to God as a single individual. … Suppose that someone meets him and says: Do you know that the Sanhedrin has stipulated flogging as punishment for preaching the Word? The apostle replies: Well, if the Sanhedrin has done that, then I shall be flogged. …

He has to be a solitary person in order to strive through suffering, in order to choose martyrdom. Conscience and a matter of conscience can be represented only through action by a solitary person and in character, by action, not by prompting a discussion that is concluded by voting ("An Open Letter" in *KW* 13:56–58).

Karl Barth took a different approach to the text: "Even in the well-known phrase of Ac. 5[29] it does not say that we should obey God and not men, but that we should obey God more than men. Hence our dutiful obedience to men is not precluded by what we have to do in obedience to God. It is included in it even in the case of a conflict with what may be required by men" (*CD* 3.4.250).

Gamaliel: Crypto-Christian? (5:33–42). Gamaliel, member of the Jewish council before whom the apostles are tried (5:33–42), was viewed by Bede (eighth century) as "a companion of the apostles" (*Comm. Acts* 5:34). His sage advice to the religious leaders to wait and see whether or not the apostles' undertaking was of God or of humans elicited the following judgment by Chrysostom: "this man all but preached the gospel!" (*Hom. Act.* 14). According to the pseudo-Clementine literature (second–fourth century), Gamaliel was a "crypto-Christian" who remained a member of the Sanhedrin and maintained secrecy about his conversion in order to provide covert assistance to fellow believers: "Gamaliel … was the head of the nation and … was, because it was advantageous, secretly our brother in the matter regarding faith" (*Clem. Rec.* 1:65.4; Syriac trans. Jones). The Eastern Orthodox Church venerates Gamaliel as a saint, assigning him the Feast Day of August 2, when tradition claims that his relics (along with those of Stephen and Nicodemus) were found.

Gamaliel figures briefly in Trollope's *Barchester Towers*. The inexperienced minister, Rev. Mr. Slope, has stirred a controversy between the ladies, on his side, and the men on the other, and serves as an anti-type of the biblical Gamaliel: "No man—that is, no gentlemen—could possibly be attracted to Mr. Slope, or consent to sit at the feet of so abhorrent a Gamaliel" (chap. 7; cited in Jeffrey 1992, 299).

Overview

Acts 6 begins with the account of the selection of the Seven to care for the needs of the Greek-speaking Jewish Christian widows (6:1–8), followed by the story of the arrest, testimony, and martyrdom of Stephen, one of the Seven (7:9–8:1a). Acts 8 is comprised of two episodes, Philip with the Samaritans and Simon (Acts 8:1–25) and Philip and the Ethiopian Eunuch (8:26–40). The story in Acts 6:1–8 was formative especially during the Reformation among Protestants who sought to use this text and others to reorganize church leadership roles, in

The Acts of the Apostles Through the Centuries, First Edition. Heidi J. Hornik and Mikeal C. Parsons.

some cases expanding those roles to include laity (such as "deacons"). Later, the passage figured prominently in the so-called Tübingen School's reconstructions of early Christian history into competing groups of conservative "Hebrew" Christians and more liberal "Hellenistic" Christians.

The text goes on to recount the arrest, testimony, and martyrdom of Stephen, one of the Seven (6:9–8:1a). Stephen has figured prominently in Christian liturgy (St. Stephen's Day), Christian art (manuscript illumination, Fra Angelico, Don Simone Camaldolese), and in later Christian literature as the proto-martyr (Søren Kierkegaard). Elements of Stephen's speech were pursued by later interpreters: Abraham, Joseph, Moses, and the law. Some interpreters distinguished between Stephen's vision in which Christ is standing (as an advocate) in 7:56 from other NT references in which Christ sits (in judgment), while still others (Calvin, etc.) think too much is made of the distinction. Finally, in a moving speech before his executioners, Sir Thomas More appeals to the story of Paul appearing at Stephen's martyrdom as evidence that both the martyred (Stephen and More) and their executioners will one day commune in heavenly harmony.

The account of Simon (Acts 8:1b–25), later called Simon Magus, was the scriptural basis for the word "simony," a prominent practice in the Middle Ages (for its critique, see Luther, below). Other interpreters question whether Simon's repentance was genuine (e.g., Chrysostom and Arator) and whether or not Philip had the authority to confer the Holy Spirit to the Samaritans (Ammonius).

As might be expected, issues of baptism emerged in the reception history of the story of the Ethiopian Eunuch (Acts 8:26–40). Was it ever proper to administer baptism without a period of catechism? The text was also a favorite among the radical dissenters who practiced "believer's baptism" (while other passages in Acts served well those who advocated infant baptism). The eunuch's response to Philip's question in 8:30 ("Do you understand what you are reading?") signaled for some interpreters the need for an ecclesial context for the interpretation of Scripture: "How can I understand unless someone guides me?" Modern interpreters have attended to the significance that the Eunuch was recognized as a person of color and one whose disability caused him to suffer ridicule in antiquity.

Reception and Interpretation

Acts 6–7

Hebrews and Hellenists (Acts 6:1–8)

Chrysostom assumes that the "Hellenists" in Acts 6 refer to Greek-speaking Jewish Christians (so also Joseph Barber Lightfoot 1865, cited by Baird 1992, 16, and many others; but see Calvin, *Commentary on Acts*, 6:1–6; Cadbury

1932, 4:64 who think they were "Gentiles" or "Greeks"). "By 'Hellenists' I suppose he means those who spoke Greek, for these, being Hebrew, spoke Greek" (Chrysostom, *Hom. Act.* 14). On "church offices," Chrysostom ponders:

> But what sort of rank these bore, and what sort of office they received, this is what we need to learn. Was it that of Deacons? And yet this was not the case in the Churches. But is it to the Presbyters that the management belongs? And yet at that time there was no Bishop, but the Apostles only. Whence I think it clearly and manifestly follows, that neither Deacons nor Presbyters is their designation: but it was for this particular purpose that they were ordained. And this business was not simply handed over to them without further ceremony, but the Apostles prayed over them, that power might be given to them (*Hom. Act.* 14).

About the custom of ordination, Ammonius wrote: "the ordination comes by the word of the leaders through their prayer and the imposition of their hands, and ... the rank of deacons was given to deacons from the beginning, and ... this custom has been observed until now" (*Catena on Acts* 6.6; ACCS, 71).

Martin Luther refers to Acts 6 in his critique of the papacy's preoccupation with worldly affairs: "They said in Acts 6[:2–4], 'It is not right that we should leave the Word of God and serve tables, but we will hold to preaching and prayer, and set others over that work.' But now Rome stands for nothing else than the despising of the gospel and prayer, and for the serving of tables, that is, temporal things. The ride [sic?] of the apostles and of the pope have as much in common as Christ has with Lucifer, heaven with hell, night with day. Yet the pope is called 'Vicar of Christ' and 'Successor to the Apostles'" ("The Christian in Society"; *LW* 44:159–60).

Luther also appealed to the examples of Stephen (6:8) and Philip (from Acts 8) in support of his view of expanded roles for laity and the priesthood of all believers:

> Another example is provided by Stephen and Philip, who were ordained only to the service at the tables [Acts 6:5, 6]. Yet the one wrought signs and wonders among the people, disputed with members of the synagogue and refuted the council of the Jews with the word of the Spirit [Acts 6:8 ff.], and the other converted Samaritans and travelled to Azotus and Caesarea [Acts 8:5 ff., 40]. By what right and authority, I ask? Certainly they were not asked or called by anyone, but they did it on their own initiative and by reason of a common law, since the door was open to them, and they saw the need of a people who were ignorant and deprived of the Word. How much more readily they would have done it had they been asked or called by anyone or by the community? ("Church and Ministry"; *LW* 40:38).

Among heirs of the Reformation, Acts 6 served as something of a blueprint for church offices and the process of electing persons into those offices. The use of Acts 6 by John Smyth (an early Baptist) in his articulation of "receiving officers into office" is extensive (1607, 7–9). This process consists of three parts: election, approbation, and ordination. This election process, he claims, "must be performed with fasting & prayer" (cf. Acts 6:5). Furthermore, the candidate for church office "must first be a member of that visible church whence he hath his calling" (cf. Acts 6:3–5) and is elected "by most voices of the Church in ful communion," although women, servants and "under age" children are not eligible to participate in these voice votes. Approbation, Smyth explains, "is the examining & finding the officer elect to be according to the rules of his office" (Acts 6:3). The ceremony of ordination includes the "imposition of hands" used in "ordeyning ordinarie Ministers" (cf. Acts 6:6). These ordinary Ministers or Deacons can be men or widows (who are of 60 years of age). The "Men Deacons collect and distribute with simplicity the churches treasury according to the churches necessities, and the Saints occasions." Acts 6:1–7 remains a scriptural touchstone as the process of electing, approbating, and ordaining church officers evolves in ecclesiology over the next four hundred years (see e.g., Barber 1651, 8; Blackwood 1653, 58–59; Danvers 1674, 4–6; Bunyan 1689, 20–21; Gill 1796, 3.2.267–69; Graham 1851, 113–14; Edgren 1948, 167; Moody 1968, 63–69; Ervin 1987, 53). Dietrich Bonhoeffer made several references to Acts 6:4 to argue for the necessity of the minister to have an active prayer life: "Acts 6:4 especially commends the office of prayer to those who are to proclaim the word. The pastor must pray more than do others, and indeed has more to pray about" (*BW* 14:932).

Acts 6 played a pivotal role in the reconstruction of early Christian history in critical scholarship. In the mid-nineteenth century, F.C. Baur, one of the founders of the so-called "Tübingen School," argued that a deeper "dislike between the two parties" lay beneath the dispute over the daily distribution (6:1). For Baur, the "Hebrews" who "adhered as nearly as possible to the Jewish religion" refused to tolerate the "liberal turn of thought" of the Hellenists, represented by Stephen. Stephen's critique of the Temple and Jewish ancestral customs epitomized the ever-increasing "division between the two elements of the Church formerly allied together" (Baur 1853, 43). Thus, early Christianity was divided into two parties, what Baur would elsewhere term the "Petrine" and "Pauline" parties, a division that found its genesis in Acts 6–7 (no matter how "unhistorical" the details of the account of Stephen's martyrdom might be, according to Baur). While there was (sometimes fierce) opposition to Baur from the beginning, Baur's views that "the Hellenists and Hebrews were distinctive ideological groups, that Stephen, the Hellenist leader, spoke against the temple (and quite possibly the law), that he was put to death for his liberal (or radical) views, and that the Hellenists and not the Hebrews were persecuted by the Jews" remain positions widely held and regarded in NT critical scholarship (Hill 1992, 11–12).

Stephen and the "Crown" of Martyrdom (6:8–15)

Much has been made of the meaning of Stephen's name ("crown") with regard to his martyrdom; Bede's comments are typical: "It was fitting that in the first martyr he [God] should confirm what he deigned to promise to all those handed over [to martyrdom] for the sake of his name" (*Comm. Acts* 6:10).

In the lessons for St. Stephen's Day (celebrated on December 26 in the Western church or December 27 in the Eastern tradition) found in the Roman breviary (based on the sermons of Fulgentius [467–532]) we read:

> Stephen, indeed, deserved to bear his name—"the crowned"—for he had armed himself with the mail of love, and conquered through it everywhere. Because of his love for God he was unshaken before the cruelty of the Jews; through his love for his neighbor he interceded even for those who stoned him. Through love he argued with the erring that they might be corrected; through love he prayed for those who stoned him lest they be punished. Strong with the might of love he overcame Saul who had compassed his death cruelly, and won his persecutor on earth as his comrade in heaven (*Roman Breviary Lesson* 6; ed. Nelson, 1950, 348–49).

An eighteenth-century St. Stephen's Day anthem proclaims:

> First of martyrs, thou whose name
> Doth thy golden crown proclaim
> … First like him in dying hour
> Witness to almighty power;
> First to follow where he trod
> Through the deep Red Sea of blood;
> First, but in thy footsteps press
> Saints and martyrs numberless
> (translated from Latin 1861;
> cited in Jeffrey 1992, 735).

The popular Christmas carol, "Good King Wencelas," recounts the legend of a Czech king caring for the poor during harsh winter weather on the day after Christmas (St. Stephen's Day): "Good King Wencelas looked out, on the feast of Stephen, when the snow lay round about, deep and crisp and even."

About Stephen's visage, Chrysostom observed: "'They saw,' it says, 'that his face was like the face of an angel' [6:15]. This was his grace. This was the glory of Moses [see Exod 34:29–35 and 2 Cor 3:13]. Gracious did God make him, now that he was about to speak, so that immediately by his very look he might strike them with amazement" (*Hom. Act.* 15).

Stephen's Speech (7:1–54)

A number of early interpreters sought to reconcile apparent discrepancies between Stephen's speech and the Genesis account regarding the timing of the event of Abraham's call (cf. Augustine, *Civ.* 733–34; Bede, *Comm. Acts* 7:2). Chrysostom commented insightfully about various aspects of Stephen's speech. On the promise made to Abraham, noted by Stephen (7:5), he said: "He shows here that the promise had been made before the place [the land of Israel], before the circumcision, before sacrifice and before the temple. He also shows that it was not by merit that these people received either circumcision or law, but that obedience alone secured the land as its reward" (*Hom. Act.* 15). Chrysostom connects God's rescue of Joseph in Acts 7:9–10 with Gamaliel's previous comment: "See how it demonstrates what Gamaliel said, 'If it comes from God, you will not be able to destroy it' (Acts 5:38–39). See how the victims of plots became the authors of salvation to those plotting against them" (*Hom. Act.* 16). Fifth-century Syrian bishop, Severian of Gabala, makes a similar point when he writes that "the plot of those who contrived against him became the way of success for the one who was envied" (*Catena on Acts* 7:9; 108.31–32; cf. 108.26–28, in which he calls the Joseph story a "type of Christ").

Ammonius practically dismisses Moses' "foreign education" except for apologetic purposes: "Neither Moses, nor the ones with Ananias and Daniel (see Dan. 1:11), would have learned the foreign education, except by the force and compulsion of a despot. For they made use of this in nothing, except where someone might have said that it was good to learn in order to refute their deceptions" (*Catena on Acts* 7:21; 112.16–19). Fourth-century theologian Gregory of Nyssa, on the other hand, appeals to the example of Moses (7:22) to justify believers receiving from "those outside the church": "such things as moral and natural philosophy, geometry, astronomy, dialectic, and whatever else is sought … since these things will be useful when in time the divine sanctuary of mystery must be beautified with the riches of reason" (*Life of Moses* 2.115; ACCS, 79; cf. Didymus the Blind, *Catena on Acts* 7:21; 112.20–29 and Augustine's balanced comments in *Civ.* 877). Fourth-century theologian Gregory of Nyssa also offers this spiritual meditation on Moses' encounter at the burning bush (7:33): "Sandaled feet cannot ascend that height where the light of truth is seen, but the dead and earthly covering skins, which was placed around our nature at the beginning when we were found naked because of disobedience to the divine will, must be removed from the feet of the soul. When we do this the knowledge of the truth will result and manifest itself" (*Life of Moses* 2:22; ACCS, 80; see also Cyril of Alexandria *Catena on Acts* 7:33; 116.19–33, who makes a similar allegory regarding the sandals; cf. Lampe 1961, 1447).

In an exposition on the Ten Commandments written from prison in June or July 1944, Dietrich Bonhoeffer reflects on Stephen's description of the ten commandments as "living oracles" (Acts 7:38):

> In every word of the Ten Commandments, God speaks fundamentally of god's self, and this is their main point. That is why they are God's revelation. It is not a law but God we are obeying in the ten Commandments, and our failure when we break them comes not from disobeying a law but from disobeying God … It is not merely unwise to disregard God's command; it is sin, and the wages of sin are death. This is the reason the New Testament calls the Ten Commandments "living words" (Acts 7:38; *BW* 16:634).

Some modern commentators have seen Stephen's remarks in 7:48 ("the Most High does not dwell in houses made with human hands") as critical of "the temple itself" (Pervo 2009, 191). This interpretation has ancient roots. Presumably drawing on common tradition, the author of *Barnabas* observed: "I will also speak to you about the Temple, since those wretches were misguided in hoping in the building rather than in their God who made them, as if the Temple were actually the house of God" (Barn. 16:1). Chrysostom thinks the temple was a mistake made by Solomon (*Hom. Act.* 18).

Later, the Reformers would use the passage to criticize institutions and practices of the Catholic Church. Balthasar Hubmaier (1480/05–1528) wrote against monasteries: "In this passage you clearly hear that we cannot make wooden, stone, silver or golden houses for Christ. Therefore, it is all in vain, the expenses that until now have been invested in such costly monasteries" (Hubmaier, *A Simple Instruction*; RCS, 93). The German theologian, Peter Riedemann (1506–56) used Acts 7:48 to criticize as idolatry the Catholic doctrine of transubstantiation, which holds that the divine presence in the element of the bread was real: "They make something idolatrous out of it, which is an abomination to our God. It is idolatry to honor as God that which is not God, and to look for him where he is not. 'God does not live in temples made by human hands.' These words are proof that he is not in the bread, because bread is always made by human hands. Therefore, God is not in the bread" (Riedemann, *Confessions of Faith*; RCS, 94).

Standing or Sitting? (7:56)

Several patristic writers commented on the fact that Stephen sees Christ standing, rather than sitting (see, e.g., Rom 8:24; Heb 1:3), at the right hand of God (7:56). St. Augustine suggests that Christ stands in order to strengthen Stephen: "As to what the most blessed martyr saw as he engaged in that final, agonizing contest, you will no doubt recall his words, which you regularly hear from the book of the Acts of the Apostles; *Behold*, he said, *I see the heavens opened, and Christ standing at the right hand of God* [Acts 7:55]. He could see Jesus standing; the reason he was standing, and not sitting, is that standing up above, and watching from above his soldier battling down below, he was supplying him with invincible strength, so that he shouldn't fall" ("Sermon: On the Birthday of St. Stephen"; *WA* 3.9.126–27).

Fourth-century Bishop of Milan Ambrose wrote along similar lines: "Jesus stood as a helpmate; he stood as if anxious to help Stephen, his athlete, in the struggle. He stood as though ready to crown his martyr. Let him then stand for you that you may not fear him sitting, for he sits when he judges" (*Letter 59*; ACCS, 86). Elsewhere Ambrose uses this same point to counter Arians who would view Christ standing as clearly inferior to the Father sitting on the throne: "He sits as Judge of the quick and the dead; he stands as his people's Advocate" (*Fid.* 3.17); since Christ is both Advocate and Judge he is in no way inferior to the Father and certainly unique and superior in comparison with the Roman emperor (Williams 1993, 319–20). Ammonius was more concerned with the metaphorical nature of Luke's description of the vision in 7:55: "It is impossible to see God; therefore it says 'the glory of God'; it calls this glory, 'God,' by a misuse of language; therefore one must note that the ones who say they have seen God, they were seeing the divine glory; whether in fire, or in a pillar of cloud, or in a kind of sapphire or amber vision" (*Catena on Acts* 7:55–56; 129.10–13).

John Calvin deems the discussion regarding the differences between Christ sitting (in judgment) or standing (as here, in advocacy) as "too subtle": "For mine own part, I think that though these speeches be diverse, yet they signify both one thing … the whole text is a metaphor, when Christ is said to sit or stand at the right hand of God the Father, and the plain meaning is this, that Christ hath all power given to him" (*Commentary on Acts*, 7:54–58; 238–39). Kierkegaard, on the other hand, sees the image of Christ standing as indicative of his continuing activity: "Yet in his loftiness he is neither indifferent nor inactive. He is always ready to appear before us with unspeakable sighs. Nor does he sit down, for when the danger is great, he rises up—as Stephen saw him" (*JP* 1:312; 1991, 269–70).

Visual Exegesis and the Martyrdom of Stephen

The Vercelli manuscript illumination from c. 1200 (**Figure 17**) depicts Stephen in prison on the right side of the composition and, on the left, Stephen has just lain down after being stoned (Eleen 1977, 263). Rocks are visible in the hands

FIGURE 17   *Stoning and Imprisonment of Saint Stephen.* c.1200. Manuscript illumination. French Biblioteca Capitolare, Vercelli. Photo: Gianni Dagli Orti/ The Art Archive at Art Resource, NY

of the three men assaulting him. A stone has just landed on Stephen's left eye and another in the center of his chest. Both rocks defy gravity to convince the viewer of the recent occurrence and a sense of the momentary. Stephen's left hand is extended open with his palm visible. It is elevated, indicating his final prayer (vv. 59–60), "Lord Jesus, receive my spirit." Although he is lying down rather than on his knees, his final words remain, "Lord, do not hold this sin against them."

The fresco example by Fra Angelico (**Figure 18**) is his only surviving papal commission. The chapel of Pope Nicholas V was intended to commemorate Saint Lawrence (m. 258) and Saint Stephen. According to tradition, Stephen's relics were brought to Lawrence's tomb in recognition of the saints' common apostolate as deacons (Ahl 2008, 173). Throughout history, both Lawrence and Stephen had been held in high regard by the papacy (Ahl 2008, 173). The lives of the martyrs extend across three walls of the chapel. The events of Stephen's life occur in three lunettes. The scenes were selected to parallel the lives of Lawrence and Stephen: ordination, preaching of the Gospel and charity to the poor. They were arrested, persecuted and martyred. The arrest of Stephen can

FIGURE 18   Fra Angelico (1387–1455). *St. Stephen Led to Torture and Stoned.*
1448–1449. Fresco. Cappella Niccolina, Vatican Palace, Vatican State. Photo: Scala.
Art Resource, NY

be seen on the left-hand side of the lunette while the stoning is visible on the
right. The wall of Jerusalem separates the scenes (Venchi 2001, 63–76; Calvesi
2001, 45–62). A hooded man brings Stephen to his doom before the Sanhedrin,
armed with the rocks that will be used to stone him. He kneels, as in the traditional manuscript "type" referred to above, as the stones are thrown into his
back. Blood gushes from the back of his head and trails down his neck onto his
garments.

Don Simone Camaldolese was active as a miniaturist for illuminated manuscripts in Florence during the period 1375–1405. The *Stoning of Stephen*
(**Figure 19**) illustrated here is from his final project, an antiphonary labeled
Codex B executed for Santa Croce in Florence (Firmani 1984, 87, 130). The
narrative appears in the historiated initial, S. It is believed that this complex
pictorial scene was painted by Don Simone himself and is among the most
elaborate of his entire career. There was a lively and productive industry of
manuscript production at the time in Florence. The *Stoning of Stephen* depicts
movement through the throwing of stones. Stephen kneels in the lowest area of
the composition. His space is clearly defined and the landscape recedes behind
him. The two individuals casting the stones are also in the lower half of
the historiated initial but are placed on the curving area of the completion of

FIGURE 19   Don Simone Camaldolese (14th–15th century). *Stoning of Saint Stephen. Illuminated intial S.* Choral B, L 32 v. Museo di S. Marco, Florence, Italy. Photo: Nicolo Orsi Battaglini/Art Resource, NY

the letter S. The opponents casting him out points at the center left or middle of the S while Jesus, holding Stephen's crown, assumes the upper space and directs the flow of the composition from upper right to lower left. The figures explode out of the initial to increase action; the two men throwing stones overlap the letter and the decorative foliage (Firmani 1984, 90). Through the curves of the historiated letter and the strong diagonals created by the dramatic gestures of the figures, a sense of movement along with the drama of the narrative is exceptional.

Paul's Participation and Stephen's "Sleep" (7:58–8:1a)

Given Stephen's status as the first or "proto-martyr" one might expect that subsequent martyrologies might take some of their narrative clues and shape from the Stephen story. Apart from some general "echoes," such as visions on the part of the martyrs (see, e.g., *Passion of Perpetua and Felicitas* 1.3, 5.3), there is little direct influence that can be traced between Stephen's martyrdom and other subsequent ones in the early church (see Musurillo 1972). There is, however, some evidence of the story's influence in a different direction. In the *Gospel of Nicodemus I/The Acts of Pilate*, Jesus is portrayed as speaking some of the words attributed to Stephen in canonical Acts: "Then Jesus cried out with a loud voice, saying: Father, let not this sin stand against them; for they know not what they do" (106).

Sir Thomas More (1478–1535) greatly admired and often appealed to the example of Saint Stephen in his writings (Cavanaugh 1965). His son-in-law and first biographer, William Roper, recorded these words by More after he was tried in Westminster Hall on July 1, 1535, and condemned to die:

> More have I not to say (my Lords) but like as the blessed Apostle St. Paul, as we read in the Acts of the Apostles, was present, and consented to the death of St. Stephen, and kept their clothes that stoned him to death, and yet be they now both twain holy saints in heaven, and shall continue there friends for ever, so I verily trust and shall therefore right heartily pray, that though your Lordships have now in earth been judges to my condemnation, we may yet hereafter in heaven merrily all meet together to our everlasting salvation (Roper, Harvard Classic reprint 1909–14, para. 5–7).

In his journal, Søren Kierkegaard included this remarkable reflection on the image of the "sleeping Stephen" (Acts 7:60).

Stephen
When he had said this, he fell asleep

(2) He fell asleep. How powerful—yes, or seen from another side, how powerless, how powerless you are, sinful world, how powerless in all your noise and rage; what do you accomplish by it—look, this is what you accomplish: he sleeps … How powerful to be able to sleep at that moment, and not only to sleep at that moment but to lay himself down to sleep at that moment. How little it usually takes to disturb a man's slumber—and then to be able to sleep this way. You are almost to be laughed at, world, for your impotence: he sleeps, he sleeps through the whole affair …

(3) When he had said this, he fell asleep. What was it he said? He said: Father, do not hold this sin against them … He prayed for them. He had prayed for himself again and again; his whole life to the very end, his sufferings, were praying for himself. Now there is only a moment left, a minute: he prays for his enemies. Yet it must be confessed that the shorter the time allotted, the easier it is, perhaps, to resolve to pray for one's enemies …

But we learn from him—to pray for ourselves, to pray for our enemies—and then to fall asleep.

So sleep then, sleep sweetly (to be continued).

[In margin: They saw that his face was like the face of an angel—so it is in death.] For 1,800 years he has been famous and eulogized; but he cares nothing about that—he sleeps (JP 4:329–30).

In *Basil Howe: A Story of Young Love*, his first novel written at the age of nineteen (but unknown until it was discovered in 1989 among his unpublished works), G.K. Chesterton, Britsh writer and Christian apologist (1874–1936), tried his hand at romance. In one scene the two female friends of the protagonist share the following exchange:

Cécile looked rather puzzled, and Gertrude tumbled over a half-laugh, as they drew up to the principal carving, a relief of St. Stephen undergoing martyrdom in the gauntest mediaeval spirit.

"Isn't it beautiful?" said Cécile, in an awe-struck voice.

"No," replied Gertrude, abruptly.

"That sweet carving not beautiful … Gertrude!" said Cécile hotly.

"I don't see anything beautiful about it," said Gertrude with bullet-headed honesty. "I don't see why St. Stephen should be so hideously starved and ugly, or why he should stand on one leg, with his head on one side, to be martyred. It isn't like people are, it isn't like people ought to be: why should I be made to like it?" (*Basil Howe*, 458).

C.S. Lewis imagined what Stephen might say to Lazarus:

> But I was the first martyr, who
> Gave up no more than life, while you,
> Already free among the dead,
> Your rags stripped off, your fetters shed,
> Surrendered what all other men
> Irrevocably keep, and when
> Your battered ship at anchor lay
> Seemingly safe in the dark bay
> No ripple stirs, obediently
> Put out a second time to sea
> Well knowing that your death (in vain
> Died once) must all be died again?
> ("Lazarus" in Atwan and Wieder
> 1993, 249–50).

Acts 8

Philip, Simon and the Ethiopian Eunuch (Acts 8:1b–40)

Philip and Simon (8:1–25). Like many other interpreters, Augustine assumed Simon Magus was not a true convert:

> The apostles came to Samaria, where the magician was and where he had been baptized. They laid their hands on the newly-baptized, who received the Holy Spirit and began to speak in tongues. Simon was amazed and dumbfounded at this divine miracle, that at the imposition of human hands the Holy Spirit should come and fill people; and he lusted after the power, not the grace. What he wanted was not something to set him free, but a gift to enhance his own reputation ("Expositions of the Psalms: Exposition 3 on Psalm 30"; *WA* 3.15.345).

Justin Martyr (c. 100/110–165) embellished the details surrounding Simon Magus:

> There was a Samaritan, Simon, a native of the village called Gitto, who ... did mighty acts of magic, by virtue of the art of the devils operating in him. He was considered a god, and as a god he was honored ... with a statue, which ... bore this inscription, in the language of Rome, *Simoni Deo Sancto*, "To Simon the holy god." And almost all the Samaritans, and a few even of other nations, worship him and acknowledge him as the first god (*1 Apol.* 26; ACCS, 90; see also Eusebius, *Hist. eccl.* 2.14).

Arator judged that "Simon the magician had been here washed indeed in the fount but not clean in the heart" (*OAA*, 1). John Chrysostom wondered why Peter baptized Simon rather than striking him down. He argued: "And how came he [Peter] to baptize Simon also? Just as Christ chose Judas ... How was it then that they did not strike him dead, as they did Ananias and Sapphira? Because even in the old times, he that gathered sticks (on the sabbath-day) was put to death as a warning to others (Num. xv. 32) and in no other instance did any suffer the same fate" (*Hom. Act.* 18).

Ammonius counters the argument that Philip did not confer the Holy Spirit upon the Samaritans because "he was only a deacon" (*Catena on Acts* 8:15–17; 138.8). Rather, Ammonius argues that, although the Scriptures do not mention him explicitly, Philip was involved along with John and Peter in praying and laying hands on the Samaritans in order that they might receive the Holy Spirit:

> Why did Philip not cause those who were baptized by him to partake of the Holy Spirit? For the one who must make a defense for the grace of God: for even if at first no one received the Holy Spirit whenever Philip baptized those in Samaria, certainly later, after John and Peter prayed, he [Philip] gave the Holy Spirit through the laying on of his hands to those who had been baptized. For by a common and indefinite name the Scripture says that through the hands of the Apostles laid upon the believers, the grace of the Spirit shone forth. It does not say that through only Peter and John, but speaking without distinction, it includes also Philip [cf. Acts 8.17]. *Catena on Acts* 8:15–17; 137.1–138.23).

Like others before him, Martin Luther traced the medieval practice of simony (the word is first used in the thirteenth century and based on the name, "Simon" in Acts 8) and offered criticism of its corrupted practice among his contemporaries:

> Simony is the purchase or sale of something spiritual for money or when someone accepts money and gives a gift or something spiritual. Thus when Simon Magus [Acts 8:17 ff.] saw that the Holy Spirit was given through the laying on of the apostles' hands, he offered them money, saying: "Give me also this power, that anyone on whom I lay my hands may receive the Holy Spirit." He wanted the Holy Spirit, purchased with money, to be in his power and to do what pleased him.
>
> From that Simon the crime is called simony. It occurs when, in accordance with Simon's example, someone thinks that the gifts of God are to be bought with or sold for money. Christ does not sell His gifts and grace, but He has redeemed us without charge.
>
> This is the true definition. Later on the canonists [interpreters of church law] distorted it in an astonishing manner; for that part of the definition, "the gift of God for money," they apply to everything men give to God. Thus they now call the revenues of the church "spiritual goods" because they are gifts of God, not gifts that God has given but gifts that men have offered to God (*Lectures on Genesis* 23.1.4; *LW* 4:199–200).

The story of Philip and the Samaritans was especially important to early adherents of "believer's baptism" over against the traditional practice of infant baptism. In their confessions, Acts 8:12 is the most cited verse in Acts (cf. True Gospel 1654, XI; Somerset 1656, XXIV; Standard Confession 1660, XI; Orthodox Creed XXXII). Others cite Acts 8:12 in their arguments against infant baptism (e.g., Blackwood 1646, 22–23; Hargreaves 1823, 10–12; Carroll 1893, 6–7) or even children of "non-age" (Hammon 1658, 38). Still others explore the relationship between baptism and the gift of the Holy Spirit (Writer 1658, 2–4; Collins 1680, 34–38; Moody 1968, 65–69; Ervin 1984, 27; 1987, 2), as well as baptism and the laying on of hands (Caffyn 1660, 16–17; Gill 1746, 859–60).

Philip and the Eunuch (8:26–40)

Fifth-century bishop Severus of Antioch commented on the Isaiah text that the eunuch was reading:

> And he [the eunuch] was diligently wrapped up in reading, but he did not understand what he was reading because of the language. And the One who sees the heart saw he had love for God, the One who desires that all people believe in order to be saved, and he sent Philip to him, one of his intimate disciples; he placed him unexpectedly on the road, and uncovering the things hidden in the words of the prophets, Philip made known to him the one proclaimed by the prophets who would draw the human race to salvation, Christ who is Jesus, the Word of God who was in flesh unchangeable for us, the one who was led like a sheep to slaughter, and the one who remained on the saving cross for us, and through resurrection destroyed the power of death, and became the first fruits from the dead, and the one who brought to us the hope of immortality through his own flesh (*Catena on Acts* 8:29–30; 143.15–31).

Elsewhere Augustine counters arguments that favor baptism immediately upon confession of faith with no period of catechism:

> They say that that eunuch whom Philip baptized said nothing other than *I believe Jesus Christ is the Son of God* [(Acts 8:37-38] and, on making this declaration, was immediately baptized. Are we content then for people only to give this answer and then be baptized straightaway? Is there nothing the catechist need say and nothing the believer need acknowledge about the Holy Spirit, nothing about the holy Church, nothing about the forgiveness of sins, nothing about the resurrection of the dead, nothing even about the Lord Jesus Christ himself except that he is the Son of God, nothing about his suffering, his death on the cross, his burial, his rising on the third day, his ascension and his sitting at the right hand of the Father? … It may be, however, that scripture was silent and left to be understood everything else that Philip did with that eunuch he was baptizing. It may be that with the words, *Philip baptized him* [Acts 8:38], it was implied that everything was carried out that we know from a continuous tradition has to be carried out, even if for the sake of brevity it is not all mentioned in scripture" ("On Christian Belief"; *WA* 3.8.235).

Acts 8:35–38 is another "magnet text" for practitioners of believer's baptism. Once again, a number of Baptist confessions cite one or more of these verses as support for their claims that baptism ought only to be administered to those making a confession of faith (e.g., London Confession 1644, xxxix, XL; Midland Confession 1655, 14; Second London 1689, 29; New Hampshire 1833, 14; Free Will Baptists 1935/2001, XVIII; American Baptists 1993, 18; Pentecostal Free Will Baptists 1999, 20.A). A number of these early confessions appeal specifically to Acts 8:37, in which Philip replies to the Eunuch's query, "See, here is water! What hinders my being baptized?" (8:36): "If you believe with all your heart, you may." And he replied, "I believe that Jesus Christ is the Son of God" (cf. Declaration of Faith 1611, 10; Somerset 1656, XXV; Orthodox Creed 1678, XXIII) or in some combination with other verses (Acts 8:36–37: Faith and Practice of Thirty Congregations 1651, 35; Orthodox Creed 1678, XXVIII; Second London 1689, 29; Acts 8:37–38: Somerset 1656, XXIV, General Baptists 1970, VIII.A.2).

Calvin recognized the importance of this verse to those arguing for believer's baptism but, drawing an analogy with Jewish circumcision, argued that infants of Christian parents should be baptized: "it is perfectly clear that infants ought to be put in another category, for in ancient times if anyone joined himself in religious fellowship with Israel, he had to be taught the Lord's covenant and instructed in the law before he could be marked with circumcision, because he was of foreign nationality, that is, alien to the people of Israel, with whom the covenant, which circumcision sanctioned, had been made" (*Instit.* 3.23). So also Bonhoeffer argues: "the presupposition of baptism is hearing the word, repentance, and faith; for congregational praxis, that means instruction, confession of sin, absolution, profession of faith to Jesus Christ [Acts 8:35; 2:38; Rom 6:2 etc.]. Hence the baptism of children—whether attested in the New Testament or not—is never baptism of nonbelievers, which is impossible in any case, but rather baptism of those who are to come to faith within the church-community" (*BW* 14:829).

An even greater number of individual seventeenth-century interpreters appeal to Acts 8:37 (either alone or in some combination with preceding or succeeding verses) as scriptural warrant for the necessity of a confession of faith to accompany baptism (see, e.g., Smyth 1609, 50; Denne 1645, 34–35; Richardson 1645, 9–11; Blackwood 1646, 29; Lawrence 1651, 75–76; Powell 1677, 99–103; Kiffin 1681, 24–25). Ironically, this verse is missing from the most ancient manuscripts of Acts (a fact unknown to these early interpreters, but cf. Robertson 1930, 111–112 and the GARBC 1934, XV, which cites vv. 36, 38, 39) and therefore missing also from the most recent translations (though the NRSV prints it in a footnote). Thus, we have the ironic situation that one of the most cited verses in Acts is no longer available in the text of any modern translation!

According to student notes from December 16, 1935, Bonhoeffer appealed to Acts 8:37 to counter attempts to unite representatives of the Reich Church with those of the Confessing Church: "The profession of faith in the church-community is Jesus is the Christ, the Lord 1 Cor 12:3. Rom. 10:9. Acts 8:37. A confession with two fronts, to the self-revealing God and against the deification of Caesar. Hence the confession, to Jesus the Lord is not a minimal confession as some would have it again today, in order to preserve the church-community itself from schism, but is a genuine confession of the church-community against the world and to its God" (*BW* 14:459).

For Calvin the Ethiopian eunuch (8:26–40) was evidence that "there were some … in the East parts which worshipped the true God, because after the people were scattered abroad there was some odor of the knowledge of the true God spread abroad with them throughout foreign countries" (*Commentary on Acts*, 8:26–31).

Karl Barth reflected on Acts 8 in his section on the need, and limits, of "scriptural interpretation":

[think] of the man (Ac. $8^{26f.}$) who was reading Is. 53 in his chariot- it was not quite unprepared that he had gone to Jerusalem to worship-and who to the question: "Understandest thou what thou readest?" had to answer: "How can I, except some man should guide me?" … At this point there commences what we may call the need of interpretation in the narrower sense … A member of the Church is as such called upon to be the third party who … intervenes between the speaker and the hearer … On the side of Scripture, he helps by attempting to illuminate its sense, on the side of the hearing or reading man, by attempting to suggest to him the fact and extent that Scripture has a meaning for him. The former task has also to be understood, of course, as a service to men, the latter as a service to Scripture (*CD* 1.2.713–14).

More recently, scholars have recognized the significance of the Ethiopian's ethnicity; in modern terms, the first Gentile convert to Christianity was a "person of color," a fact mostly overlooked in the history of interpretation. Acts 8:26–40 then is "the story of a black African … from what would be perceived as a distant nation to the south of the empire," a story that is "consistent with the Lukan emphasis on 'universalism,' a recurrent motif in both Luke and Acts, and one that is well known" (Martin 1989, 114).

Didymus the Blind (ca. 313–98) compares Philip's "translation" to Azotus (Acts 8:39) to the story of Elijah (2 Kings 2:1–11):

[Philip's] 'taking up' … is equivalent to the ascension of Elijah; and after he was taken up, Philip was carried from place to place, even as Elijah was taken up from a place near the earth in order to be carried to another region … But Elijah was raised and carried to a place *without borders*, so it has been said he had been taken up into heaven. (*Catena on Acts* 8:39; 147.13–33).

FIGURE 20   *Philip and the Ethiopian Eunuch. Saul receives letters.* 1200–25. Manuscript illumination. Cod.lat 39 fol 91r. © 2012 Biblioteca Apostolica Vaticana. Photo: By permission of Biblioteca Apostolica Vaticana, all rights reserved.

Visual Exegesis and the Ethiopian Eunuch (Acts 8:26–40)

The manuscript illumination from the Vatican library, known as Lat. 39 (**Figure 20**), illustrates the portion of the narrative where Philip and the Ethiopian are discussing the Book of Isaiah. The Ethiopian had been reading it in the chariot when Philip arrived and asked if the man understood what he was reading. The Ethiopian invited Philip to teach him and they traveled together. Luba Eleen deduced that this manuscript is part of a conversion in the manuscript tradition to a less sophisticated pictorial language in accordance with Romanesque stylistic limitations and Western iconographic practice. In this type of thirteenth-century composition, reducing the number of horses to one and flattening the figures so that the two men face each other on the same plane simplify spatial relationships. The latter changes also result in the Ethiopian neglectfully turning his back on driving (Eleen, 1977, 270, 285 fig. 13).

Overview

Acts 9 consists of three episodes. The conversion of Saul/Paul is narrated in Acts 9:1–19a (cf. also chs 22, 26) and is pivotal to Luke's account of the spread of Christianity into the Gentile world (see Chrysostom et al). Some see a dramatic reversal in Paul from persecutor of the Church to Apostle to the Gentiles. Other modern interpreters (Stendahl) have questioned whether "call" rather than "conversion" is a better description of the results of the Damascus Road experience. The scene was a favorite among artists. Caravaggio's portrayal is

The Acts of the Apostles Through the Centuries, First Edition. Heidi J. Hornik and Mikeal C. Parsons.
© 2017 Heidi J. Hornik and Mikeal C. Parsons. Published 2017 by John Wiley & Sons, Ltd.

characteristically dramatic; the presence of the horse, while missing in the biblical text, is a common feature in the visual depictions explaining how he "fell." Acts 9:19b–31 recounts various plots against Paul's early ministry in Damascus and Jerusalem. Paul's escape in a basket elicits various responses in the visual and literary traditions, including some allegorical ones (cf. Arator). Luke ends the chapter by turning attention back to the deeds of the Apostle Peter (9:32–43), who heals Aeneas (32–35) and resuscitates Tabitha (36–43). In addition to speculations regarding the symbolism of Tabitha's or Dorcas' name, the raising of Tabitha figures prominently in visual cycles of Peter's life and later becomes an important text for feminists trying to assess Luke's view of the role and importance of women in the early Church.

Reception and Interpretation

Paul's "Conversion" (Acts 9:1–19a)

The story of Paul's conversion is told three times in Acts (chs 9, 22, 26), with variations in some of the details. This first version is the most detailed. Chrysostom credits Paul's "conversion" (see Stendahl below) to the power of Christ's resurrection: "This furious assailant of Christ, the man who would not believe in his death and resurrection, the persecutor of his disciples, how should this man have become a believer, had not the power of his resurrection been great indeed?" (*Hom. Act.* 19). Origen, like many other interpreters, comments on Christ's question to Saul: "Why are you persecuting me?" (Acts 9:4): "And as a consequence of this we see that everyone who betrays the disciples of Jesus is reckoned as betraying Jesus Himself" (*Comm. Jo.* 1.62).

Caravaggio painted *The Conversion of St. Paul* (**Figure 21**) as a pair with *Crucifixion of St. Peter* to establish a theme of suffering. The suffering of Peter, the apostle to the Jews, as he is crucified upside down on a cross is immediately apparent. As the apostle to the Gentiles, Paul endured suffering and ridicule as he took the gospel to those outside the Jewish faith.

Monsignor Tiberio Cerasi, treasurer general under Pope Clement VIII, commissioned Caravaggio to paint the two pictures in his recently-acquired private chapel in Santa Maria del Popolo, Rome. On September 24, 1600, Caravaggio signed a contract to paint them on two cypress panels measuring 10×8 palmi (Hibbard 1983, 118–137; the palmo, a unit of measure based on the breadth of a human hand with the fingers splayed, was a little more than eight inches).

Keeping close to the details in the biblical accounts of the apostle's conversion (Acts 9:1–6, 22:5–11, 26:13), Caravaggio does not embellish the narrative with

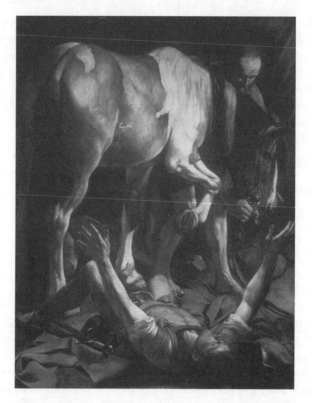

FIGURE 21   Michelangelo Merisi da Caravaggio (1573–1610). *The Conversion of Saint Paul.* 1600–01. Oil on canvas. S. Maria del Popolo, Rome, Italy. Photo: Scala/ Art Resource, NY

an apparition of God or angels. The psychological dimension of the painting is very modern: Saul, the Jewish persecutor of Christians, is knocked flat on his back before the viewers' eyes and almost into their space. He is converted through the penetrating light of God, "a light from heaven flashed about him" (Acts 9:3). He does not react in fear, but opens his arms to receive as much of the light as possible. His eyes are closed to indicate the blindness that he endures for three days. His commission to be the apostle of the Gentiles is symbolized by Caravaggio's depiction of him in Roman garb (Hornik 2010, 50–51). The presence of the horse underscores Paul's presentation as a Roman patrician (Baskett 2006, 73–75; for a similar depiction see Rubens, *Conversion of St. Paul*, Courtauld, London) and also explains the note in Acts that Paul alone "fell to the ground" (9:4), while those with him "stood there speechless" (9:7). In William Blake's watercolor of this scene, the divine commission is underscored by Christ's outstretched hand and extended index finger (cf. Butlin 1981, vol. 2, plate 575).

In his *Lectures on Galatians*, Martin Luther commented on Christ's words in Acts 9:4:

Christ Himself testifies when He says in Acts 9:4: "Saul, Saul, why do you persecute Me?" Saul had not done any violence to Christ, but only to His church. But whoever touches this, touches the apple of His eye (Zech. 2:8). The head is more sensitive and responsive in its feeling than the other parts of the body, as experience teaches. When the small toe or some other tiny part of the body is hurt, the face immediately shows that it feels this; the nose contracts, the eyes flash, etc. In the same way Christ, our Head, makes our afflictions His own, so that when we, who are His body, suffer, He is affected as though the evils were His own (*Lectures on Galatians* 16.6; *LW* 27:134; cf. *Sermons on St. John* 15.1.22; *LW* 24:276; cf. Augustine, "Sermon 279: On the Apostle Paul"; *WA* 3.8.60; cf. Bede *Comm. Acts* 9:4 [p. 87]).

In a rarely depicted detail of the text, the Rockefeller-McCormick New Testament (**Figure 22**) illustrates the moment when Paul is literally being led to Damascus (Acts 9:8). Paul has been blinded and is being led down the road by an unnamed figure in a short red dress. Paul's vulnerability is highlighted in the scene; he is totally dependent on others.

Ammonius comments on Paul's lack of sensory perception following the Damascus Road experience: "After seeing Jesus and being [unable] to endure more light, the discernment and vitality of his soul became stone; therefore, even though he seemed to have eyes, he did not see, and although he had a mouth, he did not eat, until, after believing Ananias, who spoke the word to him, he was healed. For after faith he began to see; then he was baptized, and in this way, when he partook of more spiritual nourishment, he recovered" (*Catena on Acts* 9:3–4a; 151.8–16; cf. Erasmus, *Paraphrase on Acts* 9:3–10).

A number of patristic and medieval commentators compare Paul's three days of blindness with Christ's resurrection on the third day (*inter alia*, cf. Chrysostom, *Hom. Act.* 19; Bede, *Comm. Acts* 9:9). Sixth-century Latin poet and orator Arator extends the imagery of "something like scales" falling from Paul's eyes to conclude that Paul "cast away snake-like crime and strife, and now as a teacher he wages better battles" (*OAA*, 9 [lines 708–53]; Bede, *Comm. Acts* 9:4, refers to the "scales of your pride," but see also Bede, *Comm. Acts* 9:18).

Nineteenth-century Baptist preacher C. H. Spurgeon, on the other hand, focuses on Paul's actions after his Damascus Road experience. He points to the brief description of Paul in Acts 9:11, "Behold, he prayeth," as evidence of Paul's post-conversion sincerity ("Paul's First Prayer," *The New Park Street Pulpit* [1855], 1:121; cf. Vavasor Powell 1677, 130). Furthermore, Spurgeon sees in this reference to Paul's piety "proof of this man's election" since, later, Ananias is told by Christ, "Behold, he [Paul] is a chosen vessel." Earnest, sincere prayer,

FIGURE 22   *Paul Led to Damascus.* 1269. Manuscript illumination. MS 965 fol. 115r
(Rockefeller-McCormick New Testament). Photo: Special Collections Research
Center, University of Chicago Library

Spurgeon claims, is a sure mark of "election" (1855, 121–22; cf. Dixon 1905). A
century later, charismatic Howard Ervin also commented on Paul's piety, this
time in terms of Paul's "personal Pentecost" and concluded, based on his reading of Paul's letters elsewhere (especially 1 Corinthians) that it is a "reasonable

assumption then to affirm that Paul also spoke in tongues when he received the Pentecostal gift of the Holy Spirit" (1984, 41; cf. Gordon, 1894, 83).

By "inventing" the meaning of "sheep" for the name Ananias, Augustine is able to create an interesting, if misguided, word play:

> He is taken to Ananias, and Ananias means sheep. Why, look! The ravenous wolf is brought to the sheep in order to follow it, not ravage it ... And yet such frightful reports had preceded that wolf, that the sheep couldn't help being agitated on hearing his name. You see, when the Lord Jesus told this Ananias that Paul had already come to believe, and that Ananias must go to him, Ananias said, *Lord, I have heard about this man, that he has done many bad things against your saints; and now he has received letters from the high priests, authorizing him, wherever he finds followers of your name, to drag them away. But the Lord said to him, Let it be, and I will show him what he must suffer for my name* (Acts 9:13–16).
>
> A great and wonderful thing is being enacted ... But such terrible reports about the wolf as ravager had preceded him, that when the sheep heard his name, he was seized with fear ... He is encouraged, told he needn't think of him any longer as raging, nor fear him as throwing his weight about. The lamb who died for the sheep reassures the sheep about the wolf ("Sermon 279: On the Apostle Paul"; *WA* 3.8.60; cf. *OAA*, 9 [lines 708–53]).

Aquinas uses Acts 9:15 ("But the Lord said to him, 'Go, for he is an instrument whom I have chosen to bring my name before Gentiles and kings and before the people of Israel'") in the prologue to his commentary on Romans as the scriptural *accessus* to open up his interpretation of Paul's letter, which in turn serves as an introduction to all of Paul's letters ("Prologue 1," *Comm. Rom.*; ed. Larcher). Aquinas, as was typical of medieval commentary, uses Aristotelian categories of cause—efficient, material, formal, and final—to discuss issues of authorship, content, literary style and structure, and overall purpose:

> From the words of our text, therefore, we gather the four causes of this work, i.e., of Paul's letters, which we have before us. First, the author, in the word *vessel*; second, the matter, in the words *my name*, of which the vessel is full, because this entire teaching is about the teaching of Christ; third, the manner, in the word *carry*. For this teaching is conveyed in the manner of letters which were customarily carried by messengers: *so couriers went with letters from the king and his princes* (2 Chr 30:6). Fourth, the difference of the work in the usefulness mentioned (*Comm. Rom.*, Prologue [10], 4 [Larcher]).

John Calvin suggests that the description of Paul as an "elected instrument" (*organum electrum*; Acts 9:15) "shows that men can do nothing except in so far as God uses their labour according to His will. For if we are instruments He is strictly speaking the only Doer (*auctor*); the power and the capability of acting are in His hands" (*Commentary on Acts*, 9:15). Luther links the descriptions of Paul as a "chosen instrument" with his negative (according to Luther) description of the Law as "elements of the world":

> Paul is the only one to use this phraseology, when he calls the Law of God "elements of the world" or "weak and beggarly elements" or "the power of sin" or "the letter that kills" [e.g., Gal 4:31; Col 2:8; 2 Cor 3:6]. The other apostles did not speak this way about the Law. Therefore let every student of Christian theology carefully observe this way of speaking that Paul has. Christ calls him "a chosen instrument" (Acts 9:15). Therefore He gave him a most excellent way of speaking and a unique phraseology, different from that of the other apostles, so that he, as the chosen instrument, may faithfully lay the foundations of the doctrine of justification and set it down clearly (*Lectures on Galatians* 4.1.4; *LW* 26:366).

John Calvin says that, in Acts 9, Luke "takes up what is particularly worth telling, the well-known story of Paul's conversion; how the Lord not only brought him under His own control, when he was raging like a wild beast, but immediately made a new and different man of him" (*Commentary on Acts*, 9). Partly on the basis of the account of Paul's conversion, English political philosopher John Stuart Mill (1806–1873) found Paul's writings the least objectionable in the NT: "St. Paul, the only known exception to the ignorance ... of the first generation of Christians, attests to no miracle but that of his conversion, which of all the miracles of the New Testament is the one which admits of the easiest explanation from natural causes" ("Theism," in pt. 4 in *Three Essays on Religion*; cited in Jeffrey 1992, 592).

The Cappella Palatina in Palermo, Sicily contains mosaics that, beginning with their popularity in Ravenna, became a specialty of the Greek East. Greek mosaicists were brought in by Charlemagne to work on his chapel at Aachen in the eighth and ninth centuries. Imported Greek artists created the mosaics in the new abbey church of Montecassino (Borsook 1990, 17–18). The next wave of mosaic popularity occurred in Venice and Norman Sicily. Those in Sicily were completed in less than sixty years between 1130 and 1187. In the Pope's eyes, Sicily was a fief of St. Peter's but this was not the idea of the Norman conquerors (Borsook 1990, 1). The dedication of the Capella Palatina to Peter by King Roger of Siciliy is associated with an inscription dated 1143 (Borsook 1990, 17). The "chapel" is really a small church located along the southern side of the royal palace. It functioned as a private chapel for the family as well as an audience hall. The Pauline section (biblical and apocryphal scenes) of the mosaic program occurs in the southern aisle. The *Baptism* (**Figure 23**) follows Paul's *Dispatch to Damascus and Conversion* according to Acts.

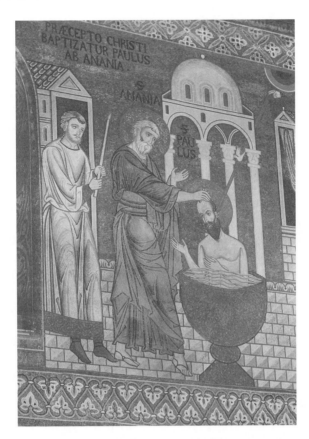

FIGURE 23   *Paul Baptized by Saint Ananias.* 1130–40. Mosaic. Cappella Palatina, Palazzo dei Normanni, Palermo, Sicily, Italy. Photo: Erich Lessing/Art Resource, NY

The inscription describes the scene (PRAECEPTO CHRISTI BAPTIZATUR PAULUS AB ANANIA; "By the Command of Christ, Paul is baptized by Ananias"). Paul's lower body disappears into a baptismal font. The water reaches the middle of his chest and he leans his head towards Ananias as he is blessed. Paul directs the viewer with his right hand towards Ananias. The action is placed in the front foreground. A servant stands to the left of Ananias and Paul. Three pieces of architecture are also visible. In the center is a dome on pendentives (triangular-shaped constructions) that form a canopy. The typical gold-leaf background is used, with white, rose, green and violet allowing the scene to be quite colorful. Paul's eyes are clear and open indicating that the scales have fallen from his eyes.

In a tongue-in-cheek passage, Kierkegaard compares the conversion of St. Paul to that of one "Dr. Hjortespring" (Johan Heiberg) who "converts" to Hegelian philosophy: "According to his own very well written report, he became an adherent of Hegelian philosophy through a miracle at Hotel Streit in Hamburg on Easter morning (although none of the waiters noticed anything)— an adherent of the philosophy that assumes that there are no miracles. ... Wondrous sign of the times, far more magnificent and important than the conversion of Paul, because Paul's conversion through a miracle to doctrine that declares itself to be a miracle is rather straightforward, but to be converted by a miracle to the teaching that accepts no miracles is rather topsy-turvy" ("Concluding Postscript, Part Two" in *KW* 12.1:184).

Early modern interpreters, like their patristic predecessors, focus much of their attention on the conversion of Christianity's first and chief antagonist, Saul of Tarsus. Francis Bampfield, a seventeenth-century British Seventh Day Baptist pastor, describes the former life of the "furious assailant" Saul in particularly vivid language that echoes Philippians 3. Paul, Bampfield asserts, after his conversion is now found "preaching up that Christian Doctrine and Discipleship, which but a little before he endeavoured to persecute down; counting all his former self-righteousness, formal-worshippings, creature-advantages, outward Church-priviledges, vain affectation of human wisdom, by Philosophic Studies, to be as dung, and as Dogs-meat, for the excellency of the Knowledg of Christ Jesus his Lord" (*A Name*, 1681). Likewise, seventeenth-century British minister and writer, John Bunyan, utilizing the rhetorical convention of a first-person monologue, puts himself and his readers in Paul's place, citing him as the chief exemplar of one who is capable of loving much because he is one who has been forgiven much:

> Oh! I shall never forget his love, nor the circumstances under which I was, when his love laid hold upon me. I was going to *Damascus* with Letters from the High Priest to make Havock of God's People there, as I had made Havock of them in other places. These bloody Letters was not imposed upon me. I went to the High Priest and desired them of him, *Acts* 9. 1, 2. And yet he saved me! I was one of the men, of the chief men that had a hand in the Blood of his Martyr *Stephen*, yet he had mercy on me! When I was at *Damascus*, I stunck so horribly like a Blood-sucker, that I became a Terrour to all thereabout: Yea, *Ananias* (good man) made intercession to my Lord against me, yet he would have mercy upon me! Yea, joyned mercy to mercy, untill he made me a monument of grace. He made a Saint of me, and perswaded me, that my transgressions were forgiven me (*Good News*, 1688, 40–42; cf. W. O. Carver 1916, 92).

After years of writer's block, partially the result of drug and alcohol addiction, country singer Johnny Cash, the "man in black," published a novel about Paul, entitled simply, *Man in White* (Cash 1986). The novel imagines events prior to and following Paul's Damascus Road conversion, but it is Paul's encounter with Christ that forms the narrative pivot of the book. Cash describes the christophany in this way:

> The earth shuddered. Or did it tremble in fear and wonder? … Before he [Paul] could cry out, he was overwhelmed by pure light. … The light, the beautiful, horrible light. And there before his eyes, manifested physically in glorified reality, for just a split second, was the figure of the Man in White. The Man, carried to the earth to appear before Saul in a stream of wonderful, dazzling beauty, a flowing stream of divine substance, came in a white so white, so pure, so brilliant that his eyes were seared and scaled over (Cash 1986, 89).

From Augustine forward, climaxing with Luther and continuing into the modern period (cf. Kierkegaard above), the dominant and consistent interpretation in Western Christianity of Paul's Damascus Road experience is one of "conversion," motivated by Paul's guilt over his past life and frustration with his inability to observe Torah. In a famous address given to the Annual Meeting of the American Psychological Association in 1961, Harvard Divinity School Dean Krister Stendahl (1921–2008) challenged this view, arguing that Paul was being read through "Lutheran lenses." Although his argument was based mostly on the undisputed Pauline Epistles, Stendahl, at least on this particular point, found Acts in agreement:

> Paul had not arrived at his view of the Law by testing and pondering its effect upon his conscience; it was his grappling with the question about the place of the Gentiles in the Church and in the plan of God, with the problem Jew/Gentiles or Jewish Christians/Gentile Christians, which had driven him to that interpretation of the Law which was to become his in a unique way. These observations agree well with the manner in which both Paul himself and the Acts of the Apostles describe his "conversion" as a call to become the Apostle to and of the Gentiles. This was the task for which he—in the manner of the prophets of old—had been earmarked by God from his mother's womb (Gal. 1:15; cf. Acts 9:15). There was not—as we usually think—first a conversion, and then a call to apostleship; there is only the call to the work among the Gentiles (Stendahl 1963, 204–05).

Stendahl's distinction between call and conversion has had a lasting impact in the study of Paul's conversion, both in Acts and in Paul's letters.

Paul's Early Ministry (9:19b–31)

After being baptized, and eating some food, Paul is very successful in regaining his strength. He spends several days with the disciples and preaching in the synagogues of Damascus. He was growing powerful and "baffled the Jews living

FIGURE 24   St. Paul Disputing in Damascus. 1130–40. Mosaic. Cappella Palatina,
Palazzo dei Normanni, Palermo, Sicily, Italy. Photo: Alinari/Art Resource, NY

in Damsacus in proving that Jesus is the Messiah" (v. 22). *St. Paul Disputation
in Damascus and his Escape* follows the *St. Paul Being Baptized* (see above) in
the Cappella Palatina mosaic cycle (**Figure 24**). The mosaic shows Paul (identified by an inscription on his right) preaching, with elevated hand, to two
learned men on the left side of the composition. The Latin inscription at the top
of the scene describes this action, "PAULUS DISPUTAT ET CONFUNDIT
EOS" (Paul disputed and confounded them [Jewish leaders]).

    In fact, Paul's success caused a conspiracy among the Jews to kill him. Paul
learns of their plan—which included guarding the city gates day and night—yet
we see him escaping in a somewhat comical manner on the right side of the
mosaic (described in the second half of the inscription above, *DEINDE
FUGIENS DAT LOCUM* ... "Then he fled that place ..."). Paul is crouched over
and squeezed into a basket as he is being lowered to safety outside the city walls
(an incident Paul mentions in 2 Cor 11:32–33). The guard is oblivious to the
event. There is no differentiation in lighting so the scene looks especially odd.
The escape was to take place during the night (9:25).

    Earlier Arator, sixth-century Latin poet and orator, had allegorized about
the basket in which Paul is lowered in his escape from Damascus: "a basket,
which is customarily woven with bulrushes and palms in turn, gives covering

to Saul, in glory retaining an allegory of the Church, for there is always contained in it the bulrush, by the waters [of baptism], and the palm by the crowns [of martyrdom]; the wave of baptism and the blood of martyrs promote the Church" (*OAA*, 9 [lines 708–53]).

Several issues of ecclesiology emerge in the early modern interpretations of Acts 9:25–43, which describes Barnabas's introduction of Paul to the disciples in Jerusalem, that apparently have no antecedents in patristic readings. British Baptist pastor and theologian William Kiffin (1616–1701), for example, seeks to counter the argument that Barnabas presented Paul to the Church at Jerusalem for acceptance without making any mention of Paul's baptism. Kiffin argues that the Jerusalem church would have been especially keen to assure that Paul, previously their arch enemy, "had at least done the first things of a disciple, of which we find all along in the History of the Acts of the Apostles, a *Being Baptized*" (Kiffin 1681, 146–49). Kiffin here is refuting the practice of "open communion" in which believer's baptism was not a prerequisite for participation in the Lord's Supper, or in some cases, church membership, a view advocated by John Bunyan (1628–88), among others.

Cuban-American Justo González has highlighted how Acts 9 presents a "harsh word" to those who find themselves "in the polarized situations of extreme suffering," where "what is natural is to hate those who are evil":

> It is at this point that this ninth chapter of Acts breaks into our set ways. When it was least expected, this Saul, who was breathing threats and murder against the disciples of the Lord, becomes a brother to Ananias and to those very disciples whom until then he persecuted. Likewise, that unbeliever who now scorns us, that inordinately wealthy one who lives it up while the people suffer, that journalist who lies about us because someone pays him to do so, and even that sergeant who tortures one of our sisters or brothers—any one of them may one day fall to the ground "on the Damascus road." In such a case, even though our natural inclination, like that of Ananias, may be exactly the opposite, we have no other alternative than to call them "brother" or "sister," and treat them as such (González 2001, 127).

Acts of Peter (9:32–43)

The chapter closes with two stories about Peter. In the story of Peter's healing of Aeneas, sixth-century Latin poet and orator Arator sees in the reference to the eight years of Aeneas's illness (9:33) an allusion to Christ's appearance to the disciples on the "eighth day after the resurrection" (*OAA*, 9 [lines 754–800]; cf. John 20:26).

Chrysostom suggests that the reason the disciples urge Peter not to delay in coming to see about the ailing Tabitha is because "she was a female disciple" (Acts 9:36; *Hom. Act.* 21). With regard to Luke's statement that the name of Tabitha means Dorcas or "deer," Chrysostom also notes that Tabitha is "as active and wakeful as an antelope" (*Hom. Act.* 21). The Venerable Bede, eighth-century British monk and exegete, is convinced that "the blessed Luke would not have provided the meaning of the name if he had not known that there was strong symbolism in it" (*Comm. Acts* 9:36). Bede then proceeds to explain that deer "dwell on high mountains, and they see all who approach no matter how far way they may be. Hence ... they are called *dorcades* from the sharpness of their vision. So it is with the saints. As they dwell on high by the merits of their works, through mental contemplation they simultaneously direct their attention with wisdom toward things above" (*Comm. Acts* 9:36). John Calvin is less positive about the meaning of Tabitha's name, claiming that it is a "wild she-goat" but arguing that the name "did not match the virtues of a holy woman" and that "the sanctity of her life easily wiped out the stigma of a rather unbecoming name" (*Commentary on Acts*, 9:36).

Citing the reference to Tabitha as a "disciple" Anglican minister Hanserd Knollys (1598–1691) further argues that "though believing Women being baptized are Disciples; Act. 9.36. and can make out Christ; yea, and some of them (by their experimentall knowledge and spirituall understanding of the way, Order, & Faith of the Gospel) may be able to instruct their Teachers, Acts 18.26. Rom 16.3. yet we do not hold, that a woman may preach, baptize, nor administer other Ordinances" (Knollys 1646, 6). Such an interpretation that reads into the text an institutional hierarchy is common in the history of Christianity.

We return to the fifteenth-century Peter cycle by Masolino and Massacio in the Brancacci chapel in the church of S. Maria del Carmine, Florence (for an introduction and background to the chapel, see the commentary on Acts 4:32–35). The life of the saint is presented as a moral exemplum for the Church that shows humankind the way to salvation. The cycle begins with temptation and expulsion (cf. Gen 3). The subjects show the plight of humanity and establish the church as its solution, as well as Peter's place in Christian history. Peter's primacy among the apostles is demonstrated through illustrating his special bond with Christ (in the frescoes on the left-hand wall), his ministry (in the altar-wall), and his miraculous powers (on the right-hand wall) (Roberts 1993, 57). There are two events from the ministry of Peter on the right side wall of the chapel. On the left half of the fresco, Peter and John are about to enter the Temple in Jerusalem (**Figure 25**). They are approached by a crippled man asking for alms (3:1–10). The miracle is about to take place.

The right half of this fresco takes place in Joppa after the death of Tabitha. The disciples sent two men to get Peter in Lydda. Despite the narrative stating

FIGURE 25 Tommaso Masolino da Panicale (1383–1447). *Curing the Crippled and the Resurrection of Tabitha.* 1425–27. Fresco. Brancacci Chapel, S. Maria del Carmine, Florence, Italy. Photo: Scala/Art Resource, NY

that Peter was brought to an upper chamber, Masolino places the event on the same level and in the same perspectival framework as the scene from Jerusalem. This is the first time that Masolino has used one-point linear perspective with a central vanishing point. The cityscape is actually Florentine. Two widows are present at the bedside of Tabitha. The miracle is happening as we watch. Peter holds his arm out and his hand is in the blessing gesture while Tabitha is sitting up in the bed. The man with Peter may well be his host in Joppa, the tanner Simon (Acts 9:43; Roberts 1993, 69). The reaction to this miracle is expressed in the various body positions of those in Tabitha's room.

The second example of the Raising of Tabitha (**Figure 26**) was painted by the Baroque artist, Gian Francesco Barbieri (called Guercino), approximately two hundred years later. Guercino was born in Cento, a small town outside the metropolis of Bologna. He became known as Guercino because he was squint-eyed (from the Italian *guercio*, "cross-eyed"), probably from a childhood accident. Guercino was a painter of the third-generation Bolognese style. He preferred a pictorial, rather violent Baroque manner that creates a deep impression and precipitated a change in the prevailing classicism.

The patron and original location of this work are unknown (Stone 1991, 62–63; Mahon 1991, 90–91). Stylistically, it is dated as an early work in 1618. The moment in the narrative occurs before that depicted by Masolino. Peter

FIGURE 26   Giovanni Francesco Guercino (1591–1666). *Raising of Tabitha.* 1617. Oil.
Galleria Palatina, Palazzo Pitti, Florence, Italy. Photo: Scala/Art Resource, NY

has raised his hand as if to command Tabitha upwards but she has yet to
respond. She lies lifeless and foreshortened. Three widows stand around and
behind Peter. Simon (apparently) points to Tabitha on Peter's right side and one
widow is at the bedside of Tabitha. In typical Baroque fashion, the gestures are
exaggerated and dramatic. The external lighting comes from the upperleft
corner and illuminates Peter's balding head, Tabitha's toes and the bedside widow's hands and white veil. The dark background adds to the drama but does not
offer any additional narrative detail. It is impossible to tell if they are in an
upper room.

   As mentioned above, many interpreters find Luke's calling Tabitha a "disciple" noteworthy. With the rise of feminist approaches to biblical studies in the
late twentieth/early twenty-first centuries, the assessment of Luke's view of the
role of women has varied greatly (see Gaventa 2004, 49– 60). Some continue to
affirm the older view that Luke's presentation of women was generally positive
or at least "reflects no particular tendency to keep women at home and subject
them to men" (Richter Reimer 1995, 267). Others characterize Luke's corpus "as

an extremely dangerous text, perhaps the most dangerous in the Bible" because Luke "deftly portrays [women] as models of subordinate service, excluded from the power center of the movement and from significant responsibilities" (Schaberg 1998, 363).

The story of Tabitha presents the debate in microcosm (see Anderson 2004, 22–48). Reading from the perspective of a "hermeneutics of suspicion," Gail O'Day notes that, despite the fact that Luke refers to Tabitha as a "female disciple" he describes her benevolence toward widows as "good works" and "acts of charity" but not as "ministry" (*diakonia*), a term reserved in Acts to describe the ministry of male disciples (O'Day 1998, 309). "One has to wonder why when men take care of widows, Luke calls it 'ministry' (6.4) but when Tabitha performs the same services Luke calls it 'good works'" (O'Day 1998, 310). Furthermore, there is also the issue of agency; few women, including Tabitha, are allowed speaking parts in Acts. This fact contributes to the "'*de facto* silencing' of women in Luke-Acts" (D'Angelo 1990, 312). Scott Spencer admits that "it is difficult to ignore that a lot of speechmaking goes on in Acts and that it all comes from male voices" (Spencer 2004, 146). Nonetheless, Spencer notes, contrary to O'Day, that while Luke avoids attributing the term "ministry" (*diakonia*) to Tabitha's activities, the terms that he does use—"good works" and "almsgiving"—align Tabitha closely with Luke's description of Jesus' overall ministry (Acts 10:38) and the deeds of Cornelius (10:2, 4) and Paul (24:17). From a post-colonialist perspective Margaret Aymer adds, "Peter calling her to life not by her colonial name but by her precolonial, Aramaic name is itself a decolonizing narrative device" (Aymer 2012, 541). However this debate is resolved, the words of contemporary biblical scholar Beverly Gaventa still seem á propos: "it would be difficult to find in recent work the glib assessments that characterize earlier generations of treatments of Luke and women" (Gaventa 2004, 53).

Overview

Acts 10–12 consists of three episodes. The first, the conversion of the Roman centurion Cornelius by Peter (10:1–11:18), is comprised of seven scenes (10:1–8; 10:9–16; 10:17–23a; 10:23b–33; 10:34–43; 10:44–48; 11:1–18). Some early interpreters focus on the character of Cornelius, his piety and acts of charity, while others contemplate the implications of Cornelius' occupation as a centurion for the issue as to whether or not Christian believers may participate in the military. Others are intrigued by Peter's vision, especially the significance and symbolism of the clean and unclean animals. The scene is rarely depicted in the visual

The Acts of the Apostles Through the Centuries, First Edition. Heidi J. Hornik and Mikeal C. Parsons.
© 2017 Heidi J. Hornik and Mikeal C. Parsons. Published 2017 by John Wiley & Sons, Ltd.

tradition, although Domenico Fetti has presented a fascinating painting of Peter's vision. The character of God as "no respecter of persons" (10:34) was a purple passage for those committed to dialogue about race relations in the mid-late twentieth century. Acts 10:38 has been a crucial text in Christological reflection, both in the creedal tradition and among Christian theologians.

The second episode deals with the activities of persons related to the Christian community at Antioch (11:19–30), especially with the actions of Barnabas (11:19–26) and Agabus (11:27–30). Especially significant is the note in Acts 11:26 that informs the reader that Antioch was the place where the first Jesus followers were called "Christians." The last episode (12:1–25) recounts the death of James, the brother of John (Luke 5:10), and the Peter's imprisonment at the hands of Herod, as well as Herod's death, and has proven fertile ground for the artistic imagination (see Montegna and Raphael).

Reception and Interpretation

Acts 10–11

The Conversion of Cornelius (10:1–11:18)

Cornelius and His Vision. In the apocryphal story of Mary's nativity, the annunciation of Mary's birth to her father Joachim echoes the appearance of an angel to Cornelius in Acts 10:4: "And when he was disturbed at his appearance, the angel who had appeared to him restrained his fear, saying: Fear not, Joachim, nor be disturbed by my appearance; for I am the angel of the Lord, sent by Him to thee to tell thee that *thy prayers have been heard, and that thy charitable deeds have gone up into His presence*" (Gos. Bir. Mary 3; italics ours).

Cornelius and Alms-giving (10:1–8). The relationship of Cornelius' faith and works of piety is of much debate among patristic interpreters (Martin 2006, 118). Augustine is concerned to point out that Cornelius "without some faith neither gave alms nor prayed. .... But if he could have been saved without the faith of Christ, the apostle Peter would not have been sent as an architect to build him up" (*Presentation of the Saints* 1.7.12; cf. Bede, *Comm. Acts* 10.1). Chrysostom, on the other hand, makes no distinction between faith and works, claiming that both Cornelius' "doctrines and his life were right" (*Hom. Act.* 22).

Ammonius strikes a balance between commending the practice of alms-giving and illuminating what is requisite to receive the Spirit. On the indispensability of alms-giving as part of the life of faith, Ammonius observes:

And if you fast without [giving] alms, then the fast does not count as a deed, certainly, such a person is worse than the glutton and the drunkard; and to such a person is a worse [punishment], as much as cruelty is more grievous than wantonness. And I say, what [good] is a fast if you show self-control and are chaste and have stood outside the bridechamber, but do not give alms? (*Catena on Acts* 10:4; 173.28–33).

But alms-giving cannot supplant the need for the believer to share in and accept the "word of faith":

> One must note that the Holy Spirit would not otherwise fall upon Cornelius and those with him, even if they are attested to be God-fearing and righteous, unless they are instructed first in the word of faith, then they can hear and believe; and in order that it might be clear from this that a gentile, even if he is altogether upright, never receives the gift of the Spirit if he has no share in and is ignorant of the true faith (*Catena on Acts* 10:44; 190.22–28; cf. 186.16–19).

Aquinas also tackles the reference to Cornelius' almsgiving in his discussion of the question: "Whether every act of an unbeliever is a sin?" To the objection that "there is no act of faith in unbelievers, they can do no good work, but sin in every action of theirs," he responds: "On the contrary, It is said of Cornelius, while yet an unbeliever (Acts 10:4. 31), that his alms were acceptable to God. Therefore not every action of an unbeliever is a sin, but some of his actions are good" (*ST* 2.2, Question 10: Of Unbelief in General).

John Calvin contrasts the piety of Cornelius with the other Italians who "were carried into the provinces to live in warfare, ran to and fro like hungry wolves to get some prey; they had for the most part no more religion than beasts; they had as great care of innocency as cutthroats; for which cause the virtues of Cornelius deserve the greater commendation, in that leading a soldier's life, which was that time most corrupt, he served God holily, and lived amongst men without doing any hurt or injury" (*Commentary on Acts*, 1.310).

Peter and His Vision (10:9–16). The note that Peter "went up" to pray indicates that he "had gone up 'to the higher,' not only in the body but also in mind and spirit" (Origen, *Hom. Lev.* 7.4.5; ACCS, 124). Chrysostom understands Peter's "trance" to be an "ecstatic vision" in which "the soul, so to speak, was caused to be out of the body" (*Hom. Act.* 22). According to Didymus the Blind (ca. 313–98), the Montanists appealed to Acts 10:9 to provide scriptural warrant for their ecstatic experiences in which they do not understand their own utterances at the time they are given. Didymus counters, "without a doubt, Peter, in a trance, followed along so as to proclaim what he saw and hear and what the signs, which he received, revealed" (*Catena on Acts* 10:10; 3.17.7; ACCS, 125). Augustine comments on the conflict between the Jerusalem believers and Peter and the symbolism of the latter's vision:

> Later some Christians from the circumcision wanted to put Peter in the wrong. They challenged him, *Why did you go into the house of uncircumcised Gentiles,*

and eat with them? (Acts 11:3). He explained to them how a dish was shown to him while he was praying, let down from heaven by four linen cloths. This dish contained all kinds of living creatures, signifying all nations. The reason why it was suspended by four linen cloths was that there are four quarters of the world, from which people would come. This is also why four gospels preach Christ, so that his grace may be understood to reach all four regions of the earth ("Exposition of Psalm 96," in *Expositions of the Psalms, 73-98*; WA 3.18.452).

Elsewhere, according to Augustine, Faustus the Manichaean criticized catholic Christians because they were inconsistent in following Peter's vision in Acts 10:14–15 which he took "to mean that one must eat all sorts of vipers, serpents, and snakes if one is going to obey the voice that Peter heard" (*Faust.* 1.20.31.3). Augustine responded:

> In saying that *for the clean all things are clean*, the apostle wanted us to understand the natures that God created, not the things of which they were symbols, in accord with which God distinguished the clean from the unclean. The apostle calls unclean and unbelieving those people who, after the revelation of the New Testament, maintained that they should still observe the symbols of what was to come and that the pagans could not be saved in Christ without the observance of those symbols. Although Manicheans carefully avoid eating meat, which they say was created by the devil, their own bodies are unclean and defile their souls. Hence, for Manicheans nothing is clean (*Faust.* 1.20.31.4).

Visual Interpretation of Peter's Vision. The Baroque painter, Domenico Fetti (1589–1623), developed his own "pictorial language" of biblical material (Askew 1961a). Fetti's depiction of the spiritual world through a series of parables enhanced the communicative power of his visual imagery and aided in the interpretation of Fetti's *Vision of St. Peter* (**Figure 27**). Growing up during the Counter Reformation, Domenico Fetti's work serves as a "response to the religious situation of his time" (Askew 1961a, 22).

Domenico Fetti's composition organizes all of the action into the left side of the composition. According to the biblical narrative, Peter goes to an upper area, such as a roof or a terrace, in order to pray (Acts 10:9). In this picture, we see Peter seated in front of a balustrade and above a landscape in the distant right. Peter appears to sleep while the subject of his vision is apparent to the viewer. To his left lies an open book, perhaps used to assist in his prayers but now discarded, taking, as it were, second place to the visionary moment (for a similar scene, see Velázquez's *St. John on Patmos* [London, National Gallery]; cf. Kovacs and Rowland 2004, 47–48). Following the Biblical text, in accordance with the stipulations of the Counter Reformation, Peter is depicted with his eyes closed, suggesting he is in a trance. The painting has been cut so the

FIGURE 27   Domenico Fetti (1589–1624). *Saint Peter's Vision of the Unclean Beasts.* 1619.
Oil. Kunsthistorisches Museum, Vienna, Austria. Photo: Erich Lessing/Art Resource, NY

vision is partially destroyed. A group of four-footed creatures (cow, lion, rabbit)
are visible on a sheet being pulled back up to heaven by angels (now only one
set of angels' legs remain). In Acts the vision is accompanied by a voice that tells
Peter three times that it is now permissible to eat these animals. These animals
are typically considered unclean by Jewish law. God has cleansed the food, in
addition to creating it, so that new laws are established for the Gentiles.

This is a very rare scene in visual art. The painting was once located in
Amsterdam and is believed to have inspired pen and ink drawings by Rembrandt
(Bevers, Hendrix, Robinson and Schatborn 2010, 152). Fetti, although born
and trained in Rome, was greatly influenced by the light and warm tones of
Venetian art. Fetti's active brushwork creates extraordinary ranges of colors
within the folds of drapery. The figure is in a natural position. The painting is
"of a translucent matter, the face of the Saint is soaked by light, as if to create a
spot light effect" (Safarik 1990, 237). Safarik asserts that "the most successful
portion of the composition ... now damaged and badly restored ... is undoubtedly

the one representing several animals rendered in the extreme realism of Bassano" (Safarik 1990, 237). However, one can still enjoy the artistic achievements of Domenico Fetti. Pamela Askew states: "It is Fetti's rich and poetic palette that imparts overtones of phantasy to his vision of nature, allies his realism with the ideal, and makes his narrative appear more spirited" (Askew 1961b, 246). Askew further comments on how Domenico Fetti's "realism is tempered toward a pleasing naturalism that visually binds his meaning to an ideal of religious sentiment" (Askew 1961b, 246). Fetti preferred themes of dreams and visions that allowed his pictures to have a sense of melancholy and calm. For Peter, representative of the world of nature, literally witnesses the world of the Spirit through his vision. Perhaps it is Fetti's affinity for allegory that leads him to paint Peter's vision.

Radical Reformer Thomas Müntzer (c.1485–1525) commented on the necessity of visions for those who have "not grasped the clear word of God in his soul …. As when Saint Peter, in the Acts of the Apostles, did not understand the law (Leviticus 11), he had doubts about food and about the Gentiles— whether he should accept them into his company—so God gave him an ecstatic vision" (*Sermon to the Princes*; RCS, 136).

Bearing Arms (Acts 10:31). Augustine appeals to Acts 10:31 in his discussion of whether or not Christians can bear arms as a soldier: "Do not suppose that no one can please God who as a soldier carries the weapons of war. Holy David carried them, and the Lord bore a great a testimony to him. …. Cornelius carried them, to whom the angel was sent and said, *Cornelius, your almsgiving was found acceptable, and your prayers have been heard* (Acts 10:31). Then he told him to send someone to the apostle Peter and to hear from him what he should do. And Cornelius also sent a pious soldier to the apostle so that he would come" ("Letter 189: Augustine to Boniface"; WA 2.3.260).

Like Augustine, Luther appeals to the example of Cornelius (amongst others) as evidence that Christians were not forbidden by Scripture to serve in the military:

> Still, neither [John the Baptist nor Jesus] condemns the vocation of mercenaries, even though they themselves were not soldiers. On the contrary, John addresses them, saying, "Rob no one by violence or by false accusation, and be content with your wages" [Luke 3:14]. Christ went to the centurion at Capernaum, who undoubtedly also served for wages, to help his servant. Yet Jesus did not bid him to forsake his vocation, but instead praised his faith above all Israel [Matt. 8:10]. And St. Peter allowed Cornelius of Caesarea to remain a centurion after his baptism, together with his troops, who were there in the pay of the Romans [Acts 10] ("On the Councils and the Church" 1.1.1 in *Church and Ministry* 3:39–40; cf. "Temporal Authority: To What Extent It Should Be Obeyed" 4 in *Christian in Society* 2:99).

No Respecter of Persons (Acts 10:34). Søren Kierkegaard alludes to Acts 10:34 in a "Letter to the Reader" in *Stages on Life's Way*: "the believer continually lies out on the deep, has 70,000 fathoms of water beneath him. However long he lies out there, this still does not mean that he will gradually end up lying and relaxing onshore. .... The person who chooses spiritual existence by virtue of the religious will have the consolation .... that he, too, suffers in life and that *before God there is no respect of persons* (*KW* 11:444–45; emphasis added). Elsewhere, he appeals to the same verse in answer to the question "What then is the eminent Christian?": "He is a Christian. As a Christian, he knows about shutting his door when he is to speak with God—not so that no one will find out that he is speaking with God but so that no one will disturb him .... He believes that there is a God in heaven who is not a respecter of persons; he believes that the person who ruled over all of humanity, if we will imagine such a one, is not the least bit more important to God than the lowliest—yes, than the sparrow that falls to the ground" (*KW* 18:50–51).

In a prophetic voice raised in 1959, ethicist T.B. Maston (1897–1988) applies Acts 10:34 ("God is no respecter of persons") to the troubled issue of race relations and prejudice: God "does not look on or judge men by the color of their skin or by their general external conditions; he looks on the heart. His relations to men are absolutely fair and unprejudiced. Since God expects his children to be like him, we should not be respecters of persons. We should be impartial; we should not play favorites" (Maston 1959; see also Baptist Manifesto 1997).

In a fascinating reflection on Acts 10 in an adult Sunday school lesson, "The Reality of Prejudice," written by and for Native Americans, we read:

> Prejudice is an attitude of prejudging someone or a group of people before you know them. This prejudging is usually based on two things: (a) what others say about the person and (b) what you have read about the people. Most Indians can identify with this attitude. Many people have formed their opinion of Indians by the things they heard from other people, television, or things they read in books. Also, many people base their opinion of Indians on what they see in the downtown areas of many small and large towns. They don't see the majority of Indians who are being educated or working. ... You may be prejudiced toward other Indians, White people, Black people, or those who don't speak your language or believe the way you do, or who live and eat differently. Pray that God will help you overcome these feelings and beliefs just as Peter did (SBC-Lifeway 1989).

Christology and Ethics (Acts 10:38). Much attention was also given to the Christology of Peter's speech, especially with regard to the relation of Christ's humanity to his divinity. The Second London Confession (1689) appeals to Acts 10:38 ("how God anointed Jesus of Nazareth with the Holy Spirit") in its explication of Christ's two natures under the article on "Christ the Mediator":

"The *Lord Jesus* in his human nature thus united to the divine, in the Person of the *Son*, was sanctified, anointed with the *Holy Spirit*, above measure ..." Interestingly, the authors of the Second London confession added the reference to Acts 10:38 to the Westminster Confession of Faith upon which the Second London is based and which does not refer to Acts 10. British cleric Matthew Caffyn's obtuse polemic against the Quakers' "Inner Light," reflects not only aspects of his emerging Hoffmannite Christology (which, by emphasizing Christ's divinity, undermined his humanity), but also his inability "to explain the Trinity to his own satisfaction" (McBeth 1987, 156):

> The Eternal Spirit which was given to, and received by the visible man, cannot be the Christ, that is in English **Anointed**, because he is said by the Apostle to be the **Anointing with which** the Saviour was anointed: as 'tis written, *how God anointed Jesus*, (that is, the Saviour) of Nazareth **with the Holy Spirit**, Act. 10.38. If the Eternal Spirit, as Spirit, was anointed, I would know with what, and wherefore? (Caffyn 1660).

Karl Barth points to Jesus' earthly activity as a benefactor (Acts 10:38) as evidence of his divinity:

> The whole sequence of the life of Jesus as recounted by Peter in his address at Cæsarea in Acts 10[38], in which we are told that Jesus of Nazareth was anointed with the Holy Ghost and with power, and went about as a Benefactor (εὐεργετῶν), "healing all that were oppressed of the devil." According to the New Testament, this sympathy, help, deliverance and mercy, this active solidarity with the state and fate of man, is the concrete correlative of His divinity, of His anointing with the Spirit and power, of His equality with God, of His wealth (*CD* 3.2.210).

Acts 10:38 was also utilized in poignant ethical reflections. Welsh nonconformist Vavasor Powell (1617–1670) claims that Jesus doing "good" (Acts 10:38) can serve as a model for a member of Parliament or a Magistrate: "If a man be a *Parliament man*, he should not loose one day of being there, to see what may be done for Gods glory. And if a man be a *Magistrate* of the City, he should observe all opportunities of glorifying God; as Christ did" (Powell 1649, 53). Ethicist T. B. Matson suggests that the "five-word biography" (he went about doing good) flowed naturally and inevitably from within His life. Jesus had been anointed with the Holy Spirit and power, and "God was with him." Will people be able to say when we come to the end of the journey, "[They] went about doing good"? (Matson 1987, 80).

Judge of the Living and the Dead (Acts 10:42). In one of the early references to Acts 10:42, Polycarp (c. 69–155) praises "our Lord Jesus Christ" whom "every breathing creature serves, who is coming as 'Judge of the living and the dead'"

(Pol. *Phil.* 2:1; cf. also Tertullian, *Virg.* 1.3). The Niceno-Constantinopolitan Creed also echoes Acts 10:42: Christ "ascended into heaven, and sitteth on the right hand of the Father. And he shall come again with glory *to judge both the quick and the dead*, whose kingdom shall have no end." Pelikan and Hotchkiss catalogue over fifty subsequent confessions and creeds that, influenced by the Niceno-Constantinopolitan Creed, allude to Christ coming to "judge the living and the dead" (Acts 10:42; *CCF*, 4:553–54).

In paragraph four of the 1689 Second London's "Christ as Mediator" article, the confession appeals to Acts 10:42 ("whom God ordained to be the judge of the living and of the dead") to describe the Glorified Lord's work in the eschaton: "[Christ] ascended into heaven: and there sitteth at the right hand of his *Father*, making intercession; and shall return to judge *Men* and *Angels* at the end of the *World*." The verse lends its words to the hymn, "He That Was Ordained of God to be the Judge of the Quick and the Dead" (1691) by Benjamin Keach (1640–1704), one of the primary forces behind the Second London Confession.

The General Baptist Orthodox Creed (1678) combined the language of Acts 10:42 with the aside in Acts 10:36, "he is Lord of all," in its articulation of liberty of conscience, one of the distinctive hallmarks of Baptist thought:

> The Lord Jesus Christ, who is king of kings, and lord of all by purchase, and is judge of quick and dead, is the only Lord of Conscience, having a peculiar right so to be. He having died for that end, to take away the guilt, and to destroy the filth of sin, that keeps the consciences of all men in thraldom, and bondage, till they are set free by his special grace. And therefore he would not have the consciences of men in bondage to, or imposed upon, by any usurpation, tyranny, or command whatsoever, contrary to his revealed will in his word, which is the only rule he hath left, for the consciences of all men to be ruled, and regulated, and guided by, through the assistance of his spirit.

British Particular Baptist pastor Samuel Medley (1800) explores other dimensions of Jesus as "Lord of all" in a hymn:

> To JESUS let us join to raise
> Our hearts and voices in his praise;
> Peace to poor sinners, great or small,
> Is preach'd thro' him, as "Lord of all."

In subsequent stanzas of the hymn, Medley celebrates Jesus as Lord of "all glory," "all grace," "all enemies," and "all blessedness above."

Baptized in the Name of Jesus (Acts 10:48). British cleric Hanserd Knollys (1598–1691), perhaps reflecting some current debate about the use of the trinitarian baptismal formula, argues that Acts 10:48 ("he commanded them to be baptized in the name of Jesus Christ") is to be understood, not as an "Exception," but rather as the equivalent to "In the Name of the Father, Son, and Holy Spirit. For these three are one in Essence. ... There is not one Baptism in the Name of the Father, Son, and Holy Spirit, [Matt. 28:19] and another Baptism in the Name of the Lord, Jesus Christ" (Knollys 1646, 2).

Katherine Sutton, a seventeenth-century prophetess and mystic, credited the "Great Commission" of Matthew 28 and Acts 10:48 with convincing her to submit to believer's baptism: "Now that which made me willing to obey the Lord, in this Ordinance was the Command of Jesus Christ in Mat. 28:19. and Act. 10:48. and the example of Christ and the practise of the Apostles, and primitive Saints, together with the promise of the gift of the Holy Ghost, anexed thereunto" (Sutton 1663, 11–12).

Christians at Antioch (11:19–30)

First Called "Christians" (Acts 11:26). Fourth-century theologian Gregory of Nyssa discusses the significance of the name "Christian": "Our good Master, Jesus Christ, bestowed on us a partnership in his revered name, so that we get our name from no other person connected with us, and if one happens to be rich and well-born or of lowly origin and poor, or if one has some distinction from his business or position, all such conditions are of no avail because the one authoritative name for those believing in him is that of Christian" (*On Perfection*; ACCS, 148). Luther discusses the reference to the believers first being called Christians in Antioch (and not Rome!) as another way to mock the claims to primacy of the Roman papacy:

> We also said above that the churches in Alexandria and Antioch were excellent churches, better than the one in Rome, gifted with special talents and people, even though they were not planted by apostles—especially the one at Antioch, which was, as Acts 11 [v. 19] says, planted by the scattered disciples during the trouble that arose over St. Stephen, but which nevertheless grew so much that the believers here were the first to be called Christians [Acts 11:26]. Oh, if the pope had the advantage that the disciples in Rome were the first to be called Christians, then all the ten heavens, as the astronomers count them, would be too small to encompass the glory of the arrogant paunch in Rome! And it still is worth nothing, for in Christ all churches are equal ("Against the Roman Papacy an Institution of the Devil," 3.1.1 in *Church and Ministry* 3:348-49).

Karl Barth also comments on the significance of the name "Christian" (Acts 11:26): "We read in Ac. 11²⁶ that they were first called Χριστιανοί in Syrian Antioch, a name of which we read in 1 Pet. 4¹⁶ that it pledged them to glorify

God. That to be a bearer of this name involves a real change of the form of human existence seems to come out in Agrippa's ironical words to Paul as reported in Ac. 26²⁸: 'Almost thou persuadest me to be made (ποιῆσαι) a Christian.' It is not without theological significance that this name—that the fact that these folk are adherents of Christ—should have prevailed" (*CD* 4.1.749; *CD* 4.3.525–26).

The Jerusalem Conference (Acts 11:27–30 and Galatians 2). Acts 11:30 reports that Barnabas and Saul delivered a relief fund to believers in Jerusalem. According to Acts, this is Paul's second visit to Jerusalem (9:25–26). In that sequence, the Jerusalem Council in Acts 15, which addresses the issue of Gentiles and the Law, is Paul's third visit and stands in tension with Paul's account in Galatians 2, which also addresses the issue of Gentiles and the Law and which many take to be reflecting the same event recorded in Acts 15. One solution is to equate Acts 11:30, described as a famine visit, and Galatians 2, presented by Paul as a private conference between himself and the Jerusalem pillars. The public Jerusalem Council in Acts 15 is then Paul's third visit and not referenced in his letters (Bruce 1978, 475). Others have proposed that Luke (or the tradition he inherited) split the second Jerusalem visit into two accounts, one that focused on famine relief (Acts 11:30) and the other (Acts 15) that addressed the Gentile issue (Wedderburn 1981, 107).

Acts 12

Death of James and Imprisonment of Peter (Acts 12:1–25)

Opposition to the new faith continues. Eusebius (260–339) refers to a lost work of Clement of Alexandria who reported that "the man who turned James [brother of John] over to the judgment of martyrdom was himself moved to confess himself a Christian. Both were led away together to punishment, and while they were being led on the way, he asked James to forgive him. He considered for a moment and said, 'Peace be to you,' and kissed him. And so both were beheaded at the same time" (*Hist. eccl.*, 2.9; cf. Bede, *Comm. Acts 12:2*). Seeking the political roots of religious persecution, Swiss Reformer Rudolf Gwalther (1519–1586) comments that tyrants seek to avoid religious unrest because "although they are void of all religion, they seek to have in their realm a uniform consent in religion" (*Homilies* 82, Acts 12:1–5; RCS, 161).

Rudolf Gwalther also commented on the angelic intervention. God sent the "angel to loosen the iron chains, he opened the doors in an amazing way, he defeated the watch of the soldiers and brought Peter out of all danger and set him at liberty when the sentence of death was already given against him" (*Homilies* 8, Acts 12:12–19; RCS, 166).

The rise of the Enlightenment threatened the existence of angels, or at least the acceptance of their existence! In an article on angel appearances in Acts, Johann Eichhorn (1752–1827) argued that Peter, upon reflecting on his remarkable release from prison (Acts 12:1–11), concluded it was the result of Providence which took the shape of angelic intervention: "the visible hand of providence had set him free: this Peter was compelled to conclude on the basis of the whole incident: Jewish theology, which always provides Providence with a host of angels to perform its purposes, could express this in no other way than that an angel of the Lord had delivered him from prison. Once this expression was chosen, everything that had happened—the shaking, the speaking, the leading—an angel of the Lord must have done" (Eichorn 1790, 398; cited in Baird 1992, 1:150).

Visual Interpretation of James' Execution and Peter's Liberation. The Overtari chapel frescoes are in the Eremitani Church in Padua, which was dedicated to the patron saints of the chapel, Saints James and Christopher. The chapel was bombed on March 11, 1944 during World War II (Salmazo, Spiazzi, Toniolo, eds. 2006), and the black and white photographs are from 1932–34. The lower left scene was *James Led to Execution*. The lower right fresco, illustrated here, was the *Execution of James* (**Figure 28**). The other scenes of the fresco cycle were *James Baptizing the Hermogenes* and the *Judgement of James*.

Andrea Mantegna completed this commission when he was only twenty-six years old. We know a lot about its young artist because archives in the cities where he worked, Padua and Mantua, are well-preserved (Finaldi 2010). After starting his professional career at a very young age (his first contract had to be signed by his older brother because he was too young), he became the leading northern Italian mainland painter of the fifteenth century. Born and raised in the university town of Padua, Mantegna's interest in classical antiquity was encouraged by a circle of university scholars and professionals.

He was greatly influenced by *Gattamelata*, the monumental equestrian sculpture in the Piazza del Santo executed by Donatello from 1443–1453, and by paintings of Jacopo Bellini of Venice, whose daughter he would marry when he was twenty-three. Mantegna also studied works by the Tuscan artists Andrea del Castagno, Filippo Lippi, and Paolo Uccello. Mantegna's own work is characterized by an unprecedented use of Roman architecture to organize and frame his compositions. He became known for precise and meticulous execution, and for his use of perspective and foreshortening as demonstrated in this destroyed fresco.

FIGURE 28   Andrea Mantegna (1431–1506). *Martyrdom of St. James.* 1454–57. Destroyed fresco. Chiesa degli Eremitani, Padua, Italy. Photo: Alinari/Art Resource, NY

Saint James lies prone and his body is drastically foreshortened so that the severed head will roll out of the picture plane and onto the floor of the chapel below. The executioner has the giant mallet already raised above his head and about to strike. The illusion is further enhanced by the rail that one of the soldiers leans over into our space. The landscape contains a hill that slopes downward culminating in the execution in the foreground. This also further heightens the drama of the narrative.

FIGURE 29 Raphael (1483–1520). *The Liberation of St. Peter from Prison*. 1514. Fresco. Stanze d'Eliodoro, Vatican Palace, Vatican State. Photo: Scala/Art Resource, NY

In Acts 12, Luke recounts how King Herod—after he ordered James, the brother of John, "killed with the sword"—imprisoned Peter for preaching the gospel about Christ. The believers in Jerusalem had identified King Herod and Pontius Pilate specifically as political leaders who conspired against Jesus (Acts 4:27); now the King was laying "violent hands upon some who belonged to the church" (Acts 12:1).

The King intended to deliver Peter for trial after the Passover, but before this happened, Peter was delivered from prison. Raphael's fresco *Liberation of St. Peter from Prison* (**Figure 29**) shows the critical elements of the story in three scenes from left to right: the soldiers in front of the prison door, the sleeping Peter being awakened by the angel, and the freed Peter walking with the angel past the sleeping soldiers.

By the beginning of the fifteenth century, the High Renaissance style was firmly established in Rome; and Raphael, known as the great assimilator, had been called to decorate the Pope's private apartments, today part of the Vatican Museum. Pope Julius II della Rovere (pontiff from 1503 to 1513) was a powerful leader who planned to create a Second Golden Age of Rome in terms of artistic production. Michelangelo was just completing the painted ceiling of the

Sistine Chapel, the Pope's private chapel, when Raphael began this Room of Heliodorus, or *Stanza d'Eliodoro*, in 1513. In addition to the Heliodorus, there are three other "Raphael Rooms" in the papal residence. Raphael was first commissioned to paint the Room of the Segnatura, which was originally a library and study. He adorned its walls with representations of Truth, Goodness, and Beauty (for a discussion of the most famous fresco in this room, *The School of Athens*, see Hornik 2009, 46–49). The Room of the Fire in Borgo originally held the meetings of the highest court of the Holy See during the time of Pope Julius II. Raphael did not fresco this room until it was appropriated as a dining room during the time of Julius' successor, Pope Leo X. This room was decorated with images of two previous popes who took the name Leo. The Room of Constantine was to be used for receptions and official ceremonies. Raphael died before this room was finished so its paintings depicting the life of Constantine were completed by the school of Raphael (see the web pages on the Raphael Rooms at *Vatican Museums* [accessed 21 July 2016], http://mv.vatican.va/3_EN/pages/sdr/sdr_00.main.html).

The Heliodorus room was used for private audiences with the Pope. Each wall is painted with an historical or legendary narrative with special significance not only for the papal devotions, but also the political aspirations of freeing Italy from French military control: the miraculous bleeding of a Eucharistic wafer during the *Mass at Bolsena*, the *Expulsion of Heliodorus* from the Temple of Jerusalem, the *Repulse of Attila* by Pope Leo I, and the *Liberation of St. Peter* (Penny 2010). Each of these scenes depicts God's miraculous protection of the Church.

The *Expulsion of Heliodorus* depicts Pope Julius II witnessing a second century BCE event recorded in 2 Maccabees 3:21–28, when God sent a horseman and two youths to drive Heliodorus out of the Temple in Jerusalem before he could steal its treasures on behalf of the King of Syria. The *Repulse of Attila* shows the legendary appearance of Peter and Paul armed with swords during a meeting between Pope Leo the Great (d. c461) and Attila which caused the Huns to desist from invading Italy in 452 C.E. In the *Mass of Bolsena*, Pope Julius II observes a miracle in 1263 that convinced worshippers that Christ was present in the Eucharist. As the Vatican Museums sums up the artistic program of this room: "Faith had been threatened (*Mass of Bolsena*), in the person of its pontiff (*Liberation of St. Peter*), in its site (*Encounter of Leo the Great with Attila*) and in its patrimony (*Expulsion of Heliodorus from the Temple*)" (*Vatican Museums* [accessed 21 July 2016], http://mv.vatican.va/3_EN/pages/SDR/SDR_02_SalaElio.html).

In the *Liberation of St. Peter*, the artist portrays the Apostle with the features of Pope Julius II. This allows the depiction of Peter's salvation to double as a celebration of a victory for the papacy over an invading French army. Pope

Julius had been praying at San Pietro in Vincoli (St. Peter in Chains)—the church in Rome where the chains that bound Peter are displayed—when he learned of an unexpected victory against the French in 1512. To commemorate the victory, that evening Julius II staged a re-enactment of the liberation of Peter and led a procession to Castel Sant'Angelo with more torches than had been previously used (Hartt and Wilkins 2011, 523).

The architectural prison setting in this fresco is inspired by the contemporary High Renaissance style of Donato Bramante (1444–1514), the architect of St. Peter's Basilica. For instance, the monumental arch is constructed of rusticated blocks seen in Roman palaces of this time. The grate continues the visual tradition established for other scenes depicting the imprisonment of John the Baptist and Peter. Raphael exhibits an exceptional handling of light in the clouds that drift in front of the Moon (in the scene on the left) and the torches that flicker off the guards' armor (on the right). The central scene truly has a transcendent and radiant light.

The contemporary New Testament scholar Susan Garrett argues that Luke regarded Jesus' death, resurrection, and ascension as an "exodus" because in these events Jesus, "the one who is stronger," led the people out of bondage to Satan. Luke believed that Satan had long exercised authority over the peoples of the world (Luke 4:6; cf. Acts 26:18). Jesus' "exodus" from Satan's power (through his resurrection and ascension) becomes a typological model for subsequent events in the life of the Church, especially Peter's miraculous release from prison and King Herod's ensuing fall. Peter (like Jesus) is freed from a horrible tyrant and "led out of bondage" and (as at the resurrection) the miraculous rescue is followed by the tyrant's demise (Garrett 1990, 659–60).

Whether the story of Peter's liberation is interpreted by a fifteenth-century artist and pope or by a twentieth-century New Testament scholar, its symbolism of freedom from spiritual and political oppression is evident (Hornik 2010b, 48–52).

Overview

Since the beginning of the seventeenth-century British missionary movement, Acts 13–14 has been known as the account of Paul's "first missionary journey" (but see Townsend 1986, 99-104). Interpretations of Acts 13–14 have tended to focus on ecclesial issues. A number of confessions appeal to Acts 13:1–3 and 14:23 for scriptural warrant in selecting church leaders and, in the case of 13:1-3, for the practice of laying on of hands for those ordained to ministry

The Acts of the Apostles Through the Centuries, First Edition. Heidi J. Hornik and Mikeal C. Parsons.
© 2017 Heidi J. Hornik and Mikeal C. Parsons. Published 2017 by John Wiley & Sons, Ltd.

(e.g. Thirty Congregations 1651; Somerset Confession 1656, XXXI; Standard Confession 1660). Others consider the character and role of the Holy Spirit in the narrative. The Conversion of the Proconsul (Acts 13:4-12) was part of Raphael's program for the cartoons and tapestry decorations of the Sistine Chapel. Various details of Paul's sermon in Pisidia occupied the attention of interpreters, but Acts 13:46–47 was a focal point in discussions of the contested relationship between Jews and Christians and 13:48 figured prominently in discussions of predestination. The sacrifice at Lystra (14:11–18) is the subject of another of Raphael's Sistine tapestries, and the stoning of Paul (14:19–20) figures in visual images.

Reception and Interpretation

Acts 13

Commissioning in Antioch (13:1–3)

Acts 13:1-3 is widely recognized as the beginning of Paul's so-called three missionary journeys in Acts. Luke does not actually enumerate Paul's missionary activity in this way, and, in fact, the first reference to "three Pauline missionary journeys," occurs in J.A. Bengel's 1742 *Gnomon Novi Testamenti* (Townsend 1986, 99–104). Further, the concept of Paul's missionary journeys was apparently "created" as part of the propaganda developed by the Society for Promotion of Christian Knowledge (founded 1698) and the Society for the Propagation of the Gospel in Foreign Parts (founded 1701). Paul's "missionary journeys" provided a biblical pattern for missionaries going out from a central location to the "ends of the earth" and then returning periodically for spiritual renewal, administrative guidance, and financial support (Townsend 1986, 99–104). The "mythical" journeys of Paul provided the biblical "foundation" necessary to persuade believers to support these missionary causes, and the romantic appeal of the three journeys is seen in their stubborn resistance as they continue to hold a place of prominence in Bible atlases, introductory New Testament textbooks, and classroom lectures and discussions in both church and academ. While Paul's mission to the Gentiles certainly occupies a central place in the second half of Luke's narrative, it may not fit the familiar pattern of "Paul's missionary journeys," no matter how attractive the map.

Many early modern interpreters appealed to Acts 13:1–3 and/or 14:23 as a biblical basis for the authority of the "visible church" to appoint officers or ministers (e.g., Smyth 1607, 7–9; Declaration of Faith 1611, article 21;

The Standard Confession 1660, Article XV; Second London Confession XXVI; The Orthodox Creed 1678, Article XXXI).Protestant dissenter John Smyth also refers to Acts 13:1 (and 1 Cor 14) in his discussion of the role of the prophet: "Prophets are men endued with gifts apt to utter matter fit to edification, exhortation, and consolation. 1 Cor. 14, 3, Act. 13, 1, Rom. 12. 6. These persons must first be appointed to this exercise by the church. 1 Cor. 14, 40, Act, 13. 1" (Smyth 1607, n.p.) While prophet and pastor are probably interchangeable for Smyth, this passage may also reflect Smyth's recognition of of the traveling prophet in the NT and in Puritan/Baptist communities. As a biblicist, Smyth always seemed to be pressing for ways to protect literalism within the various pieties/theologies he passed through in his pilgrimage.

John Calvin ruminates on the contrast between Paul's insistence in Gal 1:1 that he was called directly by God and Acts 13:2 which reports the role of the church at Antioch in setting Saul (and Barnabas) apart for service:

> Because Luke says here that Paul was ordained by the votes of the Church, it seems to disagree with Paul's statement, in which he denies that he was called by men and through men (Gal. 1.1). I reply that he was created an apostle long before he was sent to the gentiles, and that not by men voting for him; and he had already discharged his apostleship for several years when he was summoned to the Gentiles by a new oracle. … [God] now reveals by public proclamation that decision of His, which up to then was known to a few, and orders it to be sealed by the solemn approval of the Church. The meaning of the words is therefore this: the time has now come for Paul to spread the gospel among the Gentiles, and, because the wall has been destroyed [Eph 2:14] to gather a Church from the Gentiles, who had previously been outside the Kingdom of God (*Commentary on Acts*, 13:2; 353).

Others focus on the role of the Holy Spirit in the commissioning scene. Drawing specifically on Acts 13:2, Pseudo-Basil draws on Acts 13:2 in an argument against those who deny the divinity of the Spirit:

> The Acts of the Apostles taught that the Spirit directed the setting aside. If the Lord, the God of the fathers, chose him whom he had preordained, while the Son called him forth, and the Spirit, using the operation of [the divine] nature, set the same one aside, how is there a difference of nature in the Trinity in which an identity of operation is found? (Pseudo-Basil, *Against Eunomius* 5; trans. Martin 2006 159).

Particular Baptist minister Christopher Blackwood appealed to Acts 13:2 (among other texts) to answer the catechetical question: "Whether the Holy ghost is only a motion, action, or operation, whereby God works effectually in the hearts of the elect; or whether he is an understanding, willing, working substance?" The Holy Spirit who had separated Paul and Barnabas "for the work" is therefore an "understanding, willing, working, substance" or a "person indued with understanding" and not simply a "motion, action, or operation" (Blackwood 1653, 3–4). Blackwood is joining a long debate seeking to clarify the nature and operation of the Holy Spirit in relationship to the doctrine of the Trinity.

Emerging from the protest by the "Confessing Church" against the practice of state-appointed clergy in Nazi Germany, Dietrich Bonhoeffer read Acts 13:2 as providing evidence of one way in which church leaders were chosen (none of which involved the State or non-ecclesial individuals or institutions):

> The New Testament attests the appointment of church offices through God himself (1 Cor 12:28), by Christ (Eph. 4:1), by the Holy Spirit (Acts 20:28), by the church-community with the assistance of the Holy Spirit (Acts 6:5; 13:2), by the apostles and office holders after careful examination (Titus 1:5; 1 Tim. 5:23). Appointment of church offices by anyone outside the church-community is inconceivable for the New Testament, since the church-community is the body of Christ. There are, to be sure, no fixed rules governing the order of offices in the church-community. The church-community in Jerusalem is ordered differently than are those in Asia Minor. Here there is freedom as long as "all things are done for building up" (1 Cor 14:26), that is, for the proper building of the body of Christ through the power of the keys (*BW* 14:838).

Contest on Cyprus (13:4–12)

With Acts 13:4–12, we return to the Sistine Chapel and to Raphael's watercolor cartoons for the wall tapestries. *The Conversion of the Proconsul* (**Figure 30**) is a centralized, characteristically High Renaissance composition. The proconsul, the governor of a senatorial province, sits enthroned in the center of the painting. The throne is inset before an architectural niche. His attention is on the man to his left, the magician Elymas, who has just now been struck blind by Paul. Paul is on the left of the painting in green gown and rose-colored mantle with his right hand extended towards Elymas. Elymas staggers forward with eyes closed and hands and arms extended to feel his way as he walks towards Paul.

The proconsul Sergius Paulus had called Paul and Barnabas because he wanted to hear the word of God (Acts 13:7; Alexander 2001, 1044). Elymas opposed what they had to say. Elymas was a Jew, a magician and a false prophet who was turning the proconsul away from the Lord, so Paul blinded Elymas to demonstrate God's presence in his words and actions. The onlookers express amazement and converse and gesticulate amongst themselves as they witness Elymas walking as a blind man. It was common for educated Romans to have a soothsayer or diviner kept in their company.

FIGURE 30   Raphael (1483–1520). *The Conversion of the Proconsul.* 1515–16.
Watercolor mounted on canvas (tapestry cartoon), 3.4 × 4.4m. V&A Images/The Royal
Collection, on loan from HM The Queen. Victoria and Albert Museum, London,
Great Britain. Photo: V&A Images, London/Art Resource, NY

Paul sees this magician as evil. Luke describes their encounter: Paul, filled
with the Holy Spirit, looked intently at him [Elymas] and said, "You son of the
devil, you enemy of all righteousness, full of all deceit and villainy, will you not
stop making crooked the straight paths of the Lord? And, now listen—the hand
of the Lord is against you, and you will be blind for a while, unable to see the
sun" (Acts 13:10–11). Immediately mist and darkness came over him, and he
went about groping for someone to lead him by the hand.

The "Blinding of Elymas" is often stated as the title for this composition.
Shearman (1972, 58) rightly observed that this is not a good title based on the
explanatory inscription given in the painting by the artist. This is the only
tapestry that has such an inscription and Raphael directs the viewer to draw
specific meaning and place the correct emphasis on the event. The titulus,
or inscription, is "Through the preaching of Saul, Sergius Paulus, Proconsul
of Asia, embraces the Christian Faith." So what matters is not the blinding of
Elymas but the conversion to Christianity of the proconsul (governor of a

senatorial province), Sergius Paulus. Luke allows the supernatural power of this story to encourage the reader to share the astonishment and belief along with the proconsul (Alexander 2001, 1044). The story also serves to distance the Christian message from one of its closest rivals in the market place of ancient religions. A.D. Nock views the Elymas scene as demonstrating the superiority of Christian miracle to pagan magic (1933, 164–88; cited in Baird 2003, 2.430).

In an anonymous catena on Acts 13:11, the author picks up on Paul's statement that Elymas will be blind "for a time": "The phrase, 'until a time' is a sign of repentance, so that if one repents, then one may obtain salvation from God. But if one despises, in this way, both the patience and goodness of God, then he will have an irrevocable judgment" (*Catena on Acts* 13:11; 217.9–12).

Paul's Preaching and Expulsion in Pisidia (13:13–52)

While much of subsequent reception and interpretation of Paul's speech focuses on 13:46–48, some attention is paid to several other aspects of Paul's sermon. Edwin Barber (1648) tells an interesting story in which he combines Acts 13:15 and 1 Cor 14 in an application of the role of the "prophet" in an early congregation of the Radical Reformation (see also Bampfield 1681, 19; Dayton 1857, 158–59). Here Barber attempts to invoke the "Gospel priviledge" of speaking to "contradict if erroneous" the comments of a visiting preacher, a Mr. Callamy:

> Being earnestly desired by diverse of the Inhabitants of the parish to come to heare Mr. Callamy at the Moruing [sic] lecture, they promising that I should have liberty to add to what he should deliver, or contradict if erronious. ... he desired me to forbear till he had concluded, & I might speak, upon which I did forbeare till he had done and pronounced his blessing: and the desired that as he had prayed that the Gospell might be sent fort In the right order, that I might have liberty to speak according to St. Pauls exortation, 1 Cor. 14. 29. 30. Let the Prophets speak two or three, and let the other judge. If any thing be revealed to another that siteth by, let the first hold gis [sic] peace. For ye may all prophecy one by one, that all may learne and all may be comforted. &c. Which freedom was practised in the Sinagogues as Acts 13. 15. where After the reading the Law and the Prophets, the Rulers of the Sinagogues were so far from denying this priviledge that they sent unto Paul and Barnabas saying, ye men and brethren if ye have any word of exortation for the say on ... (Barber 1648).

The theology and practice of the Radical Reformation are echoed in this remarkable passage: a long-standing member of a congregation is authorized by the congregation to dissent publicly (in the role of a "prophet") when he hears something "erroneous." Further, Barber claims, on the basis of Acts 13:15, that "all" may prophesy, one by one, in this manner. Finally, it will be up to the congregation to judge which interpretation of scripture was correct. Here the individual and the community work in tandem in the church's pursuit of truth.

Bonhoeffer commented on the relationship between Christ and David (Acts 13:34): "According to the New Testament, Christ is the heir of David not only in his person but also in his *office*. The throne of David, his kingship, and his reign are the throne of Christ, his kingship, and his reign (Luke 1:32, 69).... The faithfulness God swears to David is the pledge and proof because it is in the strict sense a proof of God, God's own proof of the resurrection of Christ (Acts 13:34). The everlasting seat of David is the seat of the resurrected Christ for the sake of the promise and the faithfulness of God" (*BW* 14:872).

Luther also refers to Luke's citation of Habakkuk in Acts 13:41, noting that Luke follows the LXX rendering and explaining the difference between the Greek and Hebrew on the basis of problems in translation!

> It is apparent that he quotes from the Septuagint, for he has added many words that are not in the Hebrew. The Hebrew "Look among the nations" Luke has translated "Behold, you scoffers." This error could easily have arisen from just one letter in the Hebrew word [reading מִירְגּוֹב instead of בַּגּוֹיִם]. Perhaps it happened that the letter was changed by a mistake of the copiers. However, since all the books today agree, we also will read "among the nations." Perhaps a poor translation was made by the Seventy, in whose translation there are many other errors as well, since they were yawning and paying too little attention. It is inevitable that such errors occur when a translator is not careful and fails to keep his eyes open (*LW* 19:110).

Acts 13:46 records Paul and Barnabas's words to the Jews: "'It was necessary,' they said, 'first to proclaim the word of God to you. But since you push it away from you, and judge yourselves unworthy of eternal life, lo, we turn to the Gentiles.'" Augustine sees the fulfillment of Ps 35:6 and Isa 5:6 in Paul's turning to the Gentiles in Acts 13:46:

> [God] was reproaching that vineyard which he had expected to yield grapes, but which had yielded nothing but thorns, so he continued, *I will forbid my clouds to send rain upon it* (Is 5:6). ... and that indeed was what happened. The apostles were sent out to preach; and in the Acts of the Apostles we read that Paul wanted to preach to the Jews, but found there no grapes, only thorns, for they began to return evil for good by persecuting him. And so, as though to fulfill the prophecy,

I will forbid my clouds to send rain upon it, Paul told the Jews, *We were sent to you, but because you have rejected the word of God, we are turning now to the Gentiles* (Acts 13:46). In this way the prophecy came true. ... But the truth reached the clouds, and that made it possible for the mercy of God which is in heaven, not on earth, to be proclaimed to us [Gentiles] ("Exposition of Psalm 35:6," in *Expositions of the Psalms, 33–50; WA* 3.16.78).

Early Protestants understood Judaism to be legalistic, and viewed this Jewish legalism through their perception of the legalistic practices of the Roman church. In both cases, the malady of legalistic religion, in which one "earned" one's salvation (either through the observance of the Torah or the Roman rites and rituals), needed a Gospel remedy of justification by faith. British Baptist pastor George Hammon's comments are typical (1658):

> The Apostle endeavoureth to take the Jews from their conceit or confidence that they had of their righteousnesse through the Law, shewing them that it would not commend them (now under Gospel times) unto God, onely obedience unto Gods call (which was better than their Sacrifice) and would onely admit or inright them to blessings for (saith he) *the Gentiles which have not followed after Righteousnesse* (*viz* the righteousnesse of the Law) yet being obedient to Gods call [Act. 13.48] (in the Gospel) have attained a far better Righteousness (than that Legall Righteousness that is to be obtained through the Law) (Hammon 1658).

In a remarkable interpretation of Genesis 25, Hammon's comparison of the Jew/Gentile issue with the story of Jacob and Esau echoes patristic allegory (for example, cf. Tertullian, *Adv. Jud.* 1.3 ff. and Marc. 2.24.8 f.) and anticipates by several centuries a similar comparison (though without, of course, the indictment of Judaism) made by modern Jewish exegete, Alan Segal (1986):

> But in the 25. of Gen. is it not said children, But two Nations are in thy womb, and two manner of People shall be separated from thy bowels, and the one People shall be stronger than the other People, and the elder shall serve the younger. Hence we see the two Nations, namely, Edom and Israel, was a type of the estate and condition between Jew and Gentile, that as Jacob, and Esau strove in the womb, and Esau came out first, and yet Iacob took hold on Esaus heel: Showeth the great striving between Jew and Gentile in the Gospel, typed out, by the striving between Edom and Israel; and also sheweth, that as Esau came first, and that Iacob took hold on his heel, and also took away the blessing; so although the Jews were the first-born as in respect of having the Oracles committed first unto them, and not onely so, but the Gospel also must be first preached to them; yet the younger, namely the Gentiles took hold of their heel, that is, rise by their fall; and they refusing the Gospel, the Gentiles received it, as Act. 13, and so

while the Jews were hunting abroad in the field for venison to be accepted thereby, I mean the works of the Law; Iacob, namely the younger brother, stepped in, (viz. the Gentiles) and got the blessing, and the elder brother was wroth, and hated the younger, even the Gentiles; and this it was in the primitive time. ... " (Hammon 1658).

These comments reflect the ongoing struggle of traditional Christianity to articulate the soteriological implications of its christology. At their best, early moderns have tempered their exclusivistic claims about Christianity with core convictions regarding the religious liberty of all persons, even those with whom they fundamentally disagree. Early Baptist Thomas Helwys's famous comment to this effect is important to recall at this point: "Let them be heretics, Turks, Jews, or whatsoever, it appertains not to the earthly powers to punish them in the least measure" (*A Short Declaration*, 1612, 58). Furthermore, John Smyth's objection to the use of the Septuagint translation (in which he cites Acts 13:46–48 in support of his argument) makes a surprising gesture toward the Jews: "[the] translation of the Septuagint out of Hebrue into Greeke, is contradictory to the *Lords mercy to the Jewes church & ther special Priviledges*" (Smyth 1608, 11, emphasis added). And later, post-Holocaust, Protestant commentators are more nuanced in their appraisal of Paul's handling of the Jew/Gentile relationship. Frank Stagg's comments are illustrative:

> Turning to the Gentiles was both happy and sad. It hastened the conversion of the Gentiles, but made less probable the winning of the Jews. This weighed heavily with Paul through subsequent years (cf. Rom. 9–11). Paul's yearning for the Jews never diminished; his desire was to minister to the two as one. But if the issue was forced, *he would cast his lot with the excluded and not with the excluders.* He came to see more clearly through the years that God's purpose of the ages was to create out of Jews and Gentiles one new humanity in Christ; the Ephesian letter is his greatest statement of that ideal. But even at this earlier date, Paul could get no joy in being forced to turn from the synagogue. The proof is in the fact that he entered the next synagogue whose door was open to him (Stagg 1955, 145–46).

Karl Barth, relying heavily on Paul's letter to the Romans (11:11–32), comments poignantly on Paul's claim that Jewish rejection has led to his turning to the Gentiles:

> It is unmistakeably the case that when Paul bases his own approach to the Gentiles on his repulsion by the Jews, which is so much emphasised in Acts (13[46], 18[6], 28[28]), he sees a parallel and illustration of the greater event which came on

Jesus Christ Himself. ... If Jesus had not been delivered up by the Jews, He would not have become the Saviour of the Gentiles. If Paul had not been repulsed by the Jews, he would not have become the apostle of the Gentiles. God needed the Jews for the sake of the Gentiles. He needed their transgression. In order to bring about this transgression. He hardened them. Thus their hardening has become an integral part of salvation-history in a way that is decisive even for the Gentiles. ... The Gentile Christians are not, then, to ask whether God has now forsaken these hardened Jews. On the contrary, it is patent, and ought to be seen especially by the Gentile Christians, how very securely He holds these hardened Jews as such in His hand. ... This is God's purpose in bringing salvation to the Gentiles, in causing the Jews to commit that transgression, in giving them occasion for that transgression by hardening. In so doing, He has not then forsaken them. On the contrary, in this very hardening He has really made them more than ever His main concern. ... The existence of Gentiles as recipients of salvation has the meaning and purpose of a summons to these hardened Jews and therefore of a confirmation of their eternal election (*CD* 2.2.279).

Graham Paulson, an ordained minister of Australian aboriginal descent, extends the application of Acts 13:47 to the modern post-colonial context:

... the commandments of scripture indicate that God's people should pursue justice and be open to the stranger. The apostle Paul, however, affirms that those who believe in Jesus Christ are committed to a faith that is multi-cultural, and no Christian can impose the laws of their own culture on others (even when those laws were given to Israel by God). Both Testaments are clear that that people of every race, nation, tribe, people group and language will be redeemed before God.

If, according to the scriptures, God's salvation extends to the ends of the earth (e.g., Isa 49:6; Acts 13:47), then we can be sure that the people groups of the South Pacific are included. And to the extent that we live in the spirit of Christ, the church will seek in every place to overcome the distortions of colonial power (Paulson 2006, 317).

Acts 13:48 ("When the Gentiles heard this, they were glad and praised the word of the Lord; and as many as had been destined for eternal life became believers") figures prominently in interpretations regarding the predestination of God's elect. Consider, for example, article five in the Baptist Midland confession of 1655: "That God elected and chose, in His Eternal counsel, some persons to life and salvation, before the foundation of the world, whom accordingly He doth and will effectually call, and whom He doth so call, He will certainly keep by His power, through faith to salvation. Acts xiii.48;

Ephesians i.2–4; II Thessalonians ii.13; I Peter i.2, etc." (cf. also Keach 1698, 17). The Calvinistic overtones are clear. Calvin himself said of Acts 13:48: "For this ordaining must be understood of the eternal counsel of God alone. Neither doth Luke say that they were ordained unto faith, but unto life; because the Lord doth predestinate his unto the inheritance of eternal life. And this place teacheth that faith dependeth upon God's election" (*Commentary on Acts*, 13:48).

This is not to say, however, that Arminian Christians (who emphasize human free will) avoided the verse altogether. The Orthodox Creed (1658), a confession produced by a group of General Baptist congregations in the Midlands, England, cites Acts 13:48 in its decidedly Arminian interpretation of the atonement: "And Christ died for all men, and there is a sufficiency in his death and merits for the sins of the whole world, and hath appointed the gospel to be preached unto all" (Article XVIII, "Of Christ Dying for All Mankind"). John Wesley (1703–91) argued: "'As many as were ordained to eternal life' – St. Luke does not say fore-ordained. He is not speaking of what was done from eternity, but of what was then done, through the preaching of the Gospel. He is describing that ordination, and that only, which was at the very time of hearing it" (*ENNT*, Acts 13:48).

Visual Interpretation of Acts 13

The Saint John's Bible provides an overview of the *Life of Paul* in a full-page illumination (**Figure 31**, color plate), blending traditional style and iconography with contemporary imagery and symbolism (see the introduction to *The Saint John's Bible* Project in the commentary on Acts 2:38; see also *www.saintjohnsbible. org*). Usually, when the Apostle is depicted in art, the subject is his dramatic encounter with the risen Christ on the road to Damascus (Acts 9:3–6). The text above Paul—"I saw a light from heaven" (Acts 26:13; cf. 9:3 and 22:6)—refers to that event, but the symbols painted around him reference his later journeys and ministry. Traveling by the boat on the blue seas beneath his feet, Paul communicates the *koinonia*, or fellowship of the Christian community, to the great cities of the world. These cities, ancient and modern, are represented by a mélange of Turkish, Byzantine, Near Eastern, French Romanesque, Italian Renaissance, and contemporary buildings. Integrated into the sea waves at the bottom are the words of Paul and Barnabas's call, "I have set you to be a light for the Gentiles, so that you may bring salvation to the ends of the earth" (Acts 13:47). Though he is clothed in first-century robes, Paul is holding models of two later church buildings: an Italian Renaissance dome in one hand, and an Orthodox-style building in the other. The Apostle literally holds the Church, West and East, in his hands.

Even the technique of this illumination, reminiscent of both a Byzantine mosaic and a twentieth-century collage, bridges past knowledge with modern experiment. A mosaic traditionally used cut pieces of glass or stone to form (when viewed from a distance) a figure with a black outline around the shape; the heavy linear quality of many of the buildings echoes this type of silhouetted form. On the other hand, the use of color, the overlapping of the figures, and the flatness of the composition are typical of a modern collage method. Light, reflective colors—reminiscent of the Venetian paintings of Titian and Giorgione—are used in the upper areas of the painting where the lines are blurred as the buildings shift into abstract forms. The strong, vibrant colors in the middle of the painting are more similar to the more acidic tones of some American realists during the Industrial Revolution.

Acts 14

Success and Division in Iconium (14:1–7)

Acts 14 describes Paul's visits to other cities of Asia Minor (modern Turkey) and his return to Antioch. The additions to Acts 14:2 found in the sixth-century Codex Beza (D) may reflect an anti-Jewish tendency in that manuscript in that it sets the Jewish leaders over against the Apostles: "But the *chiefs of the synagogue of the Jews and the rulers of the synagogue stirred up for themselves persecution against the righteous* and poisoned the minds of the Gentiles against the brothers. *But the Lord soon gave peace*" (additions in italics; cf. Epp 1966, 136–7, 169).

Healing and Stoning in Iconium (14:8–20)

The Venerable Bede, eighth-century British monk and exegete, notes the parallels between the healing of the lame man in Acts 3–5 and the healing here in Iconium (14:8–20) and argues that they reflect the division of labor in which the Jerusalem apostles would go to the Jews and Paul and Barnabas to the gentiles (cf. Gal 2:9): "the former [the lame man cured by Peter and John] was cured in the earliest days of the faith, when the word was not yet believed by gentiles. The latter [i.e. the lame Lycaonian] was cured in the midst of the new joys of the converted gentile world" (Bede, *Paraphrase of Acts* 14:8). Centuries later, the Tübingen school would point to parallels such as this as evidence of a *Tendenz* on the part of the author to harmonize conflicting Petrine and Pauline forms Christianity "by making Paul appear as Petrine as possible, and correspondingly, Peter appear as Pauline as possible" (Baur 1838; cited and translated in Gasque 195, 30, 326).

The *Sacrifice of Lystra*, painted by Raphael for the Sistine Chapel illustrates the biblical text of Acts 14:11–18 in precise detail (**Figure 32**). The cartoon and tapestry project has been introduced and discussed earlier in this study (see comments on the Healing of the Lame Man at 3:1–10 and also discussion of Raphael's tapestries of the Death of Ananias, Acts 5; and Conversion of the Proconsul, Acts 13).

The scene takes place in an area in which the native tongue is not Greek but Lycaonian (Alexander 2001, 1046). Lystra was a small town in southern Asia Minor. Paul has just commanded a man whose feet have been crippled from his birth to "Stand upright on your feet." This healing occurred after Paul "looking at [the man] intently saw that he had faith to be healed" (Acts 14:9). Upon seeing the man rise up and walk, the frenzied crowd on the right, along with the priest of Zeus who brought oxen to the gates, want to offer sacrifice to Paul and Barnabas. The crowd refers to the two missionaries as Mercury/Hermes and Jupiter/Zeus, respectively (because Paul was the chief speaker).

FIGURE 32   Raphael (1483–1520). *The Sacrifice at Lystra*. 1515–16. Watercolor on paper mounted on canvas (tapestry cartoon), 3.5 × 5.6m. Victoria and Albert Museum, London, Great Britain. Photo: V&A Images, London/Art Resource, NY

Off to the left side of the composition, Paul is about to tear his green gown and red cloak as stated in the narrative. Barnabas is visible behind him in orange robes. The man, crippled from birth who had never walked, is in blue standing with hands clasped in prayer below one of the oxen still in the crowd. The now discarded crutch is visible between his legs. A man just behind him leans down to see the miracle for himself as the now muscular and functioning leg is revealed beneath the drapery.

Raphael follows every detail of the text but chooses the moment when Paul attempts to stop the crowd from making sacrifice rather than the moment of healing. Paul's subsequent speech is his first attempt to explain the gospel in totally pagan terms and it is totally consistent with the orthodox, Jewish critique of pagan religion, which stresses (against a broadly animistic religious culture) the distance separating God from the created order (Loveday Alexander 2001, 1046). Those who fail to recognize the source of creation's gifts continue to fall victim to the pagan gods and idolatry while those who believe in the one true god will have their hearts filled with food and gladness. Later, some Jews come from Antioch and Iconium and convince the crowd that Paul and Barnabas are not related to their pagan gods. They stone Paul, drag him out of the city, and leave him for dead. Only then are Paul and Barnabas able to leave the city of Lystra.

The stoning of Paul (14:19–20) is a very brief but important event in the book of Acts. It is not often represented in visual art. The two examples that we have selected are separated by a millennium. The sixth-century marble sarcophagus depicts Paul flanked by two men holding stones. It is in high relief with deeply cut figures (**Figure 33**). That Paul is standing during the episode is probably due more to the compositional and space limitations of the sarcophagus than to an kind of symbolic statement regarding Paul's being immune to such an attack (supported also by the text, which records that Paul's opponents "supposed him to be dead" (14:19); see also the comments on Figure 36 below).

The seventeenth-century painting by Jean-Baptiste de Champaigne (**Figure 34**) offers the viewer significantly more detail and drama than the sarcophagus. Twelve agitated men surround Paul who has fallen on the stairs. Five of them have rocks in their hands. It anticipates a brutal occurrence. The action is placed in the foreground of the painting as is typical of the French Baroque. It appears as a stage set with a few figures and with architecture and pagan sculptures painted in the background.

Jean-Baptiste de Champaigne was from a French family of painters of Flemish origin. He is best known for his large-scale compositions and decorative work (Garnot, 2010). He was the nephew to Phillipe de Champaigne

FIGURE 33   *The Lapidation of Saint Paul*. High relief from a sarcophagus. 6th century. Marble. St. Victor Basilica, Marseille, France. Photo: Erich Lessing/Art Resource, NY

who sent for Jean-Baptiste after Phillipe's own son died. Jean-Baptiste was his pupil and also collaborated with Nicolas de Platte Montagne. In 1658, Phillipe reluctantly allowed him to go to Italy for 18 months where he studied, and was influenced by, the works of High Renaissance master Raphael and contemporary Baroque painters working in the classicizing tradition such as Domenichino. After Jean-Baptiste returned to Paris in 1659, he worked with Phillipe for ten years on all of his major commissions.

Jean-Baptiste was received as a member of the Académie Royale in 1663, and his style began to break away from his uncle. In 1667, Jean-Baptiste de Champaigne's first independent commission was to paint *The Stoning of Paul* for the corporation of Parisian goldsmiths for Notre Dame (Lanoë 2009, 82). According to Nicolas Sainte Fare Garnot, two preparatory drawings for the painting have been identified and these works testify to Jean-Baptiste's maturity and to his becoming independent from his uncle's influence (Garnot, 2010).

FIGURE 34   Jean-Baptiste de Champaigne (1631–1681). *St. Paul Overthrown and Stoned in the City of Lystra.* 1667. Oil on canvas. 64 × 52.5cm. Photo: René-Gabriel Ojéda Musée Magnin, Dijon, France. Photo: Réunion de Musées Nationaux/Art Resource, NY

Strengthening the Disciples (14:21–28)

This section (14:21-28) describe Paul's journey back to Antioch. A number of interpreters cite 14:22 (which predicts persecutions for the faithful) as scriptural warrant for the tribulations which Christians will suffer The Somerset Confession by British Particular Baptists articulates this point in the form of a theological assertion (1656 XXXVI); John Fawcett presents this claim as the title and recurring theme of a hymn ("Through Tribulation We Must Enter the Kingdom of God"; Fawcett 1793); and John Bunyan (1628-88) narrates this suffering as a violent, two-way street in an eschatological allegory (1678, Part One, 25–28). Barth observes: "The fiercer the affliction which assails us, the stronger the confirmation of our *societas cum Christo*" (*CD* 4.2.607; cf. *CD* 4.3.643).

The comments of modern interpreter, Scott Spencer, are consonant with this point: "The Pauline mission may reach out to elite imperial authorities, like Sergius Paulus, but it does not cut any easy deals with them. It is still exceedingly 'hard … for those who have wealth to enter the kingdom of God' (Lk. 18.24–25). The lowly path of suffering remains the best way" (Spencer 2004, 162).

Acts 14:23, which describes the appointment of elders in various cities, is among a cluster of passages used to provide scriptural warrant for congregational polity, but there is an interesting contrast in the way the argument is made. Anglican turned Baptist minister Hanserd Knollys (1681), for example, speaks of the proper role of the State in relationship to matters of faith:

> Gospel-Government is ordained and appointed of God for the Well-Being of his Church: The Church of God cannot have a Well-Being without Christ's Instituted Gospel-Government. And to that end God the Father hath laid the Government of his Church up on his Son Jesus Christ, *Isa.* 9. 6, 7. To whom he gave all Power in Heaven and Earth, *Matth.* 28, 18. And he hath made Christ Lord of his House, and King of his Church, *Heb.* 3. 1–6 & *Psal.* 149.2. The Lord Jesus Christ delegated this his *Ecclesiastical* Government of the Church unto his holy Apostles, Prophets, Evangelists, Pastors and Teachers, called Bishops, Presbyters or Elders, who were *allowed of God to be put in Trust with the Gospel*, 1 *Thes.* 2. 4. And the Apostles and Evangelists did commit the same unto faithful men, 2 *Tim.* 2. 12. whom they Ordained Bishops, Presbyters or Elders in the Churches of Saints, *Titus* 1. 5, 7. *Act.* 14. 23. which Gospel-Government (*as we said before*) is not a Coercive-Power over Mens Consciences; nor is it a Dominion over their Faith, neither is it a *Lordship* over God's Clergy or Heritage; but it is a *Stewardship* of the Mysteries of God, 1 *Cor.* 4. 1, 2, 3, 4.

Particular Baptist pastor John Gill (1697–1771), on the other hand, begins his argument by appealing to the model of the civil society that "has a right to choose, to appoint, and ordain their own officer" and concludes "so churches, which are religious societies, have a right to choose and ordain their own officers … and which are ordained … for each particular church, and not another, Acts xiv. 23–27" (Gill 1796). It is likely that both Knollys and Gill (a staunch Calvinist) ground their congregational polity in the sovereignty of God, despite the difference in mode of argumentation, and it would be unwise to make too much of this difference.

Early Baptist John Smyth, appealing specifically to Acts 14:23, rejected a "triformed" presbytery of pastors, teachers, and elders (reflected in the later quotation from Knollys cited above) in favor of a "uniform" ministry of pastor/ elder (and lay deacons): "Moreover, if the Apostles had ordeyned 3. Kinds of

Elders, Act. 14.23. they would have mentioned them with the several kinds of ordination: but that is not done: for in one phrase their election and ordination is mentioned: so their ordination being one, their office is one & not three" (John Smyth 1607, 7–9). Smyth also reasons by inference that if the church calls a minister, then the church has the "powre of casting out" officers out of office; he finds scriptural warrant for his biblicist position in Acts 14:23.

Overview

Acts 15 is widely recognized as standing at the center of the book of Acts, both literally and theologically (Haenchen 1971, 461–62; Johnson 1992, 280; Witherington 1998, 439). The issue of Gentile inclusion into the family of God is finally addressed and resolved. Acts 15 divides into five thought units: The Circumcision Controversy (15:1–5); Speeches by Peter (and Paul and Barnabas) (15:6–12); Speech by James (15:14–21); the Apostolic Decree and its Distribution

The Acts of the Apostles Through the Centuries, First Edition. Heidi J. Hornik and Mikeal C. Parsons.

(15: 22–35); and Paul and Barnabas Separate (15: 37–41). Acts 15 has been important as a blueprint for solving congregational conflict (e.g., Ammonius; Calvin), though Luther points to Acts 15 to express his lack of confidence in the value of conciliar decrees. In modern times, the decision-making process of the Council was appealed to in discussions of topics as varied as Christian mission and the inclusion of gays in the church. Interpreters also offered various explanations for the dispute between Paul and Barnabas (15:37–41).

Reception and Interpretation

The Circumcision Controversy (15:1–5)

Ammonius comments on the content of the debate in Acts 15:

> ... that the believers long ago were, with much query and with much earnestness, generating discussions concerning doctrines. And that it was so great a thing for them to be helped through discussions, (and) that those from Antioch did not hesitate to send (men) to Jerusalem and to ask about the dispute—and yet not chiefly concerning the dispensation of the incarnation of the Son or concerning the Spirit, or angels, or principalities, or heaven, or any other such question; but (rather) concerning circumcision, the least part of the most inferior (parts) of the body of man. For they knew that (even) "one jot or tittle of the law" was full of spiritual significance. [(*Catena on Acts* 15:1–8; 244.22–245.6).

In his consideration of the (lack of) value of councils, Luther returns to the "first apostolic council" to show that his contemporaries were not following its decrees, despite their protests otherwise:

> Indeed, to play absolutely safe, and so that we cannot fail or worry, we shall take up the very first council of the apostles held in Jerusalem, of which St. Luke writes in Acts, chapters 15 [:1–29] and 16 [:4]. ... There we hear that the Holy Spirit (as the preachers of councils boast) commands that we eat nothing that has been sacrificed to idols, no blood, and nothing that is strangled. Now if we want to have a church that conforms to this council (as is right, since it is the first and foremost council, and was held by the apostles themselves), we must teach and insist that henceforth no prince, lord, burgher, or peasant eat geese, doe, stag, or pork cooked in blood, and that they also abstain from carp jelly, for there is blood in them, or, as cooks call it, "color." And burghers and peasants must abstain especially from red sausage and blood sausage, for that is not only fluid blood, but also congealed and cooked blood, a very coarse-grained blood. Likewise we are forbidden to eat rabbits and birds, for these are all strangled (according to hunting customs), even if they were only fried, not cooked in blood.

Should we, in obedience to this council, refrain from blood, then we shall let the Jews become our masters in our churches and kitchens; for they have an especially large book on the subject of eating blood, so large that no one could vault over it with a pole. ... For God's sake, what harried Christians we would become because of that council, just with the two items of eating blood and the meat of strangled animals! Well then, begin, anyone who wants to or can, to bring Christendom into conformity with this council; I shall then be glad to follow. If not, I want to be spared the screams of "Councils! Councils! You neither heed the councils nor the fathers!" (*LW* 41:27–20).

Elsewhere Luther comments on the Pharisaic Christians' insistence on circumcision as a denigration of the work of Christ: "It is not enough for you to believe in Christ or to be baptized. You must also be circumcised; for 'unless you are circumcised according to the custom of Moses, you cannot be saved.' [15:1] This is tantamount to saying that Christ is a good workman who has begun a building but has not completed it, and that Moses must complete it" (*LW* 26:50).

John Calvin appeals to Acts 15 as a way to acknowledge the precedence of divisions in the church:

Although we naturally dread the cross and persecution of any sort, yet greater danger comes from internal divisions, lest they should break our spirit or weaken us. When tyrants attack with all their force, the flesh is certainly afraid ... But when it comes to the brethren being in conflict with each other, and the Church being in a state of internal upheaval, weak minds will inevitably be confused, and may even give way, especially when the controversy is over doctrine, which alone is the sacred bond of fraternal unity. Finally there is nothing that damages the Gospel more than internal discords, for they not only discourage weak consciences, but provide the ungodly with an opportunity to speak evil of it ... the Lord certainly frustrates the subtlety of Satan for a wonderful purpose, because he tests the faith of His own people by such trials, He honours his Word with a glorious victory, and He makes the truth, which the wicked have tried to obscure, shine out all the more brightly (*Commentary on Acts*, 15:1, 22–23).

Across the entirety of their interpretive history, early modern Christians have looked to Acts 15:1–5 (and 15:29; cf. Powell 1650, 101–03) both as an explanation of the cause of ecclesiastical controversy (Denne 1642, 16–17) and as a model for settling differences in church (Second London Confession Article XXVI; Orthodox Creed Article XXXIX [which also advocates "majority vote" as the means to achieve resolution]; Smith 1970, 90–91). In the twentieth century, Rick Warren, pastor of Saddleback Church in Lake Forest, CA, extends the application to include debates between church and world: "Too often we let cultural differences between believers and unbelievers become barriers to getting the message out. For some Christians, any talk of 'adapting to their culture' sounds like theological liberalism. This is not a new fear. In fact, it was the reason the apostles held the Jerusalem conference in Acts 15" (Warren 1995, 195).

Speeches by Peter (and Paul and Barnabas) (15:6–12)

Acts 15:9 was one of St. Augustine's favorite verses; he quotes or alludes to it over twenty times. In a sermon on Matthew 5:3 ("Blessed are the Pure in Heart"), Augustine appeals to Acts 15:9 to explain how the believer is made pure and how genuine faith is different from demons who also have "faith":

> So if we long to see God, how is this eye going to be purified? Who wouldn't take pains, who wouldn't look for ways of purifying the instrument with which he can see the one he is longing for with all his heart? Divine authority has given us this clear answer to our question: *Purifying their hearts*, it says, *by faith* (Acts 15:9). Faith in God purifies the heart, the pure heart sees God [Matt 5:8]. But faith is sometimes defined as follows by people who wish to deceive themselves; as if it were enough merely to believe—some people, you see, promise themselves the vision of God and the kingdom of heaven for believing while living bad lives. Against these the apostle James indignantly took umbrage out of spiritual charity, so he says in his letter, *You believe that God is one.* You pat yourself on your back for your faith; you observe that many godless people assume there are many gods, and you congratulate yourself for believing that there is only one God. *You do well. The demons also believe—and shudder* (Jas 2:19). Shall they too see God? Those who are pure of heart shall see him. Whoever would say that the unclean spirits are heart-pure? And yet, *they believe—and shudder* ("Sermon 53"; WA 3.3.70–71).

Ammonius notes that circumcision itself is limited to males, while faith is gender inclusive:

> He [Peter] says, "No distinction between believers" [Acts 15:9]—whether they are Jews, or Greeks, wherever faith makes one clean from the sins which issue from the heart. And this cleansing is like circumcision. And in the place of the circumcision of the flesh the circumcision in the Spirit is given, cleansing the hidden places by faith in Jesus Christ. And in this way the carnal circumcision was not for the common benefit, because it was given to only the male gender. And nothing is kept from true persons [lit. "faces"]. For in true faith there is not male and female. There is not Greek or barbarian. But all are one [Gal 3:28] (*Catena on Acts* 15:9–10; CGPNT 245.15–23).

John Calvin appeals to Acts 15, among other texts, to establish that Peter, claimed as the first pope, was "one of the Twelve" and not "their master":

> If we gather together all the passages where it teaches what office and power Peter had among the apostles, how he conducted himself, and also how he was received by them. Run over all that is extant: you will find nothing but that he was one of the Twelve, the equal of the rest, and their companion, not their master. He indeed refers to a council anything that is to be done, and advises what needs to be done. But at the same time he listens to the others, and he not only lets them express their views, but leaves the decision to them; when they have decreed, he follows and obeys [Acts 15:5–12]. When he writes to the pastors, he does not command them from his authority, as a superior, but makes them his colleagues and gently urges them, as is customarily done among equals [I Peter 5:1 ff.] (*Instit.* 4.6.7).

Several interpreters appeal to the image of God "cleansing their [e.g., Gentiles] hearts by faith" in Acts 15:9 in their explication of God's overcoming the corruption of sin in the believer's life (cf. Knollys 1681, 37–38); for John Bunyan (1628–88) the "dust" of Original Sin (which is made worse by the Law) is "cleansed" by the Gospel (Bunyan 1678, 21–22).

Early advocates of believers' baptism (e.g., baptism of those old enough to make a confession of faith) appealed to Acts 15:10 in their arguments against infant baptism, by contesting those who made an analogy between circumcision and infant baptism. Seventeenth-century British evangelist and Quaker sympathizer, Henry Denne (ca. 1605/06–1661), for example, contends that "Circumcision under the Law was called a *Yoak*, Acts 15:10" (Denne 1645, 34–35; cf. Lawrence 1651, 74–75; Grantham 1687, 17; cf. Polhill 1992, 327). In an interesting twist, Independent Baptist minister Vavasor Powell (1617–1670) admits that baptism has the effect of binding believers "to observe the commandements of the Gospel" in the same way that circumcision had the effect of binding Jews "to keep the Law," but neither has soteriological benefits: "And as now it would be unreasonable, abusive, (and contrary to the first institution) to urge baptisme as necessary to justification and salvation, so it was then, to urge circumcision, as necessary to justification and salvation" (cf. Acts 15:24; Powell 1650, 48–49; cf. also the imagined and imaginative dialogue between Christ and the Pharisee [of the parable in Luke 18] in Powell 1677, 34–40).

Baptist minister C. H. Spurgeon (1834–92) has a fascinating sermon on Acts 15:11 ("we believe that it is by the grace of the Lord Jesus Christ that we and they shall be saved"). He observes that the text begins with "we believe" and therefore suggests the verse be called the "Apostle's Creed" and that "we may rest assured that it has quite as clear a right to that title as that highly esteemed composition which is commonly called the ... 'Apostle's Creed'" (Spurgeon 1867, 445). Spurgeon then launches into an eloquent diatribe against the state-church:

> Well, Peter, what do you believe? We are all attention. Peter's answer is, "We believe that through the grace of the Lord Jesus Christ we shall be saved, even as they." There is a great deal of talk in our day—foolish, vainglorious, idiotic, senseless talk, as we think—about apostolical succession. Some persons think they have the direct line from the apostles running right at their feet, and others believe that those who make the greatest boast about it, have the least claim to it. There are clergymen who imagine that because they happen to be in a church which is in open alliance with the state, they must necessarily be ministers of the church of which Christ said, "My kingdom is not of this world." [John 18:26] ... Whenever did Peter or Paul become state-paid ministers? In what state church did they enroll themselves? What tithes did they receive? What rates did they levy? What distraints did they make upon the Jews and the Gentiles? Were they rectors or vicars, prebends or deans, canons or curates? Did they buy their livings in the market? Did they sit in the Roman House of Lords dressed in lawn sleeves? Were they styled Right Reverend Fathers in God? Were they appointed by the prime minister of the day? Did they put on gowns, and read prayers out of a book? Did they christen children, and call them regenerate, and bury wicked reprobates in sure and certain hope of a blessed resurrection? As opposite as light is from darkness were those apostles from the men who pretend to be their divinely-appointed successors (Spurgeon 1867, 445–46; cf. also the Westminster Confession of Faith 31.2, which cites Acts 15:6–21 to make the corollary point in noting that the Jerusalem council did not seek Pilate's permission to meet).

Cuban American Justo González relates Acts 15 to the history of Christian missions:

> The Hispanic Church is a result of missionary adventures of the past. Some of them were more violent than others, and some more benevolent than others. But in all of these we learned to receive. We received missionaries. We received doctrines. We received ideas. We received money. In the midst of so much receiving, we are tempted to believe that we are somehow inferior: the important church is elsewhere, the place where the missionaries come from; the books worth reading are only those that come from over there ... We, poor little folk, must forever be receiving.
>
> But no! The case of Paul, a Pharisee of Pharisees and his contrast with these other Christians, equally Pharisees from Jerusalem, presents the matter in a different way. The place where we are, at this apparent edge, is where God is doing new things. And those who daily see the new things that God is

doing in the world have the obligation toward God and toward the rest of the Church to go back to the old centers, which often have lost much of their vision, taking to them our renewed vision of what God is doing today (González 2001, 179–80).

Speech by James (15:14–21)

Acts 15:16–18 is a focal point in early modern discussions of the authority of Scripture. The Orthodox Creed (1678, Article XXXVII) and Second London Confession (1689, chap. 1, section 8) use James' citation of Amos 9 in Acts 15:16–18 as scriptural warrant for their assertion regarding the nature and authority of Scripture. Again citing Acts 15:15–16, the Second London Confession (chap. 1, section 9) goes on to claim that Scripture has a single meaning: "the true and full sense of any Scripture (which is not manifold but one)." This stands in contrast to twentieth-century professor Clark Pinnock's claim, citing the same chapter in Acts (Acts 15:6–29) that the early "Christians did not limit themselves to the original sense of the passage, but sought the will of the Lord in the reading of the texts such that it became a Word of God to them" (Pinnock 1984, 172).

Acts 15:17–18 underpins much interpretation regarding God's providence. One of the earliest Calvinist confessions, *Propositions and Conclusions concerning True Christian Religion* (1612–14), states: "God before the foundation of the world did foresee, and determine the issue and event of all His works (Acts. xv. 18)" (Article 9; cf. Powell 1650, 8–9; The True Gospel-Faith Declared According to the Scriptures, 1654, I; Second London 1689, Article III). Quoting this verse, seventeenth-century British Particular Baptist minister Hercules Collins calls divine foreknowledge "an incommunicable property of the Divine Being" (Collins 1690, 20; cf. Gill 1796, 1:109). The Orthodox Creed invokes the language of Acts 15:18 in its article on Predestination and Election: "Now predestination unto life is the everlasting purpose of God, whereby *before the foundation of the world was laid, he hath constantly decreed in his counsel* secret to us, to deliver from curse and damnation, those whom he hath chosen in Christ" (Orthodox Creed 1678, Article 9; cf. Gill 1796, 1:109).

Didymus the Blind (ca. 313–98) appeals to Acts 15:21 to make the case that the Jewish Scriptures continued to be read in the churches after the coming of Christ:

Even though Moses alone was being read in the synagogues "on each and every Sabbath" (Acts 15:21) before the arrival of Christ, after the coming of Christ he (Moses) is still not prevented from being read in the churches. And see, if it is possible, that this came from the [saying], "for until this very day whenever Moses is read" (2 Cor 3:15). But also the [saying], "Pay attention to the public reading of scripture" (1 Tim 4:13), is spoken not about only the books of the new (testament), and neither is the [saying] "Every scripture is divinely inspired and beneficial" (2 Tim 3:16). For if the ancient writings were not being read in the churches, then he would not have rashly instructed the Galatians by letter, "Tell me, those who wish to be under the law, do you not listen to the law?" (Gal 4:21)? (*Catena on Acts* 15:21; 251.6–15).

The Apostolic Decree and its Distribution (15:22–35)

Fifth-century bishop Severus of Antioch addresses the concern that the phraseology of Acts 15:28 ("It seemed [good] to the Holy Spirit and to us") diminished the "glory of the Spirit." He draws on several OT examples to bolster his case:

> If the apostles having been joined with the Holy Spirit diminishes the glory of the Spirit, so then (does) Moses having been joined with God diminish the glory of God? For the Scripture says, "The people believed in God and in Moses." But we might also present another weapon. If the glory having been joined with the Apostles reduces the worth of the Spirit, (then) Samuel being connected (with God) also insults God and diminishes his worth. For it has been written, "And all the people feared the Lord and Samuel." [1 Sam 12:18] And again we present yet a third weapon against the impiety. If the apostles having been joined with the Spirit diminishes the worth and divine authority of the Spirit, (then) Gideon being connected with his name diminishes the worth of God: "For the whole people shouted, 'War with the Lord and with Gideon.'"[Judg 7:18] So, just as Moses has been joined with God, not as an equal, but as a prophet; and Gideon (has been joined) with God, not as an equal, but as a general of war; so also the Apostles (have been joined) with the Holy Spirit, as heralds of the gospel. Know, then, the authority, and do not insult the worth of the Spirit (*Catena on Acts* 15:28; 253.25–254.7).

The formula of Acts 15:28 ("It seemed good to the Holy Spirit and to us") was invoked by a number of subsequent ecumenical councils (Second Council of Constantinople 553; The French Confession 1559/1571, 32; Second Helvetic Confession 1566, 27.1; The Cambridge Platform 1648, 1.4; The Orthodox Confession of the Catholic and Apostolic Eastern Church by Peter Mogila 1638/1642, 1.72; cf. *CCF*, 4:100).

The German historian Adolf Harnack (1851–1930) first regarded the textual variant in the list of prohibitions in Acts 15:29 in Codex D (which removes the reference to "what is strangled") as the effort of a later editor to change the focus of the Apostolic Decree from a ritual requirement to a moral exhortation (Harnack 1899, cited in Baird 2003, 129–30). A decade later, Harnack would reverse his earlier position, crediting Luke with shaping the Decree into a document of moral instruction (Harnack 1908; Baird 2003, 131; also Machen 1921; cf. also Strange 1992).

In the second half of the twentieth century, Acts 15 became an important text for both sides in the debate over gay marriage (Perry 2010, 321–47). The earliest use of Acts 15 in this debate seems to come from a study paper produced for the United Presbyterian Church in 1978 (Shafer 1978; cf. Perry 2010, 335). Based on Acts 15, the study concluded:

> In Paul's day, there was a similar but different set of questions. Ought Gentile civilization and culture ever to have been developed? Palestinian Judaism viewed Gentile culture with great disgust. Certainly one could not remain an uncircumcised, non-Kosher Gentile and be fully obedient to God. "Ought Gentile civilization and culture ever to have been developed?" was replaced by a fact—God chose to sanctify some uncircumcised, non-kosher Gentiles (Shafer 1978, 239).

By analogy, the report goes on to ask: "Has the very question, 'Ought humans to have developed homosexual behavior?' been replaced by the fact that God has chosen to sanctify some homosexual persons?'" and tentatively to answer the question in the affirmative (Shafer 1978, 34–36; cf. Perry 2010, 335). More recently, Bishop Sally Dyck of the Northern Illinois Annual Conference points to Acts 15 as one possible starting place for a new conversation—one that does not try to change people's minds about homosexuality. "At the end of Acts 15, no one in Jerusalem had changed their minds about how they felt about gentiles, but they had somehow been convinced by the witness of Paul that there needed to be space [for them]. They found some way to be together. Are there conditions that would help us live together?" (cited in Frykholm 2014).

Contemporary biblical scholar, Jeffrey Siker, is another example of one who has used Acts 15 in support of inclusion of gays in the church:

> [J]ust as Peter's experience of Cornelius … led him to realize that even Gentiles were receiving God's Spirit, so my experience of various gay and lesbian Christians has led me to realize that these Christians have received God's Spirit as gays and lesbians and that the reception of the Spirit has nothing to do with sexual orientation. … I once thought of gays and lesbians as Peter and Paul thought of "Gentile sinners," but now, with Peter I am compelled to ask, "Can anyone withhold the water for baptizing these people who have received the Holy Spirit just as we have?" (Siker 1994, 230–31).

Biblical scholar Richard Hays, on the other hand, has questioned the analogy between inclusion of those who engage in homosexual behavior and the Gentiles of Acts 15, at least as it has been argued to date:

> Only because the new experience of Gentile converts proved hermeneutically illuminating of Scripture was the church, over time, able to accept the decision to

embrace Gentiles within the fellowship of God's people. This is precisely the step that has not—or at least not yet—been taken by the advocates of homosexuality in the church. Is it possible for them to reread the New Testament and show [that] this development can be understood as a fulfillment of God's design for human sexuality as previously revealed in Scripture? (Hays 1996, 399).

Without taking an explicit position on the issue, scholar Luke Timothy Johnson also points to Acts 15 as a biblical narrative that can serve the "cause of discernment" on this and other issues (Johnson 1983, 97).

Paul and Barnabas Separate (15: 36–41)

Several patristic writers commented on the disagreement between Paul and Barnabas recorded in Acts 15:36–41. An anonymous writer dismisses altogether the notion that it was a disagreement: "A 'sharp disagreement' among the apostles did not arise because of a quarrel, but divine dispensation. For since Paul intended to take Timothy as his companion, naturally, the Holy Spirit gave Mark over to Barnabas. But we know that Paul also loved him; listen to what he writes to Timothy: 'Take Mark and bring him with you; for he is quite useful to me for ministry' (2 Tim 4:11). I believe he wrote this because he wanted to be assisted by both of them" (*Catena on Acts* 15:39; CGPNT 258.35–259.6; cited by Brookins, Reynolds and Parsons 2011, 28).

Ammonius, on the other hand, acknowledges the strife between Paul and Barnabas but demurs from the view that Paul was "angry":

> Briefly a defense should be made concerning the apostles Barnabas and Paul. The author says that Barnabas and Paul increased strife to such a degree that they departed from one another. Mark made up his mind to go astray by abandoning them. Paul became indignant in order that Mark might be brought to his senses; and he was wanting him to experience some grief for a little while, in order that, upon feeling grief to the full, he might repent, [and might in the future resign himself not to making his own plan, but might against his own plan resign himself to following the work of the ministry. … Therefore, he wanted to discipline Mark also in this way.] But Barnabas, being simple, instead waived Mark's sin even without any consternation. Paul was exhorting Barnabas, saying, under present circumstances, not to take him back who had fled companionship, but to turn him away, because he had not insulted *them* in doing this, but rather, by despising the ministry, had rejected *God*. Paul was opposing Barnabas with this aim. He was actually not angry with him, but was exhorting him; as the Scripture says, "And Paul thought it right." … Doubtless, both men acted well in accordance with their own aims. However, they were also separated from one another on account of this difference, seeing that they were not both of one disposition. … [And they did not depart from one another as if unable to bear one another's

weaknesses—seeing that they had spent much time together, labored together, and so often risked their necks together—but rather in order that someone, seeing the inconsistency of their way of life, may not take offense at one of them, either calling Paul irascible, or calling Barnabas one who has become a despiser even of himself.] ... And, most of all, since they were about to preach to the heathen, who have no discernment of good and evil; and the heathen, perhaps from the difference of their way of life, suspecting the mystery preached by Paul and Barnabas also to be discordant, on account of the fact that their disposition was discordant—rather, having considered all of *this*, Paul and Barnabas withdrew from one another, having thus judged it to be good for the ministry of the word (*Catena on Acts* 15:39; CGPNT 259–260.12; cited in Brookins, Reynolds and Parsons 2011, 29–30).

The Venerable Bede takes a different tack when dealing with the dissension between Paul and Barnabas: "Do not think this is a moral fault, for it is not evil to be agitated. Rather it is evil to be agitated unreasonably, when no just reason demands it" (*Comm. Acts* 15:39a).

Finally, apart from the commentary tradition, there is little reflection on the dispute between Paul and Barnabas recorded in Acts 15:37–41. Scottish Reformed preacher John Knox (1513–1572) appealed to this text to dispute the view that disagreement among sincere believers was a sure sign of heresy:

That is, "It is proper to heretics to disagree among themselves" which sentence, how ancient that ever it be, if it should be so understand as the Papist doeth—that is, whosoever disagrees among themselves in matters of religion they are heretics;—if the former sentence (we say) should be so understood, then shall we accuse more of heresy then can be excused in any one age from Christ Jesus to this day. ... What shall we say of the hot contention which fell betwixt Barnabas and Paul, which separated them that before they were joined in as straight conjunction as ever were two mortal men upon the earth? If Maister Tyrie and his Jesuits will allege that these were but sudden passions, and did not concern any chief head of doctrine, the Holy Ghost will prove the contrary (*Works of John Knox*, 6b: 500).

Another notable exception is the letter, dated March 24, 1876, from Lottie Moon (1840–1912), a missionary to China (1873–1912) to Dr. Henry A. Tupper, the Foreign Mission Board corresponding secretary, in which she draws comparisons between Paul and Barnabas's disagreement and disputes among fellow missionaries:

I am sure you are much grieved at the unfortunate alienation between the two brethren. May I remind you, if it be any comfort, that it is said of Paul & Barnabas that "the contention was so sharp between them that they departed asunder one from the other"? [Acts 15:39] In China, alas! such things are not confined to missionaries of any one Board. … Cases of incompatibility are of constant occurrence on the mission field & are usually settled by one of the parties removing elsewhere. Such differences frequently are settled by the quiet withdrawal of one of the parties. … People out here are very tolerant. I suppose we must make allowances for troubles between missionaries by remembering that the very strength of character which impels them to the mission work is apt to manifest itself in sharp angles (Moon 1876).

Overview

Traditionally recognized as the inauguration of Paul's second missionary campaign, Acts 16 has been understood as the account of the Gospel crossing "over into Europe" (although Jeffrey Staley has challenged that understanding as "a colonialist geographic designation with no actual textual basis, and one that has helped foster the ideology of modern colonialist missionary movements"; Staley 2004: 177; cf. Townsend 1985: 433–37). The chapter recounts Paul's

The Acts of the Apostles Through the Centuries, First Edition. Heidi J. Hornik and Mikeal C. Parsons.
© 2017 Heidi J. Hornik and Mikeal C. Parsons. Published 2017 by John Wiley & Sons, Ltd.

circumcision of Timothy (16:1–5), the Macedonian vision (16:6–10), and stories of conversion, imprisonment and release (16:11–40).

When most readers think of Acts 17, they think of Paul's famous speech on Mars Hill. In actuality, only the second half of the chapter (17:16–34) is devoted to the Areopagus speech. The first half of the chapter records the continuation of Paul's Macedonian ministry in Thessalonica and Berea (17:1–15). Interpretations have focused on the political charge made by the Thessalonian Jews that the Christians were "turning the world upside down" by preaching Jesus as "another king" (17:7), the claims made by Paul about God as Creator and the question of "natural theology" (17:24–28), and, especially among Christian creeds and confessions of faith, Paul's call to repentance in the face of an impending day of judgment (17:30–31). There are also some isolated but intriguing insights into and applications by specific interpreters of particular verses in this chapter.

Reception and Interpretation

Acts 16

The Circumcision of Timothy (16:1–5)

Typical of the tradition, the Venerable Bede argues that Paul circumcises Timothy "not because he believed that the symbolic actions of the law could provide anything of use now that the truth of the gospel was shining through. [Paul did this] instead so that the Jewish [Christians] would not fall away from the faith because of the pretext of the gentiles" (*Comm. Acts* 16:3; cf. Tertullian, *Pud.* 211; Erasmus, *Paraphrase of Acts* 16:3–6). Likewise, Aquinas is concerned to explain an apparent inconsistency between Acts 16 and Gal 2:1–5:

> Then when he says, "but because of false brethren, unawares brought in" [Gal 2:4], he shows that he did not change on any other point. This passage is obscure and variant readings are found. It should be read thus: You say that you did not permit Titus [to be circumcised]; but why? seeing that in another case you permitted Timothy, as is read in Acts (16:3). To this the Apostle can respond that when Timothy was circumcised, it was an indifferent matter whether circumcision was observed or not; but later on, when it came to Titus [Gal 2:3], circumcision became a matter of paramount importance and I said that it is not to be observed. Hence, if I had allowed him to be circumcised, whereas I had already settled the question definitively myself, I would have been acting to the contrary. Furthermore, it was not lawful to raise this question again or to make difficulties about a matter now settled (*Comm. Gal.*, Chapter 2, Lecture 1).

Elsewhere, Aquinas answers the question about the consistency of Paul's actions by appealing to Augustine:

> However, according to Augustine, the answer is that the apostles did in very truth observe the works of the Law and had the intention of observing them; because, according to the teaching of the apostles, it was lawful at that time, i.e., before grace had become widespread, for converts from Judaism to observe them. Therefore, because Timothy was born of a Jewish mother, the Apostle circumcised him with the intention of observing the Law. But because the Galatians were putting their hope in the legal observances after the spreading of grace, as though without them grace was not sufficient to save them (*Comm. Gal.*, Chapter 5, Lecture 1).

Luther appealed to the example of Acts 16:1–5 as a rationale for dealing with papal commands that the sacrament be received annually each Easter "in one kind" (bread only). Over against this, Luther appeals to the example of Paul as one who followed his conscience as circumstance dictated:

> When he [Paul] encountered the stubborn Jews who insisted upon circumcision and the law, he took delight in teaching and doing the very opposite; he would not be coerced [Gal. 2:3–5]. But when he came to the weak and simple people he even practiced circumcision [Acts 16:3] and let the law stand, until such time as he might strengthen them and deliver them from the law. Therefore he boasts in I Cor. 12 [9:20]: "To the Jews I became as a Jew; to the Greeks I became as a Greek"; and yet he says in Gal. 3 and let the law stand, until such time as he might strengthen them and deliver them from the law. Therefore he boasts in I Cor. 12 [9:20]: "To the Jews I became as a Jew; to *LW* 36:253).

John Calvin claimed that the "circumcision of Timothy was not a sacrament, such as had been given to Abraham and his descendants, but a neutral and indifferent ceremony, which was of use only for the fostering of love, and not for the exercise of godliness" (*Commentary on Acts*, 16:3).

English Puritan statesman Henry Lawrence (1600–1664) notes that Paul consents to circumcise Timothy in order to avoid offending fellow Jews and as part of his effort in the "breaking downe of the partition wall" between Jew and Gentile [Eph 2:14]:

> It is true that *Paul* did once use a liberty in circumcising one, to wit, *Timothy*, as ye find, *Acts* 16. *Paul* was to visit the Churches, and having a desire to take *Timothy* along with him in that work who was well reported of by the brethren he took and circumcised him; *Because* (saith the Text) *of the Iewes which were in those quarters, for they knew all, that his Father was a Greek*: Lest therefore the

brethren of the Circumcision should be scandalized in the converse of a *Gentile*, the breaking downe of the partition wall being yet not manifest as was needful for the satisaction of their scrupulous consciences, *Paul* tooke the advantage of his Mothers being a Jewesse, and to avoyd the scandal and offence of those brethren, circumcised him (Lawrence 1651).

Lawrence points out that the same Paul who would "avoid the scandall of some weake brethren" by circumcising Timothy, the son of a Jew, would not sacrifice his principles and relent under the pressure of "false brethren" to circumise the Gentile, Titus (Gal 2:3).

Lawrence's interpretation echoes certain patristic interpreters and anticipates the arguments of some modern commentators. Chrysostom, for example, said that Paul "engaged in circumcision in order to abolish it" (*Catena on Acts* 16.1–3; cf. also Chrysostom, *Hom. Act.* 34; Augustine, *Letter 82.8 to Jerome*). Biblical scholar T.C. Smith (1915–2011) gives an answer similar to Lawrence's to the question, "Why did Paul circumcise Timothy when on a previous occasion, he refused to yield to the pressure of the circumcision party and require circumcision for Titus, a Greek (Gal. 2.3 f.)?":

> We have no evidence that the apostle ever opposed a Jew being circumcised. Presumably, he would find the rite acceptable in the case of mixed marriages. ... We assume that the apostle accepted the continuance of the rite of circumcision among the Jewish Christians, but we know definitely that he rejected the imposition of the Jewish custom on Gentile converts.
>
> The situation of Titus was different. He had no Jewish parentage. In circumcising Timothy, Paul did not believe that he was compromising his view. It was a case of half and half. He felt that no harm was done; yet by acceding, the Jews in the region might be less belligerent (Smith 1970, 95; cf. Stagg 1955, 165).

German theologian Dietrich Bonhoeffer makes the most of the little information available on Timothy:

> Timothy is not being asked to perform great things; instead, he is charged with living in a straightforward fashion before this truth. Timothy was not a missionary. Paul was, and it was he who built the house in which Timothy is now to live.... Who is Timothy? What interest might this question have for us? What kind of person was this servant in the house of God? What were his gifts and qualities? How did his inner development come about? What presuppositions did he bring to this vocation? We are told nothing: Acts 16:1–2; 2 Tim. 3:15; 2 Tim. 1:5; Acts 16:3. What is the unique feature all these descriptions offer us concerning Timothy? They all emerge from the exterior rather than from the interior: his family, his reputation, his education in Scripture, his circumcision. All these things, none of which says anything about his inner development, suffice to

describe this unusual man. Not a word about any particular gifts or about his personal development. Why not? Because apparently such considerations have nothing to do with service in the house of God. It suffices that he stands in the faith and that he gives no external offense.

Standing in the faith and not giving offense! We might say that this is the self-evident presupposition. Paul, however, says that that is all! Paul seems to have made different demands on those who serve the word than do we (*BW* 14:942).

The Macedonian Vision (16:6–10)

Acts 16:6–10 records the curious account of Paul and company "being forbidden them to proclaim the message in Asia" by the Holy Spirit but instead to cross over to a new mission field in Macedonia. The Second London Confession (1677) cites Acts 16:7 in support of its claim that the "Revelation of the Gospel unto Sinners" and the "Promises and Precepts for the Obedience required therein" is "merely of the Sovereign Will and good Pleasure of God" (Second London, chap. 20). Similarly, in a sermon on Acts 16:9, renowned minister C. H. Spurgeon (1834–92) claims that Paul "desires to tarry in Asia, and there throughout its length and breadth preach the gospel; but he is strictly forbidden, and the command comes to him that he is to go across to Europe, and there proclaim the gospel. Was not this sovereignty?" (Spurgeon 1858, 194). In his sermonic musings on the text, however, Harry Emerson Fosdick (1978–1969), seminary professor at Union Seminary in New York and first pastor of New York's Riverside Church, shifts the focus from God's sovereignty—though it is not entirely lacking: he does refer to God's purposes and leading—to Paul's reliance on his own religious experience when he arrives in Troas rather than his desired goal of Bithynia:

> Whatever else was shaken when he got to Troas, his conviction still was there that God had a purpose for his life, that if God had led him to Troas there must be something in Troas worth discovering, that God's purposes included Troas just as much as Bithynia, that God never leads any man into any place where all the doors are shut. Paul's religion entered in.
>
> ... What helped him most, I suspect, was that his thought went back, as it so habitually did, to the cross of his Master. That was a Troas to land on!

And in typical Fosdick-fashion, he turns the text onto his audience:

> Is there anybody here who has not wanted Bithynia and gotten Troas? We older people watch the youths come up, as we did, with their ambitions and plans for Bithynia and we wonder what they will do when they face the

inescapable experience. When they are shut out from some Bithynia and land in Troas, will they know how to handle that? Will they have the spirit and attitude and the technique to make of it their finest chance? (Fosdick 1958).

William Carey (1761–1834), missionary to India and recognized as the "father" of the modern missionary movement, had a fascinating interpretation of Acts 16:7. He claims that the Great Commission of Christ was not limited to the Apostles: "If the command of Christ to teach all nations extend only to the apostles, then, doubtless, the promise of the divine presence in this work must be so limited; but this is worded in such a manner as expressly precludes such an idea. *Lo, I am with you always, to the end of the world*" [Matt 28:19–20]. But Carey recognizes that "there are cases in which even a divine command may cease to be binding"; namely, "when we can produce a counter-revelation, of equal authority with the original command." And he cites Acts 16:7 as just such an example: "as when Paul and Silas were forbidden of the Holy Ghost to preach the word in Bythinia. Acts xvi. 6. 7. or if, in any case, there be a *natural impossibility* of putting it in execution."

Karl Barth appeals to Acts 16:9 in describing the church's obligation to the world and the world's need of the church's help, whether they realize it or not: "All those who are without are waiting not only for the understanding and solidarity and participation, but for the helping action of the Christian community, for that which it alone in the whole world can do for them. Whether they are aware of it or not, their whole being and striving and existence utters the cry of the Macedonian: 'Come over … and help us' (Ac. 16⁹)" (*CD* 4.3.778).

Conversions, Imprisonment, and Release (16:11–40)

Acts 16:10–11 ("immediately we sought to go on into Macedonia. … Setting sail therefore from Troas, we made a direct voyage to Samothrace") contains the first of the so-called "we-passages," in which the narrator identifies himself as among the company of Paul. Irenaeus was apparently the first to comment on the use of first-person narration and to connect it to Luke, the companion of Paul (Col 4.14, Phlm 24, and 2 Tim 4.11; see Introduction):

> But that this Luke was inseparable from Paul, and his fellow-labourer in the Gospel, he himself clearly evinces, not as a matter of boasting, but as bound to do so by the truth itself. For he says that when Barnabas, and John who was called Mark, had parted company from Paul, and sailed to Cyprus, "we came to Troas;" (10) and when Paul had beheld in a dream a man of Macedonia, saying, "Come into Macedonia, Paul, and help us," "immediately," he says, "we endeavoured to go into Macedonia, understanding that the Lord had called us to preach the Gospel unto them. (*Against Heresies*, 3.14.1)

Modern interpreters have evaluated the evidence of the "we" passages very differently. Some have accepted the references as indicating that the author was a some-time companion of Paul; others have viewed it as a literary device to establish the authority credibility of the writer (see Campbell 2007, 1–13).

The stories of the household conversions of Lydia and the Philippian jailer were often invoked by opponents of believers' baptism in support of infant baptism (see previous discussion at 15:10). After all, these households must surely have included infants. Martin Luther argued: "The apostles baptized entire households [Acts 16:15]. John writes to little children [I John 2:12]. St. John had faith even in his mother's womb, as we have heard [Luke 1:41]. If all of these passages do not suffice for the enthusiasts, I shall not be concerned. They are enough for me, to stop the mouth of anyone from saying that child baptism does not mean anything" (*LW* 40:257).

Many advocates of believer's baptism have also been drawn to Acts 16, not because they found in it a natural ally of their conviction regarding the New Testament witness to believers' baptism, but in order to refute the arguments of their opponents on their own playing field (in much the same way that the Apostle Paul was evidently drawn into the interpretations of the near sacrifice of Isaac by Abraham by his opponents who appealed to this story as scriptural warrant for circumcising Gentile believers; cf. Gal 2; Rom 4). The logic of Puritan Separatist John Smyth's argument is transparent, and it is worth quoting in full, especially since Baptist interpretations that take up this argument in each subsequent century have been essentially variations on the same theme:

> First, I say though infants are a part of the Family when the family hath infants in it, yet it doth not follow that whersoever there is mention made of a Family, that therefore that Family had infants in it: except therefore it bee proved that the family of Lydia, & the family of the Gaylor had infants in it, this allegation is nothing.
>
> Secondly, by this reason you might prove that Lydias Husband, & the Gaylors [jailor's] wife, & their children of 40 yeeres old, & their Servants of 60 yeeres old, were baptized. For al these are parts of a Family, yea, I supose you wil not say they were al of them baptized, except you can prove, that Lydia had a Husband, or the Gaylor had a wife, or children of 40. & servants of 60 yeeres olds; your argument therfor is weak presupposing the thing that is to question.
>
> Thirdly, if it were yeelded that ther were infants in Lydias Family, & in the Gaylors, doth it therfor follow that they were baptized nothing lesse: be that I will declare thus.
>
> 1. You say that to the baptising of the Gaylors wife, & children of yeeres of discretion ther was necessarily required Faith & repentance, or els they were not

baptized: So say I that bicause infants cannot beleeve & repent, though they were in the Family yet shal thy not be baptized. For ther is one condintn required for al persons to be baptized.

2. I say that although it be said that al that preteyned to the Gaylor were baptized, yet it is also said vs. 32. That the word was preached to all that were with his howse: &c vs. 34. Than al his howsehold beleeved, & how came their faith but by the word preached vs. 30. Seing therfor that al that were baptized in the Gaylors hows beleeved by the preaching of the word, infants that could not beleeve by the preaching of the word, were not baptized if he had any: besides it was a marvailous distempered tyme at midnight to wake children, & to bring them before the Apostles for baptisme.

3. I say: That for Lydias Family it is not said that all her howsehold was baptized or if it had been so said, yea it followeth not that every particular person of her Family was baptized. For Mat. 3.5.6. it is said that al Iudea went out to Iohn & were baptized of him, confessing their sinnes: yet hence it cannot bee concluded that all & every one that went out were baptized: or that all & every one went out to bee baptized: no more can it bee proved that bicause it is said that Lydias Family was baptized that therefore all & every particular person was baptized, but as Mat. 3.6. only they that confessed their sinnes: & as Act. 16.32–34. onley they that beleeved by the word preached were baptized, so was it with them of Lydias Family that were baptized: For the Apostles I doubt not kept one order, & required the same conditions in al that they baptized: So that by that which hath been said, the vanity of this argument is manifested: & it is proved plainly that none were baptised in the Gaylors Family, but only they that beleeved after the word preached & so infants specially are exempted, if he had any in his family which yet is not.

Hence, therfor I reason thus against baptising infants.

(Smyth 1609, 27–29; cf. Dannvers 1675; Taylor 1792, Dayton 1857; Stagg 1955).

One might be forgiven for surmising that the length of the argument testifies to the difficulities this passage presents to advocates of believers' baptisim, regardless of how much support one finds elsewhere in the New Testament.

Lydia was a native of Thyatira, a city in the province of Lydia. Hence, she is "Lydia of Lydia." On the basis of the "symbolic richness" of her name (among other things), some have recently conjectured that Lydia is a fictional character (Matthews 2004, 131; MacDonald 2004, 109–10). This need not be the case, however, as it was not uncommon for slaves and freedman (and women) to take the name of their homeland. Strabo, for example, mentioned "Lydus" as an appropriate name for a slave purchased in the region of Lydia (*Geogr.* 7.3.12). Thus, "Lydia of Lydia" could be so called because she was formerly a slave and is now a freed woman. That may say something about her social status. Traditionally, she was grouped with those "leading women" who responded favorably to Paul's message in the ensuing episodes in Thessalonica (17:12);

as a "dealer in purple cloth" she may have belonged to the category of "women of means" (Witherington 1998, 492). However, there could well be a distinction between "purple-*wearers*" and "purple-*weavers*" (Spencer 2004, 148). Plutarch, for example, claims that purple clothing is highly valued "but the dyers and salve-makers remain for us common and low craftspersons" (*Per.* 1.3–4). Such observations are causing re-assessment of Lydia's perceived social and economic status in modern scholarship (Parsons 2008: 230).

The thirteenth-century Latin New Testament manuscript, Vat.lat.39, contains a "dense cycle of illustrations of the Acts of the Apostles, a rare attribute indeed" (Eleen 1977, 255). One of those illuminations is of *Paul and Silas Beaten at Philippi* (Acts 16:18–22; **Figure 35**). The manuscript presumably shares a common ancestor with Cod. Chig.A.IV.74 (Eleen 1977, 256; see also comments on Acts 18:12–17, 18). The manuscript apparently derives from Verona (Arslan 1943, 167–41; cited in Eleen 1977, 255) and the images are "unframed text pictures within the columns of writing" (255). Like most of the other illustrations, the scene depicting the beating of Paul and Silas at Philippi (fol.98r) is systematically placed in close proximity to the text it describes, suggesting "that the scribes and artists were working with a text-picture combination that had already been proven" (Eleen 1977, 256).

Also typical of the program of the manuscript is the tendency to elaborate miracles in a sequence of two scenes (Eleen 1977, 263). On the recto of the manuscript page (not shown here) is a picture of Paul's exorcism of a possessed slave girl (Acts 16:16–18). In the following scene, Paul and Silas are shown being flogged with sticks. They are stripped to their waists, and bloody welts are visible on their upper torsos. Paul is identifiable by his balding head and beard. Both Paul and Silas have their hands raised in a gesture of prayer. They are being driven toward a prison, an imposing building complete with domes and turrets, a building similar to, but not identical with, the earlier illustration in the manuscript of the prison from which Peter is liberated (cod.lat39.fol.94r).

They are being flogged in a vertical, upright way (rather than a prone position of falling to, or lying on, the ground), a detail "peculiar to Italian iconography" in manuscript illumination (Eleen 1977, 264; cf. the more traditional prone position preserved in the cod.Barb.lat.4406, fol.97r, Vatican library, reproduced in Eleen 1977, fig. 40). While it is possible the depiction of the "standing disciples" is due to some iconographical symbolism (e.g., to demonstrate the "manliness" of Paul and Silas who remain standing, despite suffering a severe flogging), the detail may more likely be due to traces of a "compositional solution" in response to technical problems, associated with fitting an expanded sequence of scenes into an archetypal text, with multiple columns, which the artist of Vat.lat. 39 was copying (Eleen 1977, 273).

FIGURE 35   *Paul and Silas Beaten at Philippi.* 1200–25. Manuscript illumination.
Ms lat.39fol.98r. © 2012 Biblioteca Apostolica Vaticana. Photo: By permission of
Biblioteca Vaticana, all rights reserved.

Emily Dickinson also muses on the implications of the imprisonment of Paul and Silas:

> Of Paul and Silas it is said
> They were in Prison laid
> But when they went to take them out
> They were not there instead.
> Security the same insures
> To our assaulted Minds—
> The staple must be optional
> That an Immortal binds
> (Atwan and Wieder 1993, 256).

The question/answer exchange between the Philippian jailer in Acts 16:30–31 ("Sirs, what must I do to be saved?") and Paul and Barnabas ("Believe on the Lord Jesus and you will be saved.") is a favorite among evangelicals (cf. Bunyan 1689; Orthodox Creed 1678; Kiffin 1681; Knollys 1681; Keach 1693; Colby 1838; Dayton 1857; Bachelor 1873; Stagg 1955). Despite the evidence of Acts 16:15, in one place, Dietrich Bonhoeffer claims: "Child baptism is dubious" (*BW* 14:631); in another place, appealing to Acts 16:15, 33, etc. he opines: "The practice of infant baptism cannot be directly proven in the New Testament (NT), to be sure, but can nevertheless be seen as probably there" (*BW* 16:551, 553).

Karl Barth argues, "In the New Testament, so far as I can see, there is no summons to the direct defence of one's honour, but only the admonition to remember and actively to respect the honour of others." He then considers Acts 16:37, in which Paul challenges magistrates to appear in person to release him from prison as a possible counter example: "As an example of the direct defence of honour the scene in Ac. 16[35f.] naturally demands to be considered. ... We can hardly fail to see that in these undoubtedly courageous words we have an almost classic example of the desire for a restoration of disrupted order and not of vain or rancorous contention" (*CD* 3.4.685). Methodist historian Justo González observes that Paul "does not employ it [Roman citizenship and status] among the church membership in order to claim greater importance, whereas he is quite ready to employ it beyond the confines of the church, in order to demand respect for Silas and for himself and, by implication, for other believers" (González 2001, 196).

Acts 17

Paul's Macedonian Ministry in Thessalonica and Berea (17:1–15)

Within the narrative of Paul's mission in several Greek cites, Codex D introduces changes into the Alexandrian text of Acts 17 that have the effect of diminishing the importance of women in the narrative (Malick 2007,

171–75). In Acts 17:4, D changes the case of the word "women" from genitive to nominative, producing a text that reads the "wives of not a few of the prominent or leading men," rather than "not a few of the leading women." In the Alexandrian text of Acts 17:12, women are listed before men, highlighting their significance. D reverses the word order, placing "men" before "women" and thus muting their importance (Malick 2007, 175; cf. Acts 18:26).

Patristic and Reformed interpreters note that Paul continues to preach in the synagogues (17:1–9), despite his earlier assertion that he was now turning to the Gentiles (cf. 13:46), and attribute this action to his continued love and concern for his fellow Israelites (Chrysostom, *Hom. Act.* 37; Spangenberg, *Der Apostel Geschichte* 184v; Gwalther, *Homilies* 647; RCS, 238–39). Luther appeals to Acts 17:2–11 to argue for the importance of reading the Old Testament (typologically): "In Acts 17:2 ff. we read that Paul preached the faith to the Thessalonians, led them into Scripture, and expounded it to them, and that they returned to Scripture every day and searched to see whether his teachings were in agreement with it (v. 11). Therefore we must do the same thing. We must go back to the Old Testament and learn to prove the New Testament from the Old" (*The Catholic Epistles. Sermons on the First Epistle of St. Peter* 1.26; *LW* 30:18).

Thomas Monk, Joseph Wright, and Frank Stanley (1661) echo the accusations against Christians in Acts 17:6–7 in their caveat against civic Magistrates who seek to exercise authority over spiritual matters:

> … there can therefore be no security for a Magistrate that he doth well, in persecuting or putting to Death the contrary minded, in religious matters, seeing a thorow [thorough] mistake he may as soon persecute, or put to death, the true followers of the Lord Jesus, or any other; yea, in likelihood much sooner, because they in conscience towards God, cannot receive the inventions and traditions of men, in the Worship of God, but must be a witness for the eternal God against them, for which they are accounted (as the Saints of old) *pestilent fellows, movers of sedition, turners of the World upside down, enemies to Cesar*, and upon this account persecuted, when the greatest part of men being unregenerate, and have no other Spirit in them, but what is of this World; there is therefore no reason why the World should persecute and hate his own (Monk et al 1661, 17–18; cf. Richardson 1646, 46–48; 1648, 29–32).

John Calvin, on the other hand, sees the charges of Paul's opponents as "invented with too much impudence": "The Jews knew that this was being done without any harm to the Roman Empire. They knew that there was no question of those men intending to overthrow the public order, or snatch Caesar's authority away from him, but they maliciously plead this excuse for the sake of procuring ill-will" (*Commentary on Acts*, 17:7). Modern interpreters, on the other hand, have seen in this scene (taken in tandem with 1 Thess 4–5) a clear anti-imperial emphasis and suggest that the opponents' charges of a political dimension to Paul's gospel were not completely unfounded (see Donfried 1985, 336–56).

British Baptist pastor C.H. Spurgeon (1834–92) also appeals to the same verses to make a point concerning piety rather than politics:

> It is marvelous how great a change the gospel makes in a man's house too. Why, it turns his house upside down. Look over the mantle-piece—There is a vile daub of a picture there, or a wretched print, and the subject is worse than the style of the thing. But when the man follows Jesus he takes that down, and he gets a print of John Bunyan in his prison, or his wife standing before the magistrate, or a print of the apostle Paul preaching at Athens, or some good old subject representing something Biblical. There is a pack of cards and a cribbage board in the cupboard; he turns them out, and instead he puts there perhaps the monthly magazine, or mayhap a few works of old divines, just here and there one of the publications of the Religious Tract Society, or a volume of a Commentary. Every thing is upside down there [Acts 17:6] (Spurgeon 1858, 4:231).

Paul's Areopagus Address (17:16–34)

The Areopagus speech is one of the most important, beloved and frequently interpreted scenes in Acts. Tourists who visit the traditional site are greeted with a plaque embedded in a stone monument inscribed with the words of Paul's speech in Greek. This text was crucial for patristic authors who were concerned to develop a systematic Christian theology (as well for many later theologians who argued for the value of Greek philosophy as a help in interpreting the gospel). Clement of Alexandria (ca.150–ca. 215), for example, quotes Acts 17:22–28 in the context of an extended defense of his use of Greek philosophy in interpreting the Bible, introducing the text as follows: "It is possible also from the following evidence to see that the Greeks are attested as teaching certain true things.'" He refers to the Areopagus speech numerous times (see, e.g., *Strom.* 5.11.75; 5.12.82; 6.18.165).

As previously discussed in relation to the *Sacrifice of Lystra* cartoon by Raphael (see the text on Acts 1:8–20), the Jews were not accepting of Paul's gospel in Lystra. Paul has a very different experience in Athens as seen in the final discussion of a tapestry cartoon for the Sistine Chapel to be discussed here. This is often considered Paul's most dramatic speech and defines him as a preacher. Some scholars have suggested the message is received differently by country dwellers (Lystra) than city residents (Athens) (Parsons 2008, 199–200; cf. Béchard 2000). *Paul Preaching in Athens* (**Figure 36**) is the most widely copied of the Raphael cartoons.

FIGURE 36   Raphael (1483–1520). *Paul Preaching at Athens*. 1515–16. Watercolor on paper mounted onto canvas (tapestry cartoon), 3.4 × 4.4m. V&A Images/The Royal Collection, on loan from HM The Queen. Victoria and Albert Museum, London, Great Britain. Photo: V&A Images, London/Art Resource, NY

Paul had become deeply concerned about the presence of idols as he walked around the city of Athens. He wears the same vestments as in other tapestry scenes and stands on a stepped platform in front of the Areopagus as he raises his hands in gesture. He addresses the crowd, "Athenians, I see how extremely religious you are in every way. For as I went through the city and looked carefully at the objects of your worship, I found among them an altar with the inscription, 'To an unknown god'" (Acts 17:22b-23a). The statue of Mars can be seen to the right of the composition. Paul goes on to speak of God as creator and as the one who raised "the man whom he appointed," Jesus, from the dead. The mention of the Resurrection causes some in the crowd to scoff, but others believe.

The tapestry was, from an iconographic perspective, appropriately placed below Cosimo Rosselli's fresco from the Moses cycle depicting the *Adoration of the Golden Calf.* Pope Leo X had just issued a doctrine about preaching reform in the tenth session of the Lateran Council on December 15, 1515 (Shearman, 1971, 71). In this document, the Pope gives Paul the title Prince of Preachers.

The tapestries were truly a legacy of Pope Leo X but, unfortunately, when he died in 1521 the papacy was bankrupt and the tapestries had to be sold to help pay for the gathering of the cardinals to elect his successor (Hartt and Wilkins 2011, 530).

The Raphael tapestries are rich visual depictions of stories about Peter and Paul. Eight out of ten of them refer to events recorded in the Acts of the Apostles. We have discussed five of them in this book (cf. 3:1–10, Figure 11; 5:1–11, Figure 15; 13:11, Figure 30; 14:11–18, Figure 32; 17:22–31, Figure 36). As the most thorough set of paintings from Acts, they allow us to visualize the major events in the spreading of the gospel "unto the ends of the earth" (Acts 13:47).

In 1644, John Milton, British poet and nonconformist, published a speech in the form of a pamphlet that challenged the licensing order (which required authors to receive governmental sanction before publishing) and defended free speech (cf. Jeffrey 1992, 53). The title of the pamphlet, *Areopagitica*, appealed both to the *Areopagicitus* of Isocrates and Paul's speech in Acts 17:18–34. Milton points out that Paul was able to quote from the pagan philosophers (Acts 17:28), only because he had access to their books and that reading them was "both lawfull and profitable."

Reformers comment on the status of Athens in antiquity as a "learned city" (cf. Luther, *Sermon on Acts 17:16–21*; Augustine, *WA* 15:630; Gwalther, *Homilies* 658; RCS, 243), although that does not insulate its residents from idolatrous practices (cf. Calvin, *Commentary on Acts*, 17:17). Luther uses the example of Paul at Athens to argue for the transformative power of the Word of God:

> Once, when Paul came to Athens (Acts 17 [:16–32]), a mighty city, he found in the temple many ancient altars, and he went from one to the other and looked at them all, but he did not kick down a single one of them with his foot. Rather he stood up in the middle of the market place and said they were nothing but idolatrous things and begged the people to forsake them; yet he did not destroy one of them by force. When the Word took hold of their hearts, they forsook them of their own accord, and in consequence the thing fell of itself. ... For the Word created heaven and earth and all things [Ps. 33:6; John 1:3]; the Word must do this thing, and not we poor sinners ("The Second Sermon, March 10, 1522, Monday after Invocavit"; *LW* 51:77; cf. *LW* 51:83).

Chrysostom claims the reference to the Greeks' description of Paul preaching "foreign deities" in Acts 17:18 was "because he [Paul] preached unto them Jesus and the Resurrection: for in fact they supposed 'Anastasis' [the Resurrection; the Greek word is grammatically feminine] to be some deity, being accustomed to worship female divinities also" (*Hom. Act.* 38). Augustine focuses on another part of Acts 17:18 and plays on the meaning of the Greek word, *spermologos*, often rendered "babbler" in English translations. He asserts:

> That Paul spoke to the Athenians, and that those of them who were contemptuous of the preaching of the truth called him *a sower of words* (Acts 17:18). It was said, certainly, by scoffers, but it should not be rejected by believers. After all, that man was indeed a sower of words, but also a harvester of good deeds. I too, midget though I am and in no way to be compared to his pre-eminence, am sowing the words of God in God's field, which is your hearts, and am looking for a bumper harvest of good habits from you ("Sermon 150" in *Sermons on the New Testament, 148–183; WA 3.5*).

While subsequent modern scholarship most certainly would not agree with his characterization, the Venerable Bede makes an interesting comparison of Paul with the Epicurean and Stoic philosophers: "The Epicureans... put the happiness of man in the pleasure of the body alone, while the Stoics placed it solely in the virtue of the mind. ... they were united in opposition to the apostle with respect [to his belief that] a human being subsists in soul and body, a happiness that can be achieved only "by the grace of God through Jesus Christ in the glory of the resurrection" (*Comm. Acts* 17:18). William Blake depicts Paul himself as an almost divine figure, complete with radiant glory, in his 1803 pen, black chalk and watercolor drawing (**Figure 37**).

Paul's speech at Areopagus (Acts 17:23–28) appeals to what some regard as "natural theology" in its claim that the unknown God whom the Athenians worship is none other than the one, true God (see Clement of Alexandria above). British theologianWilliam Clarke (1841–1912) comments on this verse: "The outreaching of their worshipping hearts Paul regarded as an outreaching after God, even though it did not intelligently find him so as to know him as he is. If this hint of Paul is followed, it appears possible for the living God to regard himself as really though ignorantly addressed, in the praying of men who do not know him as he is, and to do them good in proportion to their possibilities, in answer to their prayer" (Clarke 1908, 98–100; cf. Clarke 1914, 420).

In an extended discussion of the Areopagus speech (*CD* 2.1.121–23), Karl Barth denies that the sermon reflects a "natural theology" that supposes "that without and before God's revelation in Jesus Christ men already stood in a relationship to God" (Barth *CD* 2.1.121). Rather, the sermon is "not an attempt to understand the world of the Athenian philosophers from their own viewpoint and to overcome it from within. It is the announcement of the judgment which comes upon this world from without—certainly upon *this* world, but upon this world *from without*. ... When Paul declared the Word of resurrection, everything immediately became clear and mockery and boredom was the answer of

FIGURE 37   William Blake (1757–1827). *St. Paul Preaching in Athens*. 1803.
Watercolor with touches of black chalk and scraping on paper. 18 × 12¼ inches. Photo:
Museum of Art, Rhode Island School of Design, Providence. Gift of the Estate of Mrs.
Gustav Radeke 31.280

the Athenian philosophers. But when he turned his back on them a few others
joined him" (*CD* 1.2.122, 121). Dietrich Bonhoeffer makes a similar point: "the
church can be led not to dispense with Christ but rather to make full proclamation of the grace of Christ's dominion. The unknown God is preached only as
the known—because revealed—God" (*BW* 16:550–51).

The Lifeway Adult Bible Study material, created by and for Native Americans,
has a fascinating, cross-cultural application of this verse:

> On many reservations traditional religious practices were outlawed by those who
> were in charge of overseeing the welfare of the tribe. When foreigners first came

to this country and overran a tribe or portion of the tribe, they forced their religious beliefs on them. This was not a new practice. …

Paul encountered a people whose culture, views, customs, and religion were different from his own. His approach to closing the cultural gap is described by the words "I observe" (v. 22) and "examining" (v. 23). Paul took the time to know the life-style, philosophy, religion, and custom of these people. The words *observe* and *examine* do not describe a casual look but indicate he studied or looked at intently. We as Christians too often make the mistake of passing judgment on people without observing them. This leads to prejudice and discrimination and leads to resentment. By doing this we build walls rather than bridges. This destroys our Christian witness. We don't need to turn people off but turn them on to Jesus.

We can draw several conclusions from Paul's actions in these two verses related to closing cultural gaps. (1) Accept people as they are. Paul did not reject them but "stood in the midst." (2) Get to know the people. Paul "observed" the people. (3) Respect the culture of the people. Paul did not tear down their practice. (4) Present the gospel in the context of the culture. Paul took what they knew and led them to Jesus. (5) Do not manipulate people. Paul was honest and direct with the people. (6) If people reject you, keep on loving and ministering to them. Paul did this throughout his ministry (SBC-Lifeway 1989, 64–65).

Acts 17:24 includes a clear affirmation of "God who made the universe and all things in it" (17:24) and was, along with Genesis 1, a verse much-quoted in early confessions concerning God as Creator. *The Propositions and Conclusions concerning True Christian Religion* (1612–14), attributed to John Smyth and British dissenters living in Amsterdam at the time, asserts: "That God in the beginning created the world viz., the heavens, and the earth and all things that are therein (Gen. i; Acts xvii. 24)" (Propositions 1612–14, chap. 11; cf. also True Gospel-Faith 1654, 192).

Acts 17:26 ("He has made of one blood every nation of men to dwell on all the face of the earth, having determined their appointed seasons and the bounds of their habitation") has also generated a wide variety of interpretations among interpreters. Non-conformist pastor William Jeffrey (et al, 1660) appeals to Paul's declaration in Acts 17:26 that God has established the political bounds of human habitation as a basis for their plea to the Monarch for justice to those whose unjust incarceration violates the "Laws of God and Nature":

GOD that hath made of one Bloud all Nations of men, for to dwell on all the face of the Earth; and hath determined the Times before appointed, and the bounds of their Habitation; hath made this Land the Place of our Nativity and Abode, by which we have an Interest in Common with others Thy Subjects in this Nation, so that none can Deprive us of that which is Propriety, and Native Birth-rights, without violating the Laws of God and Nature: Yet (may it please Thee, O King,) … We Thy Imprisoned Subjects, have (some of us) had our Houses broken open in the dead of the Night, without producing any Authority from Thee, or any inferior Minister under Thee; our Goods and Cattel taken away from some others, and yet detained from us ... (Jeffrey et al 1660, 5–6).

Centuries later, ethicist T.B. Maston (1897–1988) would use the first part of Acts 17:26 ("He has made of one blood every nation of men") in his prophetic call for racial justice: "This same God 'created all races of men.' This was true of the proud Greeks and of the equally proud, self-conscious Jews. We are 'of one' or 'from one.' Men and women of all races belong to one human race" (Maston 1987, 82–83). In the *Bethel Confession* of August 1933, to which Dietrich Bonhoeffer was a major contributor, we read this rejection of Nazi racial ideology: "No order regarding race is found in either the Bible or the Luther confessions. In this regard, we are referred to Acts 17:26, to the origin of the human race in one common ancestor" (*BW* 12:388). In the 1970s, the pro-Apartheid Dutch Reformed Church appealed to the latter part of Acts 17:26 (God "determined the boundaries of their habitation"), along with other texts (Gen 11; Deut 32:8; 1 Cor 7:17–24; Rev 5:9, 7:9; cf. comments on Acts 2; *Human Relations*, 14–15; cited in Burridge 2011, 76) in defense of its view that the diversification of humanity was divinely ordered. This interpretation implied that "such divisions must be observed in modern times" (Lombaard 2009, 276).

Origen comments on "nearness of God" (Acts 17:27): "He is thus, for his part, close, but if we ourselves make no effort, though he be close, to draw near to him, we will not enjoy his nearness. For this reason sinners are far from God" (*Palestinian Catena on Psalm 118.151*; cited in ACCS, 220). Seventeenth-century British Baptist minister Hercules Collins, on the other hand, appeals to the verse in defense of the doctrine of God's sovereignty: "if God had not first Will'd and Decreed it, it had not been. ... Yea our very Habitations where we dwell, were before time determined and appointed; [Acts 17. 26] which Doctrine *Paul* Preached to the *Athenians*, to bring them off from their Idolatry, to worship the true God who made Heaven and Earth, and all things therein, and made all Nations of one Blood ..." (Collins 1690, 6–7).

The providence of God is also defended on the basis of Acts 17:28, in which Paul claims that in God "we live and move and have our being." No fewer than eleven early modern confessions and creeds reference Acts 17:28 in their discussions of God's sovereignty and providence (cf. *CCF*, 3:1038). Seventeenth-century British Baptist Thomas Helwys observes that the doctrine of God's sovereignty can be abused "to conclude most blasphemously that God hath foredecreed that sin should come to passe: & not content to stay thē selves here, they runne on with an high hand, & because they see sin enters by actiō, & that God is the moveing cause off al thinges. For in him wee live/and move/ād have our being. Act. 17.28" (Helwys 1611). The first London Confession uses

Acts 17:28 to present God as a kind of First Mover (see also Gill 1796, 1:435): "That God is of himselfe, that is, neither from another, nor of another, nor by another, nor for another: But is a Spirit, who as his being is of himselfe, so he gives being, moving, and preservation to all other things [Act. 17. 28]" (London Confession 1644, II). The Orthodox Creed cites the verse in its explication of the "essence" of God: "WE verily believe, that there is but one only living and true God; whose subsistence is in and of himself, whose essence cannot be comprehended by any but himself; a most pure, spiritual, or invisible substance; who hath an absolute, independent, unchangeable, and infinite being; without matter or form, body, parts, or passions. [Acts 17:28.]" (Orthodox Creed 1678, Article I).

William Clarke (1841–1912), on the other hand, appeals to the verse in his articulation of a doctrine of God's immanence: "The God who is immanent in the universe is immanent in the spiritual order of which our spirits and their life form a part. 'In him we live, and move, and have our being' (Acts xvii. 28)—we, whose being does not belong altogether to this world which we behold" (Clarke 1914, 334; cf. Pinnock 1980, 35–36).

Aquinas cites this verse as evidence of the usefulness of "natural reason" for theology: "Hence sacred doctrine makes use also of the authority of philosophers in those questions in which they were able to know the truth by natural reason, as Paul quotes a saying of Aratus ... (Acts 17:28)" (*ST*, Treatise on Sacred Doctrine, Question 1). However, Karl Barth once again rejects any notion that Acts 17:28 reflects accessibility to God apart from God's revelation in Jesus Christ: "In this verse Paul made use of heathen wisdom, but he immediately gave it a Christian sense and thus in a sense baptised it. He, whom Paul proclaimed to the Athenians in these words which had once been heathen, but in his mouth were so no longer, is undoubtedly neither the classical Zeus nor Hellenistic fate" (*CD* 3.2347; cf. *CD* 1.2.305–06; *CD* 4.3.43).

Across the centuries and theological spectrums, the declaration of the need for repentance in Acts 17:30–31 has figured prominently in confessions and interpretations (True Gospel 1654; Standard Confession 1660, IV; Orthodox Creed 1678, XXII; Free Will Baptists 1935, ch. 9; Pentecostal Free Will Baptists 1999, ch. 9). The urgency of this need was anchored in the belief in a coming final and universal judgment, a conviction anchored in part in Acts 17:31 ("inasmuch as he [God] has fixed a day in which he will judge the world justly, by the Man whom he has ordained"). *Propositions and Conclusions* (1612–14, 95), produced by British dissenters living in Amsterdam at the time, asserts: "That there shall be a general and universal day of judgment, when every one shall receive according to the things that are done in the flesh, whether they be good or evil (1 Cor. v. 10; Acts xvii. 31)," but references to it continue right up to the present (Hammon 1658, 192; Second London 1689, XXXII; Philadelphia 1742, ch. 8, 34; New Hampshire 1833, 17; Allen 1873, 122–23; Free Will Baptists 1935, XXII; Baptist Faith and Message 1963, X; Talbert 1997, 164–65; Pentecostal Free Will 1999, Article 13). And while the judgment is universal, Paul says that the consequences of sin are specific and particular. Each person shall stand accountable before Christ whom God has appointed Judge. Noncomformist pastor William Jeffrey claims that anyone who "continues in disobedience to the Gospel, his punishment is eternal, in the world to come" (Jeffrey 1660). A similar sentiment is found in the Orthodox Creed's article on the last judgment (1678, Article 50): "all persons that have lived upon the earth, shall appear before the tribunal of Christ; to give an account of their thoughts, words, and deeds, and shall receive a just sentence, according to what they have done in their bodies, whether good or evil. ..." The relationship between congregational ecclesiology (a regenerate church membership) and individual eschatology (the individual before Christ in the last judgment) is understudied, but it would appear that the function of the one (ecclesiology) is in part to insure a felicitous conclusion to the other (eschatology).

Interpreters have long noted the "failure" of Paul to win many converts in Athens (Spangenberg, *Der Apostel Geschichte* 157v–158r; RCS, 250). In the Italian film series, *Atti degli Apostoli* (1968), directed by Roberto Rossellini (1906–1977), the character, Paul, reminisces about his time in Athens: "I wanted to get there to the Areopagus. It seemed so natural to be right there where Socrates and Plato lived. ... Athens is the only city from which I was not expelled, but is the only city from which I left empty-handed as a beggar. The wisdom of humans rejected the wisdom of the cross."

Some modern commentators blame Paul's preaching of a "natural theology" (but cf. above) rather than the Christian kerygma (so Dibelius 1939), but to do so is to ignore the kerygmatic elements that reverberate throughout the sermon and the fact that there are a number from the audience who respond positively to Paul's message (17:34) and others who resolve to hear more (17:32; cf. Parsons 2008, 256–58).

Acts 18–19

Overview

Acts 18 records Paul's ministry in Corinth and his visits to urban areas in the Mediterranean basin. The chapter contains scenes of Paul with fellow tent-makers Aquila and Priscilla (18:1–4); Aquila and, especially, Priscilla play an important role in the reception of Acts 18:1–4, 26, highlighting again the portrayal of women in the Christian community in Acts. Acts 19 records Paul's various encounters in Ephesus with John's disciples, itinerant Jewish exorcists,

The Acts of the Apostles Through the Centuries, First Edition. Heidi J. Hornik and Mikeal C. Parsons.
© 2017 Heidi J. Hornik and Mikeal C. Parsons. Published 2017 by John Wiley & Sons, Ltd.

and the devotees of Artemis. Questions of (re-)baptism, laying on of hands, and the miracle of the handkerchiefs figure prominently in this chapter.

Reception and Interpretation

Acts 18

Paul with Aquila and Priscilla (Acts 18:1–4)

Chrysostom viewed the artisanship of Paul, Aquila, and Priscilla as a model virtue to be extolled (Acts 18:3), especially for his urban audience who disdained manual labor and its concomitant poverty: "It was with them that [Paul] stayed, and he was not ashamed to do so; on the contrary, he stayed precisely because he had found a suitable lodging place. ... For just as to an athlete the gym is more useful than soft cushions, likewise to a warrior an iron sword is useful and not a golden one. And he worked while preaching. Let us be ashamed, we who live idle lives even though we are not occupied with preaching" (*Hom. Act.* 39).

Acts 18:2–3 was ripe for allegorizing among ancient interpreters. Sixth-century Latin poet and orator Arator allegorized both Aquila's name (= "eagle") and Paul's occupation, claiming it has "hidden good." Just as the traveler takes refuge in physical tents from harsh winters and the heat of summer, so the believers who are "driven from our first home through sin" and "scattered by exile in the world" find shelter on their journey back to the Father in Paul's camp from the "rains of sin" and the "heat of wickedness" (*OAA*, II.506–68). Echoing Arator, Bede (eighth century) compares the tentmaking trade to the tents lived in by exiles and argues that the Greek word, *skēnai*, is "etymologically derived from 'the giving of shade'" and concludes that "mystically just as Peter by fishing draws us out of the waves of the world by nets of faith, so also Paul, by erecting shady coverings of protection, defends us by his word and deeds from the rains of [our] faults, from the fierce heat of temptations, and from the winds of the snare" (*Comm. Acts* 18:3; this "mystical" interpretation becomes common in the tradition; cf. e.g., Gloss 1180D; Hugo of St. Cher 270v F).

John Calvin notes that Paul found no one to offer him hospitality in Corinth except Aquila who was "an exile both from his native land and a foreign country." "Nothing is more wretched than exile"; yet, according to Calvin, this "fortunate misfortune of Aquila's tells us that the Lord often has better regard for our welfare, when He inflicts us rather severely, than if He were to deal with us with the utmost indulgence" (*Commentary on Acts*, 18:2). Twentieth-century historian Justo González observes: "Before Paul ever reached Corinth, the Spirit of God was already preparing the way by taking Priscilla and Aquila there. God does not act only in the history of the Church and in the lives of believers, but also in the history of the world and even in the lives of unbelievers" (González 2001, 209).

James Bailey, Seventh-Day theologian, took note of references to Paul speaking in the synagogue (18:1, 4, 11) at Corinth as a culmination of synagogue sermons and concluded (1888, 66):

> Paul reasoned in the synagogue every Sabbath. He was there seventy-eight Sabbaths. There is no mention of meetings on any other days. Adding to the seventy-eight at Corinth, three at Thessalonica, one at Philippi, and two at Antioch, we have an aggregate of eighty-four Sabbaths specifically named on this mission of Paul through Asia Minor, Macedonia and Greece, embracing a period of about ten years. Of these Sabbaths named, two were in Asia Minor, four in Macedonia, and seventy-eight in Achaia, or Greece. To thus use the Sabbath, as it is said, "his manner was," leaves the indisputable impression that for the ten years he preached Christ every Sabbath. There is no mention made in all the history of this mission of meetings for worship on any other specific day. He never alludes to any change of the Sabbath under Christ. The historian of the mission, Luke, calls it Sabbath each time. The mission included the time from A.D. 45 to 55, or from twelve to twenty-two years after the resurrection.

Eighteenth-century American evangelist Henry Alline observed that not only did Christ come "in the form of a servant; poor, despised and rejected; a man of sorrows and acquainted with grief" [Isa 53:3], but "he first made choice of poor despised men, fisher-men, and tent makers [Acts 18. 3] to spread the gospel, and many of them illiterate men, so he does commonly still" (Alline and Randall 1804, 229). American missiologist W.O. Carver (1868–1954) acknowledges the "manly independence" of Paul's manual labor reflected here in Acts 18 but, appealing to the Philippian monetary gift referenced by Paul in Phil 4, Carver uses the text as an opportunity to make a not-so-veiled reference to the need to provide financial assistance to contemporary missionary endeavors:

> In large measure Paul supported himself and those who attended him in work; but was glad to be free from this necessity. He had a manly independence but he had more time to devote to his mission work when supported. ... Paul was careful to accept this only as a gift to the cause, not to himself, and to point out that its chief value was to the giving church. He fully recognizes that by this gift the givers entered into participation with his grace of being a missionary and that the results of the enlargement of his work on account of their gifts was fruit that increased to their account (Carver 1909, 202–03).

The Public Accusation before Gallio (Acts 18:12–17)

In a rarely depicted scene in the visual tradition, the thirteenth-century Latin manuscript, Codex Chigi (Cod.A.IV.74) portrays Paul before the proconsul Gallio (fol.137v; see Acts 18:12–17). Gallio is seated and raises his right hand

FIGURE 38   *Paul led to Gallio* and *Paul in Boat with Priscilla and Aquila*. 1200–25.
Manuscript illumination. fol. 137v. Cod. Chigi.A.IV.74. © 2012 Biblioteca Apostolica
Vaticana. Photo: By permission of Biblioteca Vaticana, all rights reserved.

with index finger extended as a gesture of judgment (**Figure 38**). The gesture
echoes that of Herod's depiction earlier in the same manuscript, when Herod
orders the execution of James and arrest of Peter (Cod.Chigi.A.IV.fol.130r).
There Herod wears a crown, indicating he is a "king" and is backed by a soldier
with a sword. His orders are simultaneously being carried out: another soldier
has his sword raised above the head of a kneeling St. James, and Peter is led away
by a third armed soldier. Similarly, in the scene depicting Stephen's stoning
(124v), a seated figure (presumably a leader of the Sanhedrin; this detail is missing from Acts) raises his right hand with index finger extended in judgment. In
his left hand he holds a sword, a sign of foreboding danger for the Christian community. The religious leaders are shown in the process of stoning Stephen, whose

back is turned to them as he falls to the ground, covered with stones. The present scene depicting Gallio differs somewhat, presumably because his judgment is different from that of the Sanhedrin or Herod. According to the Acts narrative, rather than enter into what he considers an intra-Jewish debate over Jewish law, Gallio renders a judgment that is essentially a non-judgment: "I refuse to be a judge of these things" (18:16). Standing next to St. Paul are two Jewish leaders indicated by their pointed, cone-shaped hats (Latin: *pilleus cornutus*). The one closer to Paul is clutching his chest as if to indicate surprise at Gallio's decision.

Paul is barefooted, indicating either (1) his status as an Apostle of Christ, or (2) his identification with society's vulnerable and disenfranchised. Beginning with the Pentecost scene (fol.117v), only the Apostles are barefooted in the illuminations (see Peter and John in Acts 3–4, fol.119r; Peter in Acts 9, fol. 127v and in Acts 10, fol.128r; James and Peter in Acts 12, fol.130r). Before the Apostles are "baptized" with the Spirit at Pentecost, the Apostles are depicted with shoes in the Ascension scene (fol. 116v, which shows Christ as barefooted); similarly, Paul has covered feet prior to his baptism (see fol. 126r). If this is the significance of the bare feet, then Barnabas (whom Luke also identifies as an "apostle" in Acts 14:14) and Silas are also granted this distinction (see fols. 132v; 135r). On the other hand, other disciples of Christ, Stephen (one of the Seven, but not an Apostle), Ananias, and other disciples, have shoes (see fol.124v, 126v). The only other barefooted character depicted in Vatican Codex Chigi is the lame man of Acts 3–4 (fol. 119r). Folio 132v seems to telescope the healing of the lame man at Lystra [Acts 14:8–10] with the scene of the Jews arriving from Antioch and Iconium to oppose Paul [Acts 14:19]. Here the man, still lame, seems to have sided with the Jews in the ensuing debate. Their shoe-lessness may also suggest an identification of the Apostles with the vulnerable of society, thus fulfilling Jesus' command to the Apostles to travel shoeless (Matt 10:10/Luke 9:3/Luke 10:4, contra Mark 6:8–9).

In "Gallio's Song," Rudyard Kipling reflects on the official's refusal to render judgment on the dispute between Paul and the religious leaders:

> All day long to the judgment-seat
> The crazed Provincials drew—
> All day long at their ruler's feet
> Howled for the blood of the Jew.
> Insurrection with one accord
> Banded itself and woke,
> And Paul was about to open his mouth
> When Achaia's Deputy spoke—
> "Whether the God descend from above
> Or the Man ascend upon high,
> Whether this maker of tents be Jove [Zeus]

> Or a younger deity—
> I will be no judge between your gods
> And your godless bickerings.
> Lictor, drive them hence with rods—
> I care for none of these things!
> Were it a question of lawful due
> Or Caesar's rule denied,
> Reason would I should bear with you
> And order it well to be tried;
> But this is a question of words and names.
> I know the strife it brings.
> I will not pass upon any your claims.
> I care for none of these things.
>   (Atwan and Wieder 1993, 360)

Paul, Priscilla, Aquila, and Apollos (Acts 18:18–28)

In an even more rare scene (bottom scene of fol. 137v in the Codex Chigi, **Figure 38**; but see also Giustiniani Codex fol. 138v), Paul is shown sailing for Syria with Priscilla and Aquila (Acts 18:18). Their hand gestures suggest they are in conversation. The structure behind Paul may represent a church building, strengthening the traditional symbolism of the ship as representative of the Christian Church. There is also an unidentified figure (a sailor?) with them in the boat. Priscilla is only the second female disciple depicted in Codex Chigi (see also Tabitha, Acts 9, in fol. 127v).

The role of Priscilla and Aquila in correcting the teacher Apollos (Acts 18:26) likewise does not go unnoticed in the exegetical tradition. Dutch humanist and theologian Desiderius Erasmus (1469–1536) notes that "Priscilla and Aquila had amended in Apollos an imperfect Christianity" and thus "have offered an example that we should courteously give help to those in whom there shines the good hope of better growth" (*Paraphrase on Acts* 18:24–19:1). Bonhoeffer also takes note of the fact that "a mature member of the congregation can teach the pastor without that being a disgrace for the pastor (Acts 18:26)" (*BW* 16:97). Under the rather innocuous heading, "Women Extended Hospitality to Preachers," Kathleen Mallory (1879–1954), Corresponding Secretary of the Southern Baptist Woman's Missionary Union, extols Priscilla as "a gracious hostess"—certainly conventional language appropriate to her mid-twentieth-century context. She continues, however, by observing that Priscilla "was a consecrated, gifted fellow worker" and further that "so diligent" were Priscilla and Aquila in their study that they "were able to instruct Apollos in the right doctrines." She concludes with this observation, remarkable for her time: "The value Paul placed upon Priscilla's service is indicated by his mentioning her name before that of her husband as he writes to the church at Rome asking to be remembered to them, 'his fellow workers'" [Rom 16:3–4] (Mallory 1949, 5–6). Nearly half a century later, scholar Charles Talbert (1997, 173) makes a similar (though more pointed) comment: "Although the *Textus Receptus* lists Aquila first, the best manuscript tradition gives Priscilla first. In Lukan practice, whichever of a pair is listed first is regarded as the dominant authority (cf. 11:30; 12:25; 13:2, 7, 13, 50). Here, then, not only is a male preacher instructed by a woman but the wife is regarded by the narrator as the dominant religious authority."

In his novel, Walter Wangerin tells the story of Paul from the perspective of various characters including Luke, Timothy, Annaeus Seneca, and Paul himself. The story begins from the perspective of Prisca (Priscilla). Later in the novel, Prisca tells of a meeting between her, Paul and Lydia [Acts 16:14–15]. Paul admits to Prisca that, until he met Lydia in Philippi, he "never thought that women could or should utter sacred words in public places. But there in Philippi I found the Spirit already working in this woman with power. How could I contradict the Spirit of God" (Wangerin 2001, 297–98). Prisca realizes Paul's words also apply to her. She asks:

> "So then it was not you, Paul … but God … who chose me to prophesy?"
> He looked at me. "God, yes. To prophesy, yes." … "To practice that spiritual gift, upbuilding the people, encouraging them, consoling them—yes Prisca. God chose you to edify the church" (Wangerin 2001, 298).

Later Paul asks Prisca to serve as Lydia's mentor, teaching her how to build a church in Thyatira. The chapter ends with a delightful double entendre about Prisca's equality with Paul, both in tent-making and in ministry: "I plucked up his [Paul's] right hand, selected the long forefinger, laid it beside mine in the light, and showed Lydia how the apostle and I had the self-same callus in the self-same place because we did the self-same work in leather and tents. "Equals," I said. Paul blinked. Lydia let out a glad whoop—and so we began" (Wangerin 2001, 300).

Acts 19

Disciples of John in Ephesus (19:1–7)

The account of Paul's conveying the Spirit on believers in Ephesus, who "knew only the baptism of John" and had not even heard of the Spirit (Acts 19:3), figured in debates about infant baptism and rebaptism. The early Baptist confession, *Propositions and Conclusions* (1612–14), appeals to Acts 19:4 ("John indeed baptized with the baptism of repentence," answered Paul, "telling the people to believe on One who was coming after him, namely, on Jesus") in its claim that "the outward church visible, consists of penitent persons only, and of such as believing in Christ bring forth fruits worthy amendment of life (I Tim. vi. 3, 5; 2 Tim. iii. l, 5; Acts xix. 4)." British pastor Henry Denne (1642: 32–34; cf. 1643, 19–20) clarifies the role of John the Baptist in the call for repentance that leads to remission of sins: "This glosse is warranted, *Act.* 19.4. *John verily Baptized with the Baptisme of Repentance, saying that they should believe in him that should come after, that is in Christ Iesus:* Thus Iohn makes low the mountains, cuts off legall prerogatives, and bringeth downe every high imagination and every thought that exalteth it selfe against God."

Baptists such as Christopher Blackwood (1646, 23) and George Hammon (1658, 38) use Acts 19:1–7 to argue (again) against infant baptism. Further, Blackwood, while acknowledging that Acts 19 states that John's disciples were baptized in the name of Jesus only, dismisses the notion that their knowledge of the Trinity was somehow insufficient: "though sometime persons were baptized in the name of the Lord Jesus, yet doubtlesse had those persons a knowledge of the Trinity. Yea, and *Iohns* Disciples also had the same knowledge; in that the Spirit descended visibly like a Dove upon Christ, at his baptisme, and a voice cried out; *This is my beloved Sonne, in whom I am well pleased.* Matth. 3. 16, 17. Where Father, Son, and Spirit, are all named."

American General Baptist A.D. Williams (1825–1894), on the other hand, claims that John's baptism:

> Lacked elements deemed by every one essential to Christian baptism,—It was not in the name of the Son or Holy Ghost. … For these reasons, Paul rebaptized certain disciples at Ephesus, who had been baptized with John's baptism. Acts 19:5. For the same reason, any Christian minister would now rebaptize any one who had been baptized only in the way John baptized. Obviously, it [sic] they had been baptized by John's baptism, it was not the baptism the Master instituted in the Great Commission [Matt 28:19–20]. At most, it was but an imperfect preparatory substitute for it, lacking essential features.

In a remarkable turn, however, Williams goes on to argue that such persons should not be excluded from the Lord's Supper:

> If we believed baptism essential to communion, we would as readily accept pedobaptist baptism, lacking only in form, as John's baptism, lacking the more essential feature of regenerating faith.
> So, when the Lord's Table is spread, all the Lord's children, however weak and erring, if so be they are his children, though feeling their unworthiness like a load upon them, should hear the Master say, "Drink ye all of it!"—and obey (Williams, *The Lord's Supper*).

Others are not so readily able to resolve the difficulties posed by this passage, especially with regard to the question of rebaptism. English Puritan Henry Lawrence (1600–1664) admits that if rebaptism were the issue of Acts 19, then water baptism would have been the mode, but Lawrence himself concludes, apparently against the claims of the text itself (cf. 19:5): "I am of opinion with those that thinke that *Paul* did not here command any to bee baptized in the Name of the Lord Jesus, which were already baptized with the baptisme of *John*, but rather taught that those who had received *Johns* baptisme were rightly baptized into Christ, and therefore had no need of any new, or other baptisme" (Lawrence 1651, 38). Later interpreters will solve this issue by claiming that, strictly speaking, the baptism of Acts 19 was not a rebaptism: "Their former immersion was with such limited understanding and intent that Paul was not able to recognize it as Christian baptism, and so baptism—not re-baptism—was now administered. The fault was in the intent, in the symbolism. This was so defective that it was no baptism. It is not well to speak of re-baptism. There is but 'one baptism.' An immersion is either baptism or it is not" (Carver 1916, 189–90; cf. Robertson 1930, 4–5; Stagg 1955, 195–97). John Wesley (1703–91) agrees that, strictly speaking, this was not a case of Christian rebaptism: "They were baptized twice; but not with the same baptism. John did not administer that baptism which Christ afterward commanded, that is, in the name of the Father, Son, and Holy Ghost" (*ENNT*, Acts 19:5). Pentecostal theologian Howard Ervin (1984, 48; 1987, 80) and Baptist theologian Dale Moody (1968, 65–69) also explore the relationship between water and Spirit baptism.

Karl Barth offers a fascinating, and in the history of interpretation practically unique, interpretation on Acts 19:1–7. Barth argues that 19:5 refers to those persons who had come to be baptized by John and *not* to John's disciples being rebaptized by Paul! In effect, Paul's quotation ends at verse 5 and not 4:

A saying which Ac. 19[4f.] attributes to Paul when he was talking to the disciples of John found at Ephesus is perhaps typical of the view of John's baptism which obviously came to be held quite generally—and it is interesting that the saying is traced back or attributed to Paul. It runs as follows: "John verily baptised with the baptism of repentance (ἐβάπτισεν βάπτισμα μετανοίας), saying unto the people that they should believe on him which should come after him, that is, on Christ Jesus. When they (not John's disciples, but the people at the Jordan) heard this, they were baptised in the name of the Lord Jesus." What needs to be said authoritatively to these disciples of John (v. 6f.) by the laying on of Paul's hands is simply that in being baptised by John they did in fact accomplish the conversion to Jesus which was the point of his baptism, they did in fact meet the requirement that they should believe in Him, and therefore, baptised in His name, they already belong to His people and are Christians. That this is so is confirmed at once by the fact that their earlier disturbed confession to Paul: "We have not so much as heard whether there be any Holy Ghost" (v. 2), is rendered pointless, since there at once comes on them that which on the Day of Pentecost had come on the disciples, who had probably been baptised by John too: "The Holy Ghost came on them; and they spake with tongues, and prophesied." Those baptised by John in the Jordan were as such truly called, invited and summoned to faith in Jesus Christ. Accepting John's baptism, they made in fact a genuine confession of Jesus Christ (*CD* 4.4.62).

In a remarkable exchange, Thomas Grantham (1633/34–1692) and Henry Danvers (ca. 1619–1687/8) debate the practice of the laying on of hands, a debate in which Acts 19:6 figures prominently. Based on his reading of Acts 8 and 19, Grantham (1671, 24–25) insists that the act "was not the laying on of Hands for extraordinarie gifts, but for the general donation of the Spirit to Disciples indifferently" and that it was to be practiced universally (and was not limited to Apostolic times). Danvers replies: "And as to that of *Ephesus*, Acts 19. 6, *Paul* it seems, finding some of the *Church* there, that had not received the Spirit after they had *believed* and were baptized, *viz.* in that visible *manner* so usually given in those days, layes his hands upon twelve men of their number; (it is not said all the Church) ... in neither of these two places [Acts 8:17 and 19:6] can we find that there was a *laying* on of hands *immediately* after *Baptism*, nor with any *certainty* upon all and every *Member* of the Church, nor to such an end as can be attainable in after-times" (Danvers 1674, 47). Grantham disputes Danvers' claim that these disciples were members of the church at Ephesus (anticipating the argument of Carver and others that these had not received Christian baptism) and infers that the laying on of hands at baptism would, in fact, have already been administered to those in the Ephesian church:

> Furthermore, Mr. *D.* [Danvers] doth certainly mistake *Act.* 19.2 in saying the Twelve Disciples at *Ephesus* were of the Church, whereas the Scripture, and Reason, do both inform us they could not be Imbodied with the Church ... Again, their great ignorance of the Holy Ghost shews plainly they were not united to the Body or Church at *Ephesus* ... And Lastly, their being Baptized again, shews plainly they were not of the Church, for if they had, why must not the Church also be Baptized again as well as they? (Grantham 1674, 20–21; cf. Orthodox Creed 1678, Article XXXII; Collins 1680, 34–36).

Paul and the Handkerchiefs (19:11–12)

The account of Paul and healing by means of handkerchiefs in Acts 19:11–12 is echoed in the testimonies regarding the healing efficacies associated with the cult of the saints in late antiquity, In the case cited below, the transfer of the martyrs' remains by Ambrose to the altar of the cathedral did no doubt help consolidate his bishopric authority in Milan (see Brown 1981, 36–37). Consider, for example, Ambrose's report to his congregation regarding the discovery of the remains of the martyrs Gervasius and Protasius in 386 C.E. He commented on the healing efficacy of the martyr's remains:

> You know—nay, you have yourselves seen—that many are cleansed from evil spirits, that very many also, having touched with their hands the robe of the saints, are freed from those ailments which oppressed them; you see that the miracles of old time are renewed, when through the coming of the Lord Jesus grace was more largely shed forth upon the earth, and that many bodies are healed as it were by the shadow of the holy bodies. How many napkins are passed about! How many garments, laid upon the holy relics and endowed with healing power, are claimed! All are glad to touch even the outside thread, and whosoever touches will be made whole (*Letter* 77.9).

Fourth-century Bishop of Milan Ambrose also reports on a miracle that occurred to a blind butcher, Severus, during the transfer of the remains for burial. Severus, Ambrose reports, was able to call as witnesses those who had previously known him.

> They [the Arians] deny that the blind man received sight, but he denies not that he is healed. He says: I who could not see now see. He says: I ceased to be blind, and proves it by the fact. They deny the benefit, who are unable to deny the fact. The man is known: so long as he was well he was employed in the public service; his name is Severus, a butcher by trade. He had given up his occupation when this hindrance befell him. He calls for evidence those persons by whose kindness he was supported; he adduces those as able to affirm the truth of his visitation whom he had as witnesses of his blindness. He declares that when he touched the hem of the robe of the martyrs, wherewith the sacred relics were covered, his sight was restored (*Letter* 77.17; NPNF 82.3.236–127).

St. Augustine, a professor at Milan at the time, also knows this story and adds the detail that the butcher touched his handkerchief to the body of the martyr and then to his eyes, achieving instantaneous recovery of sight (*Conf.* 9.7.16).

About reported miracles associated with relics, and this account by Ambrose in particular, Ronald Kydd observed: "One must avoid rank credulity when faced with these accounts. Nonetheless, I find it difficult to state categorically that nothing extraordinary ever happened. The story of Ambrose's butcher who received his sight back is remarkable by any standard" (1998, 129).

In response to criticisms regarding abuses related to medieval relics and indulgences, the Council of Trent, in its twenty-fifth session (December 1563) issued a call for reform "in the invocation of saints, the veneration of relics, and the sacred use of images" in that "every superstition shall be removed, all filthy lucre be abolished; finally, all lasciviousness be avoided." The Council of Trent also clarified the relationship between the relics and the martyrs themselves in a way consistent with Luke's emphasis that the healing bore testimony to the "extraordinary deeds" of God and not to the efficacy of the cloth or even the saint: "Also, that the holy bodies of holy martyrs, and of others now living with Christ,—which bodies were the living members of Christ, and the temple of the Holy Ghost, and which are by Him to be raised unto eternal life, and to be glorified,—are to be venerated by the faithful; through which (bodies) many benefits are bestowed by God on men; so that they who affirm that veneration and honour are not due to the relics of saints" (Session XXV, December, 1563; Martin Luther makes a similar distinction calling the "sufferings" of the martyrs the "true relics"; cf. *LW* 31:226).

Other (Protestant) commentators on Acts 19:11–12 have noted, "this practice often strikes the modern mind as too close to the relic worship that plagued the medieval church" (Polhill 1992, 402). In so doing, they echo the criticisms of the Protestant reformers who objected to the abuses of the sale of relics as part of the indulgence system. This system was widespread, very lucrative, and subject to much abuse in medieval Christianity (see Brown 1981). In his commentary on Acts 19, John Calvin wrote: "The Papists are more blockish, who wrest this place unto their relics; as if Paul sent his handkerchiefs that men might worship them and kiss them in honour of them ... Yea, rather, he did choose most simple things, lest any superstition arise by reason of the price or pomp (*Commentary on Acts*, 2:215).

The rise of critical scholarship often saw this passage treated with derision. English deist Peter Annet (1693–1769), for example, "wondered how long these aprons or handkerchiefs must have been with the holy Paul, to be thus impregnated with this healing quality" and if they "resisted sweat, or could stand a lather" (Annett n.d., 88–89; cited by Baird 1992, 51). German exegete Heinrich Ewald (1803–1875), on the other hand, found the account wholly plausible (beyond even the usually accepting Ramsey 1897; Baird 2003, 2.193):

> The healing power of the man who was always speaking such holy words, and himself living such a holy life, was so much in request that even the handkerchiefs and the short aprons which he wore on his breast at his work, were asked for and laid upon the sick while they were still warm from his skin, and in the case of certain evils, demoniacal possession for instance, relief was thereby found (Ewald 1885, 68; cited in Baird 1992, 1.292).

In contemporary times, Scott Shauf has noted "the embarrassment with which many commentators have viewed the passage on the outstanding character of Paul's miracles, especially concerning the use of Paul's garments without his active involvement" (Shauf 2005, 111). No doubt this embarrassment is due, in part, to the multiple examples of abusive misinterpretation of the verses. Consider, for example, the exploitations of various tele-evangelists,

- 3 -

Jesus is here for you! I am with you in this! Just as
His miraculous power and strength healed the woman of her
plague (when she touched the hem of His garment), I am
praying that your miracle will begin as you touch the
enclosed piece of cloth/hem that's anointed with power for
your special miracle need.

Something supernatural takes place when you release
your faith through something that is anointed and used as a
miracle point of contact. ✳It links your faith to God. ✳It
plugs your need into His miracle source of power.

Matthew 14:35-36 explains how people brought the sick
to Jesus "THAT THEY MIGHT ONLY TOUCH THE HEM OF HIS GARMENT:
AND AS MANY AS TOUCHED [His hem] WERE MADE PERFECTLY WHOLE."

The apostle Paul saw the very same miracle results in
his own ministry. Acts 19:11-12 describes how cloths from
his body were laid upon the sick, and diseases and evil
spirits departed. It says that "SPECIAL MIRACLES" took place
this way. *Do you need a special miracle?*

It was a means by which Paul could be with those who
needed to be ministered to without having to physically
stand in their presence. That anointing...that power...that
miracle presence of Jesus was somehow resident in the very
fabric of the cloth. He would send it to those who desired a
SPECIAL MIRACLE and their united faith was honored by God.

AND THAT IS HOW I AM COMING TO YOU! You are on the
brink of another miracle. I am excited about what God is
about to do for you as you release your faith and apply this
anointed prayer cloth. I BELIEVE THAT IT IS TRULY AN
ANOINTED CARRIER OF MIRACLE VIRTUE THAT HAS FLOWED FROM THE
JESUS WHO IS IN ME, TO THIS MATERIAL, TO YOU!

N✱E✱X✱T: I want to personally
MINISTER TO YOU BY PRAYING over the specific
areas of your life where you need your
SPECIAL MIRACLE.

TAKE THE ENCLOSED PRAYER REQUEST SHEET AND
CAREFULLY WRITE DOWN YOUR MIRACLE REQUESTS.
Not only do I want to be WITH YOU IN THE
SPIRIT (through this letter and anointed
prayer cloth), but I want to be WITH YOU
IN SPIRIT THROUGH POWERFUL ANOINTED
PERSONAL PRAYER!

F✱I✱N✱A✱L✱L✱Y: PUT FIRST THINGS FIRST. Instead of
going to God with your hand out, come to Him with a gift in
your hand. Sow a seed of faith that he can bless and return
to you in the form of a SPECIAL MIRACLE HARVEST. You see,
it's a law! You can't reap a harvest until you plant a seed.

*keep reading
on page 4 →
- over -*

DOCUMENT 1   Faith Healer Mailer

who have employed "prayer cloths" as part of a mass mailing campaign to fleece the pockets of the faithful. Such abuses are noted by Justo González: "The reference to Paul's handkerchiefs and aprons has provided some supposed evangelists with an opportunity to make money by selling handkerchiefs and other items they have blessed" (González 2001, 222). This point is illustrated by the handbill below received by the authors in 1991.

We might balance these obvious instances of abuse by noting other examples of "mediated grace," which are more in keeping with the Lukan purpose of demonstrating the "extraordinary deeds" of God. The use of "devotional cloths" goes back to the very beginnings of the Pentecostal Movement (Roebuck 2006, 143–44). R. Marie Griffith has collected testimonies by American Pentecostal women in the 1930s, published in several different denominational weekly organs, the *Evangel* (Church of God of Cleveland, Tennessee), *The Advocate* (Pentecostal Holiness Church), and the *Whole Truth* (African-American, Memphis-based Church of God in Christ) (Griffith 2002, 188–89). She writes: "A common practice reported in the letters printed in Pentecostal devotional materials, whether the audience was predominately white or black, was the use of 'anointed handkerchiefs' in procuring physical healings. This practice found scriptural basis in the nineteenth chapter of Acts (11–12)" (Griffith 2002, 197). Griffith cites several examples (Griffith 2002, 197–98):

> I received the letter and anointed cloths from you, for which I thank the Lord. My heart rejoiced and the power of God came upon me as I applied the cloth to my breast. I could feel the affected part being drawn, and when I applied the second cloth it completely left. I have not felt the hurting any more. I thank the Lord for being healed (Sister L. Banks, Fresno, CA, *Whole Truth* 9 [May 1933]: 2).

> I received the letter with the anointed handkerchief and wonderful blesings I received after I placed one to my body. ... I surely do feel so much better (Mrs. Minnie Johnson, *The Advocate*, Nov. 9, 1933, 15).

More often than not, these handkerchiefs came from other Pentecostal women (and not necessarily, or even often, from the hands of powerful Pentecostal preachers); e.g., Della Turtle sent out this simple request: "Will somebody send me a handkerchief?" (*The Advocate*, May 7, 1931, 13). Furthermore, there was rarely money involved, except perhaps to cover mailing costs. Sister Maxwell's offer was typical: "Many write us that they have been wonderfully blest by application of the anointed handkerchiefs. Please remember to send stamps to pay for mailing same. It is not necessary for you to send handkerchiefs, as we have the thin soft material cut in sizes suitable for mailing. We can put a dozen of these in a letter if needed" (Sister Berta Maxwell, *The Advocate*, May 23, 1935, 7). However one evaluates these testimonies, their tone and intent are markedly different from the corruptions more commonly associated with the kind of modern mass mailings of TV evangelists referenced by González above. As Griffith notes: "The handkerchiefs themselves are just the most ordinary of objects. We use them to wipe away tears or sweat, or blow our noses—just the most ordinary kinds of bodily stuff. But even as these are objects of divine grace, they are also objects of human kindness and generosity. You can see the power of asking someone for a handkerchief out of desperation—when you have tuberculosis or some degenerative disease—and all these handkerchiefs flood into you from this widespread community of people you may never have met before" (Griffith 2002).

This miracle of St. Paul at Ephesus is rarely depicted in the visual arts. The painting illustrated here, although attributed to Jean Restout by Art Resource, is not included in the exhibitions or in the lists of either the attributed or rejected works by the painter (**Figure 39**). Given the rarity of the subject and the variety of styles painted during the eighteenth century in France (Late Baroque, Rococo, Neoclassicism), for our purpose we will discuss the painting as a Restout. The painting exhibits classicizing characteristics of the Late Baroque which correspond to Jean Restout. Michael Levey stated that Jean Restout continued the

FIGURE 39   Jean Restout (1692–1768). *The Miracle of St. Paul at Ephesus.* c. 1740. Oil. Musée des Beaux-Arts, Rouen, France. Photo: Bridgeman-Giraudon/Art Resource, NY

restrained French version of the Counter Reformation and was a principal religious painter of eighteenth-century France (Levey 1985, 36).

At this time in the history of art, the most popular style was French Rococo. Rococo artists were concerned with excessive life styles, afternoon excursions and lighthearted themes and colors. This is not the case with our painting. Philip Conisbee commented when reviewing a 1970 exhibition of Restout's work in Rouen, that "it is instructive, if not wholly delightful, to take a step back from the boudoir and the cabinet and consider the 'serious' and 'committed' grand manner" (Conisbee 1970, 768).

Paul at Ephesus is presented as a miracle worker of extraordinary charismatic power. Paul's healing powers are conveyed through skin contact with inanimate objects (cloths, aprons). It is important for Luke to convey that Paul's spiritual power does not come from him but rather is a direct divine endorsement of his mission (Alexander 2001, 1052). Paul stands heroically in heavy red drapery at the top of steps and in the center of a pyramidal composition. Monumental columns and architecture flank him on both sides and further emphasize him as the center of attention. The figures (male and female) surround him and look towards Paul. Even the marble statue on the left directs the viewer's attention to Paul! We can identify the narrative as we see the white cloth being placed in front of Paul. Paul looks to heaven and blesses it with his right hand.

There are two groups of people on the stairs. The group of four to the right includes a man on a stretcher who leans towards Paul and extends both arms towards him. The cloth about to be blessed is probably his and he is hopeful and determined to receive this healing. The group of three on the lower left side of the composition have already received a cloth touched by Paul. A man wraps it around the seemingly crippled legs of another man sitting at the base of the steps in the lower left of the composition. The woman in pink gown and blue mantle looks back towards Paul as the next cloth is about to be touched, her hands facing the man whose legs are being wrapped. She will look back towards him momentarily and witness the healing. Garments painted in brilliant yellows, rich blues, and vibrant pink punctuate the composition and heighten the drama and miraculous action occurring in the painting. Restout's working methods were the traditional ones of an academic history painter. He did many preparatory drawings, in a firm and decisive style, but with freedom of touch rather than tight control (Turner and Conisbee 2012). The "Grand Manner" of history painting has been applied to a dramatic and exciting religious subject at a time when the French audience became increasingly interested in the hedonistic silk sheets of Jean-Honoré Fragonard and the afternoon excursions with wine and women of Antoine Watteau.

Acts 20–23

Overview

In Acts 20, Luke records the beginning of Paul's last journey to Jerusalem (20:1–16) and his farewell address to the Ephesian elders (20:17–38). In chapters 21–26, Paul is subjected to arrest and questioning by a series of officials: the Roman tribune, the Jewish Sanhedrin, the Roman governors Felix and Festus, and the Jewish (?) king Herod Agrippa.

The Acts of the Apostles Through the Centuries, First Edition. Heidi J. Hornik and Mikeal C. Parsons.
© 2017 Heidi J. Hornik and Mikeal C. Parsons. Published 2017 by John Wiley & Sons, Ltd.

The story of Eutychus, who falls out of a window (20:7–11) provides some comic relief and also opportunity for allegorical moralizing. Most interpretations have gravitated to two verses, Acts 20:7 and 20:28. Acts 20:7 figures prominently in debates regarding the timing of the Christian Sabbath. Acts 20:28a is important in debates regarding ecclesial leadership, and interpreters of 20:28b have been vexed by the phrase "with his own blood" (or the "blood of his Own"). As always, there are other interesting comments on isolated verses. The agraphon (an isolated saying of Jesus unattested elsewhere) quoted by Paul in Acts 20:35 ("It is more blessed to give than to receive") has generated much reflection among theologians and has been a favorite slogan in the political rhetoric of American Presidents.

Acts 21–23 records Paul's travels to and time in Jerusalem. The first half of chapter 21 recounts Paul's trip through Caesarea on his way to Jerusalem (21:1–16), and interpreters are again fascinated by the reference to Philip's prophesying daughters and the struggle between Agabus and Paul over whether he should go to Jerusalem. The second half tells of his arrival and arrest in Jerusalem (Acts 21:17–40). In Acts 22 Paul addresses the angry crowd and the Roman tribune who saved him from them (22:1-29). Luke's account of Paul before with the Sanhedrin (22:30–23:11) cuts across the traditional chapter division. Interpreters have puzzled over whether or not Paul knew the identity of the High Priest and purposefully insulted him (23:1–10). The chapter ends with a report of the foiling of a plot to kill Paul (23:12–35). These chapters garner relatively little attention by interpreters, although there is one key passage in each chapter and, as usual, some interesting comments by individual interpreters on isolated verses.

Reception and Interpretation

Acts 20

Sabbath Practices (Acts 20:7)

Acts 20:7 reports that, in Troas: "On the first day of the week we met for the breaking of bread. ..." Since patristic times (cf. Augustine, *Letter* 36.12.28), interpreters have found in this verse evidence that the earliest Christian community celebrated the Christian Sabbath on Sunday, the first day of the week. Various confessions and creeds affirm this point. The Declaration of Faith (1611) asserts: "That everie Church ought (according to exampple off CHRISTS Disciples and primitive Churches) upon everie first day of the weeke, being the LORDS day, to assemble together, to pray, Prophecie, praise GOD, and breake Bread, and performe all other partes of Spirituall communion for the worship of GOD, their owne mutuall edificacion, and the preservation off true Religion, & pietie in the church Io 20.19. Act. 2.42. and 20.7. 1 Cor. 16.2." (cf., for example, Smyth 1608, 30; The Orthodox Creed 1678 XL; Second London 1689, XXII; New Hampshire 1833, 15; Hackett 1882, 232–33; Baptist Faith and Message 1925, XIV; Robertson, 339–40; GARBC 1934, XIV; Free Will Baptists 1935/2001, XIV; Stagg 1955, 211).

There were those in the patristic period who argued that Christians should observe the "Jewish Sabbath," and Acts 20:7 played a major role in that argument. In the second century, Polycrates of Ephesus (fl. 130–196) concluded in support of Christians who were worshipping on Saturday, rather than Sunday: "Those who in our own times have revived the observance of the Jewish Sabbath, show us how much may be said on their side" (Polycrates e-catena). This view persists among later groups. For example, in the nineteenth century James Bailey, recognized as the "father" of the Seventh Day Baptist Historical Society (whose members understood Scripture to mandate community worship on Saturday rather than Sunday), offers an alternative interpretation to the dominant reading:

> This passage shows a gathering of the disciples upon *one day after the Sabbath.* The object of this coming together is also clearly stated *to break bread.* Critics are divided in opinion whether the Lord's Supper or the evening meal is referred to. The same words are used in the eleventh verse, where Paul broke bread and ate. The word is used when Christ fed the multitude and when he instituted the Lord's Supper, and when he sat at meat with the two disciples at Emmaus. The sense must be determined by the circumstances. If it was the common meal, there is no sacredness attached to the time. If it was for the Lord's Supper it still remains to be shown that it belonged to Sabbath worship, and was limited to it.
>
> The greater probability, generally accepted, that the breaking of bread was for the evening meal, and not the Lord's Supper, during the evening or night of the first day of the week, and the fact that Paul journeyed from Traos to Assos, starting at break of day, and going on foot a day's journey during the daylight of the first day of the week—leave little or no evidence that that day was observed as a Sabbath-day. It was a day of traveling, and not of Sabbatizing (Bailey 1888, 86).

Karl Barth, on the other hand, understands the Christian Sabbath to be grounded not only on Christ's resurrection on the "first day" (cf. *CD* 3.4.53); he also sees in Acts 20:7 (and other relevant passages) an echo of Gen 2 and concludes that "God's seventh day was man's first. ... The time of man begins, therefore, with a day of rest and not a day of work; with freedom and not with obligations ... with joy and not with labour and toil; under the Gospel and not under the Law. These other things will all come, but when they do they will be secondary and additional. ... it was no innovation when the early Christians adopted the first day of the week as a holiday instead of the seventh" (*CD* 3.2.457–58).

Others appeal to the same verse for the practice of observing the Lord's Supper, despite the fact that there was some debate, ancient and modern, regarding whether or not the reference to "the breaking of bread" was Eucharistic (e.g., Chrysostom, *Hom. Act.* 43, apparently views it as an ordinary meal; cf. Burnside 1827, 161–62, and Bailey 1888, 5–6, cited above, who are aware of this debate). English minister Thomas Grantham (1687, 28) notes: "The Congregation being met together, and having spent part of the day in Preaching, and Prayer, commonly towards the Evening, and ordinarily upon the Lords Day, the Table is decently prepared, and the Bread and Wine set upon it also in decent manner [Acts 20. 7]." (Grantham 1687, 28; cf. First London Confession 1644, XLI; The True Gospel-Faith 1654, XVI; Free Will Baptists 1935, XV, XVIII; Baptist Faith and Message 1963, VII).

According to Augustine, the Priscillians, a fourth-century ascetic group, fasted on the Christian Sabbath, a practice based in part on their interpretation of Acts 20:7, which they took to suggest that the Apostles regularly fasted on the Lord's Day. Augustine argued that Paul's desire to leave the Ephesians with a parting discourse took precedence on that occasion over meeting the physical need of hunger. In fact, Luke "took care to explain the reason for extending the discourse in order that we might know that, if some necessity should arise, eating should not take preference over some more urgent action" ("Letter 36: Augustine to Casulanus"; *WA* 2.1.140). Augustine goes on to point to Acts 20:11, in which Luke reports that Paul and company did break bread in Acts 20:11, and that it was, in fact, still the "first day of the week" and therefore the Lord's Day.

Eutychus (Acts 20:8–12)

About Eutychus, sixth-century Latin poet and orator Arator commented: "Why do you seek the empty chaos of the window, young man, or why are you restful in that place where you will come to disaster? It is a matter harmful for well-being to seek high, hanging [places] and to wish to snatch furtive dreams on a steep couch; you were able to recline on a better resting-place, in the word of God and on the advice of Paul to desire the coming of Him whose name is the Door, accessible by the threshold of righteousness" (*OAA*, 2.81). Later Arator (2.82) offers an elaborate allegory, suggesting Eutychus fell from the "third story," thus identifying himself with the wild beasts who occupied the third story of Noah's ark! John Wesley (1703–91) offered this pastoral comment on the Eutychus text (Acts 20:12): "But alas! How many of those who have allowed themselves to sleep under sermons, or as it were to dream awake, have slept the sleep of eternal death, and fallen to rise no more!" (*ENNT*, Acts 20:12).

The Australian poet, Rosemary Dobson (1920–2012) wrote an 11-verse poem commemorating Eutychus. It ends:

> I like this story of young Eutychus
> For I, like him, am troubled too, and weak,
> And may, like him, be too preoccupied
> To listen if a saint should come to speak.
> And yet, I think, if some event befall
> To bring me face to face with holiness,
> I should not fail to recognize the truth
> And spring to life again, like Eutychus
> (Antwan and Wieder 1993, 262).

Visual Reception of Paul and Eutychus

Figure 40, is a pen and ink and wash drawing by Domenico Tiepolo (1727–1804), today located in the Louvre. Domenico Tiepolo is the son of Giambattista Tiepolo and was born while his father was working in Udine. Father and son worked throughout the Republic of Venice in the eighteenth century. There is no contemporary account of Domenico's career subsequent to the notes of Vincenzo da Canal in his *Vita di Gregorio Lazzarini*, written in 1732, though not published until 1809 (Knox 1996: 39).

Domenico produced a long series of independent, large biblical drawings (about 12" × 19") that stand apart from the preparatory studies for paintings and etchings (Knox 1996, 49). Over the years, approximately 270 drawings from the Large Biblical Series have appeared on the art market and in published catalogs. Most of the subjects of the drawings are taken from the four Gospels and the Acts of the Apostles, but Domenico was fascinated with apocryphal stories surrounding the birth and upbringing of the Virgin, which derive from the *Protoevangelium of James* and *Pseudo-Matthew* (Knox 1996, 51).

About a third of the drawings in the Large Biblical Series portray the Acts of the Apostles, with particular attention given to illustrating the lives of saints Peter and Paul (Gealt 1996, 83). In the little-known story from Acts 20:8–12, a young man named Eutychus is listening to a rather lengthy sermon by Paul, drifts off to sleep, falls out of the window and is resuscitated. Domenico, a storyteller like Luke, chooses to divide the event into three drawings. In the first drawing Eutychus falls from the window (Guerlain 1921, pl 121). The drawing illustrated here shows him lying dead on the ground. (Domenico takes some creative license by placing the window on the first rather than the third level of the building.) The final drawing depicts his resuscitation and is in the Recueil Fayet collection.

FIGURE 40   Domenico Tiepolo (1727–1804). *St. Paul Stands Before the Body of Eutychus*. c. 1785. Pen and brown ink, brown wash, on beige paper, 48.7 × 38cm. Photo: Jean-Gilles Berizzi. Louvre, Paris, France. Photo Credit: Réunion des Musées Nationaux/Art Resource, NY

A variety of reactions occur in the Louvre drawing. A young man in the center of the drawing raises his arms in despair. The elevated arms of several others can also be seen. A young woman crosses her arms on her chest with a calm acceptance, or even a prayerful response to the accident. The majority of the remaining people slump over Eutychus' body with their hands on their knees to support the weight of their own bodies. They are examining, without touching, the body before them. Paul stands with his sword to the right side.

Biblical scholar Loveday Alexander offers an explanation as to the time of day for this event and an explanation of who Eutychus may have been based on his name and living accommodations (Alexander 2001, 1053). The event is an evening gathering, after work, which may explain why Eutychus was so tired. The extended teaching session by Paul would have occurred first, followed by the breaking of the bread and a communal meal that finished at dawn. So not only had Eutychus (a common slave name) worked all day, but he probably had not eaten. The third-story room suggests a working-class insula or apartment block rather than the atrium of a villa or town house. Paul's prompt action to save the boy recalls the miracles of Elijah and Elisha; the description of the body as dead implies that Luke intends us to see this as a real miracle, not just a lucky escape (Alexander 2001, 1053).

Paul's Farewell Address to the Ephesian Elders (Acts 20:13–38)

Before Paul takes leave of the Ephesians, he delivers a heartfelt address (20:13–38). A verse from that address, Acts 20:21, formed the basis of a sermon preached by Walter Brooks (1851–1945), a former slave who became a prominent African-American pastor of the Nineteenth Street Baptist Church in Washington, D.C. (1881–1945). In a sermon, "Repentance toward God," preached on September 15, 1940, Brooks, fond of writing poetry for his sermons, included a poem that began with these words:

> Repentance unto God [Acts 20:21]
> Is turning from your wrongs
> And rendering unto God
> What unto God belongs
> (Brooks 1945, 126).

Later in his speech (Acts 20:28), Paul issues a warning about false teachers. Acts 20:28a ("Take heed to yourselves and to all the flock of which the Holy Spirit has appointed you overseers [or "bishops"], and be shepherds of the church of God ...") is the other verse in chapter 20 that has served as the fount of much theological reflection. This first half of the verse was seen by many to speak to the issue of church leadership in terms of the kinds of officers and their function. Martin Luther appealed to Acts 20:28 as part of his critique of the bishopric:

> Therefore it should be noted that it was Paul's ordinance [Acts 20:17] that he should select "elders" (in the plural) in each city, and they are called bishops and elders. Therefore at the time of the apostles every city had numerous bishops.

Then Christianity was in outstanding condition. This meaning of the word "bishop" disappeared, and it was subjected to very long and very distorted abuse. Now it is called the human ordinance by which a man is in charge of five cities. Thus human traditions are never harmless, no matter how good they may be. ... The apostolate has now become the office of acquiring property and of putting on pomp. There is no doctrine, not to speak of words and deeds. Every city ought to have many bishops, that is, inspectors or visitors. ... This apostolic type of episcopacy has long since been done away with. In Acts 20:28 Paul speaks of the bishops of a single church: "Take heed ... in which the Holy Spirit has made you bishops." All bishops nowadays are of the devil. There is no hope of salvation in any of them. They sit in the seats of bishops, and no one of them is a teacher. If they do not function in the office of a bishop, one cannot tell who is feeding the sheep ("Lectures on Titus" 1.1; *LW* 29:16-17).

These debates were not ivory tower discussions among academics. They were real battles (including with civil authorities over civil and ecclesial jurisdiction), and the disputes had serious personal and institutional consequences (not infrequently resulting in imprisonment or even death).

The Declaration of Faith (1611, 20), formulated by the first English Baptists in Amsterdam, advocated for a "uniform" ministry (elders and deacons): "That the Officers of everie Church or congregation are either Elders, who by their office do especially feed the flock concerning their souls, Acts 20.28, Pet 5.2, 3. or Deacons Men, and Women who by their office releave the necessities off the poore and impotent brethrē concerning their bodies, Acts. 6.1–4." Early Baptist John Smyth (1608, 22) specifies that two of the four functions of elders are derived from Acts 20:28 (and 1 Pet 5:2), namely, to oversee and feed the flock (cf. Knollys 1681, 4–5). The first London Confession (1644, XXXVII) elaborates this point by asserting that elders are "carefully to feed the flock of Christ committed to them, nor for filthy lucre, but of a ready mind. [Acts 4. 23. Acts 20. 28.]." Smyth (1608, 26) uses Acts 20:28 (and 20:17) to argue that Scripture did not support the hierarchical view of a one pastor/one church (that would lay the foundation for a nascent bishopric system):

> First, it can never be proved by the Scriptures that there was, but one pastor in a Church: It is plaine, Act. 20.28. That there were many in the Church of Ephesus (that was one of those seaven Churches [Rev 2–3]) that did performe the work of the pastor which is pomainein, to leed, even all the Elders of Ephesus: Act. 20. vers 17, compared with vers. 28. And therefore ther wer many Pastors in the Church of Ephesus in Paul's tyme.

Several centuries later, J.M. Pendleton, advocate of Landmarkism (which emphasized the complete autonomy and primacy of the local congregation), makes the same point, albeit in a pithier fashion: "The Church at Ephesus had a plurality of bishops; but, so far as we know, no bishop in apostolic times had a plurality of churches" (1884, 361). The Declaration of Faith (1611, 22) makes a related point regarding the relationship of clergy to the local autonomy of churches when it claims "That the Officers of everie Church or congregacion are tied by Office onely to that particular congregacion whereoff they are chosen, Act. 14.23, and 20.17. Tit. 1.5. And therefore they cannot challeng by office anie authoritie in any other congregation whatsoever, except they would have an Apostleship."

Several interpreters mention the role of the Spirit in choosing church leaders. Puritan Henry Lawrence (1600–1664) observed: "And as the holy Ghost doth preside the Ministry of preaching, so the ordinary Officers and Elders of the Church were sayd to be made *Overseers [or "bishops"] by the holy ghost to feed the Church of God which he had purchased with his own blood, Acts* 20.28" (Lawrence 1649, 78–79; cf. Lawrence 1659, 177–79; Gordon 1894, 134–45; Pinnock 1996, 130-31).

Others focused on the last phrase of Acts 20:28b ("the church of God which he has purchased with his own blood"), a passage that has become a *crux interpretum* for Christian doctrine. There is debate regarding both textual and translation issues. Many manuscripts agree with the translation above and read "the Church of God"), while Codex D (Bezae) amongst others reads "the Church of the Lord." The difference between the two is one letter in a *nomen sacrum* ΘY (for "*theou*" "of God") and KY (for "kuriou of the Lord"; cf. Metzger 1994, 480). Most translations agree with the reading "of God." Further, there is the question of whether the phrase *dia tou aimatos tou idiou* should be translated "with his own blood" (so NIV; Barrett 1998, 2:976), which creates something of a theological problem; does God have blood (see below)? Others render the phrase "with the blood of his Own" (Darby) or, more explicitly, "with the blood of his own Son" (NRSV).

A number of early Baptist confessions refer to the divine sacrifice of Christ, based on this verse, as do individual interpreters. The Somerset Confession (1656, XV) links the verse to a standard understanding of the atonement, that through Christ's "death upon the cross, he hath obtained eternal redemption and deliverance for his church (Col 1:14; Eph. 1:7; Acts 20:28; Heb. 9:12; I Pet 1:18, 19.)." The First London Confession (1644, XVIII) explores the death of Jesus in terms of his two natures, human and divine: "hee was a sacrifice most properly according to his humane nature: whence in the scripture it is wont to be attributed to his body, to his blood; yet the chiefe force whereby this sacrifice was made effectuall, did depend upon his divine nature, namely, that the Sonne of God did offer himself for us [Act. 20. 28]" (cf. Knollys 1681, 4–5; Keach 1698, 15; Gill 1796, 343–44). The Second

London Confession (1689, VIII) further explores the two natures of Christ revealed in this verse in language reminiscent of patristic and medieval discussions: "Christ, in the work of *Mediation* acteth according to both natures, by each nature doing that which is proper to it self; yet by reason of the Unity of the Person, that which is proper to one nature is sometimes in *Scripture*, attributed to the Person denominated by the other nature [Act. 20. 28]" (cf. Orthodox Creed 1678, VI, VII).

The Second London article employs the conceptual framework of the *communicatio idiomatum* ("interchange of properties") "by which properties or actions belonging to one nature of Christ may be attributed to, or predicated of, the other nature, because of the unity of the single person of the God-man" (Pelikan 2005, 221). Leo the Great (d. 461) articulated the classic formulation of the idea in his address to the Council of Chalcedon: "It does not belong to the same nature to weep out of deep-felt pity for a dear friend, and to call him back to life again at the word of command (John 11:35–44)" (Tome of Leo 9, *CCF* 1:117–18), "since only the human nature could do the first and only the divine nature could do the second and yet the actions are both attributed to the single person of the incarnate Logos" (Pelikan 2005, 222). Thus the two natures of Christ are acknowledged as evidence of "One and the same Christ, son, Lord, Only begotten, acknowledged in two natures which undergo no confusion, no change, no division, no separation" (*Definition of Faith of the Council of Chalcedon* 16–18 [*CCF* 1:180–81; Pelikan 2005, 222]). Similarly, the Venerable Bede, eighth-century British monk and exegete, claims: "He did not hesitate to say 'the blood of God,' because of the oneness of person in two natures of the same Jesus Christ" (*Comm. Acts* 20:28b). John Calvin also knows and affirms this doctrine in his commentary on Acts 20:28:

> But because the speech which Paul useth seemeth to be somewhat hard, we must see in what sense he saith that God purchased the Church with his blood. For nothing is more absurd than to feign or imagine God to be mortal or to have a body. But in this speech he commendeth the unity of person in Christ; for because there be distinct natures in Christ, the Scripture doth sometimes recite that apart by itself which is proper to either. But when it setteth God before us made manifest in the flesh, it doth not separate the human nature from the Godhead. Notwithstanding, because again two natures are so united in Christ, that they make one person, that is improperly translated sometimes unto the one, which doth truly and indeed belong to the other, as in this place Paul doth attribute to God; because the man Jesus Christ, who shed his blood for us, was also God. This manner of speaking is called, of the old writers, *communicatio idiomatum*, because the property of the one nature is applied to the other (*Commentary on Acts*, 20; 2:256–57).

American missiologist W.O. Carver (1868–1954) opts for a different exeget-ical solution by choosing a different translation:

> The reading God is decidedly preferable here, rather than Lord as in the text. Again, the position is sacred by reason of the cost of the church flock. God "got possession of it by means of the blood of him who was his own." This translation, easily possible, obviates the difficulty of "his own blood" being God's blood, which was the cause of the confusion in the reading (1916, 205).

This passage is noteworthy because it demonstrates Carver's awareness of the textual problems associated with the verse (some manuscripts read "church of the Lord," rather than "church of God," thus easing the problem since "Lord" could refer to Christ), as well as an alternative translation proposed by earlier exegetes (in this case probably Westcott and Hort 1882, 98–100, although Carver does not follow Hort's suggested emendation that "son" had dropped out following the word "own"). Still, Carver goes beyond what most profession-ally trained NT scholars of his day would be comfortable in saying when he concludes: "Thus Paul here introduces the Trinity in relation to the church. He often introduces the Trinity in relation to some phase of the work of redemp-tion (*verse* 28)." This discussion reminds us that, across history, intepreters were fully aware of and engaged with the important doctrinal discussions and textual traditions.

Among modern commentators, Acts 20:28 has proven especially resistant to definitive interpretation. Much critical scholarship of the twentieth century on Luke/Acts has argued (or assumed) that Luke has no well-formed notion of Jesus' death as atoning, or perhaps any notion of it at all (though there is a minority but significant stream of advocates for the atoning death of the Lukan Jesus; cf. e.g., Barrett 1998, 2:977). German New Testament scholar, Hans Conzelmann (1915–1989), is identified as the most outspoken proponent of the view of an "atoneless" death, arguing that, in the Lukan writings, "there is no direct soteriological significance drawn from Jesus' suffering or death. There is no suggestion of a connection with the forgiveness of sins" (Conzelmann 1960, 201). Conzelmann recognized that Acts 20:28, with its assertion that God purchased the church with a blood sacrifice, was counterevidence to his view and was forced to dismiss the verse as a "Paulinism" ("to give the speech a Pauline stamp") and was not a view that Luke himself embraced.

Other scattered interpretations of parts of Paul's farewell address are note-worthy. Several early interpreters resonate with Paul's call for courage in the face of persecution (Acts 20:22–24, 29; cf. Denne 1641, 42–43; First London Confession 1644, LI; Blackwood 1654, 53; Fawcett 1782, 39; Colby 1838, 1:37–38; 1:104). Others appeal to Paul's warning to the Ephesian elders to beware the false teachers who, after his departure, would infiltrate the church like "fierce wolves" as a caveat against erroneous teaching in the "visible church" of their own day (cf. Acts 20:29–31; Denne 1646, 6–7; Chillenden 1653, 8–9; Orthodox Creed 1678, XXX; Keach 1682, 858–59).

Drawing on Acts 20:35 ("Remembering the words of the Lord Jesus, how he himself said 'It is more blessed to give than to receive'"), Karl Barth claims that the primary characteristic of loving is giving: "It is because it is a matter of giving that we must insist so strongly that love cannot be a merely inward action" (*CD* 4.2.786). Søren Kierkegaard has a rich and complicated interpretation of Acts 20:35, in which he addresses the apparent inequality presumed between the giver and receiver of a gift by subordinating both giver and receiver to the Gift:

> "It is more blessed to give than to receive." The words express the difference that prevails in earthly existence—without mirroring human passions or borrowing its expression from them—that it is better, happier, more glorious, more desirable to be able to give than to be obliged to receive. The one who gives admits that he is more insignificant than the gift; after all, it was this confession that the apostle's words gladly accepted from the individual as willingly given or extorted from him against his will. The person who receives confesses that he is more insignificant than the gift, because it was this admission that the words gave as the condition in order to exalt him, and indeed this admission in all its humility is often heard in the world. But if the person who gives is more insignificant that the gift and the person who receives is more insignificant than the gift, then equality has indeed been effected—that is, equality in insignificance in relation to the gift, because the gift is from above and therefore actually belongs to neither or belongs equally to both-that is, it belongs to God. The imperfection, then, was not that the needy one received the gift but that the rich one possessed it, an imperfection he removed by giving away the gift (*Eighteen Upbuilding Discourses*; *KW* 5:146–50).

In a letter published in the December 1887 issue of *Foreign Mission Journal*, missionary Lottie Moon (1840–1912) aims the dominical agraphon of Acts 20:35 ("It is more blessed to give than to receive") at her fellow Baptist women in an appeal for financial support for missions:

> I wonder how many of us really believe that "it is more blessed to give than to receive." A woman who accepts that statement of our Lord Jesus Christ as a fact, and not as "impractical idealism," will make giving a principle of her life. She will lay aside sacredly not less than one-tenth of her income or her earnings as the Lord's money, which she would no more dare to touch for personal use than she would steal. How many there are among our women, alas! alas! who imagine that because "Jesus paid it all," they need pay nothing, forgetting that the prime object of their salvation was that they should follow in the footsteps of Jesus Christ in

bringing back a lost world to God, and so aid in bringing the answer to the petition our Lord taught his disciples: "Thy kingdom come."

Acts 20:35 has also played an important role in the rhetoric of the American Presidency. Harry Truman quoted this verse in his Thanksgiving appeal in which he urged people "of every faith" to "assist in the efforts ... to aid the undernourished, the sick, the aged, and all sufferers in war-devastated lands" during the Thanksgiving season (Proclamation 2756; November 10, 1947; American Presidency Project, UCSB). John F. Kennedy made a similar appeal during the lighting of the National Christmas tree on December 17, 1962; Lyndon Johnson repeated President Kennedy's words the following year on December 22, 1963, at the same event and barely a month after Kennedy's assassination (American Presidency Project, UCSB). Gerald Ford also quoted the verse at the tree lighting ceremony on December 18, 1975 and, nearly fifty years after Kennedy began the tradition (December 6, 2012), President Obama also quoted Acts 20:35 at the lighting of the National Christmas tree, although with no explicit reference to its use on previous such events. Acts 20:35 was a favorite verse of President Clinton, who quoted it at least three times, including in his remarks on August 9, 1999 at the graduation ceremony of the AmeriCorps National Civilian Community Corps, an organization whose members contribute thousands of volunteer hours to various non-profit entities (American Presidency Project, UCSB).

Finally, the emotional scene of Paul's departure from the Ephesians ("And they all began, with loud lamentations, to throw their arms about his neck, and to kiss him lovingly again and again, sorrowing most of all for the words that he had spoken, that after that day they should look upon his face no more." Acts 20:37–38) is the source of inspiration for the last verse of John Fawcett's beloved hymn (1782), "Blessed Be the Tie That Binds" ("When we asunder part, It gives us inward pain; But we shall still be joined in heart, And hope to meet again") and the text for a eulogy preached by John Gill (1697–1771) at the funeral of a colleague, Rev. Samuel Wilson (1750).

Acts 21

Philip's Daughters (Acts 21:9)

Erasmus (1469–1536) connects the reference to Philip's prophesying daughters to the prophecy in Joel 2:28–29 (cited in Acts 2:17–18) (cf. Erasmus, *Paraphrase on Acts* 21; 126). Attention to the significance of the reference to the prophesying of Philip's unmarried daughters continues in the early twentieth century. Missionary Joanna Moore (1832–1916) mentioned Philip's daughters along with Phoebe and a long list of women in Romans 16 who were Paul's co-workers. She concluded:

> Those women were doing something more than simply cooking dinners for preachers and collecting money for the churches. That service is all right, but her work does not end there. Beloved sisters, your greatest work will doubtless be a quiet one in your own home and in the homes of your neighbors. The women we have mentioned knew their Bibles, or they could not have been teachers. Sisters, study the Word of God (1902, 132).

Missiologist W.O. Carver (1916, 209) and New Testament scholar A.T. Robertson (1863–1934) also take note of these women prophesying, although they are quite cautious in their application of the text to their contemporary context. Robertson observes: "Today in our Sunday schools the women do most of the actual teaching. The whole problem is different and calls for restraint and reverence. One thing is certain and that is that Luke appreciated the services of women for Christ as is shown often in his writings" (1930, 363). By 2007, Professor Carolyn Blevins appeals to Philip's daughters as providing a "liberating" word for women:

> In early English and American Church history, women were accepted leaders as deacons and preachers. Women of the twentieth century who responded to the call to serve as preacher or deacon were merely progressing back to our earlier ... heritage. Placing women in leadership positions was not initiating a twentieth-century innovation but was reclaiming our deepest roots. ... Women of the twentieth century claimed a theology of liberation (Gal. 3:28; Acts 21:9). ... The Bible's message is one of liberation, not limitation (Blevins 2008)

On the other hand, more recent feminist scholars note that these prophesying daughters disappear from the scene as a result of Luke's reticence to highlight women's leadership roles lest Christianity be associated with other movements of "social disorder, of magic" (D'Angelo 1990, 461). More balanced is Beverly Gaventa, who asks: "What ever happened to those prophesying daughters? The women in Acts, although for the most part they do not speak, are nevertheless present in the narrative and in ways that distinguish them at least from some of the literature in Luke's world. They do not exist in the story merely as the possession of men, nor are they depicted solely as mothers or described in terms of their physical appearance" (Gaventa 2004, 60).

Paul and the Prophet Agabus (Acts 21:10–16)

Louis Chéron painted in the late sixteenth and early seventeenth-centuries in Paris and London. Like Jean-Baptiste Champaigne (see Acts 14:18–20), he was commissioned by the Goldsmiths Guild of Notre Dame, Paris to provide paintings. *The Prophet Agabus Predicting Saint Paul's Suffering at Jerusalem* (**Figure 41**) was very likely produced during this period, when he was at the height of his career, although we cannot be certain if this painting was part of the Notre Dame commission. Chéron was the son of Henri Chéron, a painter and draftsman under whom he studied, and he was awarded the Premier Prix

FIGURE 41   Louis Chéron (1660–1715). *The Prophet Agabus Predicting Saint Paul's Suffering at Jerusalem*. c. 1700. Musée des Beaux-Arts, Caen, France. Photo: Bridgeman-Giraudon/Art Resource, NY

de Rome. His subjects are mostly religious. The artist was a committed Protestant who had to flee France to escape prosecution in 1695 when he moved to London. He remained in London until his death in 1715 (Chéron, Louis).

Caesarea is the location of the event and the setting for the painting. Again like the work of Jean-Baptiste Champaigne (See **Figure 34**), the painting is very theatrical and presented much like a play with a stage set and overly emotionalized responses evident in all of the characters present. Paul, along with several other disciples, stayed at the house of Philip the evangelist. The next day they go to the city center. Chéron painted a blue sky complete with fluffy clouds and a landscape that emerged beyond the first-century architecture in the right distance. But, as the viewer focuses on the scene in the center, the darkened cloud about the leading characters is quite apparent.

Philip, in the scene to the right of the composition, is in conversation with another man while his four unmarried daughters are all visible in the right foreground and reacting to the event happening in center stage. A prophet named Agabus came from Judea and is seated in the center of the painting with an eye-catching blue cloth draped across his lower body. He is telling Paul (who is in the red cloak standing next to Luke on the left side of the scene) that he will be imprisoned by the Jews and given to the Gentiles. A red band is visible around the hands and feet of Agabus. His left leg is placed prominently on the ledge where he is seated so that the reference to his binding his own hands and feet (21:11) is understood by the audience/viewer. Above Agabus is a column, creating a strong vertical in the center of the composition. Philip's daughters and the three other apostles all react in despair, begging Paul not to go to Jerusalem (21:12). Paul does not change his mind and gestures towards Agabus with open hand in acceptance of God's will. The biblical scene climaxes with a joint appeal from the local Christians and Paul's traveling companions. Paul is moved but unshakable in continuing (Alexander 2001, 1054). This is the exact moment Louis Chéron depicts in this late French Baroque picture.

Reception of Various Verses in Acts 21

Several other verses in Acts 21 have distinctive, almost idiosyncratic, interpretations. English Anglican minister Hanserd Knollys (1681, 70–72) finds in Paul's kneeling in prayer with the Ephesian elders (21:5) a biblical base for one of the appropriate postures to be adopted in worship (!). Noncomformist minister Thomas Harrison (1660, 42–43) appeals to Paul's resolve in Acts 21:13 to suffer and die in Jerusalem if need be as scriptural warrant that "suffering for Christ" is "a strong Argument of his Electing love." American missiologist W.O. Carver (1868–1954) uses the throwaway comment in Acts 21:16 that Paul and company took lodging in the house of Mnason "as an example of how *many a well-to-do Christian would feel it an honor and grace to back the missionaries with his money*" (Carver 1918, 52). Finally, Origen cited Acts 21:26 (among other texts) to counter Celsus' charge that Jews who converted to Christianity were forced to abandon "the laws of the ancestors": "why do I mention that even Paul himself became as a 'Jew to the Jews, that he might gain the Jews?' Wherefore also in the Acts of the Apostles it is related that he even brought an offering to the altar, that he might satisfy the Jews that he was no apostate from their law" (*Contra Celsus* 2.1).

The Lifeway Adult Sunday School literature on Acts 21:20–26 prepared by and for Native Americans notes that Paul "never told the Jews it was wrong to practice their customs just as long as they did not trust in them for salvation. He further taught them not to make their customs a test of fellowship" (1993, 36). Then the writer identifies with Paul who had been accused of forsaking the "old customs" of Moses:

> Paul was trying to do what was right. He was living out the message that he preached. Through his actions, he was showing that being a Christian did not change his nationality. He could continue to be a Hebrew and do Hebrew things. Only he would not do anything that would compromise the message of the cross.
>
> I know somewhat what Paul faced. I have, at times, been accused of trying to destroy the Indian culture by the message I preached. I have faced the crisis of disappointment and rejection because of such rumors. Through it all, I have grown closer to the Lord and more committed to the message. My forefathers were brave, honest, and respectful. I can see no other way to regain those attributes except in Christ.
>
> I believe that Paul recognized that being a good Hebrew had little to do with color or culture. It had everything to do with the condition of the heart. We would do well to learn this lesson also (1993, 36).

Acts 22

Paul's Conversion, Again (Acts 22:1–11)

The *Recognitions of Clement 1* suggests that Paul went to Damascus to persecute Christians (Acts 22:5) "because he believed that Peter had fled thither" (*Clem. Rec.* 1.64). Karl Barth comments on the significance of Paul's conversion, which Paul himself narrates in Acts 22 (and 26 in addition to the third-person account in **9**): "What is it that makes his conversion so important to Paul himself for his mission to Jews and Gentiles, and so scandalous and strange to his non-Christian hearers? … Jesus of that earlier time is still at work. The life and work of the apostles is wholly and utterly dependent on His presence. Their whole recollection and tradition concerning Him is not centred on a figure of the past, on a dead man, but on One who even after His earthly time is still an acting Subject, doing new things, creating in history" (*CD* 3.2.471). Elsewhere, Barth gives an extended ten-page treatment of Paul's call narrative, with a view toward assessing the cause of the impact of the Damascus event on the Apostle:

> What happened to this man was that now he could and should receive something which he had not previously been able or willing to receive, and that in this transition from non-reception to reception he became a new man and moved from an old way to a new. We have to consider this incident in the present context because in it there is unmistakeably revealed (1) the radical meaning of what is called knowledge in the Bible, (2) the historical character of this knowledge, and in particular (3) the teleological orientation of this history as we have just considered it (*CD* 4.3.198–211; esp. 198).

Baptism and the "Washing Away" of Sins (Acts 22:16)

Acts 22:16, where Paul cites the words Ananias spoke to him after his Damascus experience ("And now why do you wait? Rise and be baptized, and wash away your sins, calling upon his name") is, by far, the most cited verse in this section among interpreters. Some emphasize the urgency for baptism (Blackwood 1646, 10); others claim that baptism represents the remission or "washing away" of sins (Denne 1646, 22–23; Somerset Confession 1656, XXIV; Lawrence 1659, 8–10, 22–24; Second London 1689, XXIX; Kiffin 1681, 26–27; Crosby 1738–40, 2:412–13; Gill 1796, 976; Baptist Manifesto 1997, Article 3). Still others warned that the relationship between baptism and the remission of sins is "not actual, but symbolic and formal" (Pendleton 1878, 350) and does not teach "baptismal remission or salvation by means of baptism" (Robertson 1930, 392) or "baptismal regeneration" (Stagg 1955, 228; Polhill 1992, 461), as some denominations seemed to insist (cf. Acts 2).

Barth does not dismiss out of hand a sacramental interpretation of the passage (in which baptism effects, rather than marks, forgiveness) but views a "non-sacramental exposition" as "decidedly the more probable" (*CD* 4.4.112). Elsewhere Barth appeals to Acts 22:16 (and Luke 3) as scriptural warrant for his view that, in its essence, baptism is an act of prayer, a calling upon the name of the Lord (*CD* 4.4.210, 213). Bonhoeffer appeals to the image expressed in Acts 22:16 to express the connection between faith and baptism in the NT: "Baptism is the actual consummated transfer of the human being into the church-community of the end times and incorporation into the body of Christ by means of a physical action instituted by Christ. Within it occur the washing away of sin [Acts 22:16], being born again, dying and rising with Christ, conformation with the image of Christ, reception of the Holy Spirit, sealing within the eschatological church-community for the day of judgment" (*BW* 16:556–57). He also notes that the phrase "'have oneself baptized' [the Greek verb is in the middle voice] ... occurs in the NT only one single time (Acts 22:16); the passive is used everywhere else. The person is baptized. The faith that receives baptism—and only in faith can baptism be received—can in no way be understood as an active cooperation in baptism; it is pure reception and only real in the very act of reception" (*BW* 16:558–59).

Acts 23

Paul's Rebuke of the High Priest and Dispute with Saduccees and Pharisees (Acts 23:1–11)

Several patristics writers rush to the defense of Paul in his encounter with the High Priest recorded in Acts 23:1–3, although they do not necessarily agree on the intent of Paul's rebuke ("Whitewashed wall, and do you sit judging me according to the law?"). Chrysostom suggests that Paul "did not know it was the high priest, since he had returned after a long absence, was not having continuous association with Jews, and was seeing him amid a crowd of many others" (*Scholion on Acts 23:1–2*; CGPNT 366.1–20; on the identity of the author as Chrysostom, see Brookins et al 2011: 37–38 n. 49). Chrysostom reasons that Paul was further emboldened by the fact that the commander had not scourged Paul, and Paul who "did not want to appear contemptible to the commander" responds boldly against the one who ordered him struck. Even so, Chrysostom argues, one could not accuse Paul of insolence unless one were willing to accuse Christ himself of insolence for calling the Pharisees "whitewashed tombs" [Matt 23:27]! An anonymous writer and Severus take a different tack, arguing that Paul does, indeed, know the high priest. Paul speaks, not simply to revile the high priest, but to "expose the high priest's outward display as hypocrisy" (Anonymous on Acts 23:3–5; CGPNT 366.30–31) and because "his understanding was full of lawlessness" (Severus on Acts 23:3–5; CGPNT 367.4–5).

The Venerable Bede, eighth-century British monk and exegete, takes a different tack, appealing to the grammar of the passage: "He [Paul] did not say this because he was stirred by passion in his mind. Rather he surely spoke by way of prophesying ..., that is why he said *God will strike you*. He did not say, 'May God strike you'. In fact he signified by the indicative mood that this thing was going to happen; he did not utter a curse by using the optative mood. He showed by the response which followed [23:5] with what a tranquil mind he said these things" (*Comm. Acts* 23:3; 175). Erasmus (1469–1536), on the other hand, admits that "Paul was filled with disdain," explaining in an aside that "such a thing [striking the accused] usually does not occur even in pagan courts of justice" (*Paraphrase on Acts* 23).

Various other aspects of the account of Paul before the Sanhedrin also attracted the attention of early modern interpreters. British minister Benjamin Keach (1640–1704) explored the background of Paul's reference to the chief priest as a "whited wall," which Keach concludes was an allusion to a wall "made of mud, that is a slight wall of untempered mortar, as Ezek. xiii. 10, which had no solid or durable substance in the inside, but was curiously whited with lime on the outside" (Keach 1682, 171). While the 1934 confession of the General Association of Regular Baptist Churches (Article XVII) cites Acts 23:5 ("Brothers, I did not know that he was the high priest," exclaimed Paul, "for it is written, *Thou shall not speak evil of a ruler of my people*") as straightforward scriptural evidence that "civil government is of divine appointment for the interests and good order of human society," not a few Baptist interpreters note the possibility of irony and sarcasm in Paul's "confession" not to have "recognized" the high priest (Carver 1916, 223–24; Smith 1970, 129; though cf. Stagg 1955, 232).

The Lord's appearance to Paul, following the confrontation with the Sadducees and Pharisees (23:6–11), is described by Erasmus (1469–1536) as the "time for God to support his athlete with some consolation in the midst of such storms, especially when even fiercer ones were threatening" (*Paraphrase on Acts* 23:11–22; 134).

Acts 24–26

Overview

Acts 24–26 records Paul's various trials and speeches before the Roman governor Felix (ch. 24) and his successor Festus. The characters, Tertullus and Felix (and Drusilla), draw significant interest among subsequent readers, who attempt to plumb the depths of their personalities as well as add historical detail to their portraits. Paul's appeal to Caesar before Festus (25:11) intrigues exegetes, anxious to understand the legal and theological implications of such

The Acts of the Apostles Through the Centuries, First Edition. Heidi J. Hornik and Mikeal C. Parsons.

an appeal. Paul's account of his conversion before King Agrippa (ch. 26) is the third time the event has been narrated, and both Paul's speech and Agrippa's response interest readers. The episode ends with Agrippa's pronouncement that Paul "is doing nothing for which he deserves death or imprisonment" (26:31). Despite this apparent acquittal, Paul is handed over to a centurion for transport to and trial at Rome (cf. Acts 27–28).

Reception and Interpretation

Acts 24

Tertullus' Speech (Acts 24:1–9)

Tertullus (24:1–8), the prosecuting attorney appointed by the high priest, does not fare well in subsequent interpretation. Erasmus's description of Tertullus' speech as "flat" (*frigidus*; Acts 24:1–13; *LB* 7:757–758 [p. 136]) "calls attention to the rhetorical character of the speech" as "ineffective" (cf. Cicero, *De or.* 2.63.256; Quintilian, *Inst.* 8.5.30; Erasmus, *Paraphrase on Acts*, 317 n. 6). The reformer Johann Spangenberg (1484–1550) refers to Tertullus as a hired speaker who was a "tongue-slinger [*Zungendrescher*] and scandalmonger" (*Der Apostel Geschichte*, 219 r-v; RCS, 325). John Wesley (1703–91) criticized both the character of Felix and the speech of Tertullus: "Felix was a man of the most infamous character, and a plague to all the provinces over which he presided. ... The eloquence of Tertullus was as bad as his cause: a lame introduction, a lame transition, and a lame conclusion. Did not God confound the orator's language?" (*ENNT*, Acts 24:2, 4).

A number of interpreters refer to Tertullus' accusation that Paul was a "pestilent fellow" (24:5; which Helen Barrett Montgomery [1861–1934] simply translates as "pest"; on the etymology of the term, see Keach 1682, 162). John Clarke, minister and co-founder of the colony of Rhode Island, claims this charge against Paul was false, but that such "pestilent fellows" (which he defines as "contagious and smitting hereticks") do exist and should be avoided by the "sober humble, discreet Christian"! (Clarke 1646, 29–30) Others apply the term more generally to "true followers of the Lord Jesus" who are falsely accused by the civil magistrates of being "pestilent fellows" and who are persecuted because of their beliefs (Monk, Wright, and Stanley 1661, 17–18). Missionary James Hargreaves (1768–1845) also generalizes about civil leaders who have overstepped their bounds: "It was the sin of the rulers, not that they did not employ civil power to propagate Christianity, but that they employed it against the Redeemer's cause; their business was, as armed with the sword, neither to bless religion at all, nor to curse it at all, but to let it alone" (Hargreaves 1823, 22).

Martin Luther drew an analogy between the accusations brought against him and his fellow reformers and those once hurled at the apostles by the religious leaders (24:5):

> So they invented the charge that the Apostles, too, were seditious—as we face that same thing today—and called them subversives of civil society and of kingdoms, and men who granted license to every evil. What shall we do? We must bear it. They will be prophets for themselves. For them we shall actually be disturbers and destroyers of kingdoms, not in act, but because the opposite of what they have in mind will occur. Since they persecute the Word which we teach, they will drive ahead and invite judgment on their necks. Thus they will be destroyed, as were the Jews in the case of Christ (*Commentaries on the Psalms* 45.5.17; cf. *Sermons on St. John* 7.1.63; *Lectures on Galatians* 4.1.30).

The Venerable Bede, eighth-century British monk and exegete, suggests that referring to the Christian movement as the "sect of the Nazarenes" (Acts 24:5) was intended "as an insult" (*Comm. Acts* 24.5). Reformer Rudolf Gwalther (1519–1586) explains the insult as "intimating that they [the Christians] have an obscure and ignoble origin as this sect. For Nazareth was a small town of no regard, as it is shown when, to Philip's proclamation of Jesus of Nazareth, Nathaniel responds, 'Can anything good come out of Nazareth?'" (*Homilies* 152; Acts 24:1–9; RCS 326). John Calvin acknowledges the term may refer to Christians, but he also suggests that Tertullus meant "those turbulent assassins who took on a worthy name and boasted that they were zealots" (*Commentary on Acts*, 24:5).

Most manuscripts do not include 24:6b–8a, which explain that the Sanhedrin did not deal with Paul because the Roman captain Lysias seized him (for comments on the omission, see Introduction). John Chrysostom, however, appeals to these verses to explain how this matter came before Felix: "'We seized him,' he says,' and would have judged him according to our law'[24:6b]. He claims that it was unpleasant to them to come to foreign courts and that they would have not given trouble to [Felix], if he had not forced them and that it was not right for Lysias to take Paul away" (cf. 24:7; *Catena on Acts* 24.7–9; cited by ACCS, 284). Gwalther also appeals to this now regarded dubious text in his praise of the Roman tribune whose actions hindered the religious authorities from judging Paul on the spot (*Homilies* 152; Acts 24:1–9; RCS, 327).

Paul's Speech and Felix's Response (Acts 24:10–27)

Regarding Paul's response to Tertullus' charges (24:10–21), John Wesley (1703–91) argued that he dealt with them systematically:

As it may be observed, his answer exactly corresponds with the three articles of Tertullus's charge: sedition, heresy, and profanation of the temple. As to the first, he suggests, that he had not been long enough at Jerusalem to form a party and attempt an insurrection: (for it was about twelve days since he came up thither; ... As to the second, he confesses himself to be a Christian; but maintains this to be a religion perfectly agreeable to the law and the prophets, and therefore deserving a fair reception, ver. 14, 16. And as for profaning the temple, he observes that he behaved there in a most peaceful and regular manner, so that his innocence had been manifest even before the sanhedrim, where the authors of the tumult did not dare to appear against him (*ENNT*, Acts 24:10).

John Calvin appealed to Acts 24:12 (and other texts) as scriptural warrant against those who opposed all legal actions by believers:

As for those who strictly condemn all legal contentions, let them realize that they therewith repudiate God's holy ordinance, and one of the class of gifts that can be clean to the clean [Titus 1:15]; unless, perchance, they wish to accuse Paul of a shameful act, since he both repelled the slanders of his accusers, exposing at the same time their craft and malice [Acts 24:12 ff.], and in court claimed for himself the privilege of Roman citizenship [Acts 16:37; 22:1, 25], and, when there was need, appealed from the unjust judge to the judgment seat of Caesar [Acts 25:10–11] (*Instit.* 4.19).

Erasmus (1469–1536) understands the reference to the "Way" in 24:14 to refer to "the tradition of the Pharisees" (*Paraphrase on Acts*, 137; see also his paraphrase of 24:22). Some isolated uncertainties regarding the meaning of the expression do exist in the earlier exegetical tradition. For example, the thirteenth-century French Dominican friar and cardinal, Hugo of Saint-Cher (1200–1263), observed "The way of truth that was found in Paul; or of the unrighteousness they were committing against Paul" (279 recto A; cited in *Paraphrase on Acts*, 318 n. 9). Typically, the term "Way" has been understood to refer to the Christian movement (see Ammonius, *Catena on Acts* 24.14; ACCS, 285). Earlier references to the "way" in Acts 19:9 and 23 were understood by Hugo to refer to "evangelical teaching" (274 verso E; see also Nicholas of Lyra 1187C; cited in *Paraphrase on Acts* 296 n. 12 and 298 n. 28).

Other interpreters were also drawn to Acts 24:14. This affirmation that Paul believes "everything that is according to the Law, or is written in the Prophets" resonates with the Protestant conviction that the Scriptures are the authoritative source of their faith and practice, a conviction evidenced in the following British Baptist confessions of faith. The Standard Confession (1660) cites this verse at the conclusion of its Prologue, and the Second London Confession begins its statement on "Saving Faith" with these words (1689,

XIV): "By this *Faith* a Christian believeth to be true [Act. 24. 14.] whatsoever is revealed in the *Word* for the authority of *God* himself" (cf. Orthodox Creed 1678, XXIII).

In his discussion of biblical authority, Rick Warren, a popular evangelical preacher and writer, quotes the verse in his best-selling devotional book, *Purpose-Driven Life*:

> The most important decision you can make today is to settle this issue of what will be the ultimate authority for your life. Decide that regardless of culture, tradition, reason, or emotion, you choose the Bible as your final authority. Determine first to ask, "What does the Bible say?" when making decisions. Resolve that when God says to do something, you will trust God's Word and do it whether or not it makes sense or you feel like doing it. Adopt Paul's statement as your personal affirmation of faith: "*I believe everything that agrees with the Law and that is written in the Prophets.*" [24:14] (Warren 2002, 187).

In the course of his defense speech before Felix, Paul claims that he, like his fellow Jewish accusers has "a hope toward God … that there is to be a resurrection both of the just and unjust" (24:15). Paul's hope in a general resurrection is referenced in a number of Baptist confessions. The Somerset Confession (1656, XL) shares Paul's hope "THAT there is a day appointed, when the Lord shall raise the unjust as well as the righteous, and judge them all in righteousness (John 5:28, 29; Acts 24:15)." This hope is a refrain in writings from the seventeenth century (Standard Confess 1660, XX; Orthodox Creed 1678, XLIV; Second London 1689, XXXI) right through to the nineteenth (e.g., Dayton 1866, 287; Allen 1873, 118) and twentieth centuries (Baptist Faith and Message 1925, XVI; Polhill 1992, 482–83).

In a meditation on the example of Anna (Luke 2) as one who practiced "patience in expectancy," Kierkegaard exhorts his audience, alluding to Acts 24:15: "But you, my listener, you have not placed your expectancy in that which is deceitful even when it comes; your expectancies are not disappointed. You are expecting the resurrection of the dead, of both the righteous and the unrighteous [Acts 24:15]; you are expecting a blessed reunion with those whom death took away from you and with those whom life separated from you. … this expectancy is not disappointed because the time of its fulfillment has not yet arrived" (*KW* 5:216).

John Calvin wished to clarify that the source of Paul's "clear conscience" (Acts 24:16) was God alone (*Instit.* 3.16; cf. 3.4). John Wesley (1703–91), on the other hand, focuses on the opposition to Paul and his message [Acts 24:19]: "But the world never commits greater blunders, even against its own laws, than when it is persecuting the children of God" (*ENNT*, Acts 24:19).

Wesley also seems to be drawing (perhaps indirectly) on Josephus, first-century Jewish historian, to add historical details regarding Felix and Drusilla (24:24):

> And after Paul had been kept some days in this gentle confinement at Cesarea, Felix, who had been absent for a short time, coming thither again, with Drusilla, his wife … The daughter of Herod Agrippa, one of the finest women of that age. Felix persuaded her to forsake her husband, Azizus, king of Emessa, and to be married to himself, though a heathen. She was afterward, with a son she had by Felix, consumed in an eruption of Mount Vesuvius (*ENNT*, Acts 24:24).

After naming Agrippa as Drusilla's son, Josephus writes "This youth and his wife disappeared at the time of the eruption of Mount Vesuvius" (*Ant.* 20.7.2). The reference to "this youth" is most likely to Agrippa (Felix would no longer have been a young man in 79 CE) and the "woman" (Greek: *gunē*) a reference to his (otherwise unnamed) wife. Wesley's suggestion that Drusilla and her son, Agrippa, both died in the Vesuvian eruption is apparently the reading of Wesley (or his source) of the word "woman" (Greek: *gunē*) as referring to Agrippa's mother and not his wife (so also González, 262). It is, however, much more likely that the reference is to Agrippa's wife as the modern Loeb translation by Louis Feldman indicates (see above).

Augustine detects echoes Luke 12:34–36 and Ps 34:14 in Paul's words in Acts 24:25:

> That's why he wanted our loins to be girt and our lamps burning [Luke 12:35]. What's the significance of having loins girt? *Turn aside from evil.* And of shining? Of having lamps burning? That means *And do good* (Ps 34:14). And what's the meaning of what he went on to say, *And you are like people waiting for their lord, whenever he may come from the wedding* (Lk 12:36), if not what follows in that psalm, *Seek peace and pursue it?* These three things, namely abstaining from evil, and doing good, and hoping for an eternal reward, are listed in the Acts of the Apostles, where it is written that Paul was teaching them *about continence, about justice and the hope of eternal life* (Acts 24:25). To continence you can refer *Let your loins be girt*; to justice refer *and lamps burning*; to the expectation of the Lord refer *hope of eternal life*" (Augustine, *Sermon 108.2*).

John Wesley notes the appropriateness of Paul's speech, given the personal qualities of Felix: "And as he [Paul] reasoned of justice, temperance, and judgment to come—This was the only effectual way of preaching Christ to an unjust, lewd judge (*ENNT*, Acts 24:25).

Kierkegaard likewise commented on the exchange between Paul and Felix:

> Immortality and judgment are one and the same. Immortality can be discussed properly only when there is discussion about judgment, and of course when there is discussion about judgment there is discussion about immortality. This was why

Felix became afraid of Paul's discussion about immortality. Paul refused to speak in other way than to speak about judgment, about the separation between the righteous and the unrighteous. If Paul had been willing to speak in a different way, had separated, according to modern taste, judgment and immortality, had spoken, or babbled, about immortality without saying a word about judgment, spoken about immortality and pretended that there is no judgment—well, then I am sure that Felix would not have become afraid, that Felix surely would have listened with the attentiveness of a cultured man and afterward would have said, "It is really entertaining to listen to the man, although it is a kind of fanaticism that nevertheless can be diverting as long as one listens to it; it has something in common with a fireworks display" (*KW* 17:205–06; cf. *KW* 16:207).

For a period of time, it was popular in modern scholarship to view Acts as an apology for the Romans to Luke's community, vindicating them for any blame in persecuting Christians (e.g., Haenchen 1971, 106, 693). John Chrysostom, however, argued that Luke presented the unvarnished truth, noting the explanation that Felix spoke frequently to Paul, not because he admired him or wished to believe but because he expected a bribe (Acts 24:26). Roman justice in Acts is something of a farce: "Observe on all occasions how the governors try to keep off from themselves the annoyance of the Jews, and are often compelled to act contrary to justice, and seek pretexts for deferring: for of course it was not from ignorance that he deferred the cause, but knowing it" (*Hom. Act.* 51). Chrysostom concludes: "This man [Felix] is succeeded in his office by another [Festus], and he leaves Paul a prisoner: and yet he ought not to have done this; he ought to have put an end to the business: but he leaves him, by way of gratifying them" (*Hom. Act.* 51).

Popular English preacher C. H. Spurgeon (1858, 50–51) showed great interest in this section of Acts, with sermons on 24:25 (Paul before Felix), 26:14 ("It is hard for thee to kick against the pricks"), and 26:28 ("thou almost persuadest me to be a Christian"; cf. Gill 1796, 999). Consider one passage from his evocative sermon on Acts 24:25 ("And as he reasoned about morality, self-control, and the future judgment, Felix was terrified, and said, 'For the present go on your way, and when I find a convenient season, I will send for you'"), in which Spurgeon invites his audience to imagine the specifics of Paul's "reasoning" before Felix:

> I can imagine how he would bring before the mind of Felix, the widow who had been defrauded of inheritance, the fatherless children who, cast from affluence, were led to beg their bread. I can suppose how he brought before the mind of that base man the many bribes that he had taken, when he sat upon his judgment-seat. He would recall to him the false decisions that he had given; he would remind him how the Jews as a nation had been oppressed—how by taxation they had

been ground to the earth; he would bring before him one scene after another, where avarice had overridden equity, boldly and sternly depicting the exact character of the man; and then at the end declaring that such men could have no inheritance in the kingdom of God—bidding him repent of this his wickedness, that his sins might be forgiven him [cf. also on this verse, Keach 1682, 795; Gill 1796, 988–89; Robertson 1930, 3.422–23].

William Blake captures this moment visually in his pen and watercolor drawing, *Felix Trembled*, in which a hunkered-over Felix (and Drusilla) raise their hands, pleading with Paul, chained but standing tall and erect, to cease his discourse (1800–03, private collection; Butlin 1981, vol. 1, plate 607).

Erasmus (1469–1536) could not resist the temptation to moralize about Felix's decision to leave Paul in prison (24:27): "he preferred to gratify the Jews rather than to set free, out of a sincere conscience, the innocent. He, therefore, left Paul a prisoner. So difficult it is for the treat of this world to follow the right path in everything" (*Paraphrase on Acts*, 139).

Acts 25

Paul's Trial Before Festus (Acts 25:1–12)

According to John Calvin, the transfer of power from Felix to Festus left Paul in a vulnerable position, especially in the early days of Festus' reign (Acts 24:27–25:4): "We know that new rulers, because they will win the favor of those who are in the provinces, use to grant them many things at their first coming; so that it was to be thought that the death of Paul should be to Festus a fine means to win favor with all" (*Commentary on Acts*, 25:1–4).

Aquinas refers to Paul's appeal to Caesar in Acts 25:11 as counter-evidence against those who would condemn clergy for going to the law courts for protection: "we can adduce proofs that holy men are at times justified in availing themselves of the protection of the law. 1. St. Paul, when in danger of being delivered to the Jews, appealed to the hearing of Augustus (Acts xxv), i.e., he appealed to the Roman law. An appeal is to go to a higher judgment. Therefore, perfect men may go to law (Aquinas, *Apol. Rel.* 1.15.8).

This "appeal to Caesar" continued to vex later interpreters. Reformers pointed to the appeal as evidence that the divinely ordained political office and its regulations must be respected. Reformer Johann Spangenberg distinguished between the "majesty of the emperor" and the "person of the emperor" (Spangenberg, *Brief Exegesis of Acts 25:8*; RCS, 334). Likewise, Swiss reformer Heinrich Bullinger observed that "the defense of Paul is also the same [as in Acts 24], except the mention of Caesar. ... They truly thought that Paul was transgressing against Caesar in this matter, because he had stirred up a crowd in Jerusalem or because he preached another king, namely, Jesus [Acts 17]. … Now the apostles were not preaching that Jesus was King or Messiah so that they could reject Caesar, for the Lord himself had said, 'Give to Caesar what is Caesar's, and to God what is God's'" (Luke 20:25; Bullinger, *Commentary on Acts*, 25:6–8; RCS, 334; cf. also the comment by Calvin above on Acts 24:12 in *Instit.* 4.19).

Roman historians, A.N. Sherwin-White and A.H.M. Jones have argued that the events in Acts following Paul's appeal to Caesar correspond closely to the political process that prevailed until the end of the first century (but not beyond), thus concluding that the author of Luke was writing in proximity to the events and certainly within the first century (Sherwin-White 1963 and Jones 1960; cited by Gasque 1975, 278–79). This conclusion has not gone unchallenged (Pervo 2006).

Clarence Jordan founded Koinonia Farm, an interracial farming community in the 1940s. He was also author of the Cotton Patch translation of the New Testament, in which he tried to make the New Testament resonate with the struggles of the Civil Rights Movement by putting the NT into Southern idiom. His rendering of Acts 25:6–12 demonstrates how translation is also and always interpretation!

> The next day he ["Judge Foster" a.k.a. Festus] convened court and ordered Paul's case to be called. During the proceedings, the whites who had come from Atlanta leveled many serious accusations against him, but they couldn't make them hold any water. In making his defense, Paul denied that he had committed any crime against the laws and customs of local whites, against the church, or against the Federal government. But Judge Foster, with an eye to making himself popular with the good white folks, asked Paul, "Would you be willing to go to Atlanta and let me hear your case there?" Paul replied, "I am standing in a Federal court right now, where I should be tried. I have done no harm to the white people, as you yourself know beyond all doubt. If indeed I have broken a law, or committed some crime punishable even by death, I ask for no mercy. But if there's no basis for the things these people are charging me with, nobody can let them put their cotton picking hands on me! I'm appealing to the Supreme Court!"
>
> Judge Foster then conferred with his associates, and gave Paul an answer. "You have appealed to the Supreme Court. To the Supreme Court you shall go." (Jordan 2004, Acts 25).

Festus Consults Agrippa (Acts 25:13–27)

In his "Warning to His Dear German People" (1531), Martin Luther contrasts the Roman policy articulated by Festus to King Agrippa "not to condemn a man without a hearing," reflected in Acts 25:16, with the treatment he and other protestors had received from contemporary civil and religious leaders

(*Christians in Society* 4.1.21; *LW* 47). John Wesley (1703–91) also praised the example of the Romans: "It is not the custom of the Romans - How excellent a rule, to condemn no one unheard! A rule, which as it is common to all nations, (courts of inquisition only excepted,) so it ought to direct our proceedings in all affairs, not only in public, but private life" (*ENNT*, Acts 25:16).

John Calvin takes Festus' description of the dispute between Paul and the chief priests and elders as being over "a certain Jesus" (Acts 25:19) as indicative of Festus' inattention and dismissiveness: "he [Festus] showeth plainly how negligently he heard him when he disputed of Christ. ... For the wicked do lightly pass over whatsoever is spoken, as if a man should tell them a fable of Robin Hood" (*Commentary on Acts*, 2.288).

In a curious note that refers to Acts 25:24, Luther claims that Jews refer to Jesus by the "hateful" name of "Thola" ("Lectures on Titus" 1.1 in *Selected Pauline Epistles* 2:5–6). Elsewhere, Luther defines "Thola" as "hanged one" (*Selected Commentaries on Psalms* 5.109.1.18; *LW* 14:269). Luther learned about this word, apparently a derivative from the Hebrew *talui* ("hanged one"), as an invective for Jesus in an interview with two Jewish rabbis (*LW* 14:269 n. 25). It is not clear how Acts 25:24 (or Acts 17:5, the other text Luther references) attests, even indirectly, to the use of this term among Jews, either in the first or sixteenth centuries.

Acts 26

In his discussion of biblical macarism or blessing, Karl Barth argues that no-one can pronounce him or herself "blessed" (Greek: *makaraios*) especially as the term is used in the Gospels. Barth dismisses Paul's use of the term for himself in his defense speech in Acts 26:2 (translated "fortunate" in the NRSV) as a "rhetorical" use by Paul (*CD* 4.2.188). Barth also appeals to the conversion of Paul as evidence that Christ is not merely remembered by his followers, but actively reveals himself in his resurrection power: "He Himself is the acting Subject who lifts the barrier of yesterday and moves into today, making himself present and entering in as the Lord" (*CD* 3.2.471). Elsewhere, Barth comments on what the Damascus Road experience (narrated three times in Acts) reveals about Paul: "what is envisaged is the total transformation which takes place with the rise of specific knowledge. What happened to this man was that now he could and should receive something which he had not previously been able or willing to receive, and that in this transition from non-reception to reception he became a new man and moved from an old way to a new" (*CD* 4.3.198).

Barth also ponders the comparison between the conversion accounts in Acts and Paul's own claims in Galatians 1:1. Barth notes that in neither of the Acts accounts that mention Ananias (9, 22; he is not mentioned in 26) does Luke indicate that Ananias imparted any doctrine to Paul; thus, the two accounts do not contradict each other. On a positive note, the presence of Ananias, as representative of the church, indicates that "Jesus Christ and His ekklesia [church] constitute an interrelated totality, so that He can represent His community, and it can represent Him" (*CD* 4.3.206).

Barth also views the Lukan accounts of Paul's conversion as analyses or commentaries on the pithy statements found in Paul's own letters: "In this third account in Acts [26] the appearance of Jesus, the calling of Saul as an apostle and the beginning of his work as such constitute an integrated whole which is presented rather more expressly than in the Pauline sayings" (*CD* 4.3.203).

Luther comments on the meaning of the rather obscure words from the heavenly voice: "It is hard for you to kick against the goads" (Acts 26:14):

> But is this not only a ridiculous but also a harmful battle, that someone is so angry that in in his anger he kicks a goad [cattle prong] with his foot ... [resulting in] self-harm? So this is a very noteworthy and comforting word for the poor, persecuted Christians, that we understand that whoever persecutes Christ is kicking against a sharp goad. Their foot will either become maimed or at the very least they certainly won't have much success (*House Postil for Saint Paul's Conversion*; RCS, 342).

Acts 26:18 has generated an enormously wide variety of interpretations. In the verse, Paul is recounting for Agrippa his Damascus Road conversion, and at this point in the speech Paul is quoting Jesus' commission to him to go to the Gentiles "to open their eyes so that they may turn from darkness to light, and from the power of Satan unto God, in order to receive remission of sins and an inheritance among those who are sanctified by faith in me." Some focus on the darkness or "ignorance" in which humans dwell and which requires "the Prophetical office of Christ to relieve them" (London Baptist Confession of Faith1644, XXXIII). Others, such as Hanserd Knollys (1598–1691), use the language of Acts 26:18 to articulate a doctrine of conversion that takes both Satan and Sin seriously: "God doth in the work of Conversion *actually* and *really* turn the converted person from darkness to light, from the power of Satan and Sin unto God, *Act*. 26. 18. Before Conversion the Sinner was under the Vasalage of Satan, who had dominion over him, and ruled and worked in him, *Eph*. 2. 2. And he was then the servant of sin, which had also dominion over him, and reigned in him, *Rom*. 5. 21" (Knollys 1681, 32–33; Second London Confession 1689, XXI).

Still others appeal to Acts 26:18, not for their understanding of faith and conversion or justification, but rather of faith and sanctification. The Somerset

Confession cites Acts 26:18 as part of a catenae of scripture passages in its claim "THAT this faith being wrought in truth and power, it doth not only interest us in our justification, sonship, and glory, but it produceth as effects and fruits, a conformity, in a measure, to the Lord Jesus, in his will, graces and virtues" (1656, XXIII; cf. Caffyn 1660, 13; Baptist Faith and Message 1925, IX). Likewise, several interpreters explore Paul's insistence on obedience to Christ in the next verse (Acts 26:19) as a hallmark and virtue of the Christian life (Blackwood 1654, 42–43; Keach 1682, 731; Maston 1987, 83–84).

In Acts 26:24, another accusation is made against Paul. "Festus exclaimed in a loud voice: 'Paul, you are raving mad; your great learning is driving you mad!'" American missiologist W.O. Carver (1868–1954) captures the dilemma often faced by persons of deep faith and commitment, like Paul: "It is a sad commentary on human nature that men who are enthusiastic for the deep things of the spirit subject themselves to suspicion of their sanity. A missionary to India said that his friends in America thought he was a fool for going, and the Indians thought he was a fool for coming" (1916, 250–51).

Chrysostom thought Paul had misunderstood Agrippa's comment that Paul was seeking to persuade him to become a Christian *en oligō* (i.e., within a short period of time" (26:28; NRSV "quickly") as "with little cost or trouble," which Chrysostom thought required something *like ex oligou*. Chrysostom attributes the misunderstanding to Paul's lack of learning (*idiotēs*; *Hom. Act.* 52).

John Calvin also attends to the history of interpretation this verse (and in implicit disagreement with Chrysostom):

> Interpreters give different explanations of the phrase *en oligo*. Valla thought that it ought to be translated like this, 'You are very near to making me a Christian.' Erasmus (1469–1536) renders it, 'in a small degree.' The Vulgate has the simpler reading, 'in a little,' because in rendering it word for word, it has left readers free to make up their own minds. And it certainly can be made to apply to time well, as if Agrippa had said, 'You will make me a Christian all at once, or in a single moment.' If anyone objects that Paul's reply does not fit in with that, there is an easy solution. Because his words were ambiguous, Paul skillfully referred what had been said about time to the situation. Therefore, when Agrippa meant that he was almost made a Christian in a short time, Paul added that he wished that both he and his companions might ascend from small beginnings to higher levels of progress" (*Commentary on Acts*, 26:28).

What Chrysostom credits to Paul's lack of learning, Calvin attributes to Paul's rhetorical skill!

John Wesley (1703–91), on the other hand, focuses on how Festus, Paul, and Agrippa provide examplesfor his reader: "See here, Festus altogether a heathen, Paul altogether a Christian, Agrippa halting between both. Poor Agrippa! But almost persuaded! So near the mark, and yet fall short! Another step, and thou art within the vail. Reader, stop not with Agrippa; but go on with Paul" (*ENNT*, Acts 26:28).

Chrysostom asserts that the reference to Paul's chains (Acts 26:29) is evidence that his speech was "devoid of flattery." He claims: "This man [Paul], who glories in his bonds [Phil 1:12–14; 2 Tim 2:9], who displays them as if they were a gold chain, deprecates them for these men. For they were still too weak, and he had spoken rather in condescension. For what is better than those chains, which often appear in his epistles, as in 'Paul, a prisoner of Jesus Christ'" (*Hom. Act.* 52). Elsewhere, Chrysostom argues that this accommodation (i.e., being in chains) is necessary also with unbelieving contemporaries: "We must therefore condescend. For once they learn of the true life, they will also know the beauty of this iron and the distinction that comes from these chains" (*Hom. 1 Cor.* 33.7; ACCS, 298).

John Wesley also complimented Paul's speech before Agrippa (Acts 26): "Nothing can be imagined more suitable or more graceful, than this whole discourse of Paul before Agrippa; in which the seriousness of the Christian, the boldness of the apostle, and the politeness of the gentleman and the scholar, appear in a most beautiful contrast, or rather a most happy union" (*ENNT*, Acts 26:3).

Kierkegaard commented on Acts 26 as it reflects on the character of an "apostle":

> We find no hostile references to humankind in any remark by an apostle. They [the apostles] are so reconciled with God, with the thought of being sacrificed, and so exclusively concerned with their relation to God that on that account they have entirely forgotten their relation to people. …
>
> Paul does not judge King Agrippa, does not attack him in his speech, does not wound him with a word. On the contrary, he deals gently with him; his words are gentle and conciliatory when he says: I would to God that not only you but also all who hear me this day might become such as I am—except for these chains. An apostle suffers: he does not struggle with people, not because he proudly and superiorly elevates himself about their attack—by no means, but because he is solely concerned with his own relation to God (*KW* 15:335).

Finally, several interpreters explore the image of Paul in chains (Acts 26:1, 29). In his interpretation of Acts 26:1 ("Paul stretched forth his hand and began to make his defense"), Horatio Hackett (1808–1875) observed: "The gesture was the more courteous, because the attention asked for was certain, from the known curiosity of the hearers. *On the arm which Paul raised hung one of the chains* to which he alludes in v. 29" (our emphasis; Hackett 1882, 281–82; cf. Blackwood 1653, 19–20; Polhill 1992, 508–09).

Overview

The final chapters of Acts (27–28) recount Paul's sea voyage to Rome. A storm at sea and shipwreck on Malta occupy the entirety of Acts 27. Various details of the shipwreck story are taken up by interpreters and given symbolic significance. Further, the chapter has spawned considerable reflection on divine providence. After a brief stay on Malta (28:1–10) in which Paul's encounter with a viper has been the topic of much verbal *and* visual interpretation, Paul journeys to Rome

The Acts of the Apostles Through the Centuries, First Edition. Heidi J. Hornik and Mikeal C. Parsons.

(28:11–16), a passage of much interest to Luther in his polemic against the "Papists." The closing verses (28:17–31) record Paul's encounters with the Jews at Rome during his house arrest there and is the basis for continued reflection on Jewish–Christian (and other race) relations and the puzzling, "open-ended" conclusion to the book.

Reception and Interpretations

Acts 27

Various Interpretive Issues in Acts 27

Few interpreters comment on the events (27:1–12) leading up to the "more exciting shipwreck passage that follows" (Chung and Hains 2014, 348). German Lutheran theologian Johann Spangenberg, however, does remark on the friendship and kindness that Paul experiences: "God gave Paul two good companions, Luke and Aristarchus, who were no little consolation to him on such a trip. The centurion Julius treated him kindly and allowed him to go to his friends and to be cared for. It is not a small refreshment to a poor, deserted person when in the midst of stress and grief he finds people who befriend him and treat him well" (Spangenberg, *Brief Exegesis of Acts 27*; RCS, 349). Calvin thinks that Luke singles out Aristarchus among Paul's companions, because he was a wealthy believer who had paid Paul's expenses over the past three years (*Commentary on Acts*, 27:2).

A number of interpreters comment on Paul's speech to the crew and passengers in the midst of the storm. Reformer Rudolf Gwalther (1519–1586), for example, notes that Paul "did not despair and was not overcome with fear in the middle of dangers instead through prayer he fled to God, who comforted him, so that he was able to comfort and strengthen others. By this example we are taught that we must not by and by despair in time of danger but put our whole hope and trust in God" (*Homilies* 168, Acts 27:21–26; see also Heinrich Bullinger, *Commentary on Acts* 27:21–26; RCS, 352).

Karl Barth observes that the angel who appeared to Paul in Acts 27:23 is similar to *the* angel of Yahweh in the "history of salvation":

> He opens the prison for the apostles in $5^{19f.}$ and for Peter in $12^{7f.}$. He orders Philip to the place where he will meet the Ethiopian eunuch (8^{26}), and tells Cornelius to get into touch with Peter ($10^{3f.}$). He comforts Paul in the storm (27^{23}), and smites Herod, the enemy of the community, at the very moment when the people say of him that his voice is that of a god and not of a man (12^{23}). And even here it seems to be the case that he owes his singular position and designation to the singular

task ascribed to him. ... *The* angel is *the* witness of God. With his appearance, words and acts he attests the work of God as such in the history of salvation and therefore in primal and eschatological history (*CD* 3.3.487, 488).

Augustine accused the Manichees of advocating for fasting on the Sabbath as an established "sacred practice." Augustine conceded that special circumstances might dictate the need for Sabbath fasting as it did for Paul in the midst of a sea storm (Acts 27:31, 33), but he concluded, "We ought not to have the least doubt that the Lord's Day should not be included among the days of fast" (*Letter* 36.29).

Most interpreters are reluctant to see the meal on the ship (Acts 27:33–38) as having Eucharistic overtones (despite the similarity in Paul's actions—taking bread, giving thanks, breaking it—to those preceding meal scenes which are recognized as eucharastic (e.g. Luke 9, Luke 24, Acts 2, and, of course, Luke 22). German Reformer Johannes Brenz, although he too stops short of viewing the scenes as Eucharistic, comments on the detail of Paul's prayer before the meal: "Dishes of food or vegetables are not sufficiently oiled or seasoned if they are prepared with external butter or salt, but they must also be prepared by the Lord's Prayer. This is the heavenly condiment, whereby food that is otherwise of very poor quality is yet rendered very delicious for a pious person" (Brenz, *Homily 118 on Acts 27*; RCS, 356). Swiss Reformed preacher Rudolf Gwalther appeals to the fact that Luke has specified the number of persons on the ship (276) as evidence that "God put forward his hand in that he brought so many together safe and sound to the shore. Here we see that it is easy for God to save many or a few" (*Homilies*, Acts 27:34–44; RCS, 356).

Symbolic Imagery in Ancient Interpretations of the Shipwreck (27:14–44)

Augustine suggests many of those shipwrecked with Paul (27:14–44) lost all their worldly possessions, yet the gain of those who had faith in God far outstripped their loss. Some of those with Paul "were lovers of this world; they were wrecked but escaped naked, and they not only lost all their external goods but found the house of their heart empty too. Paul, unlike them, carried his inheritance in his heart, his precious faith. That could not be snatched from him by any waves or storms, so, though he too escaped naked, he escaped a rich man" (*Exposition of Psalm 123.9; on 123:4–5*). Similarly, the Venerable Bede, eighth-century British monk and exegete, likens the shipwreck with "the fate of a mind attached to this world. When such a one has made no effort to trample mundane desires underfoot, he fixes the prow of his intention radically upon the earth, and therefore with waves of care he dashes to pieces the whoe structure of works that follow [from that intention]" (*Comm. Acts* 27:41b).

Some, like Augustine, understood the harbor to refer to heaven, the church's final resting place: "If God enables seafarers to come safely to port, is he going to leave his Church to her fate, and not bring her through to the final haven of rest?" (*Sermon 75.4 "On Matthew 14:24–33, the calming of the storm"*).

In *Liber contra Symmachum*, Prudentius (348–402/05) offered a distinctive, if not unique, interpretation of the ship and other symbols in Acts 27–28. The preface to book 1 of *c. Symm.* (1.1–44) is a paraphrase of Acts 27:13–28; 28:1–6 and anticipates the themes developed in the rest of the preface; it also parallels the preface of *c. Symm.* book 2, which parapharases the account of Peter walking on water in 14:22-33 (Partoens 2003: 38). In both examples, as was typical of patristic interpretation, the storm was understood to represent the persecutions faced by the church. For Prudentius, the storm of Acts 27 represented Roman persecutions of the past (*c. Symm.* 1.34–50/59–61/63–64). Paul's snakebite on the isle of Malta represented the recent, venomous attacks on Christianity by Symmachus (cf. Tertullian who likens heretical attacks on the Christian faith to scorpion stings and also cites the incident on Malta, *Scorp.* 1), who in c. 402 C.E. repeated earlier arguments in favor of restoring the altar and statue of the pagan goddess, Victory, in the Roman curia (Partoens 2003, 38). Paul's resistance to the viper's poison (1.76–79) represented the defense of the Christian faith by Prudentius and others (1.643-52).

Prudentius had to "modify" certain details of the Acts narrative in order to make it conform to his "idiosyncratic allegorical interpretation" (Partoens 2003, 38). For example, (1) Prudentius' description of the storm focuses on Paul (1.7–9) whereas, in Acts, Luke includes the reactions and responses of all those on board the ship. By focusing on Paul, Prudentius is also able to ignore the fact that most of the other passengers were likely not Christians. This omission enables Prudentius to equate the ship with the Christian church. (2) In Prudentius' paraphrase, the storm ends before the ship makes landfall and the ship enters the harbor easily and intact (10–14); in Acts, of course, the ship goes aground, is broken apart, and survivors are forced to swim ashore to Malta or cling to pieces of the ship's wreckage. For Prudentius, the harbor represents the period following the earlier Roman persecution and not heaven, the ultimate goal of the Church's journey (see as Augustine, cited above, says). These details allow Prudentius to argue that the church had survived intact the past period of persecution and would also be able to defend itself against these more recent attacks by Symmachus and others. (3) No Maltese locals receive Paul nor react to his snakebite. Again, by eliminating any reference to pagans in his paraphrase, Prudentius is more easily able to equate the snakebite to the heretical and venomous rhetoric of Symmachus to which Paul, Prudentius and the church would prove immune (Partoens 2003, 40–51).

Prudentius' allegory is distinct from those who see in the shipwreck scene a figure of Christ's death and resurrection (Arator) or Christian baptism in which the "old person" is cast off in the "shipwreck of baptism" (Paulinus, *Epistulae* 49.11; cited by Partoens 2003, 50).

The Providence of God and the Shipwreck of Paul (Acts 27)

Early in the interpretive tradition, Ammonius denies that the storm was the result of fate: "He [Paul] was not able to convince them to spend the winter in Crete, so that it was not fate that dragged them into danger but their will" (*Catena on Acts* 27:10; ACCS, 301). Pointing to Acts 27:32, Chrysostom comments that the sailors "did not believe Paul through providence, so that they might believe him after the experience of the facts" (*Hom. Act.* 53.2). For most of the history of interpretation, however, the providence of God, evidenced in the sea storm and Paul's (and others') response to it, is the source of much reflection on Acts 27.

Comparing Acts 27:44 to Genesis 19:22, in which God spares the city of Zoar in response to Lot's intercession, Luther notes that "because of Paul alone all who were sailing in the same ship were preserved in the shipwreck" (*Lectures on Genesis* 19.1.24). Luther makes a similar point about divine preservation later in lectures on Genesis, only now it is the ship (and not only its occupants) which reaches the harbor safely (despite the fact that Acts states explicitly that the ship is broken apart by the storm):

> But because there are some godly men, or only one godly man, in the same ship, the ship must reach port safe and sound, however much it has been tossed about by a heavy storm, even though a thousand devils have been fighting in opposition and causing tumult in the same ship. So also for the sake of Paul alone, a ship is saved and 276 men who were with him in the ship, as we read in Acts 27:37. In the same manner, the world continues for the sake of the church in the world. Otherwise heaven and earth would be burned up in one moment, for the world is not worthy of one grain of wheat since it is full of blasphemies and godlessness. But because the church is in the midst of the ungodly, God for its sake permits also the ungodly to enjoy the common blessings of this life (*Lectures on Genesis* 34.1.30; Jerome makes a similar point in *Jov.* 2.24).

Similarly, John Wesley (1703–91) observed about Acts 27:24: "And rather will many bad men be preserved with a few good, (so it frequently happens,) than one good man perish with many bad. So it was in this ship: so it is in the world" (*ENNT*, Acts 27:24). Calvin, however, was careful to note that the sparing of the evil was not due in any way to the merits of the righteous: "Here ariseth a question, how far the integrity of the saints doth profit the wicked? First, we must remove the superstition of the Papists, who, when they hear that God is good to the bad, for the good's sake, dream that they be mediators, who obtain salvation for the world through their merits" (*Commentary on Acts*, 27:24; 2.644).

In its article on "Divine Providence," the Second London Confession (1689, V) states: "God, in *his* ordinary *Providence* [Act. 27. 31, 44.] maketh use of means, yet is free to work, without, above, and against them at *his* pleasure." The comments by Particular Baptist pastor John Gill (1697–1771) serve to unpack the logic of Second London (Gill 1796, 1007–8):

> God had determined to save the whole ship's crew, and that in the same way and manner; they were all to be shipwrecked; some were not to leave the ship beforehand, and save themselves in the boat, but they were all to be exposed to equal danger, and then be saved; and till that time came, the proper and prudent means were to be made use of, who were the shipmen, who best knew how to manage the ship in this extremity: this teaches us that the end and means, in the decrees of God, are not to be separated; nor is any end to be expected without the use of means; and means are as peremptorily fixed, and are as absolutely necessary, and must as certainly be accomplished, as the end.

Modern commentators have noted this emphasis on God's providence too, albeit with a bit more attention to the narrative flow of the text. Charles Talbert, for example, notes that the shipwreck was caused by the season of the year (27:9), but that the passengers' and crew's deliverance was divinely planned and designed to demonstrate God's judgment of Paul's innocence (Talbert 1997, 220–21, 235). Likewise, John Polhill comments:

> At each point when the situation seemed most desperate, there came a word of encouragement from Paul—his God would not abandon them, take heart, eat, be of good cheer. Then final deliverance came. All were saved. Paul's God had indeed not abandoned them to the anger of the seas. One cannot miss the emphasis on the divine providence, and it is precisely through the detailed telling of the story that the lesson has its greatest impact. It is "narrative theology" at its best (1992, 514).

John Wesley meditates on the dynamic and necessary interaction between divine agency and human response evident in 27:31:

> We may learn hence, to use the most proper means for security and success, even while we depend on Divine Providence, and wait for the accomplishment of God's own promise. He never designed any promise should encourage rational creatures to act in an irrational manner; or to remain inactive, when he has given them natural capacities of doing something, at least, for their own benefit. To expect the accomplishment of any promise, without exerting these, is at best vain and dangerous presumption, if all pretense of relying upon it be not profane hypocrisy (*ENNT*, Acts 27:31).

Citing passages in Acts 27, twentieth-century theologian W.T. Conner also enlarges his horizon to consider the interplay between divine sovereignty and human contingency:

Here we must remember that a thing may be certain from the standpoint of God's purpose and yet humanly conditioned and from that point of view contingent. A good illustration of this is found in Paul's experience in the storm on his way to Rome as a prisoner (Acts 27:14 ff.). In the midst of the storm Paul told the company on the ship that God had assured him that they would all, without the loss of a man, be saved (vv. 22–25). Yet later on when the sailors were about to escape in the boat, Paul told the soldiers that, if the sailors got out in the boat, they (the soldiers) could not be saved (vv. 30–32).

The salvation of a man elected to salvation is from all eternity certain in the mind and purpose of God, yet it is conditioned upon faith; and it is conditioned upon a faith that perseveres and conquers. A man may be elected to salvation and yet his salvation conditioned upon the fact that somebody shall preach to him the gospel (Conner 1924, 245).

African-American pastor, Walter Brooks, reflected poetically on Paul as the agent of the miraculous event of the shipwreck:

> On seas unknown; 'neath starless skies;
> With chart and compass swept away
> A Ship was breaking on the rocks,
> When, for a fortnight, driven on
> By all the fury of the deep,
> It sought, by soundings, for a port.
> Oh, what a wreck! That proud old ship!
> Its precious cargo all a loss,
> Engulfed, and buried in the sea!
> And yet *no man* on board was harmed!
> The lives of all were saved, through One,
> Who wore the chains of martyrdom
> (Brooks 1945, 153).

Acts 28

Paul and the Viper on Malta (Acts 28:1–10)

Augustine argues that it was possible for deadly creatures, such as lions and vipers, originally to have been created harmless "if no occasion had arisen for punishing vices … or testing virtue." As an example of the latter, Augustine cites the example of Paul who "had a deadly viper clinging to his arm and doing him no harm" (*Gen. litt.* 3.15 [3.24]; Augustine's Latin at this point rings quite lyrical: *in ipsius apostoli manu mortifera vipera inhaesit nec laesit*).

A number of apocryphal Gospels, perhaps inspired by the story of Paul and the viper in Acts 28:1–6, recount a narrative about the boy Jesus healing James (his "half-brother," son of Joseph) who was collecting sticks (*Inf. Gos. Thom.* 16 [version A]) or vegetables (*Ps.-Mt.* 41) and was bitten on the hand by a viper. In both stories, Jesus blows on James's hand; James is healed and the viper dies.

John Calvin sees value in the locals' assumption that Paul is a murderer since he was bitten by a viper (28:4) as evidence of divine justice: "This judgment was common in all ages, that those who were grievously punished had grievously offended. Neither was this persuasion conceived of nothing; but it came rather from a true feeling of godliness. For God, to the end he might make the world without excuse, would have this deeply rooted in the minds of all men, that calamity and adversity, and chiefly notable destruction, were testimonies and signs of his wrath and just vengeance against sins" (*Commentary on Acts*, 28:4; so also Wesley, *ENNT*, Acts 28:4), but, appealing to the example of Job, Calvin asserts that this judgment cannot be taken as a general principle: God does "not punish every man according to his deserts in this life; and sometimes the punishments of the godly are not so much punishments as trials of their faith and exercises of godliness" (*Commentary on Acts*, 28:4). Furthermore, the residents of Malta err in their judgment because they have not taken measure of Paul's whole life nor are they privy to the scope of history; in other words, they do not see from God's point of view: "We see now wherein the men of Melita were deceived, to wit, because having not scanned Paul's life, they judge him to be a wicked man, only because the viper doth bite him; secondly, because they stay not the end, but give judgment rashly" (*Commentary on Acts*, 28:4).

English cleric and poet John Donne (1572–1631) sees in the response of the Maltese locals a witness to the truth that God "had taught him [Paul] how to want and how to abound; how to bear honor and dishonor. … So God proceeded with him here in Malta, too. He passed him in their mouths from extreme to extreme. A viper seizes him and they condemn him for a murderer; he shakes off the viper and they change their minds and say he is a *god*" (Donne, *Sermon on the Sunday of Saint Paul's Conversion*; *Works* 2:334; RCS, 360). Wesley also notes that the locals quickly flip-flop in their assessment, but draws a different conclusion: "A little before he was a murderer; and presently he is a God: … nay, but there is a medium. He is neither a murderer nor a God but a man of God. But natural men never run into greater mistakes, than in judging the children of God" (*ENNT*, Acts 28:6; so also Ammonius, *Catena on Acts* 28:5).

Fourth-century bishop of Caesarea Basil sees in the Malta episode a demonstration of Paul's faith and fulfillment of Scripture: "The beasts are the proof of faith. Do you have confidence in the Lord? You will tread upon an asp and an adder and you will trample a lion and a snake under foot [Ps 90.13 LXX]. And you have through faith authority to tread upon serpents and scorpions [Lk. 10.19]. Do you not see the viper when it latched on to Paul who was gathering

FIGURE 42   Maarten de Vos (1532–1603). *Saint Paul Bitten by a Viper*. 1566–68.
Wood. 124 × 199 cm. Louvre, Paris, France. Photo: Erich Lessing/Art Resource, NY

firewood, inflicted no damage, because the Holy One was found a fulfiller of
faith?" (*Catena on Acts* 28:3; 407.32–408.4).

Saint Paul Bitten by a Viper, a painting by Flemish artist Maarten de Vos,
includes many details from Luke's narrative of the snakebite (**Figure 42**; Acts
28:1–10). Paul and the man who presumably built the fire are closest to the
center. Paul had gathered a bundle of sticks and put them in the fire. The viper
who came out of the fire is seen spiraling up Paul's right hand (William Blake
chose to depict the next narrative moment in the pen and watercolor drawing,
St. Paul Shaking off the Viper, 1800–03; private collection; Butlin 1981, vol. 2,
plate 608).

There is a large group of onlookers to the event. They are a blend of
members of the patron's family and friends with characters from the biblical
account. According to the Musée du Louvre, that owns and has the painting
on view, it is from a suite of five panels commissioned by the Calvinist
merchant Aegidius Hooftman from Antwerp that were intended to decorate
his dining room. The paintings depicted scenes from the Life of Paul. Two
other panels survive and are in the Brussels Museum and in a French private
collection (Site officiel du musée du Louvre, http://cartelfr.louvre.fr/cartelfr/
visite?srv=car_not_frame&idNotice=8174 [accessed 21 July 2016]). This
commission represented a significant breakthrough to an important segment
of the wealthy of Antwerp.

Members of the Hooftman family and friends are strategically integrated into the painting. The two young people sitting in the front, lower left of the painting in contemporary 16th-century dress may be the patron's children. Behind the children stand a group of three turbaned men who probably represent the natives who, upon seeing the viper hanging from Paul's hand, determine that he must be a murderer. According to Luke, they are thinking that Paul escaped death at sea but now justice has caught up with him and will cause his death by poison.

The head of a woman is positioned between the first and second turbaned man in that group. It is most likely a portrait of Mrs. Hooftman who is also dressed in contemporary garb. Continuing in a clockwise direction around the back of the picture to identify the remaining onlookers, another older male is sitting in judgment of what is happening and, behind him, a man carries wood to the fire. Several Roman soldiers are visible in the back of the painting directly behind Paul and in the group positioned next to the tree. There are women present who are most likely natives of Malta rather than travellers on the ship with Paul and his companions.

The final grouping includes Aegidius Hooftman himself, visible just behind a turbaned man and a Maltese woman on the right side of the painting in the foreground. The placement of the patron's wife on one side balanced with the husband on the other is quite common and, given the placement of these panels in the family dining room, these identifications are very probable.

At the time of this painting, Maarten de Vos was enrolled as a master in the Antwerp Guild of St Luke. Maarten de Vos was successful as both a draughtsman and a painter. He was trained by his father. De Vos was documented as a Lutheran as of 1584, but by the following year he had apparently adapted to the prevailing Catholicism. Maarten chose to remain in Antwerp, forgoing the general amnesty granted by Alessandro Farnese, Duke of Parma, that would have enabled him to leave Antwerp without hindrance within four years from August 1585. Maarten de Vos ranks among the most important painters of altarpieces in Antwerp during the 1590s. Due, in part, to the Counter Reformation, there was a renewed demand for altarpieces to replace those lost during iconoclastic riots in 1566 or the reformist movement of 1581. Except for a short stay in Ghent in the summer of 1589, he spent the rest of his career in Antwerp (Schuckman 2012).

The miracle at Malta represents a kind of interlude after the drama of the storm and shipwreck. Malta is the westernmost point of Paul's epic voyage and, according to Loveday Alexander, has a deserted island feel to it. Luke refers to the natives as *barbaroi* in Greek, and they are kindly but superstitious (Alexander 2001, 1060). When they see that Paul does not swell up and/or die from the viper bite, they change their minds about him and believe that he is a god.

Another depiction contains *Paul Bitten by a Viper,* from the Carrand ivory diptych in Florence that dates from the late fourth or early fifth century (**Figure 43**). There are actually three scenes on this vertically-oriented ivory. The uppermost scene is Paul seated before one man to whom he is talking and another man, standing behind him listens attentively. Kessler suggests that,

FIGURE 43   *Paul and Viper, Healing of Publius' Father.* c. 400. Marble. Carrand Diptych, Museo del Bargello, Florence. Photo: With permission from the Ministero per i Beni e le Attività Culturali di Firenze

although the depiction could refer to any of Paul's encounters (Paul Preaching in Athens, Acts 17, 15, has been proposed), in this context, Paul's defense before Festus or Agrippa (Acts 25–26) seems more likely (Kessler, 1979, 113–114).

The central scene shows Paul bitten by a viper with three men of Malta watching what will result from this seemingly fatal occurrence. These may be the same three men grouped together on the left side of the Maarten de Vos painted version discussed above. However, Kessler identifies one of the three as the chief magistrate, Publius, who will become integral to the next scene in Acts (28:7–10) and the third scene on the diptych (Kessler 1979, 114). Publius, according to Acts, is not even present when Paul is bitten by the viper. In the Carrand diptych, Publius is given a central position of power and focus.

The fire is visible between Paul and Publius. Publius and the two men on the right react with raised arms and turned heads. The diptych is detailed and beautifully carved. The garments are striated and vary in type and shape. The facial features and bodies are each individualized. Publius is certainly portrayed as a *princeps insulae* (Shelton 1986, 177).

The Carrand ivory diptych integrates the stories of *Paul Bitten by a Viper* with the *Healing of Publius' Father and Another Sick Man* in the central and lower sections. Paul is the leftmost figure in the middle register. Associations between the patron, Publius, and the function of the ivory have been subjects of recent art historical discussion. Kathleen Shelton suggested that the patron of the fifth-century ivory was probably a member of the aristocracy and, by relating himself to Publius, emphasized Publius' witness to the faith (Shelton 1986, 180). As a consular diptych, it would have been given as a gift to the two newly-appointed chief magistrates (consuls) of the Roman state selected annually. The consular diptychs serve to mark time and record history (Bowes 2001, 338–357).

Another interesting feature of this diptych has to do with the formal arrangement of the figures, their stories and perspective in the ivory. In the lowest register, the emaciated man, presumably Publius' father, is led by another man to Paul for healing. Another male resident of Malta comes for healing by Paul as well. The figure farthest to the right points upward to Paul as he directs this sick friend to do the same. All of the figures in the lowest register must, in fact, "look up" to be involved with the characters depicted in the central register. This is quite an inventive and effective manner in which to portray depth and perspective. Being "above" implies being further back in the distance. "Under" refers to figures "in front of or before" those "above" them. Once the viewer realizes this conveyance of perspectival relationships, the scene can be understood and recognized. Although the construct of "above" referring to figures in the distance has been done for some time in ivories, the sophistication of integrating two seemingly separate figural scenes is remarkable.

A diptych is a two-part panel, thus a brief discussion of the subject of the companion leaf is in order. It depicts a reclining Adam naming the beasts in Paradise. The formal arrangement is more typical than the Paul leaf, with Adam placed at the top to signify that the beasts below him stand "in front" or "before" him. Iconographically, there are parallels between Adam and Paul via the writings and sermons of Basil and Ambrose: "The Carrand ivory presents a parallel between Adam's dominion over the animals through reason and Paul's dominion over the serpent through faith. The Diptych stresses the importance of faith for me to achieve salvation and to perfect once again the divine image which he [Adam] possessed in Paradise but tarnished in the Fall" (Konowitz 1984, 488).

The healing scenes in Malta serve as proof that the god whom Paul serves is still with him and that, far from demeaning Paul, the whole shipwreck has served to load him with honour (Alexander 2001, 1060). Kessler observed, "the carver of the Carrand ivory emphasized the apostle's authority as one of Christ's successors. The artist reinforced the allusion to Christ by showing one of the 'other sick people on the island' as a man with a paralyzed arm, recalling thereby the miraculous cure of a man with a withered hand effected by Christ (Matt 12, 9–13, Mk 3, 1–6, and Luke 6, 6–11)" (Kessler 1979, 114). This concept of ancestors, lineage and successors described here between Paul and Christ represents a Christianizing of chronology and dovetails with Kim Bowes' notion that "like the consular diptychs, re-inscribed with the names of Christian saints, the Carrand's patrons adoption of Publius and Paul as Christian ancestors witnessed the birth of a new Christian chronology, one which would replace the 1,000-year-old system of civic judges with which the Romans marked their time and history" (Bowes 2001, 353).

Paul's Arrival in Rome (28:11–29)

While ships were often take to symbolize the Church (see above), John Calvin assumes the ship which Paul boards in Malta (28:11) is "polluted with wicked sacrilege" being dedicated to idols, the Twins (Castor and Pollux). Still, because Paul did not choose to travel on the vessel he "is not polluted"; rather "Paul was no more defiled by entering into this ship, than when he did behold the altars at Athens; because, being void of all superstition, he knew that all the rites of the Gentiles were mere illusions" (*Commentary on Acts*, 28:11; see also Luther, *3rd Sermon at Wittenburg* 12.1).

Luther appeals to Acts 28:11 to argue against acts of violence against the Roman church, even though he had fundamental and sharp disagreements with the "Papists": "St. Paul travelled in a ship that carried as its figurehead the idols called the Twin Brothers, but he did not tear to pieces either the figurehead or the ship. I too have denounced vigorously the idolatry of the pope, more vigorously perhaps than anyone else; but I have never yet laid hands on it, nor asked anyone else to do so except those who have the authority and the power from God. We have done more than enough if we preach against it and set consciences free" (*Receiving Both Kinds in the Sacrament* 3.1.2).

Luther uses the fact that only Paul in the New Testament is said to have been in Rome (28:14) in order to poke fun at Petrine succession: "I do not want to be the judge as to whether or not St. Peter was in Rome; for probably only St. Paul, who certainly was there (as Luke writes in Acts [28:14] and he himself writes in his epistles), can have ordained the church and the bishop in Rome. But I can cheerfully say, as I have seen and heard in Rome, that in Rome one doesn't know where the bodies of St. Peter and St. Paul lie, or if they lie there at all! Pope and cardinals know very well that they do not know that" (*Against the Roman Papacy an Institution of the Devil* 3.1.1).

Appealing to the example of encouragement and fellowship that Paul experienced with fellow believers following his travails at sea (28:15), Martin Luther extolled the importance of seeking community when facing adversity: "This is my only and my best advice: Don't remain alone when you are assailed! Flee solitude! Do as that monk did who, when he felt tempted in his cell, said, 'I won't stay here; I'll run out of the cell to my brethren.' So it's reported of Paul in the book of Acts that he suffered for fourteen days from severe hunger and from shipwreck and afterward was received by his brethren and took courage. This is what I do too. I'd rather go to my swineherd John, or even to the pigs themselves, than remain alone" (*Table Talk* 6.29 [No. 3799]; see also *Table Talk* 3.41 [No. 1385]; *Lectures on Genesis* 13.1.7). Elsewhere, Luther cites this same verse in which the great Apostle is encouraged by anonymous believers in Puteoli as support of his contention that "even the greatest saints have seasons in which they are weak but others are strong" (*Commentary on Psalm* 90.2.9).

In the last episode of the epic Italian serial, *Atti Degli Apostoli* (1968) directed by Roberto Rossellini, Paul, who in the film is generally unaware of the impact he and other Christian evangelists are having on the larger culture, is genuinely surprised to learn that he is known and even admired by the relatively large Christian community in Rome.

From Paul's adversity—he is in custody "with a soldier" and debating his adversaries, "the local leaders of the Jews" (28:16–17)—Chrysostom draws the lesson "that always through the things which seem to be against us, all things turn out for us." He elaborates by comparing Paul's predicament with that of Moses (and others): "Unless the infants had been cast forth, Moses would not have been saved, he would not have been brought up in the palace. When he was safe, he was not in honor; when he was exposed, then he was in honor" (*Hom. Act.* 54).

No doubt aware of the popularity of his preaching due to his powerful rhetorical skills, British Baptist pastor C.H. Spurgeon (1834–92) uses Acts 28:24 ("Some began to believe what he said, but some were unbelieving") in a pastoral reflection to suggest that this "is the only proper way to calculate the results of our ministry. We just want the account-book ruled with two columns. On one side we must put down the long list of the some that believe not; and on the brighter side we may enter what is too often, the far less number of the some that believe. This is the only true method, I repeat it, by which we can hold a stock-taking so as to ascertain the net profit of the preaching of the gospel" (Spurgeon 1863, 9:349–50, 355–56).

In this last recorded meeting with the Jews, Paul quotes Isaiah 6 (Acts 28:25; Isa 6:9–10 is cited multiple times, elsewhere in the NT: Matt 13:14/Mark 4:12/Luke 8:10; John 12:39). The Venerable Bede, eighth-century British monk and exegete, observes: "Lest we think that their hardness of heart" ... [is] "attributable to their nature and not to their will, he added a fault, their free will, saying, 'And they have closed their eyes'" (*Comm. Acts* 28:27; cf. Isa 6:9–10 LXX).

Appealing to Romans 9, 10 to imagine how Paul would approach his fellow Jews, American missiologist W. O. Carver (1868–1954) attempts to capture the pathos in this final scene. With "deep yearning, like that of Jesus over Jerusalem [Luke 19:41], he [Paul] had to tell them that a time came when God's message became a rejecting, hardening judgment against unbelievers rather than a calling invitation to redemption. ... God cannot wait forever on the religious pride that calls for first place in election, but will take no place in true religion" (Carver 1916, 267–68). The Native American writer of the SBC Lifeway Adult Sunday School lesson on Acts 28:28 reflects on the way in which the Jews' resistance to the Gospel opens the door for the Gentiles:

> Our people need to be evangelized. We need to love them and reach out to them. However, we are not the only people on this planet. In our visitation efforts, we should never skip any house. Our churches should never be for just one race—Jesus died for all people. Whenever we become exclusive, we are bereft of the power of God. In choosing to proclaim the gospel, we must realize it was given for all people. ...
>
> Paul loved his people. Paul understood the Jews and their culture. He sacrificed a great deal in preaching to them. He could speak the language and identify with all that they did. He knew their prejudices because he had at one time been that way. It was not any easier for Paul to go to other nationalities than it is for you or me. However, he went knowing that it was the Father's will.
>
> If Paul had declined the opportunity to go to the Gentiles, we might not have heard the gospel. He chose to be involved rather than to be insensitive. Someone in your community is waiting for you. He may be an Indian, then again he may not. If he is in darkness, he needs your light (SBC-Lifeway 1993, 48–49).

The Ending of Acts (Acts 28:30–31)

There has been much debate, ancient and modern, regarding the way Acts ends inconclusively, with Paul confined in Rome preaching for two years "without hindrance." There is no mention of his trial and death. British philosopher John Locke (1632–1704) compared the ending of Acts with John's Gospel (20:30–31), arguing that Luke, like John, recorded only what was "necessary and sufficient to be believed for the attaining eternal life" (*The Reasonableness of Christianity* 1695, 101). Professor Frank Stagg (1911–2001) develops what he believes to be a major theme of Acts, based on the final word of the book, "unhindered":

AN ADVERB is a strange word with which to end a book, but Luke did just that. In fact, the two-volume work, Luke-Acts, is brought to a dramatic close and epitomized in an adverb. Throughout his two volumes, Luke never lost sight of his purpose, and he planned well the conclusion to it all, achieving the final effort by the last stroke of the pen. "Unhinderedly," Luke wrote, describing the hard-won liberty of the gospel. This liberty came only after many barriers had been crossed, and it was won because its first home was in the mind and intention of Jesus himself. ... The conclusion of Acts is unexcelled for its dramatic power. The major issues are brought together in the last paragraph, and the major message is reaffirmed in the very last word of the book, in the adverb, "unhinderedly" (Stagg 1955, 266).

After Acts

The influence of Acts extends far beyond the words on the page. But at what point does Acts end and its interpretation begin? Some commentators have sought a more satisfying literary ending for Acts, arguing that the Pastoral Epistles were the third volume of a planned trilogy by Luke (Wilson 1979; Quinn 1978). Others see a kind of literary legacy continued in the apocryphal acts, though that legacy may be in terms of competition with (*Acts of Peter*?), or supplement to (*Acts of Philip*?), or continuation of (*Acts of Paul*?), the canonical Acts (Bovon 2003, 191; on the contested relationships between canonical and apocryphal Acts, cf. Bauckham 1993; Stoops and MacDonald 1997). The early

The Acts of the Apostles Through the Centuries, First Edition. Heidi J. Hornik and Mikeal C. Parsons.
© 2017 Heidi J. Hornik and Mikeal C. Parsons. Published 2017 by John Wiley & Sons, Ltd.

sections of the *Ecclesiastical History* by the church's first full-fledged historian, Eusebius of Caesarea (260–339), can, in part, be viewed as an attempt to expand canonical Acts by filling in the gaps of missing details of the apostles' lives (cf. Frede 1999, 223–250).

However one solves the conundrum of Acts' literary ending, commentators are agreed that, at least with respect to the story of Paul contained within its pages, the narrative is unfinished. Citing Dionysius of Corinth, Eusebius of Caesarea (260–339), among others, reports the tradition concerning Paul's death: "Paul was beheaded in Rome itself ... under Nero" (*Hist. eccl.* 2.25). The image of the martyred Paul sparked the imaginations of artists down the centuries, who often portrayed Paul with a sword, the iconographical symbol of his martyrdom [cf. Eph 6:17], even when portraying a different scene from his life (see, e.g., paintings by Massacio 1426; El Greco 1606).

Other artists chose to depict the arrest of Paul by Roman soldiers just before his death. Such is the case with one of the most famous and complicated programs for Early Christian relief sculpture, which occurs on the sarcophagus of the Roman city prefect named Junius Bassus (**Figure 44**). The inscription on the sarcophagus documents him being a "neofitus" (newly baptized) at his death in 359 (Malbon 2012). The sarcophagus was rediscovered in 1597, and today is in the Treasury Museum (Museo Tesoro) of St. Peter's basilica in Rome. Originally, it was placed near the tomb of St. Peter. An excellent plaster cast is displayed in the Museo Pio Cristiano of the Vatican Museum, Rome. Stylistically, the high relief carvings illustrate the transition from the classical Roman to the Early Christian. This was produced just after Constantine legalized Christianity in Rome but before it became the official state religion of Rome.

Iconographically, the program includes Old Testament scenes that prefigure New Testament events. It is a double-register columnar sarcophagus with a carved lid. There are five scenes on each register and stories from both testaments appear in both the upper and lower registers. Elizabeth Struthers Malbon suggests an iconographic explanation based on its mid fourth-century context as well as considering earlier and contemporary conventions of sepulchral art (Malbon 1990, ix).

The seizure or arrest of Peter or Paul "always signifies the Death of Christ and the victory he won by his Death: the death of a martyr as a triumph over death was proof of his fellowship with Christ" (Malbon 1990, 48, citing Gertrud Schiller). The second and fourth scenes on the upper register are arrest scenes of Peter and Christ, respectively. Between them is a beardless, youthful Christ enthroned over Coelus (personification of the universe). Below the Enthroned Christ is the Triumphal Entry of Christ *into Jerusalem*. Various Christological interpretations and analogies have been drawn about the relationships of these four scenes.

FIGURE 44   *Saint Paul Being Led Toward Martyrdom.* Detail of relief from the lower panel of the sarcophagus of Junius Bassus. 4th century. Marble. Museum of the Treasury, St. Peter's Basilica, Vatican State Photo: Erich Lessing/Art Resource, NY

Saint Paul Being Led Toward Martyrdom, illustrated here, is the fifth and final scene on the lower register. Its relationship to the other four scenes on the lower register seems a bit more convoluted. Although Malbon finds this to be a post-figuring of Christ's arrest, she continues, "The scene of Paul's arrest, however, lacks the strict parallelisms in arrangement and treatment that link the arrest scenes of Peter and Christ. The representation of Paul is not centered in its niche, and both Paul and the guards show more movement than the upper-register figures" (Malbon 1990, 47).

The scenes in the lower register are *Job's Distress, Adam and Eve in the Garden, Triumphal Entry, Daniel in the Lions' Den,* and *Paul Being Led to Martyrdom. Pilate's Judgment* is directly above the arrest of Paul. Malbon's typological reading, focused on a program of salvation, finds that the lower register, like the upper register, presents three emphases: (1) patience or endurance in the *sacrifice* of wellbeing or of life itself, suggested in the outermost pairing of

Job and Paul; (2) *obedience* in reference to the promise of salvation, pictured negatively in Adam and Eve and positively in Daniel; and (3) the *victorious Christ* portrayed in the triumphal entry in the center (Malbon 1990, 68).

Job prefigures the sacrificed lives of Christ and Paul. Fritz Saxl states that the *Judgment of Pilate* is "the only scene that indicates Christ's suffering, and His bowed head is the only sign of his impending martyrdom" (Saxl 1957, 1:55). Paul, like Christ, bows his head with the same resolve of his impending death.

We arrive at the end of this (all too brief) exploration of the reception and influence of the Acts of the Apostles through the centuries. As T. S. Eliot observed "to make an end is to make a beginning. The end is where we start from." After all, he continues, "the end of all our exploring Will be to arrive where we started/And know the place for the first time" (*The Four Quartets*, "Little Gidding" V). So we, too, are ready finally to begin our (re-)reading of the Acts of the Apostles: "In the first book, O Theophilus, I have dealt with all that Jesus began to do and teach...."

Citations of the Acts of the Apostles in
Creeds & Confessions of Faith in the Christian Tradition[1]

Acts 1 – First Helvetic Confession (1536), Chapter 11
Acts 1:1, 2 – Second Vatican Council (1962–65), §8, Chapter 5.19
Acts 1:2 – First London Confession (1644), Article 36.a; United Presbyterian Church
    Confessional Statement (1925), Article 13
Acts 1:2, 3 – Mennonite Articles of Faith (1766/1895/1902), Article 14.2

[1] Jaroslav Pelikan and Valerie Hotchkiss, eds, *Creeds & Confessions of Faith in the Christian Tradition* (3 vols; New Haven: Yale University Press, 2003).

The Acts of the Apostles Through the Centuries, First Edition. Heidi J. Hornik and Mikeal C. Parsons.
© 2017 Heidi J. Hornik and Mikeal C. Parsons. Published 2017 by John Wiley & Sons, Ltd.

Acts 1:2-11 – French Confession (1559/1571), Article 36.a

Acts 1:3 – Mennonite Articles of Faith (1766/1895/1902), Article 15.3; Mennonite Articles of Faith (1766/1895/1902), Article 24.2; Richmond Declaration of Faith (1887), Article 2.30; Metrophanes Critopoulos *Confession of Faith* (1625), Article 3.13

Acts 1:4 – Assemblies of God, *Statement of Fundamental Truths* (1916), Article 5

Acts 1:5 – French Confession (1559/1571), Article 28.b

Acts 1:7 – Mennonite Articles of Faith (1766/1895/1902), Article 33.4; Mennonite Articles of Faith (1766/1895/1902), Article 34.9; United Presbyterian Church *Confessional Statement* (1925), Article 40; Evangelical Lutheran Synod (1932), Article 42; Cumberland Presbyterian Church, *Confession of Faith* (1814/1883), Article 9.e

Acts 1:8 – Mennonite Articles of Faith (1766/1895/1902), Article 14.2[2]; Second Vatican Council (1962–65), §5.1, Chapter 3.19; Second Vatican Council (1962-65), §5.1, Chapter 3.21; Lausanne Covenant (1974), Article 6; Lausanne Covenant (1974), Article 14; Mennonite Confession of Faith (1963), Article 7; Second Vatican Council (1962–65), §5.1, Chapter 3.24; The Orthodox Confession of the Catholic and Apostolic Eastern Church (1638/1642), Article 84; Ulphilas, *Confession of Faith* (383; Jeremias II, *Reply to Augsburg Confession* (1576), §13 [P&H, II.430]; Assemblies of God, *Statement of Fundamental Truths* (1916), Article 5; United Presbyterian Church *Confessional Statement* (1925), Article 13; Gregory Palamas, *Confession of Orthodox Faith,* Article 2; Catechesis and Confession of Faith of Polish Brethren (1574), [C] Question 1.4 [P&H, 722]; Second Vatican Council (1962-65), §5.1, Chapter 2.17

Acts 1:8–11 – Lausanne Covenant (1974), Article 15

Acts 1:9 – Heidelberg Catechism (1563), Question 46.g; Zwingli, *A Reckoning of the Faith* (1530), 8 [P&H, IV.264]

Acts 1:9, 10 – The First Confession of Basel (1534), Article 6.c

Acts 1:9–11 – United Presbyterian Church *Confessional Statement* (1925), Article 12; The First Confession of Basel (1534), Article 4.b; Heidelberg Catechism (1563), Question 76.f

Acts 1:9–12 – Mennonite Articles of Faith (1766/1895/1902), Article 15.3

Acts 1:11 – Moravian Church (1749), *Easter Litany*, 2 [P&H, 151]; United Presbyterian Church *Confessional Statement* (1925), Article 40; Westminster Confession of Faith (1647), Chapter 8.4.i; Catechesis and Confession of Faith of Polish Brethren (1574), [C].6 Question 7 [P&H, IV.742]; Richmond Declaration of Faith (1887), Article 2.32; Heidelberg Catechism (1563), Question 46.i; Zwingli, *A Reckoning of the Faith* (1530), 8 [P&H, IV.264]; Geneva Catechism (1541/1542), [Question] 83; First London Confession (1644), Article 19.a; The Orthodox Confession of the Catholic and Apostolic Eastern Church (1638/1642), Article 56; Bohemian Confession (1535), Article 6.[2]; New Hampshire Confession (1833/1853), Article 18.o; Southern Baptist Convention, *Baptist Faith and Message* (1925), Article 17

Acts 1:14 – Second Vatican Council (1962–65), §5.1, Chapter 8.59; True Confession (1596), Article 35.b; Catechesis and Confession of Faith of Polish Brethren (1574), [C].4 Question 16 [P&H, IV.736]

Acts 1:15–17 – First Helvetic Confession (1536), Article 17.b

Acts 1:15-26 – Edict of Justinian (551), Article 12

Acts 1:16 – New Hampshire Confession (1833/1853), Article 1.a; United Presbyterian Church, *Confessional Statement* (1925), Article 3

Acts 1:17 – Second Vatican Council (1962-65), §5.1, Chapter 3.24

Acts 1:20 – United Presbyterian Church, *Confessional Statement* (1925), Article 28

Acts 1:21 – French Confession (1559/1571), Article 31.e

Acts 1:21–26 – Commission on Faith and Order (1982), Article 3.A.9

Acts 1:23 – Cambridge Platform (1648), Chapter 8.5.a; Cambridge Platform (1648), Chapter 10.2.a

Acts 1:23, 24 – Dordrecht Confession (1632), Article 9

Acts 1:24 – Mennonite Articles of Faith (1766/1895/1902), Article 24.3; Mennonite Articles of Faith (1766/1895/1902), Article 34.6; New Hampshire Confession (1833/1853), Article 9.b; Evangelical Lutheran Synod (1932), Article 25

Acts 1:24, 25 – True Confession (1596), Article 45.a

Acts 1:25 – Westminster Confession of Faith (1647), Chapter 32.1.d; Second Vatican Council (1962-65), §5.1, Chapter 3.24

Acts 1:47 – True Confession (1596), Article 24.a

Acts 2 – Heidelberg Catechism (1563), Question 49.c; Decrees of Union of the Council of Basel-Ferrara-Florence-Rome (1431–45), *Bull of Union with the Armenians*, November 1439, 15 [P&H, III.760]; Cambridge Platform (1648), Chapter 12.6; Commission on Faith and Order (1982), Article 1.C.5

Acts 2:1 – Mennonite Articles of Faith (1766/1895/1902), Article 23.7; United Presbyterian Church, *Confessional Statement* (1925), Article 29

Acts 2:1–3 – Second Vatican Council (1962–65), §5.1, Chapter 3.24; Zwingli, *A Reckoning of the Faith* (1530), 7 [P&H, IV.260]

Acts 2:1–4 – Mennonite Articles of Faith (1766/1895/1902), Article 14.2; Mennonite Articles of Faith (1766/1895/1902), Article 24.2; United Presbyterian Church *Confessional Statement* (1925), Article 13

Acts 2:1–21 – Mennonite Confession of Faith (1963), Article 7

Acts 2:1–36 – Second Vatican Council (1962–65), §5.1, Chapter 3.19

Acts 2:1–42 – The Orthodox Confession of the Catholic and Apostolic Eastern Church (1638/1642), Article 104

Acts 2:3 – Catechesis and Confession of Faith of Polish Brethren (1574), [C] Question 1.5 [P&H, IV.722]; Synodical Tome of 1351, Article 45 [P&H, II.366]

Acts 2:4 – Second Vatican Council (1962–65), §5.1, Chapter 3.21; Assemblies of God, *Statement of Fundamental Truths* (1916), Article 6; Metrophanes Critopoulos *Confession of Faith* (1625), Article 1.9 [P&H, II.480]

Acts 2:6 – Cambridge Platform (1648), Chapter 7.2.c

Acts 2:7 – The First Confession of Basel (1534), Article 4.b

Acts 2:16–21 – Mennonite Confession of Faith (1963), Article 11

Acts 2:17 – Richmond Declaration of Faith (1887), Article 10.5; Heidelberg Catechism (1563), Question 32.h

Acts 2:17, 18 – Second Vatican Council (1962–65), §5.1, Chapter 4.35

Acts 2:21 – The Reply to the Augsburg Confession (1576), Article 20; Synodical Tome of 1341, Article 50 [P&H, II.332]

Acts 2:22 – True Confession (1596), Article 3.m

Acts 2:23 – Westminster Confession of Faith (1647), Chapter 3.c; United Presbyterian Church *Confessional Statement* (1925), Article 4; United Presbyterian Church *Confessional Statement* (1925), Article 6; Mennonite Confession of Faith (1963),

Article 5.2; French Confession (1559/1571), Article 8.c; Heidelberg Catechism (1563), Question 51; Westminster Confession of Faith (1647), Chapter 5.2.h; Westminster Confession of Faith (1647), Chapter 5.4.o

Acts 2:23, 24 – Heidelberg Catechism (1563), Question 17.b; French Confession (1559/1571), Article 8.e; Westminster Confession of Faith (1647), Chapter 8.4.d

Acts 2:24 – Geneva Catechism (1541/1542), [Question] 65; Hubmaier, *A Christian Catechism* (1526), [Q.] 19.a [P&H, IV.678]

Acts 2:26 – Moravian Church (1749), *Easter Litany*, 5 [P&H, V.153]

Acts 2:27 – Westminster Confession of Faith (1647), Chapter 8.4.d; Metrophanes Critopoulos *Confession of Faith* (1625), Article 3.9.a [P&H, II.502]; Metrophanes Critopoulos *Confession of Faith* (1625), Article 3.10.b [P&H, II.502]; Eunomius, *Confession of Faith* (383), Article 3.g

Acts 2:28 – Dordrecht Confession (1632), Article 7.a; True Confession (1596), Article 21.e

Acts 2:30 – Belgic Confession (1561), Article 18

Acts 2:31 – Cumberland Presbyterian Church, *Confession of Faith* (1814/1883), Article 30.c

Acts 2:31–36 – The Transylvanian Confession of Faith (1579), Article 1

Acts 2:32–36 – Assemblies of God, *Statement of Fundamental Truths* (1916), Article 13.i

Acts 2:32–39 – Lausanne Covenant (1974), Article 4

Acts 2:33 – Second Vatican Council (1962–65), §5.1, Chapter 1.5; Catechesis and Confession of Faith of Polish Brethren (1574), [B] Question 22 [P&H, IV.720]; The First Confession of Basel (1534), Article 1.a; Geneva Catechism (1541/1542), [Question] 79.a; United Presbyterian Church *Confessional Statement* (1925), Article 11; United Presbyterian Church *Confessional Statement* (1925), Article 12; Epistle of the Apostles (c. 150), Chapter 3.b [P&H, I.54]

Acts 2:33–36 – Mennonite Articles of Faith (1766/1895/1902), Article 16.1

Acts 2:36 – Second Vatican Council (1962–65), §5.1, Chapter 1.5; Westminster Confession of Faith (1647), Chapter 8.3.w; Catechesis and Confession of Faith of Polish Brethren (1574), [B] Question 11 [P&H, IV.715]; First London Confession (1644), Article 25.i

Acts 2:36–38 – Catechesis and Confession of Faith of Polish Brethren (1574), [C].5 Question 7 [P&H, IV.738]

Acts 2:37 – First London Confession (1644), Article 33; Cambridge Platform (1648), Chapter 12.5

Acts 2:37, 38 – New Hampshire Confession (1833/1853), Article 8.j; First London Confession (1644), Article 39.f; Second Helvetic Confession (1566), Chapter 20.[1]

Acts 2:38 – Dordrecht Confession (1632), Article 7; Westminster Confession of Faith (1647), Chapter 28.6.r; Faith and Practice of Thirty Congregations (1651), Article 47; Mennonite Articles of Faith (1766/1895/1902), Article 19.1; New Hampshire Confession (1833/1853), Article 14.i; Hubmaier, *A Christian Catechism* (1526), [Q.42], [P&H, IV.681]; Metrophanes Critopoulos *Confession of Faith* (1625), Article 5.2.b; Dogmatic Decrees of the Council of Trent (Session 14.25 November 1551), Chapter 1 [P&H, IV 849]; Cumberland Presbyterian Church, *Confession of Faith* (1814/1883), Article 43.b; Heidelberg Catechism (1563), Question 66.c; Evangelical Lutheran Synod (1932), Article 21; Catechesis and Confession of Faith of Polish Brethren (1574), [C].5 Question 1.b [P&H, IV.736]; United Presbyterian Church *Confessional Statement* (1925), Article 13; Catechesis and Confession of Faith of

Polish Brethren (1574), [C] Question 1.2 [P&H, IV.722]; Heidelberg Catechism (1563), Question 69; Ten Articles (1536), Article [2].[8]; Westminster Confession of Faith (1647), Chapter 28.6.r; Schleitheim Confession (1527), Article 1.a; Dogmatic Decrees of the Council of Trent (Session 6.13 January 1547), Chapter 6 [P&H, IV.829]; Faith and Practice of Thirty Congregations (1651), Article 20; Lutheran General Synod, *Definite Platform* (1855), Part 2. Topic 5 [P&H, V.309]; United Presbyterian Church *Confessional Statement* (1925), Article 18

Acts 2:38, 39 – Westminster Confession of Faith (1647), Chapter 28.4.m; Cumberland Presbyterian Church, *Confession of Faith* (1814/1883), Article 54.f; True Confession (1596), Article 35.i; Westminster Confession of Faith (1647), Chapter 10.3.m; Cumberland Presbyterian Church, *Confession of Faith* (1814/1883), Article 102.h; Heidelberg Catechism (1563), Question 74.a

Acts 2:38–40 – Mennonite Articles of Faith (1766/1895/1902), Article 17.1

Acts 2:38–41 – United Presbyterian Church, *Confessional Statement* (1925), Article 30

Acts 2:38–42 – Cambridge Platform (1648), Chapter 12.2

Acts 2:39 – Richmond Declaration of Faith (1887), Article 10.6; Cumberland Presbyterian Church, *Confession of Faith* (1814/1883), Article 26.e; Westminster Confession of Faith (1647), Chapter 25.2.c; Cumberland Presbyterian Church, *Confession of Faith* (1814/1883), Article 94.h; Lutheran General Synod, *Definite Platform* (1855), Part 2. Topic 5 [P&H, V.310]

Acts 2:40 – Metrophanes Critopoulos *Confession of Faith* (1625), Article 5.2.b; Lausanne Covenant (1974), Article 4; True Confession (1596), Article 17.b

Acts 2:40, 41 – First London Confession (1644), Article 51.c

Acts 2:40–42 – True Confession (1596), Article 42.a

Acts 2:41 – Westminster Confession of Faith (1647), Chapter 28.6.r; Faith and Practice of Thirty Congregations (1651), Article 47; Faith and Practice of Thirty Congregations (1651), Article 50; Mennonite Articles of Faith (1766/1895/1902), Article 9.5; Mennonite Articles of Faith (1766/1895/1902), Article 16.2; Mennonite Articles of Faith (1766/1895/1902), Article 25.4; Cumberland Presbyterian Church, *Confession of Faith* (1814/1883), Article 109.g; Protestant Christian Batak Church, *Confession of Faith* (1951), Article 10; Cumberland Presbyterian Church, *Confession of Faith* (1814/1883), Article 101.g; First London Confession (1644), Article 34.f; Cambridge Platform (1648), Chapter 12.5; True Confession (1596), Article 17.c; Catechesis and Confession of Faith of Polish Brethren (1574), [C].5 Question 7 [P&H, IV.738]; Westminster Confession of Faith (1647), Chapter 28.6.r; Westminster Confession of Faith (1647), Chapter 28.3.k; Cambridge Platform (1648), Chapter 17.1.a; United Presbyterian Church *Confessional Statement* (1925), Article 35

Acts 2:41, 42 – New Hampshire Confession (1833/1853), Article 13.d; New Hampshire Confession (1833/1853), Article 14.l; True Confession (1596), Article 33.b^2 ; The First Confession of Basel (1534), Article 5.d; North American Baptist Conference (1982), Article 6

Acts 2:41–43 – First Helvetic Confession (1536), Article 23.a

Acts 2:42 – Dordrecht Confession (1632), Article 10.a; Mennonite Articles of Faith (1766/1895/1902), Article 23.7; Westminster Confession of Faith (1647), Chapter 21.5.w; Westminster Confession of Faith (1647), Chapter 21.6.i; Cumberland Presbyterian Church, *Confession of Faith* (1814/1883), Article 57.c; True Confession

(1596), Article 35.a, b; Catechesis and Confession of Faith of Polish Brethren (1574), [C].6 Question 2 [P&H, IV.741]; Cumberland Presbyterian Church, *Confession of Faith* (1814/1883), Article 78.f; Cumberland Presbyterian Church, *Confession of Faith* (1814/1883), Article 97.c; Assemblies of God, *Statement of Fundamental Truths* (1916) [P&H, V.427]; First London Confession (1644), Article 33.d; Westminster Confession of Faith (1647), Chapter 26.2.d; United Presbyterian Church *Confessional Statement* (1925), Article 35; Heidelberg Catechism (1563), Question 103.b; Cambridge Platform (1648), Chapter 2.6.a; Evangelical Lutheran Synod (1932), Article 44; Second Vatican Council (1962–65), §5.1, Chapter 2.13; Second Vatican Council (1962–65), §8, Chapter 2.10; Commission on Faith and Order at Bangalore, *Common Statement* (1978), Part 1 [P&H, V.784]

Acts 2:42–47 – Commission on Faith and Order (1982), Article 3.A.9; Second Vatican Council (1962–65), §5.1, Chapter 2.10

Acts 2:44 – Jeremias II, *Reply to Augsburg Confession* (1576), §20 [P&H, II.452]

Acts 2:44, 45 – Lausanne Covenant (1974), Article 9; Westminster Confession of Faith (1647), Chapter 26.2.e; Presbyterian Reformed Church in Cuba, *Confession of Faith* (1977), §3.C

Acts 2:46 – Dordrecht Confession (1632), Article 10; Mennonite Articles of Faith (1766/1895/1902), Article 26.3; Cumberland Presbyterian Church, *Confession of Faith* (1814/1883), Article 97.c; Westminster Confession of Faith (1647), Chapter 26.2.d; Heidelberg Catechism (1563), Question 103.b; Cambridge Platform (1648), Chapter 3.4.c

Acts 2:47 – Mennonite Articles of Faith (1766/1895/1902), Article 16.2; New Hampshire Confession (1833/1853), Article 13.d; Lausanne Covenant (1974), Article 4; North American Baptist Conference (1982), Article 6; First London Confession (1644), Article 34.f; First London Confession (1644), Article 42.a; Westminster Confession of Faith (1647), Chapter 25.2.f; Cambridge Platform (1648), Chapter 17.1.a; United Presbyterian Church *Confessional Statement* (1925), Article 35; Cambridge Platform (1648), Chapter 4.6.a

Acts 3:1 – Cambridge Platform (1648), Chapter 14.8

Acts 3:1–10 – Hubmaier, *A Christian Catechism* (1526), 2nd Part Q.16.a [P&H, IV.687]

Acts 3:12–14 – Second Helvetic Confession (1566), Chapter 4.[3].a

Acts 3:14 – Second Vatican Council (1962–65), §5.1, Chapter 5.39

Acts 3:18 – United Presbyterian Church *Confessional Statement* (1925), Article 3

Acts 3:19 – Mennonite Articles of Faith (1766/1895/1902), Article 19.1; Westminster Confession of Faith (1647), Chapter 33.2.e; Cumberland Presbyterian Church, *Confession of Faith* (1814/1883), Article 43.b

Acts 3:19–23 – Jehovah's Witnesses, *Statement of Faith* (1918), Article 6

Acts 3:20 – Catechesis and Confession of Faith of Polish Brethren (1574), [B] Question 8 [P&H, IV.714]

Acts 3:20, 21 – Heidelberg Catechism (1563), Question 76.f

Acts 3:21 – The First Confession of Basel (1534), Article 6.d; Westminster Confession of Faith (1647), Chapter 29.6.m; New Hampshire Confession (1833/1853), Article 1.a; United Presbyterian Church *Confessional Statement* (1925), Article 40; Westminster Confession of Faith (1647), Chapter 32.1.c; Cumberland Presbyterian Church, *Confession of Faith* (1814/1883), Article 105.c; United Presbyterian Church

Confessional Statement (1925), Article 2; True Confession (1596), Article 35; Catechesis and Confession of Faith of Polish Brethren (1574), [C].6 Question 7 [P&H, IV.742]; Second Helvetic Confession (1566), Chapter 11.[12]; United Presbyterian Church *Confessional Statement* (1925), Article 12; French Confession (1559/1571), Article 36.a; Bohemian Confession (1535), Article 6.[2]; New Hampshire Confession (1833/1853), Article 18.o; The Transylvanian Confession of Faith (1579), Article 1; Second Vatican Council (1962–65), §5.1, Chapter 7.48

Acts 3:22 – Westminster Confession of Faith (1647), Chapter 8.1.b; True Confession (1596), Article 8.e; First London Confession (1644), Article 16.a; Heidelberg Catechism (1563), Question 31.b; Catechesis and Confession of Faith of Polish Brethren (1574), [B] Question 8 [P&H, IV.714]; Second Helvetic Confession (1566), Chapter 13.[1]; Cumberland Presbyterian Church, *Confession of Faith* (1814/1883), Article 27.f

Acts 3:22, 23 – Mennonite Articles of Faith (1766/1895/1902), Article 14.1; New Hampshire Confession (1833/1853), Article 8.l; First London Confession (1644), Article 8.d; First London Confession (1644), Article 14.e

Acts 3:22–24 – True Confession (1596), Article 13.c

Acts 3:22–26 – Heidelberg Catechism (1563), Question 19.g

Acts 3:23 – First Helvetic Confession (1536), Article 25.c

Acts 3:26 – Mennonite Articles of Faith (1766/1895/1902), Article 15.5; Mennonite Articles of Faith (1766/1895/1902), Article 17.3; Catechesis and Confession of Faith of Polish Brethren (1574), [B] Question 22 [P&H, IV.721]; Catechesis and Confession of Faith of Polish Brethren (1574), [B] Question 8 [P&H, IV.714]

Acts 4:1–3 – Cambridge Platform (1648), Chapter 17.1.a

Acts 4:8-13 – Mennonite Articles of Faith (1766/1895/1902), Article 29.3

Acts 4:11 – Second Vatican Council (1962-65), §5.1, Chapter 1.6

Acts 4:12 – True Confession (1596), Article 12.b; Dordrecht Confession (1632), Introduction [P&H, IV.774]; Lausanne Covenant (1974), Article 3; Bohemian Confession (1535), Article 6.[5]; French Confession (1559/1571), Article 24.i; French Confession (1559/1571), Article 18; Church of England, *Thirty-Nine Articles* (1571), Article 18; Second Helvetic Confession (1566), Chapter 11.[16].a; First Helvetic Confession (1536), Article 22; Westminster Confession of Faith (1647), Chapter 10.3.o; Westminster Confession of Faith (1647), Chapter 10.4.s; United Presbyterian Church *Confessional Statement* (1925), Article 12; Heidelberg Catechism (1563), Question 29; Synodical Tome of 1341, Article 50 [P&H, II.332]; First London Confession (1644), Article 13.d; Peter Abelard (1139-42), Article 1; Smalcald Articles (1537), Article 1.[5] [P&H, IV.126]; Zwingli, *A Reckoning of the Faith* (1530), 3 [P&H, IV.255]; Second Helvetic Confession (1566), Chapter 5.[4]; The Irish Articles (1615), Article 31; The Transylvanian Confession of Faith (1579), Article 4; Decrees of the Council of Trent (Session 5.17 June 1546), Chapter 3 [P&H, IV.825]; Protestant Christian Batak Church, *Confession of Faith* (1951), Article 7; Mennonite Confession of Faith (1963), Article 17

Acts 4:17 – French Confession (1559/1571), Article 26.f

Acts 4:17–19 – French Confession (1559/1571), Article 40.a

Acts 4:18, 19 – True Confession (1596), Article 40.f

Acts 4:18–20 – New Hampshire Confession (1833/1853), Article 16.h

Acts 4:19 – Lausanne Covenant (1974), Article 13; Mennonite Confession of Faith (1963), Article 19; Cumberland Presbyterian Church, *Confession of Faith* (1814/1883), Article 72.f; True Confession (1596), Article 42.a; First London Confession (1644), Article 51.c; First Helvetic Confession (1536), Article 26.b; United Presbyterian Church *Confessional Statement* (1925), Article 37; A Confession of Faith Containing XXIII Articles (1673), Article 22

Acts 4:19, 20 – French Confession (1559/1571), Article 26.f; Mennonite Articles of Faith (1766/1895/1902), Article 28.2; Mennonite Articles of Faith (1766/1895/1902), Article 29.3; Westminster Confession of Faith (1647), Chapter 20.2.l; Second Vatican Council (1962–65), §9.11.31

Acts 4:20 – First London Confession (1644) [P&H, V.48]

Acts 4:22, 23 – Mennonite Articles of Faith (1766/1895/1902), Article 16.2

Acts 4:23 – First London Confession (1644), Article 37.c

Acts 4:24 – True Confession (1596), Article 45.a; Irenaeus, The Rule of Faith in *Adversus haereses* and *Epideixis* (c. 180-200), Adversus haereses 1.10.1.a

Acts 4:25, 26 – The Transylvanian Confession of Faith (1579), Article 1.b

Acts 4:27 – Second Vatican Council (1962–65), §5.1, Chapter 5.39; Catechesis and Confession of Faith of Polish Brethren (1574), [B] Question 15 [P&H, IV.717]

Acts 4:27, 28 – Westminster Confession of Faith (1647), Chapter 3.c; United Presbyterian Church *Confessional Statement* (1925), Article 4; French Confession (1559/1571), Article 8.e; Heidelberg Catechism (1563), Question 38.f; Westminster Confession of Faith (1647), Chapter 5.4.o

Acts 4:28 – Mennonite Articles of Faith (1766/1895/1902), Article 9.3; French Confession (1559/1571), Article 8.c

Acts 4:29 – Second Vatican Council (1962-65), §9.14.37

Acts 4:30 – Second Vatican Council (1962-65), §5.1, Chapter 5.39

Acts 4:31 – North American Baptist Conference (1982), Article 2; Second Vatican Council (1962-65), §9.11

Acts 4:32 – Mennonite Articles of Faith (1766/1895/1902), Article 23.6; Jeremias II, *Reply to Augsburg Confession* (1576), §28 [P&H, II.472]

Acts 4:32, 33 –Mennonite Articles of Faith (1766/1895/1902), Article 16.2

Acts 4:34, 35 – Lausanne Covenant (1974), Article 9

Acts 4:35 – Cambridge Platform (1648), Chapter 7.3

Acts 5 –The First Confession of Basel (1534), Article 6.d

Acts 5:1–6 – Jeremias II, *Reply to Augsburg Confession* (1576), §27 [P&H, II.467]; The Orthodox Confession of the Catholic and Apostolic Eastern Church (1638/1642), Article 16

Acts 5:1–10 – Bohemian Confession (1535), Article 11.4

Acts 5:1–13 – Mennonite Articles of Faith (1766/1895/1902), Article 27.8

Acts 5:3 – The Orthodox Confession of the Catholic and Apostolic Eastern Church (1638/1642), Article 70

Acts 5:3, 4 – New Hampshire Confession (1833/1853), Article 2.k; Heidelberg Catechism (1563), Question 53.a

Acts 5:4 – Westminster Confession of Faith (1647), Chapter 26.3.g; The Orthodox Confession of the Catholic and Apostolic Eastern Church (1638/1642), Article 70

Acts 5:7 – Richmond Declaration of Faith (1887), Article 2.32

Acts 5:11 – New Hampshire Confession (1833/1853), Article 13.c; Cumberland Presbyterian Church, *Confession of Faith* (1814/1883), Article 16.d

Acts 5:12 – Cambridge Platform (1648), Chapter 3.4.c

Acts 5:14 – Mennonite Articles of Faith (1766/1895/1902), Article 25.5; Cumberland Presbyterian Church, *Confession of Faith* (1814/1883), Article 109.g; Evangelical Lutheran Synod (1932), Article 24

Acts 5:19 – The Orthodox Confession of the Catholic and Apostolic Eastern Church (1638/1642), Article 19

Acts 5:28, 29 – True Confession (1596), Article 40.f; True Confession (1596), Article 42.a; French Confession (1559/1571), Article 5.e; First London Confession (1644), Article 51.c; A Confession of Faith Containing XXIII Articles (1673), Article 22

Acts 5:29 – Zwingli, *Sixty-Seven Articles* (1523), 38; Zwingli, *Sixty-Seven Articles* (1523), 42; Lausanne Covenant (1974), Article 13; North American Baptist Conference (1982), Article 7; Mennonite Confession of Faith (1963), Article 19; Cumberland Presbyterian Church, *Confession of Faith* (1814/1883), Article 72.f; Westminster Confession of Faith (1647), Chapter 20.2.l; Protestant Christian Batak Church, *Confession of Faith* (1951), Article 10; True Confession (1596), Article 42; Bohemian Confession (1535), Article 16.[6]; New Hampshire Confession (1833/1853), Article 16.h; First Helvetic Confession (1536), Article 26.b; Second Vatican Council (1962–65), §9.11; Jeremias II, *Reply to Augsburg Confession* (1576), §16 [P&H, II.443]; Jeremias II, *Reply to Augsburg Confession* (1576), §28 [P&H, II.470]; Eastern Confession of the Christian Faith (1629 [1633]), Chapter 18; Augsburg Confession (1530), Article 16.[7] [P&H, IV.67]; Augsburg Confession (1530), Article 28.[75] [P&H, IV.116]; Treatise on Power and Primacy (1537), Article 38.b; Heidelberg Catechism (1563), Question 94.m; Westminster Confession of Faith (1647), Chapter 23.3.29; Lutheran General Synod, *Definite Platform* (1855), Article 16

Acts 5:30, 31 – First London Confession (1644), Article 19.a; First London Confession (1644), Article 25.i

Acts 5:31 – Mennonite Articles of Faith (1766/1895/1902), Article 15.5; Mennonite Articles of Faith (1766/1895/1902), Article 18.3; Cumberland Presbyterian Church, *Confession of Faith* (1814/1883), Article 27.f; True Confession (1596), Article 10.l; First London Confession (1644), Article 10.j

Acts 5:38, 39 – Zwingli, *A Reckoning of the Faith* (1530), 12 [P&H, IV.271]

Acts 5:41 – True Confession (1596), Article 42.a; First London Confession (1644), Article 51.c

Acts 5:81 – United Presbyterian Church *Confessional Statement* (1925), Article 9

Acts 6 – First Helvetic Confession (1536), Article 19.a; Protestant Christian Batak Church, *Confession of Faith* (1951), Article 9

Acts 6:1–3 – French Confession (1559/1571), Article 31.e

Acts 6:1–6 – Catechesis and Confession of Faith of Polish Brethren (1574), [C].3 Question 3 [P&H, IV.728]

Acts 6:2 – Cambridge Platform (1648), Chapter 10.10.a; Cambridge Platform (1648), Chapter 3.4.c; Cambridge Platform (1648), Chapter 10.8.d

Acts 6:2, 3 – Cambridge Platform (1648), Chapter 7.2.d; Cambridge Platform (1648), Chapter 7.3; True Confession (1596), Article 19.m; Cambridge Platform (1648), Chapter 8.4

Acts 6:2–4 – First Helvetic Confession (1536), Article 17.b

Acts 6:2–5 – Mennonite Articles of Faith (1766/1895/1902), Article 24.3

Acts 6:2–6 – Commission on Faith and Order (1982), Article 3.A.9; Second Vatican Council (1962-65), §5.1, Chapter 3.20.4

Acts 6:3 – Mennonite Articles of Faith (1766/1895/1902), Article 24.3; Cambridge Platform (1648), Chapter 7.3.f; Cambridge Platform (1648), Chapter 8.2.b; Cambridge Platform (1648), Chapter 8.3.c; Cambridge Platform (1648), Chapter 8.4; True Confession (1596), Article 20.b; True Confession (1596), Article 21.d; True Confession (1596), Article 23.g; Cambridge Platform (1648), Chapter 10.5.d; First London Confession (1644), Article 36.a; Faith and Practice of Thirty Congregations (1651), Article 66

Acts 6:3, 4 – Cambridge Platform (1648), Chapter 11.4; Cambridge Platform (1648), Chapter 5.2.e; Cambridge Platform (1648), Chapter 10.2.a; Faith and Practice of Thirty Congregations (1651), Article 64

Acts 6:3–5 – Cambridge Platform (1648), Chapter 8.5.a

Acts 6:3–6 – Dordrecht Confession (1632), Article 9; North American Baptist Conference (1982), Article 6

Acts 6:5 – Mennonite Articles of Faith (1766/1895/1902), Article 24.3; Cambridge Platform (1648), Chapter 10.5.d

Acts 6:5, 6 – True Confession (1596), Article 35.g; True Confession (1596), Article 20.b; True Confession (1596), Article 21.d; True Confession (1596), Article 23.g; Cambridge Platform (1648), Chapter 9.2.c; Cambridge Platform (1648), Chapter 9.2

Acts 6:6 – Cambridge Platform (1648), Chapter 7.3.f

Acts 6:34 – French Confession (1559/1571), Article 29.c

Acts 7:2 – Westminster Confession of Faith (1647), Chapter 2.2.b; Cumberland Presbyterian Church, *Confession of Faith* (1814/1883), Article 6.b

Acts 7:5 – Dositheus and the Synod of Jerusalem, *Confession* (1672), Decree 10

Acts 7:37 – The First Confession of Basel (1534), Article 11.b

Acts 7:48 – French Confession (1559/1571), Article 1.g

Acts 7:51 – Evangelical Lutheran Synod (1932), Article 37; Cumberland Presbyterian Church, *Confession of Faith* (1814/1883), Article 41.g; A Confession of Faith Containing XXIII Articles (1673), Article 11; Evangelical Lutheran Synod (1932), Article 13; United Presbyterian Church *Confessional Statement* (1925), Article 13; The Remonstrance, or The Arminian Articles (1610), Article 4

Acts 7:53 – United Presbyterian Church *Confessional Statement* (1925), Article 7

Acts 7:55, 56 – The First Confession of Basel (1534), Article 6.c; Catechesis and Confession of Faith of Polish Brethren (1574), [B]. Question 21.c [P&H, IV.719]; Heidelberg Catechism (1563), Question 80.d

Acts 7:56 – True Confession (1596), Article 35

Acts 7:58 – Mennonite Articles of Faith (1766/1895/1902), Article 32.5

Acts 7:59 – The Transylvanian Confession of Faith (1579), Article 3

Acts 7:59, 60 – Catechesis and Confession of Faith of Polish Brethren (1574), [B]. Question 21.c [P&H, IV.719]

Acts 8:1 – New Hampshire Confession (1833/1853), Article 13.c; Cambridge Platform (1648), Chapter 13.4.b; Evangelical Lutheran Synod (1932), Article 27; United Presbyterian Church *Confessional Statement* (1925), Article 32; Second Vatican Council (1962–65), §5.1, Chapter 3.26.50

Acts 8:6 – Cambridge Platform (1648), Chapter 6.2.b

Acts 8:11 – Dordrecht Confession (1632), Article 7.a

Acts 8:12 – Mennonite Articles of Faith (1766/1895/1902), Article 25.5; New Hampshire Confession (1833/1853), Article 14.i; United Presbyterian Church, *Confessional Statement* (1925), Article 30; Catechesis and Confession of Faith of Polish Brethren (1574), [C].5 Question 10 [P&H, IV.739]

Acts 8:13 – Westminster Confession of Faith (1647), Chapter 28.5.p; Cumberland Presbyterian Church, *Confession of Faith* (1814/1883), Article 103.a

Acts 8:14–16 – First Helvetic Confession (1536), Article 17.b; First Helvetic Confession (1536), Article 23.a

Acts 8:14–17 – Decrees of Union of the Council of Basel-Ferrara-Florence-Rome (1431-45), *Bull of Union with the Armenians*, November 1439, 15 [P&H, III.759]

Acts 8:17 – United Presbyterian Church *Confessional Statement* (1925), Article 13; The Orthodox Confession of the Catholic and Apostolic Eastern Church (1638/1642), Article 104; The Orthodox Confession of the Catholic and Apostolic Eastern Church (1638/1642), Article 109

Acts 8:18, 19 – Zwingli, *Sixty-Seven Articles* (1523), 56

Acts 8:20 – Richmond Declaration of Faith (1887), Article 10.9

Acts 8:20, 21 – Second Helvetic Confession (1566), Chapter 14.12

Acts 8:21 – Mennonite Articles of Faith (1766/1895/1902), Article 19.3; Mennonite Articles of Faith (1766/1895/1902), Article 25.4

Acts 8:22 – Mennonite Articles of Faith (1766/1895/1902), Article 27.4

Acts 8:23 – Westminster Confession of Faith (1647), Chapter 28.5.p; Cumberland Presbyterian Church, *Confession of Faith* (1814/1883), Article 103.a

Acts 8:30–35 – United Presbyterian Church *Confessional Statement* (1925), Article 26

Acts 8:32, 33 – Catechesis and Confession of Faith of Polish Brethren (1574), [C].5 Question 10.a [P&H, IV.739]

Acts 8:35 – United Presbyterian Church *Confessional Statement* (1925), Article 3

Acts 8:36 – Mennonite Articles of Faith (1766/1895/1902), Article 25.4; Cumberland Presbyterian Church, *Confession of Faith* (1814/1883), Article 100.f; Schleitheim Confession (1527), Article 1.a

Acts 8:36, 37 – Faith and Practice of Thirty Congregations (1651), Article 35; Creedal Statements in New Testament [P&H, I.33]

Acts 8:36–38 – First London Confession (1644), Article 39.f; Catechesis and Confession of Faith of Polish Brethren (1574), [C].5 Question 10.a [P&H, IV.739]

Acts 8:36–39 – New Hampshire Confession (1833/1853), Article 14.i

Acts 8:37 – Lutheran General Synod, *Definite Platform* (1855), Part 2. Topic 5 [P&H, V.309]; Cambridge Platform (1648), Chapter 12.1; Cambridge Platform (1648), Chapter 12.2; Cambridge Platform (1648), Chapter 3.2.b; Biblical and Primitive Rules of Faith [P&H, I.27]

Acts 8:37, 38 – Mennonite Articles of Faith (1766/1895/1902), Article 25.2; United Presbyterian Church, *Confessional Statement* (1925), Article 30; Westminster Confession of Faith (1647), Chapter 28.4.l

Acts 8:38 – Cumberland Presbyterian Church, *Confession of Faith* (1814/1883), Article 100.f; First London Confession (1644), Article 40.g

Acts 8:38, 39 – Metrophanes Critopoulos *Confession of Faith* (1625), Article 7.10 [P&H, II.514]

Acts 8:62 – Lutheran General Synod, *Definite Platform* (1855), Part 2. Topic 5 [P&H, V.309]

Acts 9:1–18 – Mennonite Articles of Faith (1766/1895/1902), Article 32.4

Acts 9:8 – Jeremias II, *Reply to Augsburg Confession* (1576), §20.a [P&H, II.456]

Acts 9:11 – United Presbyterian Church *Confessional Statement* (1925), Article 27

Acts 9:15 – Second Vatican Council (1962-65), §5.1, Chapter 3.24

Acts 9:17 – Cambridge Platform (1648), Chapter 9.7

Acts 9:18 – Dordrecht Confession (1632), Article 7.a

Acts 9:25 – Cambridge Platform (1648), Chapter 13.4.b

Acts 9:26 – Cambridge Platform (1648), Chapter 13.6; Cambridge Platform (1648), Chapter 12.1; Cambridge Platform (1648), Chapter 4.6.a; Cambridge Platform (1648), Chapter 10.5.d

Acts 9:26, 27 – True Confession (1596), Article 37.l

Acts 9:29, 30 – Cambridge Platform (1648), Chapter 13.4.b

Acts 9:31 – Mennonite Articles of Faith (1766/1895/1902), Article 22.1; True Confession (1596), Article 40.e; Heidelberg Catechism (1563), Question 53.d; First London Confession (1644), Article 50.b

Acts 9:34 – Catechesis and Confession of Faith of Polish Brethren (1574), [B] Question 22.d [P&H, IV.721]

Acts 9:36 – Mennonite Articles of Faith (1766/1895/1902), Article 22.5

Acts 10 – Second Helvetic Confession (1566), Chapter 1.[5]; Catechesis and Confession of Faith of Polish Brethren (1574), [C].4 Question 10 [P&H, IV.735]

Acts 10:1, 2 – Cumberland Presbyterian Church, *Confession of Faith* (1814/1883), Article 86.g; Westminster Confession of Faith (1647), Chapter 23.2.d

Acts 10:1–3 – Smalcald Articles (1537), Article 8.[8] [P&H, IV.145]

Acts 10.2 – Westminster Confession of Faith (1647), Chapter 28.5.o; Mennonite Articles of Faith (1766/1895/1902), Article 25.5; Westminster Confession of Faith (1647), Chapter 21.6.f; Smalcald Articles (1537), Article 8.[8] [P&H, IV.145]

Acts 10:3 – Doctrinal Chapters of Synod of Orange (529), [P&H, III.698]

Acts 10:4 – Westminster Confession of Faith (1647), Chapter 28.5.o

Acts 10:5 – Hubmaier, *A Christian Catechism* (1526), 2nd Part Q.33 [P&H, IV.691]

Acts 10:14, 15 – French Confession (1559/1571), Article 24.a

Acts 10:22 – Westminster Confession of Faith (1647), Chapter 28.5.o; Smalcald Articles (1537), Article 8.[8] [P&H, IV.145]

Acts 10:25, 26 – French Confession (1559/1571), Article 24.k

Acts 10:31 – Westminster Confession of Faith (1647), Chapter 28.5.o

Acts 10:33 – Westminster Confession of Faith (1647), Chapter 21.5.t

Acts 10:34 – Dositheus and the Synod of Jerusalem, *Confession* (1672), Decree 3; Dositheus and the Synod of Jerusalem, *Confession* (1672), Decree 3.b; Shaker Church, *A Concise Statement of the Principles of the Only True Church* (1790), Article 4.a

Acts 10:34, 35 – New Hampshire Confession (1833/1853), Article 17.j

Acts 10:34–43 – Heidelberg Catechism (1563), Question 22.a; Heidelberg Catechism (1563), Question 2.k

Acts 10:35 – Mennonite Articles of Faith (1766/1895/1902), Article 23.4; Second Helvetic Confession (1566), Chapter 16.[9]; Faith and Practice of Thirty Congregations (1651), Article 40; United Presbyterian Church *Confessional Statement* (1925), Article 10; Second Vatican Council (1962–65), §5.1, Chapter 2.9

Acts 10:37 – First London Confession (1644), Article 33

Acts 10:38 – True Confession (1596), Article 11.a; Mennonite Articles of Faith (1766/1895/1902), Article 13.3; Richmond Declaration of Faith (1887), Article 2.16; Westminster Confession of Faith (1647), Chapter 8.3.t; Cumberland Presbyterian Church, *Confession of Faith* (1814/1883), Article 29.b; United Presbyterian Church *Confessional Statement* (1925), Article 13; United Presbyterian Church *Confessional Statement* (1925), Article 12; Catechesis and Confession of Faith of Polish Brethren (1574), [C] Question 1.4 [P&H, IV.722]; Catechesis and Confession of Faith of Polish Brethren (1574), [B] Question 11 [P&H, IV.716]

Acts 10:41 – True Confession (1596), Article 9.f

Acts 10:42 – Polycarp, *Epistle to the Philippians* (c. 150), Chapter 3:1; Bohemian Confession (1535), Article 10.[1]; Mennonite Articles of Faith (1766/1895/1902), Article 34.2; Westminster Confession of Faith (1647), Chapter 8.4.i; Cumberland Presbyterian Church, *Confession of Faith* (1814/1883), Article 27.f; Heidelberg Catechism (1563), Question 46.i; New Hampshire Confession (1833/1853), Article 18.p

Acts 10:43 – Mennonite Articles of Faith (1766/1895/1902), Article 17.1; Heidelberg Catechism (1563), Question 19.g; United Presbyterian Church *Confessional Statement* (1925), Article 3; Bohemian Confession (1535), Article 6.[5]; French Confession (1559/1571), Article 20.f; Second Helvetic Confession (1566), Chapter 11. [16].a; Westminster Confession of Faith (1647), Chapter 11.1.c; True Confession (1596), Article 9.f; Evangelical Lutheran Synod (1932), Article 9; United Presbyterian Church *Confessional Statement* (1925), Article 17; New Hampshire Confession (1833/1853), Article 5.k; Evangelical Lutheran Synod (1932), Article 18

Acts 10:44–46 – Assemblies of God, *Statement of Fundamental Truths* (1916), Article 6

Acts 10:44–48 – Zurich Agreement (1549), Article 19

Acts 10:45 – Westminster Confession of Faith (1647), Chapter 28.5.o

Acts 10:47 – Dordrecht Confession (1632), Article 7.a; Westminster Confession of Faith (1647), Chapter 28.5.o; Cumberland Presbyterian Church, *Confession of Faith* (1814/1883), Article 100.f; Heidelberg Catechism (1563), Question 74.b

Acts 10:47, 48 – Mennonite Articles of Faith (1766/1895/1902), Article 25.5; New Hampshire Confession (1833/1853), Article 14.j; Cumberland Presbyterian Church, *Confession of Faith* (1814/1883), Article 102.h; Assemblies of God, *Statement of Fundamental Truths* (1916), Article 11

Acts 10:48 – Protestant Christian Batak Church, *Confession of Faith* (1951), Article 10

Acts 10:47–49 – First Helvetic Confession (1536), Article 14.b

Acts 11:2 – True Confession (1596), Article 25.c

Acts 11:2, 3 – The Orthodox Confession of the Catholic and Apostolic Eastern Church (1638/1642), Article 84; First London Confession (1644), Article 43.b

Acts 11:4 – True Confession (1596), Article 25.c

Acts 11:14 – New Hampshire Confession (1833/1853), Article 1.b

Acts 11:14–16 – Assemblies of God, *Statement of Fundamental Truths* (1916), Article 6

Acts 11:15–17 – French Confession (1559/1571), Article 28.b

Acts 11:17, 18 – The Orthodox Confession of the Catholic and Apostolic Eastern Church (1638/1642), Article 84

Acts 11:18 – Mennonite Articles of Faith (1766/1895/1902), Article 19.5; Mennonite Articles of Faith (1766/1895/1902), Article 23.7; Westminster Confession of Faith

(1647), Chapter 15.1.a; Cumberland Presbyterian Church, *Confession of Faith* (1814/1883), Article 42.a; New Hampshire Confession (1833/1853), Article 8.i

Acts 11:21 – Evangelical Lutheran Synod (1932), Article 10

Acts 11:22 – The Orthodox Confession of the Catholic and Apostolic Eastern Church (1638/1642), Article 84

Acts 11:26 – New Hampshire Confession (1833/1853), Article 15.e; Heidelberg Catechism (1563), Question 32.g; United Presbyterian Church *Confessional Statement* (1925), Article 35

Acts 11:28 – Cambridge Platform (1648), Chapter 6.2.b

Acts 11:29 – Cambridge Platform (1648), Chapter 15.2

Acts 11:29, 30 – Westminster Confession of Faith (1647), Chapter 26.2.e; The Orthodox Confession of the Catholic and Apostolic Eastern Church (1638/1642), Article 94

Acts 11:30 – Second Vatican Council (1962–65), §5.1, Chapter 3.20.4

Acts 11:31 – New Hampshire Confession (1833/1853), Article 13.c

Acts 12:3 – Cambridge Platform (1648), Chapter 5.2.e

Acts 12:5 – The Orthodox Confession of the Catholic and Apostolic Eastern Church (1638/1642), Article 93

Acts 12:7 – The Orthodox Confession of the Catholic and Apostolic Eastern Church (1638/1642), Article 19

Acts 12:7–11 – United Presbyterian Church *Confessional Statement* (1925), Article 7

Acts 12:11 – The Orthodox Confession of the Catholic and Apostolic Eastern Church (1638/1642), Article 19

Acts 12:12–16 – Mennonite Articles of Faith (1766/1895/1902), Article 23.7

Acts 12:23 – Cumberland Presbyterian Church, *Confession of Faith* (1814/1883), Article 70.d; Cumberland Presbyterian Church, *Confession of Faith* (1814/1883), Article 15.c

Acts 13:1 – United Presbyterian Church *Confessional Statement* (1925), Article 32; Second Vatican Council (1962–65), §5.1, Chapter 3.20.4

Acts 13:1–3 – Mennonite Articles of Faith (1766/1895/1902), Article 23.7; Lausanne Covenant (1974), Article 8; North American Baptist Conference (1982), Article 6; Jeremias II, *Reply to Augsburg Confession* (1576), §14 [P&H, II.436]

Acts 13:2, 3 – United Presbyterian Church *Confessional Statement* (1925), Article 34; Cambridge Platform (1648), Chapter 9.2.c; The Orthodox Confession of the Catholic and Apostolic Eastern Church (1638/1642), Article 109

Acts 13:2–4 – First Helvetic Confession (1536), Article 16.a, b

Acts 13:3 – Faith and Practice of Thirty Congregations (1651), Article 73; The Orthodox Confession of the Catholic and Apostolic Eastern Church (1638/1642), Article 88; Cambridge Platform (1648), Chapter 9.2; Cambridge Platform (1648), Chapter 9.3.a; Cambridge Platform (1648), Chapter 9.5; Cambridge Platform (1648), Chapter 9.7

Acts 13:8–11 – Mennonite Articles of Faith (1766/1895/1902), Article 27.8

Acts 13:15 – True Confession (1596), Article 34.e; Cambridge Platform (1648), Chapter 7.2.d; Cambridge Platform (1648), Chapter 10.8.d

Acts 13:22 – Sixth Ecumenical Council: Constantinople III (680–81), [P&H, I.223]

Acts 13:24 – French Confession (1559/1571), Article 35.g

Acts 13:29 – United Presbyterian Church *Confessional Statement* (1925), Article 4; Heidelberg Catechism (1563), Question 41.a

Acts 13:30 – Cumberland Presbyterian Church, *Confession of Faith* (1814/1883), Article 30.c

Acts 13:35 – Metrophanes Critopoulos *Confession of Faith* (1625), Article 3.9.a [P&H, II.502]; Metrophanes Critopoulos *Confession of Faith* (1625), Article 3.10.b [P&H, II.502]

Acts 13:36 – Westminster Confession of Faith (1647), Chapter 32.1.a; Cumberland Presbyterian Church, *Confession of Faith* (1814/1883), Article 112.c

Acts 13:37 – Westminster Confession of Faith (1647), Chapter 8.4.d; Cumberland Presbyterian Church, *Confession of Faith* (1814/1883), Article 30.c; Eunomius, *Confession of Faith* (383), Article 3.g

Acts 13:38 – First London Confession (1644), Article 5.l

Acts 13:38, 39 – Mennonite Articles of Faith (1766/1895/1902), Article 17.2; Mennonite Articles of Faith (1766/1895/1902), Article 20.1; Westminster Confession of Faith (1647), Chapter 11.1.c; First London Confession (1644), Article 28.i; Second Helvetic Confession (1566), Chapter 15.1

Acts 13:39 – Mennonite Articles of Faith (1766/1895/1902), Article 17.1; United Presbyterian Church *Confessional Statement* (1925), Article 25; First Helvetic Confession (1536), Article 14.b; New Hampshire Confession (1833/1853), Article 5.j; Bohemian Confession (1535), Article 6.[10]; Westminster Confession of Faith (1647), Chapter 19.6.l; Lutheran-Roman Catholic Dialogue, *Joint Declaration on the Doctrine of Justification* (1999), Article 1 (11); United Presbyterian Church *Confessional Statement* (1925), Article 19

Acts 13:40–46 – Mennonite Articles of Faith (1766/1895/1902), Article 36.3

Acts 13:42 – Westminster Confession of Faith (1647), Chapter 21.6.i; Cumberland Presbyterian Church, *Confession of Faith* (1814/1883), Article 57.c

Acts 13:44 – New Hampshire Confession (1833/1853), Article 15.e

Acts 13:46 – Dordrecht Confession (1632), Article 5; Mennonite Articles of Faith (1766/1895/1902), Article 9.6; Evangelical Lutheran Synod (1932), Article 37; New Hampshire Confession (1833/1853), Article 6.b; Evangelical Lutheran Synod (1932), Article 13

Acts 13:47, 48 – Heidelberg Catechism (1563), Question 54.i

Acts 13:48 – The Canons of the Synod of Dort (1618–19), §5.b [P&H, IV.578]; Evangelical Lutheran Synod (1932), Article 35; Evangelical Lutheran Synod (1932), Article 36^2; Evangelical Lutheran Synod (1932), Article 37; New Hampshire Confession (1833/1853), Article 9.n; Second Helvetic Confession (1566), Chapter 16.[3]; Metrophanes Critopoulos *Confession of Faith* (1625), Article 3.14 [P&H, II.503]; True Confession (1596), Article 3.b; United Presbyterian Church *Confessional Statement* (1925), Article 10; First London Confession (1644), Article 3.d; Zwingli, *A Reckoning of the Faith* (1530), 6^2 [P&H, IV.258]; The Canons of the Synod of Dort (1618-19), Article 10 [P&H, IV.573]; The Canons of the Synod of Dort (1618–19), §1 [P&H, IV.576]

Acts 14:8–10 – Hubmaier, *A Christian Catechism* (1526), 2nd Part Q.16.a [P&H, IV.687]

Acts 14:11 – Westminster Confession of Faith (1647), Chapter 2.1.g

Acts 14:11–13 – Second Helvetic Confession (1566), Chapter 4.[3].a

Acts 14:15 – Dordrecht Confession (1632), Article 1.c; French Confession (1559/1571), Article 24.k; Westminster Confession of Faith (1647), Chapter 2.1.g; Cambridge Platform (1648), Chapter 10.10.a; Irenaeus, The Rule of Faith in *Adversus haereses* and *Epideixis* (c. 180–200), Adversus haereses 1.10.1.a

Acts 14:15–17 – Heidelberg Catechism (1563), Question 27.b

Acts 14:16 – Westminster Confession of Faith (1647), Chapter 5.4.p; The Canons of the Synod of Dort (1618–19), §5 [P&H, IV.590]

Acts 14:17 – Mennonite Articles of Faith (1766/1895/1902), Article 1.2; Mennonite Articles of Faith (1766/1895/1902), Article 36.3; United Presbyterian Church *Confessional Statement* (1925), Article 2; Evangelical Lutheran Synod (1932), Article 21; Heidelberg Catechism (1563), Question 125

Acts 14:21–23 – True Confession (1596), Article 35.g

Acts 14:22 – Evangelical Lutheran Synod (1932), Article 42

Acts 14:22, 23 – Second Vatican Council (1962–65), §5.1, Chapter 3.26.50

Acts 14:23 – Mennonite Articles of Faith (1766/1895/1902), Article 24.2; New Hampshire Confession (1833/1853), Article 13.h; Evangelical Lutheran Synod (1932), Article 31; Lausanne Covenant (1974), Article 11; Cumberland Presbyterian Church, *Confession of Faith* (1814/1883), Article 111.b; Cambridge Platform (1648), Chapter 8.2.b; True Confession (1596), Article 20.b; True Confession (1596), Article 21.d; True Confession (1596), Article 23.g; True Confession (1596), Article 19.m; Cambridge Platform (1648), Chapter 10.10.a; United Presbyterian Church *Confessional Statement* (1925), Article 33; Cambridge Platform (1648), Chapter 5.2.e; Cambridge Platform (1648), Chapter 6.1; Cambridge Platform (1648), Chapter 10.2.a; Cambridge Platform (1648), Chapter 10.5.d; Cambridge Platform (1648), Chapter 8.5.a; Cambridge Platform (1648), Chapter 9.1.b; Cambridge Platform (1648), Chapter 9.2; Second Vatican Council (1962-65), §5.1, Chapter 3.20.4

Acts 14:26–28 – North American Baptist Conference (1982), Article 6

Acts 14:27 – Cambridge Platform (1648), Chapter 3.4.c

Acts 15 – North American Baptist Conference (1982), Article 6; Westminster Confession of Faith (1647), Chapter 31.1.40; Protestant Christian Batak Church (1951), Article 14; True Confession (1596), Article 24.b; Cambridge Platform (1648), Chapter 16.5; Cambridge Platform (1648), Chapter 16.3; Second Helvetic Confession (1566), Chapter 17.[10]; Mennonite Confession of Faith (1963), Article 8

Acts 15:1, 2 – True Confession (1596), Article 36.h; Cambridge Platform (1648), Chapter 16.4.a

Acts 15:2 – Westminster Confession of Faith (1647), Chapter 31.1.a; Westminster Confession of Faith (1647), Chapter 31.1.c; Cumberland Presbyterian Church, *Confession of Faith* (1814/1883), Article 110.a; The Orthodox Confession of the Catholic and Apostolic Eastern Church (1638/1642), Article 84; Cambridge Platform (1648), Chapter 16.6; Cambridge Platform (1648), Chapter 15.2

Acts 15:2, 3 – True Confession (1596), Article 23.g

Acts 15:2–15 – Cambridge Platform (1648), Chapter 16.1

Acts 15:2-23 – Cambridge Platform (1648), Chapter 16.2

Acts 15:2–29 – United Presbyterian Church *Confessional Statement* (1925), Article 33

Acts 15:4 – Westminster Confession of Faith (1647), Chapter 31.1.a; Westminster Confession of Faith (1647), Chapter 31.1.c; Cumberland Presbyterian Church, *Confession of Faith* (1814/1883), Article 110.a

Acts 15:6 – Westminster Confession of Faith (1647), Chapter 31.1.a; Cumberland Presbyterian Church, *Confession of Faith* (1814/1883), Article 110.a; Cambridge Platform (1648), Chapter 15.2; Mennonite Confession of Faith (1963), Article 10

Acts 15:6, 7 – French Confession (1559/1571), Article 32.g; Cambridge Platform (1648), Chapter 16.4.a

Acts 15:8, 9 – Assemblies of God, *Statement of Fundamental Truths* (1916), Article 6

Acts 15:9 – Mennonite Articles of Faith (1766/1895/1902), Article1; Cumberland Presbyterian Church, *Confession of Faith* (1814/1883), Article 53.e; True Confession (1596), Article 35.f; United Presbyterian Church *Confessional Statement* (1925), Article 17; United Presbyterian Church *Confessional Statement* (1925), Article 18; United Presbyterian Church *Confessional Statement* (1925), Article 21; Smalcald Articles (1537), Article 13.[1] [P&H, IV.147]

Acts 15:10 – Bohemian Confession (1535), Article 15.[6]; Second Helvetic Confession (1566), Chapter 27.[1]; Augsburg Confession (1530), Article 28.[42] [P&H, IV.111]

Acts 15:10, 11 – Westminster Confession of Faith (1647), Chapter 20.1.g; Augsburg Confession (1530), Article 26.[27] [P&H, IV.93]

Acts 15:11 – New Hampshire Confession (1833/1853), Article 4.c; Westminster Confession of Faith (1647), Chapter 14.2.i; Second Helvetic Confession (1566), Chapter 11.[16].a; Westminster Confession of Faith (1647), Chapter 7.6.s

Acts 15:12 – First London Confession (1644), Article 46.f

Acts 15:14 – New Hampshire Confession (1833/1853), Article 9.n; Lausanne Covenant (1974), Article 1

Acts 15:15 – Westminster Confession of Faith (1647), Chapter 31.3.d; Westminster Confession of Faith (1647), Chapter 1.8.s; Cumberland Presbyterian Church, *Confession of Faith* (1814/1883), Article 4.c

Acts 15:15, 16 – Westminster Confession of Faith (1647), Chapter 1.9.y

Acts 15:15–18 – Assemblies of God, *Statement of Fundamental Truths* (1916), Article 13.a

Acts 15:18 – Westminster Confession of Faith (1647), Chapter 3.2.d; Mennonite Articles of Faith (1766/1895/1902), Article 9.1; Westminster Confession of Faith (1647), Chapter 5.1.e; Westminster Confession of Faith (1647), Chapter 2.2.l; True Confession (1596), Article 3.m; The Canons of the Synod of Dort (1618–19), Article 6 [P&H, IV.572]

Acts 15:19 – Westminster Confession of Faith (1647), Chapter 31.3.d

Acts 15:20 – Augsburg Confession (1530), Article 28.[32] [P&H, IV.109]; Augsburg Confession (1530), Article 28.[65] [P&H, IV.114]

Acts 15:21 – Westminster Confession of Faith (1647), Chapter 21.5.r

Acts 15:22 – New Hampshire Confession (1833/1853), Article 13.h; True Confession (1596), Article 23.g; First London Confession (1644), Article 36.a

Acts 15:22, 23 – Westminster Confession of Faith (1647), Chapter 31.2.c; Cumberland Presbyterian Church, *Confession of Faith* (1814/1883), Article 110.a; North American Baptist Conference (1982), Article 6; Cambridge Platform (1648), Chapter 16.6; Cambridge Platform (1648), Chapter 15.2

Acts 15:22–25 – Westminster Confession of Faith (1647), Chapter 31.1.40

Acts 15:22–28 – The Orthodox Confession of the Catholic and Apostolic Eastern Church (1638/1642), Article 84

Acts 15:23 – Cambridge Platform (1648), Chapter 15.1.c

Acts 15:24 – Westminster Confession of Faith (1647), Chapter 31.3.d; Cambridge Platform (1648), Chapter 16.4.b

Acts 15:25 – French Confession (1559/1571), Article 32.g; Westminster Confession of Faith (1647), Chapter 31.2.c; Cumberland Presbyterian Church, *Confession of Faith* (1814/1883), Article 110.a; True Confession (1596), Article 23.g; First London Confession (1644), Article 36.a

Acts 15:27–31 – Westminster Confession of Faith (1647), Chapter 31.3.d

Acts 15:28 – French Confession (1559/1571), Article 32.g; Second Helvetic Confession (1566), Chapter 27.[1]; Cambridge Platform (1648), Chapter 1.4; The Orthodox Confession of the Catholic and Apostolic Eastern Church (1638/1642), Article 72; Cambridge Platform (1648), Chapter 4.g; Second Vatican Council (1962–65), §5.3, Chapter 3.1.18

Acts 15:28, 29 – A Confession of Faith Containing XXIII Articles (1673), Article 19; Cambridge Platform (1648), Chapter 16.4.b; Fifth Ecumenical Council: Constantinople II (553), [P&H, I. 187]

Acts 15:29 – Augsburg Confession (1530), Article 28.[32] [P&H, IV.109]; Bohemian Confession (1535), Article 15.[8]; Jeremias II, *Reply to Augsburg Confession* (1576), §28 [P&H, II.470]

Acts 15:31 – Cambridge Platform (1648), Chapter 16.2

Acts 15:38 – Cambridge Platform (1648), Chapter 3.4.c

Acts 16:1, 2 – Faith and Practice of Thirty Congregations (1651), Article 70

Acts 16:1–3 – Fifth Ecumenical Council: Constantinople II (553), [P&H, I. 195]

Acts 16:2 – Cambridge Platform (1648), Chapter 8.3.c

Acts 16:4 – Westminster Confession of Faith (1647), Chapter 31.3.d; Cumberland Presbyterian Church, *Confession of Faith* (1814/1883), Article 111.b; The Orthodox Confession of the Catholic and Apostolic Eastern Church (1638/1642), Article 84; Cambridge Platform (1648), Chapter 16.2; United Presbyterian Church *Confessional Statement* (1925), Article 33

Acts 16:6 – Zwingli, *A Reckoning of the Faith* (1530), 10 [P&H, IV.268]; Eastern Orthodox Patriarchs, *Response to Pope Pius IX* (1848), Article 6 [P&H, V 270]

Acts 16:6, 7 – The Canons of the Synod of Dort (1618–19), §5 [P&H, IV.590]

Acts 16:7 – United Presbyterian Church *Confessional Statement* (1925), Article 13

Acts 16:9 – Zwingli, *A Reckoning of the Faith* (1530), 10 [P&H, IV.268]; Metrophanes Critopoulos *Confession of Faith* (1625), Article 17.2; Second Helvetic Confession (1566), Chapter 18.[1]

Acts 16:13 – Cumberland Presbyterian Church, *Confession of Faith* (1814/1883), Article 57.c

Acts 16:14 – Second Helvetic Confession (1566), Chapter 1.[6]; Dordrecht Confession (1632), Preface [P&H, IV.770]; Mennonite Articles of Faith (1766/1895/1902), Article 18.6; Formula of Concord (1577), Article 2.4.3 [P&H, IV.173]

Acts 16:14, 15 – Catechesis and Confession of Faith of Polish Brethren (1574), [C].5 Question 11.b [P&H, IV.739]; Cumberland Presbyterian Church, *Confession of Faith* (1814/1883), Article 102.h

Acts 16:15 – True Confession (1596), Article 35.i; True Confession (1596), Article 37.k; The First Confession of Basel (1534), Article 5.d; Cumberland Presbyterian Church, *Confession of Faith* (1814/1883), Article 26.e; United Presbyterian Church, *Confessional Statement* (1925), Article 30; Cambridge Platform (1648), Chapter 16.2; Mennonite Articles of Faith (1766/1895/1902), Article 25.5; Dositheus and the Synod of Jerusalem, *Confession* (1672), Decree 16

Acts 16:20 – True Confession (1596), Article 42.a

Acts 16:26 – New Hampshire Confession (1833/1853), Article 3.m

Acts 16:30 – Mennonite Articles of Faith (1766/1895/1902), Article 18.4

Acts 16:30, 31 – New Hampshire Confession (1833/1853), Article 8.j

Acts 16:30–34 – Catechesis and Confession of Faith of Polish Brethren (1574), [C].5 Question 11.b [P&H, IV.739]

Acts 16:31 – Cumberland Presbyterian Church, *Confession of Faith* (1814/1883), Article 46.e; Westminster Confession of Faith (1647), Chapter 14.2.i; North American Baptist Conference (1982), Article 2

Acts 16:31–33 – Schleitheim Confession (1527), Article 1.a

Acts 16:32–34 – New Hampshire Confession (1833/1853), Article 14.i

Acts 16:33 – Dordrecht Confession (1632), Article 7.a; True Confession (1596), Article 35.i; True Confession (1596), Article 37.k; Protestant Christian Batak Church, *Confession of Faith* (1951), Article 10; The First Confession of Basel (1534), Article 5.d; Cumberland Presbyterian Church, *Confession of Faith* (1814/1883), Article 101.g; Cumberland Presbyterian Church, *Confession of Faith* (1814/1883), Article 26.e; United Presbyterian Church, *Confessional Statement* (1925), Article 30; Westminster Confession of Faith (1647), Chapter 28.3.k

Acts 16:34 – Mennonite Articles of Faith (1766/1895/1902), Article 25.5

Acts 17:2, 3 – New Hampshire Confession (1833/1853), Article 15.e

Acts 17:3, 4 – True Confession (1596), Article 17.b

Acts 17:6, 7 – True Confession (1596), Article 42.a

Acts 17:11 – New Hampshire Confession (1833/1853), Article 1.f; United Presbyterian Church *Confessional Statement* (1925), Article 26; Westminster Confession of Faith (1647), Chapter 31.4.e; Westminster Confession of Faith (1647), Chapter 20.2.n; Cumberland Presbyterian Church, *Confession of Faith* (1814/1883), Article 77.e; Tetrapolitan Confession (1530), Chapter 1

Acts 17:23 – French Confession (1559/1571), Article 1.g

Acts 17:24 – Westminster Confession of Faith (1647), Chapter 4.1.c; Westminster Confession of Faith (1647), Chapter 21.1.a; French Confession (1559/1571), Article 8.c

Acts 17:24, 25 – Heidelberg Catechism (1563), Question 121.c; Westminster Confession of Faith (1647), Chapter 7.1.a; Westminster Confession of Faith (1647), Chapter 2.2.e; Cumberland Presbyterian Church, *Confession of Faith* (1814/1883), Article 6.b; United Presbyterian Church *Confessional Statement* (1925), Article 5; Geneva Catechism (1541/1542), [Question] 145.a

Acts 17:24–26 – First Helvetic Confession (1536), Article 6.c

Acts 17:24–28 – Heidelberg Catechism (1563), Question 27.a

Acts 17:25 – Mennonite Articles of Faith (1766/1895/1902), Article 3.1; Mennonite Articles of Faith (1766/1895/1902), Article 6.1; Westminster Confession of Faith (1647), Chapter 21.1.b; United Presbyterian Church *Confessional Statement* (1925), Article 6; French Confession (1559/1571), Article 6.g; Heidelberg Catechism (1563), Question 125; Heidelberg Catechism (1563), Question 28.f; Second Helvetic Confession (1566), Chapter 5.[2]

Acts 17:25, 26 – Westminster Confession of Faith (1647), Chapter 5.1.b

Acts 17:25–28 – Second Vatican Council (1962–65), §5.1, Chapter 2.16

Acts 17:26 – Dordrecht Confession (1632), Article 1; Mennonite Articles of Faith (1766/1895/1902), Article 5.3; United Presbyterian Church *Confessional Statement*

(1925), Article 38; Lausanne Covenant (1974), Article 5; Westminster Confession of Faith (1647), Chapter 6.3.f; French Confession (1559/1571), Article 8.c

Acts 17:26, 27 – Mennonite Articles of Faith (1766/1895/1902), Article 28.1; Bohemian Confession (1535), Article 20.[1]; United Presbyterian Church *Confessional Statement* (1925), Article 2

Acts 17:26–29 – United Presbyterian Church *Confessional Statement* (1925), Article 11

Acts 17:27 – Mennonite Articles of Faith (1766/1895/1902), Article 1.3; Mennonite Articles of Faith (1766/1895/1902), Article 17.3 s; United Presbyterian Church *Confessional Statement* (1925), Article 10

Acts 17:27–29 – First Helvetic Confession (1536), Chapter 9.a

Acts 17:28 – Mennonite Articles of Faith (1766/1895/1902), Article 5.2; United Presbyterian Church *Confessional Statement* (1925), Article 1; Evangelical Lutheran Synod (1932), Article 21; United Presbyterian Church *Confessional Statement* (1925), Article 6; French Confession (1559/1571), Article 8.c; Westminster Confession of Faith (1647), Chapter 5.1.b; Heidelberg Catechism (1563), Question 28.f; True Confession (1596), Article 2.e; Second Helvetic Confession (1566), Chapter 6.[1]; First London Confession (1644), Article 2.f

Acts 17:29 – Heidelberg Catechism (1563), Question 96.o

Acts 17:30 – Mennonite Articles of Faith (1766/1895/1902), Article 9.3; United Presbyterian Church *Confessional Statement* (1925), Article 2; Mennonite Articles of Faith (1766/1895/1902), Article 17.2; Cumberland Presbyterian Church, *Confession of Faith* (1814/1883), Article 43.b; Smalcald Articles (1537), Article 3.[34] [P&H, IV.140]

Acts 17:30, 31 – Westminster Confession of Faith (1647), Chapter 15.3.g

Acts 17:31 – Mennonite Articles of Faith (1766/1895/1902), Article 34.2; Westminster Confession of Faith (1647), Chapter 33.1.a; Cumberland Presbyterian Church, *Confession of Faith* (1814/1883), Article 114.e; Westminster Confession of Faith (1647), Chapter 8.1.g; Richmond Declaration of Faith (1887), Article 2.39; Second Helvetic Confession (1566), Chapter 11.[13].a; New Hampshire Confession (1833/1853), Article 18.c; Lausanne Covenant (1974), Article 5

Acts 17:34 – Jeremias II, *Reply to Augsburg Confession* (1576), §7 [P&H, II.414]

Acts 18:3 – Metrophanes Critopoulos *Confession of Faith* (1625), Article 19.5.a

Acts 18:4 – Cumberland Presbyterian Church, *Confession of Faith* (1814/1883), Article 57.c

Acts 18:8 – New Hampshire Confession (1833/1853), Article 14.i; First London Confession (1644), Article 39.f; Lutheran General Synod, *Definite Platform* (1855), Part 2. Topic 5 [P&H, V.309]

Acts 18:9, 10 – Fifth Ecumenical Council: Constantinople II (553), [P&H, I. 187]

Acts 18:14–16 – Westminster Confession of Faith (1647), Chapter 23.3.29

Acts 18:17 – Faith and Practice of Thirty Congregations (1651), Article 31

Acts 18:18 – Cumberland Presbyterian Church, *Confession of Faith* (1814/1883), Article 77.e; United Presbyterian Church, *Confessional Statement* (1925), Article 31

Acts 18:21 – Cumberland Presbyterian Church, *Confession of Faith* (1814/1883), Article 16.d

Acts 18:27 – Cambridge Platform (1648), Chapter 13.9.a; Cambridge Platform (1648), Chapter 13.7; Cambridge Platform (1648), Chapter 15.2

Acts 19:1 – Cambridge Platform (1648), Chapter 2.4.e

Acts 19:4 – French Confession (1559/1571), Article 35.g; Schleitheim Confession (1527), Article 1.a

Acts 19:4, 5 – French Confession (1559/1571), Article 28.b

Acts 19:8 – Cambridge Platform (1648), Chapter 12.2

Acts 19:9 – Mennonite Articles of Faith (1766/1895/1902), Article 27.5; True Confession (1596), Article 17.b

Acts 19:10 – French Confession (1559/1571), Article 24.k

Acts 19:18 – True Confession (1596), Article 37.j; The Orthodox Confession of the Catholic and Apostolic Eastern Church (1638/1642), Article 113

Acts 19:23–27 – Hubmaier, *A Christian Catechism* (1526), 2nd Part Q.17.b [P&H, IV.687]

Acts 19:27 – True Confession (1596), Article 39.c

Acts 20:2 – Second Helvetic Confession (1566), Chapter 17.[8].a

Acts 20:7 – Westminster Confession of Faith (1647), Chapter 29.3.f; Mennonite Articles of Faith (1766/1895/1902), Article 23.7; Mennonite Articles of Faith (1766/1895/1902), Article 26.3; True Confession (1596), Article 33.d; Cumberland Presbyterian Church, *Confession of Faith* (1814/1883), Article 79.g; First London Confession (1644), Article 41.i; New Hampshire Confession (1833/1853), Article 15.a; United Presbyterian Church, *Confessional Statement* (1925), Article 29; Westminster Confession of Faith (1647), Chapter 21.7.l

Acts 20:7, 8 – True Confession (1596), Article 35.a

Acts 20:17 – Cumberland Presbyterian Church, *Confession of Faith* (1814/1883), Article 111.b; True Confession (1596), Article 20.b; United Presbyterian Church *Confessional Statement* (1925), Article 33; Cambridge Platform (1648), Chapter 6.3; Second Vatican Council (1962–65), §5.1, Chapter 3.20.4; Second Vatican Council (1962–65), §5.1, Chapter 3.26.50

Acts 20:17–28 – Westminster Confession of Faith (1647), Chapter 30.1.a

Acts 20:18 – First London Confession (1644), Article 37.c

Acts 20:20 – Mennonite Articles of Faith (1766/1895/1902), Article 14.2; Cambridge Platform (1648), Chapter 7.2.e

Acts 20:21 – Mennonite Articles of Faith (1766/1895/1902), Article 9.5; Westminster Confession of Faith (1647), Chapter 15.1.b; Cumberland Presbyterian Church, *Confession of Faith* (1814/1883), Article 42.a; North American Baptist Conference (1982), Article 5; Assemblies of God, *Statement of Fundamental Truths* (1916), Article 11; First London Confession (1644), Article 33.d; United Presbyterian Church *Confessional Statement* (1925), Article 18

Acts 20:23 – First London Confession (1644), Article 51.c

Acts 20:23, 24 – True Confession (1596), Article 42.a

Acts 20:24 – Mennonite Articles of Faith (1766/1895/1902), Article 14.2; Second Vatican Council (1962–65), §5.1, Chapter 3.21; Evangelical Lutheran Synod (1932), Article 21; Formula of Concord (1577), Article 5.6.5.b [P&H, IV.182]

Acts 20:25–27 – Second Vatican Council (1962–65), §5.1, Chapter 3.20.5

Acts 20:26–28 – Mennonite Articles of Faith (1766/1895/1902), Article 24.4

Acts 20:27 – Lausanne Covenant (1974), Article 6; The Orthodox Confession of the Catholic and Apostolic Eastern Church (1638/1642), Article 76; French Confession (1559/1571), Article 5.c; Cumberland Presbyterian Church, *Confession of Faith* (1814/1883), Article 9.e

Acts 20:27, 28 – True Confession (1596), Article 19.m; First London Confession (1644), Article 44.c

Acts 20:28 – True Confession (1596), Article 17.f; Mennonite Articles of Faith (1766/1895/1902), Article 17.2; Mennonite Articles of Faith (1766/1895/1902), Article 27.1; Evangelical Lutheran Synod (1932), Article 31; Second Vatican Council (1962-65), §5.1, Chapter 3.20; True Confession (1596), Article 26.d; Metrophanes Critopoulos *Confession of Faith* (1625), Article 23.4; The Orthodox Confession of the Catholic and Apostolic Eastern Church (1638/1642), Article 85; First London Confession (1644), Article 18.h; Cambridge Platform (1648), Chapter 7.2; Cambridge Platform (1648), Chapter 7.6.a; United Presbyterian Church *Confessional Statement* (1925), Article 32; United Presbyterian Church *Confessional Statement* (1925), Article 33; Second Vatican Council (1962-65), §5.1, Chapter 2.9; Cambridge Platform (1648), Chapter 3.5; Cambridge Platform (1648), Chapter 6.3; Cambridge Platform (1648), Chapter 10.8; Cambridge Platform (1648), Chapter 9.6.a; Cambridge Platform (1648), Chapter 9.6; Mennonite Articles of Faith (1766/1895/1902), Article 23.1; Mennonite Confession of Faith (1963), Article 10; Formula of Concord (1577), Article 8.14.9 [P&H, IV.191]; Westminster Confession of Faith (1647), Chapter 8.7.o; Dogmatic Decrees of the Council of Trent (Session 23.15 July 1563), Chapter 4 [P&H, IV.866]; A Confession of Faith Containing XXIII Articles (1673), Article 16; Eastern Orthodox Patriarchs, *Response to Pope Pius IX* (1848), Article 18 [P&H, V 283]; Eastern Orthodox Patriarchs, *Response to Pope Pius IX* (1848), Article 22.c [P&H, V 286]

Acts 20:28–31 – Eastern Orthodox Patriarchs, *Response to Pope Pius IX* (1848), Article 18 [P&H, V 283]

Acts 20:29 – Eastern Orthodox Patriarchs, *Response to Pope Pius IX* (1848), Article 21.a [P&H, V 286]; Eastern Orthodox Patriarchs, *Response to Pope Pius IX* (1848), Article 21 [P&H, V 285]

Acts 20:30 – Evangelical Lutheran Synod (1932), Article 29

Acts 20:32 – Westminster Confession of Faith (1647), Chapter 14.1.d; Westminster Confession of Faith (1647), Chapter 13.1.a; A Confession of Faith Containing XXIII Articles (1673), Article 11; Cambridge Platform (1648), Chapter 7.2; United Presbyterian Church *Confessional Statement* (1925), Article 21; Second Vatican Council (1962–65), §8, Chapter 6.21

Acts 20:33, 34 – A Confession of Faith Containing XXIII Articles (1673), Article 16

Acts 20:33–35 – Richmond Declaration of Faith (1887), Article 10.7, 9

Acts 20:35 – Bohemian Confession (1535), Article 9.[11]; Mennonite Articles of Faith (1766/1895/1902), Article 23.6

Acts 21:14 – Cambridge Platform (1648), Chapter 13.3.a

Acts 21:18 – Cambridge Platform (1648), Chapter 7.2; Cambridge Platform (1648), Chapter 10.9.e

Acts 21:19 – Second Vatican Council (1962–65), §5.1, Chapter 3.24

Acts 21:22, 23 – Cambridge Platform (1648), Chapter 7.2; Cambridge Platform (1648), Chapter 10.9.e

Acts 22:8, 9 – French Confession (1559/1571), Article 24.k

Acts 22:10 – Mennonite Articles of Faith (1766/1895/1902), Article 19.3

Acts 22:16 – Mennonite Articles of Faith (1766/1895/1902), Article 25.2; Mennonite Articles of Faith (1766/1895/1902), Article 25.6; New Hampshire Confession (1833/1853), Article 14.k; Mennonite Confession of Faith (1963), Article 11; Heidelberg Catechism (1563), Question 66.c; Evangelical Lutheran Synod (1932),

Article 21; French Confession (1559/1571), Article 34.e; French Confession (1559/1571), Article 35.f; Heidelberg Catechism (1563), Question 71.e; United Presbyterian Church, *Confessional Statement* (1925), Article 30; Commission on Faith and Order (1982), Article 1.B.4; Lutheran General Synod, *Definite Platform* (1855), Part 2. Topic 5 [P&H, V.311]; Tetrapolitan Confession (1530), Chapter 17.e

Acts 22:18, 19 – French Confession (1559/1571), Article 5.d

Acts 23:6–9 – Mennonite Articles of Faith (1766/1895/1902), Article 29.3

Acts 23:11 – Second Helvetic Confession (1566), Chapter 6.[4]

Acts 23:12 – Cumberland Presbyterian Church, *Confession of Faith* (1814/1883), Article 84.e; Westminster Confession of Faith (1647), Chapter 22.7.q

Acts 23:12–14 – United Presbyterian Church, *Confessional Statement* (1925), Article 31

Acts 23:14 – Westminster Confession of Faith (1647), Chapter 22.7.q

Acts 24:14 – Westminster Confession of Faith (1647), Chapter 14.2.e; Bohemian Confession (1535), [P&H, III.799]; True Confession (1596), Article 44

Acts 24:14–16 – First London Confession (1644), Article 53.b

Acts 24:15 – Mennonite Articles of Faith (1766/1895/1902), Article 33.1; United Presbyterian Church *Confessional Statement* (1925), Article 41; Westminster Confession of Faith (1647), Chapter 32.3.g; Cumberland Presbyterian Church, *Confession of Faith* (1814/1883), Article 113.d; Richmond Declaration of Faith (1887), Article 7.1; New Hampshire Confession (1833/1853), Article 18.p; A Confession of Faith Containing XXIII Articles (1673), Article 23

Acts 24:16 – Mennonite Articles of Faith (1766/1895/1902), Article 32.4

Acts 24:25 – Mennonite Articles of Faith (1766/1895/1902), Article 19.3

Acts 25:8 – Cambridge Platform (1648), Chapter 17.2

Acts 25:9–11 – Westminster Confession of Faith (1647), Chapter 23.4.n

Acts 26:6, 7 – Westminster Confession of Faith (1647), Chapter 16.3.o

Acts 26:13–15 – Jehovah's Witnesses, *Statement of Faith* (1918), Article 10

Acts 26:17, 18 – Second Vatican Council (1962–65), §5.1, Chapter 3.24

Acts 26:18 – Mennonite Articles of Faith (1766/1895/1902), Article 19.4; Westminster Confession of Faith (1647), Chapter 20.1.b; Evangelical Lutheran Synod (1932), Article 10; First London Confession (1644), Article 33.c; First London Confession (1644), Article 14.h; Westminster Confession of Faith (1647), Chapter 10.1.d

Acts 26:19 – Cambridge Platform (1648), Chapter 6.2.b

Acts 26:20 – United Presbyterian Church *Confessional Statement* (1925), Article 18

Acts 26.23 – Mennonite Articles of Faith (1766/1895/1902), Article 33.2

Acts 27:22 – Second Helvetic Confession (1566), Chapter 6.[4]

Acts 27:24 – United Presbyterian Church *Confessional Statement* (1925), Article 6; Cumberland Presbyterian Church, *Confession of Faith* (1814/1883), Article 13.a

Acts 27:31 – United Presbyterian Church *Confessional Statement* (1925), Article 6; Richmond Declaration of Faith (1887), Article 7.2; Westminster Confession of Faith (1647), Chapter 5.3.k; Cumberland Presbyterian Church, *Confession of Faith* (1814/1883), Article 13.a; Second Helvetic Confession (1566), Chapter 6.[4]

Acts 27:34 – Second Helvetic Confession (1566), Chapter 6.[4]

Acts 27:44 – Westminster Confession of Faith (1647), Chapter 5.3.k

Acts 28:25 – Westminster Confession of Faith (1647), Chapter 1.10.z

Acts 28:26, 27 – Westminster Confession of Faith (1647), Chapter 5.6.b

Biographies and Glossary

Abelard, Peter (1079–1142). Medieval French scholastic philosopher and dialectic theologian.

Alexander, Loveday (1947–). Emeritus Professor at University of Sheffield. Author of numerous studies on Luke/Acts, especially within their Greco-Roman environment.

Alline, Henry (1748–1784). One of the most famous evangelical preachers during the Great Awakening in North America.

Ambrose of Milan (c. 333–397; fl. 374–397). Bishop of Milan and famed "Doctor of the Church," who was the teacher of Augustine.

Ammonius (c. 175–242). Third-century theologian in Egypt.

The Acts of the Apostles Through the Centuries, First Edition. Heidi J. Hornik and Mikeal C. Parsons.
© 2017 Heidi J. Hornik and Mikeal C. Parsons. Published 2017 by John Wiley & Sons, Ltd.

Annett, Peter (1693–1769). English deist and staunch critic of orthodox theologians.

Aquinas, Thomas (c.1225–74). A Dominican priest, philosopher, and the medieval church's major systematic theologian.

Arator (490–550). Latin poet and orator, perhaps of Milan. He is known for his epic *On the Acts of the Apostles*.

Athanasius (296–373), anti-Arian Bishop of Alexandria.

Augustine (354–430), Bishop of Hippo and influential theologian of Western Christianity.

Bailey, James (d. 1893). Father of the Seventh Day Baptist Historical Society and author of *The Complete Sabbath Commentary* (1888).

Bampfield, Francis (1614/5–1683/4) served congregations at Rampisham and Sherborne and was prebend of Exeter Cathedral. Later, he became a Seventh Day Baptist.

Barber, Edward (d. 1663) was an outspoken British non-Conformist leader. Along with being among the first to publish in favor of immersion baptism, he also advocated religious liberty.

Barth, Karl (1886-1968). Swiss Reformed theologian and leader of "neo-Orthodox" movement, whose *Church Dogmatics* established him as one of the most influential twentieth-century theologians.

Basil, (b. c. 330; fl. 357–379). One of the Cappadocian fathers, bishop of Caesarea and champion of the teaching on the Trinity propounded at Nicea in 325. Founded a monastic rule.

(Pseudo-)Basil. Unknown fourth-century author whose work was attributed to Basil the Great (ca.330–379).

Baur, Ferdinand Christian (1792–1860). Professor of Church History and Dogmatics in Tübingen. Famous for his dialectical view of primitive Christianity in which "catholic Christianity" emerged from a conflict between the Pauline Gentile Christianity and the Petrine Jewish Christianity.

Bede, the Venerable (673–735). Northumbrian monk, chronicler of English Christianity, and biblical exegete. Bede wrote the first history of Christianity in Britain and one of the first commentaries on Acts.

Blackwood, Christopher (1607/8–1670). A Particular Baptist minister of churches of Ireland and England. He was a staunch supporter of believer's baptism, and added his signature in 1661 to a public denouncement of the Fifth Monarchist insurrection.

Blevins, Carolyn DeArmond (1936–). Taught in the Religion Department at Carson-Newman from 1977 until her retirement in 2006.

Bonhoeffer, Dietrich (1906–45). German Lutheran theologian and pastor. A founding member of the Confessing Church, Bonhoeffer opposed Adolf Hitler. He was executed on the orders of Heinrich Himmler.

Brenz, Johannes (1499–1570). German Lutheran theologian and pastor. Helped establish Lutheran orthodoxy through treatises, commentaries and catechisms.

Bullinger, Heinrich (1504–75). A Swiss reformer and follower of Zwingli. An influential second-generation Reformer, he was chief minister in Zurich for more than forty years.

Bunyan, John (1628–88). A preacher and member of an independent congregation in Bedford, who was imprisoned for his beliefs. Famous for his spiritual classic, *The Pilgrim's Progress*.

Caffyn, Matthew (1628–1714). An influential minister for more than sixty years. Actively debated Anglicans, Presbyterians, and Quakers, earning the nickname "battle-axe of Sussex."

Calvin, John (1509–64). Pre-eminent Reformed theologian and biblical interpreter. His commentary on Acts anticipates a historical-critical approach by focusing on the "original" meaning of the text in its literary and historical contexts.

Campbell, Alexander (1788–1866). A Scot-Irish immigrant who is recognized as one of the founders and architects of the Stone-Campbell Movement, whose goal was to restore Christianity to its New Testament form.

Cash, Johnny (1932–2003). One of the most widely influential singers and song-writers in twentieth-century American popular culture. Known as the "Man in Black," Cash authored a novel about the Apostle Paul, *Man in White.*

Cassian, John (360–435). An ascetic monk who introduced the rules of Eastern monastic life to the West.

Cassiodorus (c. 485–c.580). A statesman and later founder of the monastery of Vivarium, Calabria, where monks transcribed classic sacred and profane texts, Greek and Latin, preserving them for the Western tradition.

Carey, William (1761–1834). Recognized as the "father of the modern missionary enterprise." Carey spent forty-one years as a missionary in India, earning a reputation as a learned linguist and noted botanist.

Carver, William Owen (1868–1954). Educator and theologian who taught Missions at The Southern Baptist Theological Seminary in Louisville, KY, from 1896 until his retirement in 1943. Wrote a commentary on Acts.

Chesterton, G. K. (1874–1936). British writer, poet, humorist, and Christian apologist.

Chrysostom, John (345–407). Deacon and presbyter in Antioch and Bishop of Constantinople. Preached a series of Homilies on the Acts of the Apostles.

Clarke, John (1609–1676). Baptist minister and physician. Co-founder of Colony of Rhode Island and Providence Plantations.

Clarke, William Newton (1841–1912). Pastor and theologian. Wrote a systematic theology that rejected many traditional categories of theology and used "religious sentiment" (and not the "facts") as its guiding principle.

Clement of Alexandria (c.150–c.215). Christian theologian who taught at the catechetical school in Alexandria and used Greek philosophy to assist in his interpretation of the Bible.

Collins, Hercules (d. 1702). Active minister in the late seventeenth century, participating in the Particular Baptist assembly approving the Second London Confession of Faith.

Conner, Walter Thomas (1877–1952). Professor of Theology at Southwestern Seminary (1910–1949). Author of fifteen books.

Conzelmann, Hans (1915–1989). German New Testament scholar, whose works, *The Theology of St. Luke*, was influential on twentieth-century Lukan scholarship.

Cyprian (200–258). Bishop of Carthage. Important Latin writer of Western Christianity.

Cyril of Alexandria (c. 376–444). Bishop of Alexandria and all Egypt and one of the most important theologians of the fourth and fifth centuries.

Cyril of Jerusalem (c. 315–86). Bishop of Jerusalem who wrote influential *Catechetical Lectures*.

Danvers, Henry (c. 1619–1687/8). Controversial General Baptist preacher in seventeenth-century England.

Denne, Henry (1605/6–1661). British evangelist and preacher, associated with Levellers, who displayed sympathy for some Quaker views.

Didymus the Blind (c. 313–98). Alexandrian theologian and biblical exegete who was headmaster of the Christian Catechetical School in Alexandria.

Donne, John (1572–1631). An English cleric and poet.

Eichorn, J. G. (1752–1827). German Old Testament scholar at Göttingen, who wrote critical introductions to both the Old and New Testaments.

Emerson, Ralph Waldo (1803–1882). American poet and essayist, famous for his associations with the Transcendentalist Movement of the nineteenth century.

Erasmus, Desiderius (1469–1536). Renowned Dutch Humanist priest and theologian who, although critical of the abuses within the Roman Catholic church, remainedwithin it.

Erwin, Howard (1915–2009). Professor of theology at Oral Roberts University for forty years. Charismatic who wrote extensively on the Holy Spirit.

Eusebius (260–339). Bishop of Caesarea and prolific author. Most remembered for his *Ecclesiastical History*.

Ewald, Heinrich (1803–1875). German Protestant and biblical exegete. His *History of Israel* included a section on the Apostolic Age, which commented on the Acts of the Apostles.

Fifth Monarchists. Group of Christians active from 1649–1660, who believed they were appointed to reign with Christ (as part of the fifth and final monarchy predicted in the book of Daniel) during his thousand-year reign (which they believed would begin in 1666).

Fosdick, Henry Emerson (1878–1969). Taught homiletics and practical theology at Union Theological Seminary (1908–1946). In 1926, became the first pastor of the Riverside Church, New York City.

Fulgentius of Ruspe (c. 467–532). Bishop of Ruspe and author of many orthodox sermons and tracts under the influence of Augustine.

Garr, A. G. (1874–1944). Holiness pastor who visited Azusa Street Revival and received the gift of speaking in tongues. Went to India as a missionary, but reported that tongues as a missionary language failed; still remained a Pentecostal.

Gaventa, Beverly Roberts (1948–). Formerly Helen H. P. Manson Professor of New Testament Literature and Exegesis at Princeton Theological Seminary and currently Distinguished Professor of New Testament, Baylor University. Numerous writings on New Testament, including commentary on Acts (2003).

General Baptists. Stream of Baptists who identify with Arminianism and an emphasis on general atonement (the belief that Christ had died for the whole world and not just the elect).The first Baptist congregation, led by Thomas Helwys and John Smyth, were General Baptists.

Gill, John (1697–1771). Erudite and influential eighteenth-century Particular Baptist pastor. Wrote a multi-volume *Exposition of the Old and New Testaments*.

Graham, Billy (1918–). American evangelist who has conducted countless evangelistic crusades all over the world. Has written numerous best-selling volumes in popular Christianity.

Grantham, Thomas (1633/34–1692). English minister, theologian, and controversialist. Signed the 1660 reprint of *A Brief Confession or Declaration of Faith*, the 1661 *Second Humble Addresse* and *The Third Address*.

González, Justo (1937–). Cuban American Methodist historian and theologian who wrote a commentary on Acts that gave special attention to Latino/a concerns.

Gregory of Nyssa (c. 335–394). Bishop of Nyssa and brother of Basil the Great. A Cappadocian father and author of catechetical orations.

Gwalther, Rudolf (1519–1586). Swiss Reformed preacher. Chief religious officer and preacher of the Reformed church in Zurich. Translated the works of Zwingli into Latin.

Hackett, Horatio (1808–1875). Professor of New Testament at Rochester Theological Seminary and published a commentary on Acts, among his writings.

Haenchen, Ernst (1894–1975). German New Testament scholar. Published a widely-influential commentary on Acts (1956; ET 1971).

Hammon, George (d. 1680?). British Baptist pastor who wrote pamphlets on a variety of issues including original sin, believer's baptism, baptism by immersion, and religious liberty. From prison he addressed *The Humble Petition and Representation* (along with William Jeffrey, John Reve, and James Blackmore) to King Charles II, arguing that, in matters of faith, civil rulers have no authority.

Hargreaves, James (1768–1845). Active in home and foreign missionary work and published a number of works from a moderate Calvinist theological viewpoint.

Harnack, Adolf von (1851–1930). German historian and theologian who published an influential multi-volume *History of Dogma* (1896–99) and a monograph on the *Acts of the Apostles* (1909).

Harrison, Thomas (1619–1682). Noncomformist minister, trained for ministry in New England and became chaplain to governor of Virginia. After protesting against the governor's expulsion of Puritan ministers from Virginia for their views, Harrison returned to England, eventually founding a prominent dissenting congregation in Dublin, Ireland.

Hawthorne, Nathaniel (1804–1884). American novelist whose book, *The Scarlet Letter* (1850) met with immediate and lasting acclaim.

Helwys, Thomas (1550–1615). Along with John Smyth, led a band of Puritan Separatists to Amsterdam in 1609 and founded the world's first Baptist congregation. Architect of the 1611 *A Declaration of Faith of English People*. Died in prison in 1616.

Hippolytus (d. 235). A leader and later schismatic bishop of the Church in Rome.

Hugo of St. Cher (1200–1263). French Dominican friar who became a cardinal and famed biblical commentator.

Irenaeus of Lyons (c. 125–c. 200). Early Christian bishop who was one of the first commentators on Luke and Acts.

Jeffrey, William (seventh century). Non-conformist pastor who wrote a tract, *The Humble Petition*, from prison, protesting the involvement of civic authorities in ecclesial affairs.

Jerome (c. 340–420). Biblical scholar responsible for the Vulgate, the Latin translation of the Bible.

Josephus (37– c. 100). Jewish politician, soldier, and historian who wrote a history of the Jews and an account of the Jewish war against the Romans.

Justin Martyr (c. 100/110–165). Philosopher convert to Christianity. Wrote apologies against both pagans and Jews, combining Greek philosophy and Christian theology.

Keach, Benjamin (1640–1704). English minister who published forty-three works including six on baptism. His most famous work is *Tropologia, or a Key to Open Scripture Metaphors.*

Kenrick, Timothy (1759–184). Welsh Unitarian minister and biblical commentator.

Kierkegaard, Søren (1813–55). Danish philosopher and theologian who offered critiques of the cultural accomodation of the Danish Christendom in which he lived.

Kiffin, William (1616–1701). English minister, prolific author, and theologian. Involved in heated debate with John Bunyan over the correct relationship between believer's baptism and local church membership as well as a debate over whether or not to allow the singing of hymns during worship.

Kipling, Rudyard (1865–1936). English poet (e.g., "Gunga Din") and novelist (e.g., *The Jungle Book*). In 1907, he was the first English speaker to win the Nobel Prize in Literature. Made frequent allusions to the Bible in his writings.

Knollys, Hanserd (1598–1691). Anglican minister in Lincolnshire who became involved (whether voluntarily or not) in the Fifth Monarchist Insurrection. Despite being imprisoned on multiple occasions, he published numerous polemical works and—toward the end of his life—became a formative figure in the organization of the Baptist movement.

Knox, John (1513–1572). Scottish Reformed preacher. He was a fiery preacher to monarchs and a zealous defender of high Calvinism, and was a chief architect of the reform of the Scottish church (Presbyterian), serving as one of the authors of the *Book of Discipline* and writing many pamphlets and sermons.

Lake, Kirsopp (1872–1946). Winn Professor of Ecclesiastical History at Harvard Divinity School and co-editor of *The Beginnings of Christianity*, a five-volume study of the Acts of the Apostles.

Lawrence, Henry (1600–1664). An English Puritan statesman and occasional religious author, including penning *A Plea for the Use of Gospel Ordinances* in 1652, and who was identified within Parliament as associating with "the baptized people."

Leo the Great (?– 461). Pope who exerted great religious and political leadership. Wrote a tome that provided the Council of Chalcedon with guidance on how to formulate the divinity of Christ (one divine person with two natures, human and divine).

Lightfoot, John (1602–1675). British cleric and Vice-Chancellor, Cambridge University. Hebraist best known for *Horae Hebraicae et Talmudicae*. Also wrote a commentary on Acts (1645).

Locke, John (1632–1704). English philosopher and influential Enlightenment thinker. His *Reasonableness of Christianity* (1695) attempted to reconcile biblical narrative with human reason.

Luther, Martin (1483–1546), Augustinian monk, Professor of Biblical Literature at Wittenberg, and leader of the Protestant Reformation in Germany. Although he did not publish a commentary on Acts, his writings made ample references to that work.

Mallory, Kathleen (1879–1954). Corresponding Secretary of the Woman's Missionary Union, an auxiliary to the Southern Baptist Convention. Wrote the *Manual of WMU Methods* (1917).

Maston, Thomas Buford (1897–1988). Professor of Christian Ethics at Southwestern Baptist Theological Seminary in Fort Worth, TX. Was especially well known (and sometimes despised) for his progressive views on race relations.

Medley, Samuel (1738–1799). Particular Baptist pastor for twenty-seven years of the First Baptist Church, Liverpool, England.

Mill, John Stuart (1806–1873). English social and political philosopher. His *Three Essays on Religion* was in part an attempt to read the Bible in the light of standards of rationalistic Deism.

Milton, John (1609–74). Poet, Nonconformist, anti-monarchist and apologist for the Commonwealth in England. Famous for *Paradise Lost,* Milton also wrote a tract, *Areopagiticus,* in defense of free speech that drew in part on Paul's Areopagus speech.

Mitchell, Ella Pearson (1917–2008). An ordained Baptist minister who taught at Virginia Union School of Theology and Berkley Baptist Divinity School and the first female dean at Spellman College. Wrote *Women: To Preach or Not to Preach* and edited five volumes of *Those Preaching Women.*

Monk, Thomas (seventeenth century). British pastor who (along with six others) published *Sions Groans for her Distressed* (1661) which expressly denies the magistrate's right or claim to regulate the worship of God.

Moody, Dale (1915–1992). Professor of Theology at Southern Seminary in Louisvill, KY (1948–84). In addition to a systematic theology, *The Word of Truth,* he wrote a volume on the doctrine of the Holy Spirit, *Spirit of the Living God,* in which he dealt extensively with the Acts of the Acpostles.

Montgomery, Helen Barrett (1861–1934) Biblical scholar and denominational leader. Involved in the women's rights movement; produced *Centenary* translation of the New Testament for American Baptists.

Moon, Charlotte "Lottie" (1840–1912). Missionary to China for nearly forty years. In her honor, Southern Baptists established the Lottie Moon Christmas Offering for Foreign Missions in 1918.

Moore, Joanna Patterson (1832–1916). Missionary whose career began with work in refugee camps for freed slaves. Later established a Training School for Mothers in Little Rock, Arkansas in 1891. Her missionary career was marked by her efforts on behalf of economic and educational opportunities for African-Americans.

Müntzer, Thomas (c.1485–1525). A radical reformer, whose mix of mysticism with the practice of revolutionary change led him to participate in the Peasant's Revolt, in which he was defeated and executed in 1525.

O'Donovan, Oliver (1945–). Professor Emeritus of Christian Ethics and Pastoral Theology at the University of Edinburgh. Examined the theological claims and political implications of Jesus' resurrection and ascension in *Resurrection and the Moral Order* (1986).

Oladipo, Caleb Oluremi (1955–). A Nigerian of the Yoruba tribe, Oladipo is currently serving as Duke K. McCall Professor of Christian Mission and World Christianity at The Baptist Seminary in Richmond, Virginia.

Origen (c.185–235). A leading third-century theologian and exegete, based in Alexandria and later in Caesarea.

Pachomius (292–348). Founder of cenobitic or communal monasticism. After his death, the movement grew to number more than 7,000 monks.

Papias (c. 70–163). Bishop of Hierapolis and early witness to the chiliastic tradition in second-century Christianity. Fragments of his work are preserved by Irenaeus and Eusebius.

Parham, Charles (1873–1929). Along with William Seymour, one of the founders of the Pentecostal movement. Believed speaking in tongues was speaking in known, but unstudied languages and was therefore useful for mission field preaching.

Particular Baptists. Group of Baptists influenced by Reformed theology who believed in limited atonement (the view that Christ's death was for the chosen elect). The views of Particular Baptists gradually came to dominate the Baptist scene in England. John Gill and, later, C. H. Spurgeon were important Particular Baptists.

Pelikan, Jaroslav (1923–2006). Yale Sterling Professor of History. Wrote an influential five-volume history of Christian doctrine, a commentary on Acts, and co-edited *Creeds and Confessions in the Christian Tradition*.

Pendleton, J. M. (1811–1891). Baptist minister and Professor of Theology at Union University in Murfreesboro, TN. Later became editor of *The Tennessee Baptist* denominational circular, which advocated the ecclesiology of Landmarkism (which emphasized the complete autonomy and primacy of the local congregation).

Pervo, Richard I. (1942–). Harvard-trained New Testament scholar whose commentary on Acts (2009) in the Hermeneia series replaced the older work by Hans Conzelmann.

Peter Olivi (1248–98). "Spiritual" of the Franciscan Order who argued against personal or communal possession of property based on his reading of Acts 2 and 4.

Pinnock, Clark H. (1937–). Professor Emeritus of Systematic Theology at McMaster Divinity College in Hamilton, Ontario. Authored a dozen books, including *The Openness of God* (1994), in which he lays out his case for "open theism."

Polhill, John B. (1939–) Professor Emeritus at Southern Baptist Theological Seminary. A specialist in Paul and Acts, he wrote a commentary on Acts.

Polycarp (c. 69–155). Bishop of Smyrna who vigorously fought heretics such as the Marcionites and Valentinians. Leading Christian figure in Roman Asia in the middle of the second century.

Polycrates of Ephesus (fl. 130–196). Bishop of Ephesus. During the "Quartodecimanian" controversy (regarding the date of Christian observance of Passover), Polycrates defended the local practice of following the Jewish calendar to establish the date of the Christian Passover and Easter.

Pope Felix II (reigned 483–492). Embroiled in a controversy with Emperor Zeno, Felix repudiated Zeno's *Henoticon*, which was an attempt to reconcile Miaphysite and Chalcedonian Christians.

Pope John Paul II (1920–2005). First non-Italian Pope in over four hundred years. A native of Poland, he was Pope for nearly thirty-two years. Popular for his bridge-building efforts between cultures and religions, as evidenced by his 1979 Pentecost homily.

Powell, Vavasor (1617–1670). Independent Baptist minister, influential and itinerant preacher, and civil activist in seventeenth-century Wales. A well-known opponent of both the protectorate and Quakers, associated with Fifth Monarchists, he was arrested several times, and published numerous sermons, evangelical tracts, and polemical writings.

Prudentius (348–402/05). Christian poet known for his allegory, *Psychomachia* ("Battle of Souls"), which described the struggle of faith against idolatry. He also wrote the treatise, *Libri contra Symmachum*, against the Roman senator Symmachus' demands for the restoration of the pagan altar of victory to the Senate house.

Randall, Benjamin (1749–1808). Established the first Free Will Baptist church in 1780 in New Hampshire. Amended and printed many of Alline's works, including *Two Mites*.

Rauschenbusch, Walter (1861–1918). Architect of the Social Gospel movement. Served as pastor of the congregation near "Hell's Kitchen" in New York City. Taught at Rochester Seminary from 1897 until his death in 1918. Author of *Christianity and the Social Crisis* and *A Theology of the Social Gospel*.

Robertson, Archibald Thomas (1863–1934). Greek scholar and professor at The Southern Baptist Theological Seminary (1888–1934). Best remembered for *A Grammar of the Greek New Testament in Light of Historical Research* (1914) and his six-volume *Word Pictures of the New Testament* (1930).

Robinson, Henry Wheeler (1872–1945). Old Testament scholar and theologian at Regent's Park College, Oxford University (1920–1942). Widely-published author in Old Testament studies, especially in the field of Hebrew psychology.

Robinson, John A. T. (1919–1983). Anglican Bishop of Woolwich and Dean of Trinity College, Cambridge University. Iconoclastic theologian who championed the "secular theology" movement. Known especially for *Honest to God* (1963) and *Redating the New Testament* (1976).

Rossellini, Roberto (1906–1977). Italian film director and screenwriter. Produced the popular, critically-acclaimed miniseries, *Atti degli apostoli*, based on the book of Acts.

Savonarola, Girolamo (1452–1498). Italian Dominican Friar in Florence, Italy, whose fiery denunciation of clerical corruption and apocalyptic visions and preaching resulted in his excommunication and eventual execution.

Schaberg, Jane (1938–2012). Feminist theologian and Professor of Religious Studies and Women's Studies at the University of Detroit Mercy. Published feminist studies of infancy and resurrection narratives and authored the commentary on Luke in the *Women's Bible Commentary* (1982).

Severian of Gabala (fl. c. 400). Contemporary of John Chrysostom and a highly-regarded preacher in Constantinople.

Severus of Antioch (fl. 488– 538). A monophysite theologian, consecrated bishop of Antioch in 522. Born in Pisidia, he studied in Alexandria and Beirut, taught in Constantinople and was exiled to Egypt.

Smith, Taylor Clarence (1915–2011). Professor of New Testament at The Southern Baptist Theological Seminary, the Divinity School of the University of Chicago, Berkeley Baptist Divinity School, the Graduate Theological Union of Berkeley, and later Furman University, where he retired as Professor Emeritus. He published books on Acts, Revelation, and Christian worship.

Smyth, John (1570–1612). Along with Thomas Helwys, he led a band of Puritan Separatists to Amsterdam in 1609 and founded the world's first Baptist church. Published *Principles and Inferences concerning the Visible Church*, which laid out many early Baptist doctrines.

Scholiasticus, Socrates (c. 380–c. 439). Christian church historian in Constantinople whose history of the church covered the fourth and early fifth centuries.

Spangenberg, Johannes (1484–1550). German Lutheran pastor and catechist. Published the *Postilla Teütsch*, a six-volume work meant to prepare children to understand the lectionary readings. Also wrote a postil for the Acts of the Apostles.

Spencer, F. Scott (1954–). Professor at the Baptist Theological Seminary in Richmond, who wrote a commentary on Acts, *Journeying Through Acts.*

Spurgeon, Charles Haddon (1834–92). Baptist minister renowned for his sermons. He pastored at New Park Street Chapel which, under his leadership, moved to the Metropolitan Tabernacle.

Stagg, Frank (1911–2001). Professor at New Orleans Baptist Theological Seminary (1945–64), and later, The Southern Baptist Theological Seminary (1964–71). Published a commentary on Acts, *The Struggle for an Unhindered Gospel* (1955).

Stanley, Frank (seventeenth century). British pastor who (along with six others) published *Sions Groans for her Distressed* (1661) which expressly denies the magistrate's right or claim to regulate the worship of God.

Stendahl, Krister (1921–2008). Professor and Dean at Harvard Divinity School and later Bishop of the Lutheran church in Stockholm, Sweden. His view that Paul was "called" rather than "converted" (1963) has been highly influential.

Strauss, D. F. (1808–1874). German liberal Protestant theologian, whose work especially challenged the miracle account in the Bible.

Sutton, Katherine (1630–1663). Christian prophetess who flourished during the mid-seventeenth century. Best known for her gift of "spiritual singing."

Talbert, Charles H. (1934–). Distinguished Professor of Religion Emeritus at Baylor University (1997–2012). Wrote many articles and books on the Lukan writings, including commentaries on both Luke and Acts.

Tertullian (c. 155–c. 240). Important theologian in Latin Christianity. Treatises were on issues addressing doctrinal, moral, polemical and apologetic topics.

Textus Receptus. Latin for the "received text." The Greek text of the New Testament, published by Erasmus in 1516, which became the basis for many subsequent translations, including the King James Version.

Wangerin, Walter (1944–). Author of more than thirty novels, most notably, *The Book of God* and *Paul: A Novel.* Research Professor at Valparaiso University.

Warfield, B. B. (1851–1921). Professor of Theology at Princeton Seminary. Conservative Presbyterian who advocated the doctrine of cessation, e.g., that speaking in tongues and miracles ceased at the end of the apostolic age.

Warren, Richard "Rick" (1954–) is pastor and founder of Saddleback Church in Lake Forest, California, and also leads the *Purpose Driven Network* of churches, a global coalition of congregations in 162 countries.

Williams, A. D. (1825–1894). President of Oakland City College, an institution of the General Baptists. Authored or edited several books including *The Rhode Island Free will Baptist Pulpit* and *The Christian Church and its Institutions.*

Wesley, Charles (1707–88). Anglican priest, brother of John Wesley, who wrote over 8,000 hymns.

Wesley, John (1703–91). Anglican priest, itinerant preacher, and founder of Methodism. His *Notes on the Whole Bible* (1754) include extensive references to Acts.

Winstanley, Gerrard (1609–1676). Leader of the "Diggers" who wrote a pamphlet, "The New Law of Righetousness," in which he argued for shared communal ownership of land, based on Acts 4 (and other texts).

Wright, Joseph (seventeenth century). British pastor who (along with six others) published *Sions Groans for her Distressed* (1661) which expressly denies the magistrate's right or claim to regulate the worship of God.

Wright, N. T. (1948–). Former Anglican Bishop of Durham and currently Professor of New Testament at St. Andrews University. Prolific writer and popular speaker.

Yoakum, Finis (1851–1920). Physician and supporter of the Pentecostal movement who claimed to be the recipient of a miraculous healing. Established many social ministries among the poor and indigent, including the Pisgah Home in Los Angeles for drug addicts, the terminally ill, and the homeless.

Yong, Amos (1965–). Pentecostal theologian now teaching at Fuller Seminary. Heavily involved in issues concerning theology and disability studies.

Zwingli, Huldrych (1484–1531). Swiss Reformed humanist, preacher and theologian. Influenced by the writings of Erasmus, he enacted reform through sermons, public disputations and conciliation with the town council, abolishing the Mass and images in the church.

Bibliography

Ahl, Diane Cohl. 2008. *Fra Angelico*. New York: Phaidon.
Alexander, Loveday C. A. 2000. "What if Luke Had Never Met Theophilus?" *Biblical Interpretation* 8: 161–70.
Alexander, Loveday. 2001. "The Acts of the Apostles." Pages 1028–61 in *The Oxford Bible Commentary*. Edited by John Muddiman, John Barton, et al. Oxford; New York: Oxford University Press.
Alexander, Loveday. 2006. *Acts: The People's Bible Commentary*. Oxford: Bible Reading Fellowship.
Allen, Reuben. 1873. "The Resurrection." In *The Rhode Island Free Will Baptist Pulpit*. Edited by A. D. Williams. Boston: Gould and Lincoln.

The Acts of the Apostles Through the Centuries, First Edition. Heidi J. Hornik and Mikeal C. Parsons.
© 2017 Heidi J. Hornik and Mikeal C. Parsons. Published 2017 by John Wiley & Sons, Ltd.

Alline, Henry, with Benjamin Randall. 1804. *Two Mites, cast into the offering of God for the benefit of mankind*. Samuel Bragg, publisher. The Baptist Library Online.

Allison, Dale C. 2005. *Resurrecting Jesus: The Earliest Christian Tradition and its Interpreters*. New York: T&T Clark.

Ambrose. 1896. *St. Ambrose: Selected Works and Letters*. Edited by Philip Schaff and Henry Wace. Translated by H. de Romestin, E. de Romestin, and H. T. F. Duckworth. NPNF 10. Second series. New York: Christian Literature Company. Reprint: Peabody, MA: Hendrickson, 1994.

Ambrose. 1954. *Letters*. Translated by Mary Melchior Beyenka. Fathers of the Church 26. Washington, D. C.: The Catholic University of America Press.

American Baptist Association. 1993. "Doctrinal Statement." Accessed from http://www.abaptist.org/ABA/believe.html.

Anderson, Janice Capel. 2004. "Reading Tabitha: A Feminist Reception History." Pages 22–48 in *A Feminist Companion to the Acts of the Apostles*. Edited by Amy-Jill Levine with Marianne Blickenstaff. Feminist Companion to the New Testament and Early Christian Writings 9. London and New York: T&T Clark.

Anderson, Robert Mapes. 1979. *Vision of the Disinherited*. New York and Oxford: Oxford University Press.

Annet, Peter. *The History and Character of St. Paul, Examined: In a Letter to Theophilus, a Christian Friend*. London: F. Page.

Aquinas, Thomas. 1902. *An Apology for the Religious Orders*. Translated by John Procter. London: Sands. Reprint: Westminster, MD: Newman, 1950.

Aquinas, Thomas. *Summa Theologiae*. Accessed from *Christian Classics Ethereal Library* (www.ccel.org).

Aquinas, Thomas. 1966. *Commentary on St. Paul's Epistle to the Galatians*. Translated by F. R. Larcher. Albany, NY: Magi Books.

Aquinas, Thomas. 2012. *Commentary on the Letter of Saint Paul to the Romans*. Translated by Fabian R. Larcher. Edited by John Mortensen and Enrique Alarcón. Lander, WY: The Aquinas Institute for the Study of Sacred Doctrine.

[Arator]. 1987. *Arator's On the Acts of the Apostles*. Edited and translated by Richard J. Schrader. Co-translated by Joseph L. Roberts III and John F. Makowski. Classics in Religious Studies 6. Atlanta: Scholars Press.

Arslan, Edoardo. 1943. *La Pittura e la scultura Veronese dal secolo VIII al secolo XIII*. Milan: Fratelli Bocca.

Askew, Pamela. 1961a. "The Parable Paintings of Domenico Fetti." *The Art Bulletin* 43: 21–45.

Askew, Pamela. 1961b. "Fetti's 'Martyrdom' at the Wadsworth Atheneum." *The Burlington Magazine* 103: 245–52.

Athanasius (259–373). 1892. *St. Athanasius: Select Works and Letters*. Edited by Philip Schaff and Henry Wace. NPNF 4. Second series. New York: Christian Literature Company. Reprint: Peabody, MA: Hendrickson, 1994.

Athanasius. 1950. *The Life of St. Antony*. Translated by R. Meyer. ACW 10. Westminister, MD: Newman.

Atti degli Apostoli. 1968. Directed by Roberto Rossellini.

Atwan, Robert and Laurance Wieder. 1993. *Chapters into Verse: Poetry in English Inspired by the Bible*. Volume Two: Gospels to Revelation. Oxford: Oxford University Press.

Augustine. *The Works of Saint Augustine*. Edited by Boniface Ramsey. 50 volumes. Hyde Park, NY: New City Press, 1990–.

Aymer, Margaret. 2012. "Acts of the Apostles." Pages 536–46 in *Women's Bible Commentary*. 3rd edition. Edited by Carol A. Newsom, Sharon H. Ringe, and Jacqueline E. Lapsley. Louisville: Westminster John Knox.

Bachelor, Tappan Hilton. 1873. "Salvation Conditional." In *The Rhode Island Free Will Baptist Pulpit*. Edited by A. D. Williams. Boston: Gould and Lincoln.

Bailey, James. 1888. *The Complete Sabbath Commentary*. Accessed from http://home. inwave.com/sabhist/sabbath-5.htm.

Baird, William. 1992–2013. *History of New Testament Research*. 3 volumes. Minneapolis: Fortress.

Bampfield, Francis. 1681. *A Name, An After-One, or, An Historical Declaration of the Life of Shem Archer*. Early English Books Online.

Barasch, M. 1987. *Giotto and the Language of Gesture*. New York: Cambridge University Press.

Barber, Edward. 1648. *A Declaration and Vindication of the Carriage of Edward Barber*. Early English Books Online.

Barber, Edward. 1651. *The Storming and Totall Routing of Tythes*. Early English Books Online.

Barr, Beth Allison, Bill J. Leonard, Mikeal C. Parsons, and C. Douglas Weaver, eds. 2009. *The Acts of the Apostles: Four Centuries of Baptist Interpretation*. The Baptists' Bible. Waco, TX: Baylor University Press.

Barrett, David B. ed. 1982. *World Christian Encyclopedia*. Oxford: Oxford University Press.

Barrett, C. K. 1994–98. *A Critical and Exegetical Commentary on the Acts of the Apostles*. 2 volumes. ICC. Edinburgh: T&T Clark.

Barrett, C. K. 1961. *Luke the Historian in Recent Study*. London: Epworth.

Barth, Karl. 1936–77. *Church Dogmatics*. 4 volumes. Edinburgh: T&T Clark.

Baskett, John. 2006. *The Horse in Art*. New Haven: Yale University Press.

Batastini, Robert J., Michael A. Cymbala, eds. 1994. *Gather Comprehensive Hymnal*. Chicago: GIA Publications.

Bauckham, Richard. 1993. "The Acts of Paul as a Sequel to Acts." Pages 105–52 in *The Book of Acts in Its First Century Setting. Vol 1. The Book of Acts in its Ancient Literary Setting*. Ed. Bruce W. Winter and Andrew D. Clarke. Grand Rapids: Eerdmans.

Bauckham, Richard. 1998. "For Whom Were Gospels Written?" Pages 9–48 in *The Gospel for All Christians: Rethinking the Gospel Audiences*. Edited by Richard Bauckham. Grand Rapids: Eerdmans.

Baur, F. C. 1838. "Über der Ursprung des Episcopats in der christlichen Kirche. Prüfung der neuesten von Hrn. Dr. Rothe hierüber aufgestellten Ansicht." *Tübinger Zeitschrift für Theologie* 11: 1–185.

Baur, F. C. 1863. *Geschichte der christlichen Kirche*. Tübingen: Verlag und Druck von L. Fr. Fues.

Baur, F. C. 1887. *The Church History of the First Three Centuries*. 3rd edition. 2 volumes. Translated by Allan Menzies. Theological Translation Fund Library. London: Williams & Norgate.

Bax, Douglas. 1983. "The Bible and Apartheid 2." Pages 112–43 in *Apartheid is a Heresy*. Edited by J. de Gruchy and C. villa-Vicencio. Grand Rapids: Eerdmans.

Béchard, Dean Philip. 2000. *Paul Outside the Walls: A Study of Luke's Socio-Geographical Universalism in Acts 14:8–20*. Rome: Editrice Pontificio Istituto Biblico.

Bede, The Venerable. 1939. *Expositio actuum apostolorum et retractatio*. Edited by M. L. W. Laistner. Mediaeval Academy of America Publication 35. Cambridge, MA: The Mediaeval Academy of America. ET: The Venerable Bede, *Commentary on the Acts of the Apostles: Translated, with an Introduction and Notes*. Translated by Lawrence T. Martin. Kalamazoo, MI: Cistercian Publications, 1989.

Berry, Amanda Lee Wylie. 1992. "John Chrysostom and his Homilies on the Acts of the Apostles: Reclaiming Ancestral Models for the Christian people." Ph.D. dissertation, Princeton Theological Seminary.

Bevers, Holm, Lee Hendrix, William W. Robinson, and Peter Schatborn. 2010. *Drawings by Rembrandt and His Pupils: Telling the Difference*. Los Angeles: J. Paul Getty Museum.

Blackwood, Christopher. 1646. *Apostolicall Baptisme: A Sober rejoinder to a book written by Mr. Thomas Black entitled Infants Baptism*. Early English Books Online.

Blackwood, Christopher. 1653. *A Soul-Searching Catechism*. Early English Books Online.

Blackwood, Christopher. 1654. *A Christian's Groans*. Early English Books Online.

Blass, F. 1895. *Acta Apostolorum sive Lucae ad Theophilum liber alter*. Editio Philologica. Göttingen: Vandenhoeck & Ruprecht.

Blevins, Carolyn DeArmond. 2007. "Baptists and Women's Issues in the Twentieth Century." Pages 61–73 in *No Longer Ignored: A Collection of Articles on Baptist Women*. Edited by Charles W. Deweese and Pamela R. Durso. Atlanta: Baptist History and Heritage Society.

Boccacio, Giovanni. 1351. *The Decameron*. Project Gutenberg Ebook. Accessed from http://www.gutenberg.org/files/23700/23700-h/23700-h.htm.

Bockmuehl, Markus N. A. 2005. "Why Not Let Acts Be Acts? In Conversation with C. Kavin Rowe." *Journal for the Study of the New Testament* 28: 163–66.

Boismard, M. E., and A. Lamouille. 1984. *Le texte occidental des actes des apôtres: reconstitution et rehabilitation*. 2 volumes. Synthèse 17. Paris: Editions Recherche sur les civilisations.

Bonhoeffer, Dietrich. 1996–2014. *Dietrich Bonhoeffer's Works*. 17 volumes. Philadelphia: Fortress.

Boring, M. Eugene. 1997. *Disciples and the Bible: A History of Disciples Biblical Interpretation in North America*. St. Louis, MO: Chalice Press.

Borsook, Eve. 1990. *Messages in Mosaic. The Royal Programmes of Norman Sicily 1130–1187*. Oxford: Oxford University Press.

Bovon, François. 2006. "The Reception of the Book of Acts in Antiquity." Unpublished paper presented to the Book of Acts Section at the Society of Biblical Literature, Washington, D.C., November.

Bovon, François. 2002–2012. *A Commentary on the Gospel of Luke*. 3 volumes. Hermeneia: A Critical and Historical Commentary on the Bible. Minneapolis: Fortress.

Bowes, Kim. 2001. "Ivory Lists: Consular Diptychs, Christian Appropriation and Polemics of Time in Late Antiquity." *Art History* 24: 338–57.

Brenz, Johannes. 1535. *In Acta Apostolica Homiliae Centvm Viginiti Duas*. Haganau: Peter Braubach.

Brookins, Timothy, Peter Reynolds, and Mikeal Parsons. 2011. "In Defense of Peter and Paul: The Contribution of Cramer's Catena to the Early Reception of Paul in Acts." *Journal of Early Christian History* 1: 22–39.

Brooks, Walter Henderson. 1945. *The Pastor's Voice: A Collection of Poems*. Washington, D.C.: Associated Publishers.

Brown, Peter. 1981. *The Cult of the Saints: Its Rise and Function in Latin Christianity*. Chicago: University of Chicago Press.

Brown, Peter. 2012. *Through the Eye of a Needle: Wealth, the Fall of Rome, and the Making of Christianity in the West, 250–550 AD*. Princeton, NJ: Princeton University Press.

Bruce, F. F. 1978. *Paul: The Apostle of the Heart Set Free*. Grand Rapids: Eerdmans.

Bruun, Niels W., and Finn Gredal Jensen. 2010. "Kierkegaard's Latin Translations of the New Testament: A Constant Dialogue with the Vulgate." Pages 221–36 in *Kierkegaard and the Bible*. Volume 2. Edited by Lee C. Barrett. Farnham: Ashgate.

Bullinger, Heinrich. 1533. *In Acta Apostolorum*. Zurich: Christoph Froschauer.

Bunyan, John. 1678. *The Pilgrim's Progress from this World to That which is to Come*. Early English Books Online.

Bunyan, John. 1689. *Jerusalem-Sinner Saved; or, Good News for the Vilest of Men*. Volume 11 of *Miscellaneous Works of John Bunyan*. Early English Books Online.

Burgess, Stacey, and Gary McGee, eds. 1988. *Dictionary of Pentecostal and Charismatic Movements*. Grand Rapids: Zondervan.

Burnside, Robert. 1827. *Remarks on the Different Sentiments entertained in Christendom Relative to the Weekly Sabbath*. Joseph Stillman, publisher.

Burridge, Richard A. 2007. *Imitating Jesus: An Inclusive Approach to New Testament Ethics*. Grand Rapids: Eerdmans.

Burridge, Richard A. 2011. "Apartheid." *Dictionary of Scripture and Ethics*. Edited by Joel B. Green. Grand Rapids: Baker Academic.

Butlin, Martin. 1981. *The Paintings and Drawings of William Blake*. Two volumes. New Haven: Yale University Press.

Byrom, G. H., and Bet McLeod. 2012. "Limoges." *Grove Art Online. Oxford Art Online.* Oxford University Press. Accessed from http://www.oxfordartonline.com/subscriber/article/grove/art/T051125

Cadbury, Henry J. 1920. *The Style and Literary Method of Luke*. Cambridge, MA: Harvard University.

Cadbury, Henry J. 1927. *The Making of Luke-Acts*. New York: Macmillan.

Cadbury, Henry J. 1932. *English Translation and Commentary*. Volume 4 in *The Beginnings of Christianity, Part 1: The Acts of the Apostles*. Edited by F. J. Foakes Jackson and Kirsopp Lake. London: Macmillan and Co.

Cadbury, Henry J. 1933. "Lexical Notes on Luke-Acts V. Luke and the Horse-Doctors." *Journal of Biblical Literature* 52: 55–65.

Cadbury, Henry J. 1955. *The Book of Acts in History*. London: A. and C. Black.

Caffyn, Matthew. 1660. *Faith in God's Promises*. Early English Books Online.

Calvesi, Maurizio. 2001. "Gli affreschi del Beato Angelico nella Cappella Niccolina." Pages 45–62 in *Il Beato Angelio e la Cappella Niccolina*. Edited by Francesco Buranelli. Rome: Musei Vaticani and Istituto Geografico de Agostini.

Calvin, John. 1960. *Institutes of the Christian Religion (1559)*. Edited by John T. McNeill. Translated by Ford Lewis Battles. Library of Christian Classics 20–21. Philadelphia: Westminster. Accessed: *Past Masters Online*.

Calvin, John. 1965–66. *The Acts of the Apostles*. 2 volumes. Translated by John W. Fraser and W. J. G. McDonald. Edited by David W. Torrance and Thomas F. Torrance. Calvin's New Testament Commentaries 6–7. Grand Rapids: Eerdmans. Accessed: *Christian Classics Etheral Library*.

Campbell, Alexander. 1828. "Ancient Gospel – No.VII. Christian Immersion." *Christian Baptist* 5: 454–55.

Campbell, William Sanger. 2007. *The "We" Passages in the Acts of the Apostles: The Narrator as Narrative Character*. Leiden: Brill.

Cannon-Brookes, P. 1968. "Botticelli's Pentecost." *Apollo* 87: 274–77.

Cardiphonia. 2011. "Pentecost Songs."

Carey, William. 1792. *An enquiry into the Obligations of Christians to Use Means for the Conversion of the Heathens*. London.

Carroll, B. H. 1893. *Baptist: Its Law, its Administrators, its Subjects, its Form, its Design*. Baptist Standard Steam Press Print.

Carver, W. O. 1909. *Missions in the Plan of the Ages*. New York: Fleming H. Revell.

Carver, W. O. 1916. *The Acts of the Apostles*. Nashville: Broadman.

Carver, W. O. 1918. *All the World in All the Word: Twelve Bible Studies in Missions for Use in Women's Missionary Union and Other Study Classes*. Southern Baptist Convention Sunday School Board.

Cash, Johnny. 1986. *Man in White: A Novel about the Apostle Paul*. Nashville: WestBow Press.

Cassiodorus. 1990–91. *Explanation of the Psalms*. Translated by P. G. Walsh. 3 volumes. ACW 51–53. New York: Paulist Press.

Cavanaugh, J. R. 1965. "The Saint Stephen Motif in Saint Thomas More's Thought." *Moreana* 8: 59–66.

Cavina, Anna Ottani. 2008. "Poussin and the Roman Campagna: In Search of the Absolute." Pages 39–49 in *Poussin and Nature. Arcadian Visions*. Edited by Pierre Rosenberg and Keith Christiansen. New Haven and New York: Yale University Press in association with Metropolitan Museum of Art.

"CHÉRON, Louis." *Benezit Dictionary of Artists. Oxford Art Online*. Oxford University Press. Accessed from http://www.oxfordartonline.com/subscriber/article/benezit/B00036954

Chesterton, G. K. 2001. *Basil Howe: A Story of Young Love*. London: New City. Accessed: *Past Masters Online*.

Childs, Brevard. 1977. "The *Sensus Literalis* of Scripture: An Ancient and Modern Problem." Pages 80–93 in *Beiträge zur Alttestamentlichen Theologie: Festschrift für Walther Zimmerli zum 70. Geburtstag*. Edited by Walther Zimmerli, Herbert Donner, Robert Hanhart, and Rudolf Smend. Göttingen: Vandenhoeck & Ruprecht.

Chillenden, Edmund. 1653. *Nathan's Parable*. Early English Books Online.

Chrysostom, John. 1889. *Homilies on the Acts of the Apostles and the Epistle to the Romans*. NPNF 11. First series. Edited by Philip Schaff. New York: Christian Literature Company. Reprint: Peabody, MA: Hendrickson, 1994. Accessed from *Christian Classics Ethereal Library* (www.ccel.org).

Chung-Kim, Esther, and Todd R. Hains, eds. 2014. *Acts*. Reformation Commentary on Scripture, New Testament 6. Edited by Timothy George. Downers Grove, IL: IVP Academic.

Cicero. *On the Orator: Books 1–2*. Translated by E. W. Sutton and H. Rackham. LCL 348. Cambridge, MA: Harvard University Press, 1942.

Clark, Albert C. 1933. *Acts of the Apostles, A Critical Edition, with Introduction and Notes on Selected Passages*. Oxford: The Clarendon Press.

Clarke, John. 1646. *Leaven, corrupting the children's bread; or Christs caveat to beware of sectaries and their dangerous doctrines*. Early English Books Online.

Clarke, William Newton. 1908. *A Study of Christian Missions*. New York: Young People's Missionary Movement of the United States and Canada.

Clarke, William Newton. 1914. *The Christian Doctrine of God*. New York: Charles Scribner & Sons.

Clinton, Bill. 1999. "Graduation Ceremony of the AmeriCorps National Civilian Community Corps." *The American Presidency Project*. Accessed from http://www.presidency.ucsb.edu

Colby, John. 1838. *The Life Experience and Travels of John Colby, Preacher of the Gospel*. N. Thurston and A. Watson, publishers. Originally published 1815–19.

Collins, Hercules. 1680. *An Orthodox Catechism*. Early English Books Online.

Collins, Hercules. 1690. *Mountains of Brass*. Early English Books Online.

Conisbee, Philip. 1970. "Jean Restout at Rouen." *The Burlington Magazine* 112: 768–70.

Conner, W. T. 1924. *A System of Christian Doctrine*. Nashville: Southern Baptist Convention Sunday School Board.

Conzelmann, Hans. 1960. *The Theology of St. Luke*. New York: Harper & Bros.

Cornelius á Lapide. 1662. *Commentaria in Acta Apostolorum*. Antverpiae: Apud Iacobum Meursium.

Corns, Thomas N., Ann Hughes, and David Loewenstein, eds. 2009. *The Complete Works of Gerrard Winstanley*. 2 Volumes. Oxford: Oxford University Press.

Cramer, J. A. 1840. *Catenae Graecorum partum in Novum Testamentum*. 8 volumes. Oxford: Clarendon Press.

Crosby, Thomas. 1738–40. *The History of the English Baptists*. London.

CroweTipton, Vaughn. 1999. "*Ad Theophilum*: A Socio-Rhetorical Reading of Peter in Acts in Codex Bezae Cantabrigiensis." Ph.D. Dissertation, Baylor University.

Cullmann, Oscar, ed. 1963. *Infancy Gospel of Thomas*. Translated by A. J. B. Higgins. Pages 388–401 in *New Testament Apocrypha, Volume One: Gospels and Related Writings*. Edited by Wilhelm Schneemelcher. Translated by R. McL. Wilson. Philadelphia: Westminster.

Culy, Martin M., and Mikeal C. Parsons. 2003. *Acts: A Handbook on the Greek Text*. Waco, TX: Baylor University Press.

Cyprian. 1958. *Treatises*. Translated and edited by Roy J. Deferrari. Fathers of the Church 36. Washington, D.C.: The Catholic University of America Press.

Cyril of Jerusalem. "The Catechetical Lectures of S. Cyril, Archbishop of Jerusalem." *S. Cyril of Jerusalem, S. Gregory Nazianzen*. Edited by Philip Schaff and Henry Wace. Translated by R. W. Church and Edwin Hamilton Gifford. NPNF 7. Second series. New York: Christian Literature Company, 1894. Reprint: Peabody, MA: Hendrickson, 1994.

Daley, Brian. 2010. "The Divinization of the Theotokos: Fifth-Century Christological Controversy and the Figure of Mary." Unpublished lecture, Villanova University, October 23.

Dalton, O. M. 1911. *Byzantine Art and Archaeology*. Oxford: Clarendon Press. Reprint: New York: Dover, 1961.

D'Angelo, Mary Rose. 1990. "Women in Luke-Acts: A Redactional View." *Journal of Biblical Literature* 109: 441–461.

Danvers, Henry. 1674. *A Treatise of Laying on of Hands*. Early English Books Online.

Danvers, Henry. 1675. *A Treatise of Baptism*. Early English Books Online.

Darby, J. N. 1967. *The "Holy Scriptures": A New Translation from the Original Languages*. Kingston-on-Thames: Stow Hill Bible and Tract Depot.

Dayton, A. C. 1857. *Theodosia Ernest, or The Heroine of Faith and Ten Days' Travel in Search of the Church*. 2 volumes. American Baptist Publication Society. Reprint 1903.

Dayton, A. C. 1866. *Emma Livingston, the Infidel's Daughter: or Conversations upon Atheism, Infidelity and Universalism*. Baptist Publishing Company.

Denne, Henry. 1642. *The Doctrine and Conversation of John Baptist, Delivered in a Sermon at a Visitation holden at Baldock, in the county of Hereford: December 9, 1641*. Early English Books Online.

Denne, Henry. 1645. *Antichrist Unmasked in Two Treatises*. Early English Books Online.

Denne, Henry. 1645. *The Man of Sin Discovered: Whom the Lord shall destroy with the brightnesse of his Coming*. Treatise 2 of *Antichrist Unmasked in Two Treatises*. Early English Books Online.

De Selincourt, B. 1905. *Giotto*. London: Duckworth and Co.

da Voragine, Jacobus. 1993. *The Golden Legend: Readings on the Saints*. Translated by William Granger Ryan. Princeton, NJ: Princeton University Press.

Dewald, Ernest T. 1915. "The Iconography of the Ascension." *American Journal of Archaeology* 19: 277–319.

Dibelius, Martin. 1939. *Paulus auf dem Areopag*. Heidelberg. Reprinted in *Aufsätze zur Apostelgeschichte*. Edited by Heinrich Greeven. Göttingen: Vandenhoeck & Ruprecht, 1951. ET: *Studies in the Acts of the Apostles*. Translated by Mary Ling. New York: C. Scribner's Sons, 1956.

Dixon, Amzi Clarence. 1905. *Evangelism Old and New: God's Search for Man in all Ages*. New York: American Tract Society.

Donfried, Karl. 1985. "The Cults of Thessalonica and the Thessalonian Correspondence." *New Testament Studies* 31: 336–56.

Donne, John. 1839. *The Works of John Donne*. 6 volumes. Edited by Henry Alford. London: John Parker.

Donne, John. 1912. *The Poems of John Donne*. Edited by Herbert J. C. Grierson. Oxford: Clarendon Press.

Dunn, James D. G. 1970. *Baptism in the Holy Spirit*. Philadelphia: Westminster.

Dutch Reformed Church, South Africa. 1975. "Human Relations and the South African Scene in Light of Scripture."

"e-Catena: Compiled Allusions to the NT in the Ante-Nicene Fathers." Accessed from http://www.earlychristianwritings.com/e-catena/

Edgren, John Alexis. 1948. *Fundamentals of Faith*. Translated by J. O. Backlund. Chicago: Baptist Conferences Press. Originally published 1890.

Eichhorn, Johann Gottfried. 1790. "Versuch über die Engels-Erscheinungen in der Apostelgeschichte." *Allgemeine Bibliothek der biblischen Litteratur* 3: 381–408.

Eleen, Luba. 1977. "Acts Illustrations in Italy and Byzantium." *Dumbarton Oaks Papers* 31: 253, 255–78.

Eliot, T. S. 1943. *Four Quartets*. New York: Harcourt.

Ephrem the Syrian. 1926. "Commentary on Acts." Translated and edited by Frederick C. Conybeare. Pages 373–453 in *The Text of Acts*. Edited by J. H. Ropes. Volume 3 of *The Beginnings of Christianity, Part 1: Acts of the Apostles*. 5 volumes. Edited by F. J. Foakes Jackson and Kirsopp Lake. London: Macmillan, 1920–33.

Epiphanius. *Panarion*.

Epp, Eldon Jay. 1966. *The Theological Tendency of Codex Bezae Cantabrigiensis in Acts*. London: Cambridge University Press.

Erasmus, Desiderius. 1524. *In Acta Apostolorum Paraphrasis*. Basel: J. Froben. In *Desderii Erasmi Roterodami Opera Omnia*. 10 volumes. Edited by Jean LeClerc. Leiden: Van der Aa, 1704–1706. Reprint: Hildesheim: Georg Olms, 1961–62. ET: *Paraphrase on the Acts of the Apostles*. Edited by John J. Bateman. Translated by Robert D. Sider. Collected Works of Erasmus 50. Toronto: University of Toronto Press, 1995.

Ervin, Howard M. 1984. *Conversion-Initiation and the Baptism in the Holy Spirit*. Peabody, MA: Hendrickson.

Ervin, Howard M. 1987. *Spirit-Baptism: A Biblical Investigation*. Peabody, MA: Hendrickson.

Evans, Mark, and Clare Browne, eds. 2010. *Raphael. Cartoons and Tapestries for the Sistine Chapel*. London: V & A Publishing.

Eusebius of Caesarea. 1953. *Ecclesiastical History: Books 1–5*. Translated by Roy J. Deferrari. FC 19. Washington, D.C.: The Catholic University of America Press.

Eusebius of Caesarea. 1981. *Proof of the Gospel*. 2 volumes. Translated by W. J. Ferrar. London: SPCK, 1920. Reprint: Grand Rapids: Baker.

Executive Council of the DRC, ed. 1976. *Human Relations and the South African Scene in Light of Scripture*. Cape Town: Dutch Reformed Church Publishers.

Ewald, Heinrich. 1885. *The History of Israel, VII: The Apostolic Age*. Translated by J. Frederick Smith. London: Longmans, Green.

Farrow, Douglas. 1999. *Ascension and Ecclesia: On the Significance of the Doctrine of the Ascension for Ecclesiology and Christian Cosmology*. Grand Rapids: Eerdmans.

Fawcett, John. 1782. "None of These Things Move Me." Pages 39–41 in *Hymns: Adapted to the Circumstances of Public Worship, and Private Devotion*. Eighteenth Century Collection Online.

Fawcett, John. 1782. "Blessed Be the Tie That Binds." In *Hymns: Adapted to the Circumstances of Public Worship, and Private Devotion*. Eighteenth Century Collection Online.

Fawcett, John. 1793. "Through Tribulation We Must Enter the Kingdom of God." Pages 167–68 in *Hymns and Spiritual Songs*. Eighteenth Century Collection Online.

Felix II. "Letter to Emperor Zeno." 1868. Pages 247–50 in *Epistulae Romanorum Pontificum Genuinae*. Edited by Andreas Thiel. Brunsbergae. ET from Hugo Rahner, *The Church and State in Early Christianity*. Translated by Leo Donald Davis. San Francisco: Ignatius Press, 1992.

Fermor, Sharon. 1996. *The Raphael Tapestry Cartoons: Narrative, Decoration, Design*. London: Scala.

Fermor, Sharon. 1998. "The Raphael Tapestry Cartoons Re-examined." *Burlington Magazine* 140: 236–50.

Finaldi, Gabriele. 2010. "Mantegna, Andrea." *Grove Art Online. Oxford Art Online.* Oxford University Press. Accessed from http://www.oxfordartonline.com/subscriber/article/grove/art/T053902

Firmani, Domenico Gus. 1984. "Don Simone Camaldolese and Manuscript Production in Late Trecento Florence: A Codicological Examination." Ph.D. dissertation, University of Maryland.

Fitzmyer, Joseph. 1981–1985. *The Gospel according to Luke: Introduction, Translation, and Notes.* 2 volumes. Anchor Bible 28–28A. Garden City, NY: Doubleday.

Fitzmyer, Joseph. 1989. *Luke the Theologian: Aspects of His Teaching.* New York: Paulist.

Ford, Gerald. 1975. "Lighting of the National Christmas Tree." *The American Presidency Project.* Accessed from http://www.presidency.ucsb.edu

Fosdick, Harry Emerson. 1958. *Riverside Sermons.* New York: Harpers.

Frede, Michael. 1999. "Eusebius' Apologetic Writings." Pages 223–250 in *Apologetics in the Roman Empire.* Edited by Mark Edwards, Martin Goodman, and Simon Price, in association with Christopher Rowland. Oxford: Oxford University Press.

Frykholm, Amy. 2014. "A Time to Split? Covenant and Schism in the UMC." *The Christian Century* (April 3). Accessed from http://www.christiancentury.org/article/2014-03/time-split

Garnsey, Peter. 2012. "Peter Olivi on the Community of the First Christians at Jerusalem." Pages 35–49 in *Radical Christian Voices and Practice: Essays in Honor of Christopher Rowland.* Edited by Zoë Bennett and David B. Gowler. Oxford: Oxford University Press.

Garnsey, Peter. 2007. *Thnking about Property: From Antiquity to the Age of Revolution.* Cambridge: Cambridge University Press.

Garnot, Nicolas Sainte Fare. 2010. "Champaigne, de." *Grove Art Online. Oxford Art Online.* Oxford University Press. Accessed from http://www.oxfordartonline.com/subscriber/article/grove/art/T015839

Garr, H. G. 1908. "Tongues in the Foreign Field: Interesting Letters." *Confidence* 2: 21–23.

Garrett, Susan R. 1990. "Exodus from Bondage: Luke 9:31 and Acts 12:1–24." *Catholic Biblical Quarterly* 52: 656–80.

Gasque, Ward. 1975. *A History of the Criticism of the Acts of the Apostles.* Beiträge zur Geschichte der biblischen Exegese 17. Tübingen: J. C. B. Mohr.

Gaventa, Beverly Roberts. 2004. "What Ever Happened to Those Prophesying Daughters?" Pages 49–60 in *A Feminist Companion to the Acts of the Apostles.* Edited by Amy-Jill Levine with Marianne Blickenstaff. Feminist Companion to the New Testament and Early Christian Writings 9. London; New York: T&T Clark.

Gealt, Adelheid M. 1996. "The Telling Line: Domenico Tiepolo as Draftsman/Narrator." Pages 62–109 in *Domenico Tiepolo: Master Draughtsman.* Edited by Adelheid M. Gealt and George Knox. Bloomington: Indiana University Press; Milan: Electa.

General Association of General Baptists. 1970. "Statements of Faith." Revised edition. Accessed from http://storage.cloversites.com/generalbaptistministries/documents/StatementsOfFaith.pdf

Gilbert, Creighton. 1987. "Are the ten tapestries a complete series or a fragment?" Pages 533–50 in *Studi su Raffaello; atti del congresso internazionale di studii: Urbino-Firenze, 6–14 Aprile 1984.* Edited by Micaela Sambucco Hamoud, Maria Letizia Strocchi, and Cristinia Acidini Luchinat. Urbino: QuattroVenti.

Gill, John. 1746. *An Exposition of the New Testament*. 3 volumes. London. Eighteenth Century Collection Online.

Gill, John. 1750. *A Funeral Sermon preached Oct. 14, 1750—death of Rev. Samuel Wilson*. Eighteenth Century Collection Online.

Gill, John. 1796. *A Complete Body of Doctrinal and Practical Divinity*. 2 volumes. Eighteenth Century Collection Online.

Goff, James R., Jr. 1988. *Fields White Unto Harvest: Charles F. Parham and the Missionary Origins of Pentecostalism*. Fayetteville, AR: The University of Arkansas Press.

González, Justo L. 1990. *Faith and Wealth*. New York: Harper and Row.

González, Justo L. 2001. *Acts: The Gospel of the Spirit*. Maryknoll, NY: Orbis.

Gordon, Adoniram Judson. 1895. *The Ministry of the Spirit*. Philadelphia: American Baptist Publication Society.

Graham, Billy. 1978. *The Holy Spirit: Activating God's Power in Your Life*. Waco, TX: Word Books.

Graham, Daniel M. 1851. *The Life of Clement Phinney*. Dover, NH: William Burr.

Grantham, Thomas. 1671. *A Sigh for Peace*. Early English Books Online.

Grantham, Thomas. 1687. *Hear the Church*. Early English Books Online.

Gregory, Andrew. 2003. *The Reception of Luke and Acts in the Period Before Irenaeus: Looking for Luke in the Second Century*. Tübingen: Mohr Siebeck.

Gregory, Andrew F., and C. Kavin Rowe. 2010. *Rethinking the Unity and Reception of Luke and Acts*. Columbia, SC: University of South Carolina Press.

Gregory of Nazianzus. 1894. "Select Orations of Saint Gregory Nazianzen." In *S. Cyril of Jerusalem, S. Gregory Nazianzen*. Edited by Philip Schaff and Henry Wace. Translated by Charles Gordon Browne and James Edward Swallow. NPNF 7. Second series. New York: Christian Literature Company. Reprint: Peabody, MA: Hendrickson, 1994.

Gregory of Nyssa. 1967. "On Perfection." Pages 91–122 in *Ascetical Works*. Translated by Virginia Woods Callahan. Fathers of the Church 58. Washington, D.C.: The Catholic University of America Press. Reprint: Peabody, MA: Hendrickson, 1994.

Gregory of Nyssa. 1978. *Gregory of Nyssa: The Life of Moses*. Translated by A. J. Malherbe and E. Ferguson. Classics of Western Spirituality. New York: Paulist Press. Reprint: Peabody, MA: Hendrickson, 1994.

Griffith, R. Marie. 2002. "Prayer Cloths." *Material History of American Religion Project*. Accessed from http://www.materialreligion.org/journal/handkerchief.html

Gurney, John. 2007. *Brave Community: The Digger Movement in the English Revolution*. Manchester: Manchester University Press.

Gurney, John. 2013. *Gerrard Winstanley: The Digger's Life and Legacy*. London: Pluto.

Guerlin, Henri. 1921. *Giovanni Domenico Tiepolo: Au temps du Christ*. Tours: A. Mame.

Gwalther, Rudolf. 1557. *In Acta Apostolorum per Divum Lucam Descripta Homiliae CLXXIIII*. Zurich: Christoph Froschauer. ET: *An Hundred, Threescore and Fiftene Homelyes or Sermons, upon the Actes of the Apostles*. Translated by John Bridges. London: Henrie Denham, 1572.

Hackett, Horatio. 1882. *A Commentary on the Acts of the Apostles*. Philadelphia: American Baptist Publication Society.

Haenchen, Ernst. 1971. *The Acts of the Apostles: A Commentary*. Translated by Bernard Noble and Gerald Shinn. Philadelphia: Westminster.

Hammon, George. 1658. *Syons Redemption and Original Sin Vindicated*. Early English Books Online.

Hansen, Lindsey. 2011. "Acts of Witnessing: The Munich Ivory of the Ascension, Medieval Visuality and Pilgrimage." *Hortulus: The Online Graduate Journal of Medieval Studies* 7. Accessed from http://hortulus-journal.com/journal/volume-7-number-1-2011/hansen/

Hargreaves, James. 1823. *Hints on the Nature of a Christian Church, and on the Principles of Dissent: Comprised in an Introductory Discourse at the Ordination of Thomas Hopley, Over the Baptist Church at Hemel-Hempstead, on Tuesday July 8, 1823*. W. Jones, publisher.

Harnack, Adolf von. 1899. "Das Aposteldecret (Act. 15,29) und die Blassische Hypothese." *Sitzungsberichte der Königlich Preussischen Akademie der Wissenschaften zu Berin*: 150–76.

Harnack, Adolf von. 1908. *Beiträge zur Einleitung in das Neue Testament III: Die Apostelgeschichte*. Leipzig: J. C. Hinrichs. ET: *New Testament Studies III: The Acts of the Apostles*. Translated by J. R. Wilkinson. Crown Theological Library 27. New York: G. P. Putnam's Sons, 1909.

Harrison, Thomas. 1660. *The Speeches and Prayers*. Early English Books Online.

Hartt, Frederick, and David G. Wilkins. 2011. *History of Italian Renaissance Art: Painting, Sculpture, Architecture*. 7th edition. Upper Saddle River: Prentice Hall.

Hawthorne, Nathaniel. 1850. *The Scarlet Letter*. Reprint: Edited by Seymour Gross. Norton Critical Edition. New York: Norton, 1988.

Hays, Richard B. 1996. *The Moral Vision of the New Testament: Community, Cross, New Creation*. San Francisco: Harper.

Heaven, T. 2010. "Personal Correspondence" with Diane Nelson, April 13.

Helwys, Thomas. 1611. *A Short and Plaine Proof by the Word*. Early English Books Online.

Helwys, Thomas. 1612. *A Short Declaration of the Mistery of Iniquity*. Early English Books Online.

Hemer, Colin. 1989. *The Book of Acts in the Setting of Hellenistic History*. Tübingen: Mohr-Siebeck.

Hengel, Martin. 1980. *Acts and the History of Earliest Christianity*. Translated by John Bowden. Philadelphia: Fortress.

Herder, J. G. 1967. *Sämtliche Werke*. Reprint: Hildesheim: Olms.

Hibbard, Howard. 1983. *Caravaggio*. New York: Harper & Row.

Hill, Craig. 1992. *Hellenists and Hebrews: Reappraising Division within the Earliest Church*. Minneapolis: Fortress.

Hobart, William Kirk. 1882. *The Medical Language of St. Luke: A Proof from Internal Evidence that "The Gospel according to St. Luke" and "The Acts of the Apostles" Were Written by the Same Person, and that the Writer was a Medical Man*. Dublin: Hodges, Figgis. Reprint Grand Rapids: Baker, 1954.

Holder, Arthur G. 1990. "Bede and the Tradition of Patristic Exegesis." *Anglican Theological Review* 72: 399–411.

Hood, William. 1993. *Fra Angelico at San Marco*. New Haven and London: Yale University Press.

Hornik, Heidi J. 2009. "Pursuing Knowledge." *Christian Reflection* 31: 46–49.

Hornik, Heidi J. 2010a. "What Is to Prevent Me from Being Baptized?" *Christian Reflection* 35: 48–49.

Hornik, Heidi J. 2010b. "Apostle to the Gentiles." *Christian Reflection* 35: 50–51.

Hornik, Heidi J. 2010c. "Liberation from Tyranny." *Christian Reflection* 39: 48–52.

Hornik, Heidi J., and Mikeal C. Parsons. 2004–2007. *Illuminating Luke*. 3 volumes. Harrisburg, PA: Trinity Press International.

Howe, Eunice D. 1996. "Luke." Pages 787–89 in Volume 19 of *The Dictionary of Art*. 34 volumes. Edited by Jane Turner. New York: Grove's Dictionaries.

Irenaeus. 1885. "Against Heresies." Pages 309–567 in *The Apostolic Fathers with Justin Martyr and Irenaeus*. ANF 1. Edited by Alexander Roberts, James Donaldson, and A. Cleveland Coxe. Buffalo, NY: Christian Literature. Reprint: Peabody, MA: Hendrickson, 1994.

Isidore of Seville. 2006. *Etymologies*. Translated by Stephen A. Barney, W. J. Lewis, J. A. Beach, and Oliver Berghof. New York: Cambridge University Press.

Jackson, F. J. Foakes, and Kirsopp Lake. 1920–33. *The Beginnings of Christianity, Part 1: The Acts of the Apostles*. 5 volumes. London: Macmillan and Co.

Jacobsen, Douglas, ed. 2006. *A Reader in Pentecostal Theology: Voices from the First Generation*. Bloomington, IN: Indiana University Press.

Jeffrey, David Lyle, ed. 1992. *A Dictionary of Biblical Tradition in English Literature*. Grand Rapids: Eerdmans.

Jeffery, William. 1660. *The Humble Petition*. London: Francis Smith, Elephant and Castle.

Jenkins, Philip. 2002. *The Next Christendom: The Coming of Global Christianity*. Oxford: Oxford University Press.

Jenkins, Philip. 2006. *The New Faces of Christianity: Believing the Bible in the Global South*. Oxford: Oxford University Press.

Jerome. 1893. *Letters and Select Works*. Edited by Philip Schaff and Henry Wace. Translated by W. H. Fremantle. NPNF 6. Second series. New York: Christian Literature Company. Reprint: Peabody, MA: Hendrickson, 1994.

Jerome. 1892. "Lives of Illustrious Men." Translated by Ernest Cushing Richardson. In *Theodoret, Jerome, Gennadius, & Rufinus: Historical Writings*. Edited by Philip Schaff and Henry Wace. NPNF 3. Second series. New York: Christian Literature Company. Reprint: Peabody, MA: Hendrickson, 1994.

Jerome. 1964. *The Homilies of Saint Jerome (1–59 on the Psalms)*. Translated by Marie Liguori Ewald. Fathers of the Church 48. Washington, D.C.: The Catholic University of American Press.

Jervell, Jacob. 1972. *Luke and the People of God*. Minneapolis: Augsburg Publishing House.

Joannides, Paul. 1993. *Masaccio and Masolino: A Complete Catalogue*. London: Phaidon.

Johnson, Luke Timothy. 1983. *Decision Making in the Church: A Biblical Model*. Philadelphia: Fortress.

Johnson, Luke Timothy. 1992. *The Acts of the Apostles*. Sacra Pagina 5. Edited by Daniel J. Harrington. Collegeville, MN: Liturgical Press.

Johnson, Luke Timothy. 2004. "Review of Illuminating Luke: The Infancy Narratives in Italian Renaissance Painting." *Bible Review* 20/6: 41.

Johnson, Lyndon B. 1963. "Lighting of the National Christmas Tree." *The American Presidency Project.* Accessed from http://www.presidency.ucsb.edu

Jones, A. H. M. 1960. *Studies in Roman Government and Law.* New York: Praeger.

Jones, F. Stanley. 1995. *An Ancient Jewish Christian Source on the History of Christianity: Pseudo-Clementine Recognitions 1.27–71.* Atlanta: Scholars Press.

Jordan, Clarence. 2004. *The Cotton Patch Version of Luke and Acts: Jesus' Doings and the Happenings.* Macon: Smyth & Helwys Press.

Josephus. 1928. *The Jewish War, Volume III: Books 5–7.* Translated by H. St. J. Thackeray. LCL 210. Cambridge, MA: Harvard University Press.

Josephus. 1937. *Jewish Antiquities, Volume IV: Books 9–11.* Translated by Ralph Marcus. LCL 326. Cambridge, MA: Harvard University Press.

Josephus. 1965. *Jewish Antiquities, Volume VIII: Books 18–19.* Translated by Louis H. Feldman. LCL 433. Cambridge, MA: Harvard University Press.

Juel, Donald. 1983. *Luke-Acts: The Promise of History.* Atlanta: John Knox Press.

Junghans, Helmar. 1982. "Acht Sermone D M Luthers von ihm gepredigt zu Wittenberg in der Fasten (Invocavitpredigten), 1522." Pages 520–58 in Volume 2 of *Martin Luther Studienausgabe.* Edited by Hans-Ulrich Delius. Berlin: Evangelische Verlagsanstalt.

Justin Martyr. 1885. "First Apology." *The Apostolic Fathers with Justin Martyr and Irenaeus.* ANF 1. Edited by Alexander Roberts, James Donaldson, and A. Cleveland Coxe. Buffalo, NY: Christian Literature. Reprint: Peabody, MA: Hendrickson, 1994.

[Justin]. 1885. "Fragments of the Lost Work of Justin on the Resurrection." Translated by M. Dods. *The Apostolic Fathers with Justin Martyr and Irenaeus.* ANF 1. Edited by Alexander Roberts, James Donaldson, and A. Cleveland Coxe. Buffalo, NY: Christian Literature. Reprint: Peabody, MA: Hendrickson, 1994.

Keach, Benjamin. 1682. *Tropologia, or a Key to Open Scripture Metaphors.* Early English Books Online.

Keach, Benjamin. 1691. *He That Was Ordained of God to be the Judge of the Quick and the Dead.* Early English Books Online.

Keach, Benjamin. 1693. *The Ax Laid to the Root, or, One Blow More at the Foundation of Infant Baptism and Church-Membership.* Early English Books Online.

Keach, Benjamin. 1698. *Christ Alone the Way to Heaven.* Early English Books Online.

Keener. Craig. 2012–15. *Acts: An Exegetical Commentary.* Four volumes. Grand Rapids: Baker Academic.

Kelhoeffer, James A. 2000. *Miracle and Mission: The Authentication of Missionaries and Their Message in the Longer Ending of Mark.* WUNT II 112. Tübingen: Mohr-Siebeck.

Kennedy, John F. 1962. "Lighting of the National Christmas Tree." *The American Presidency Project.* Accessed from http://www.presidency.ucsb.edu

Kenrick, Timothy. 1828. *An Exposition of the Historical Writings of the New Testament,* volume 3: *The Acts of the Apostles, and Chronological Tables, etc.* Boston: Munroe and Francis.

Kessler, Herbert L. 1979. "Scenes from the Acts of the Apostles on Some Early Christian Ivories." *Gesta* 18, no. 1, Papers Related to Objects in the Exhibition "Age of Spirituality", The Metropolitan Museum of Art (November 1977–February 1978): 109–119.

Kessler, Herbert. 2007. "The Word Made Flesh in Early Decorated Bibles." Pages 141–68 in *Picturing the Bible: The Earliest Christian Art.* Edited by Jeffrey Spier. New Haven: Yale University Press; Fort Worth: Kimbell Art Museum.

Kierkegaard, Søren. 1967–78. *Søren Kierkegaard's Journals and Papers.* 7 volumes. Edited and translated by Howard V. Hong and Edna H. Hong, with Gregor Malantschuk. Bloomington: Indiana University Press, 1967–78.

Kierkegaard, Søren. 1978–2000. *Kierkegaard's Writings.* Edited by Howard V. Hong and Edna H. Hong. Princeton, NJ: Princeton University Press.

Kierkegaard, Søren. 2007–. *Kierkegaard's Journals and Notebooks.* 11 volumes. Edited by Bruce H. Kirmmse. Princeton, NJ: Princeton University Press.

Kiffin, Williams. 1681. *A Sober Discourse of Right to Church-Communion.* Early English Books Online.

Klaassen, Walter. 1986. "Eschatological Themes in Early Dutch Anabaptism." Pages 15–31 in *Dutch Dissenters: A Critical Companion to their History and Ideas.* Edited by Irvin Horst. Leiden: Brill.

Klein, Dorothee. 1933. *St. Lukas als Maler der Maria: Ikonographie der Lukas-Madonna.* Berlin: Oskar Schloss Verlag.

Knollys, Hanserd. 1646. *The Shining of a Flaming Fire in Zion.* Early English Books Online.

Knollys, Hanserd. 1681. *The World that Now is; and the Word that is to Come.* Early English Books Online.

Knox, George. 1996. "Domenico Tiepolo: The Drawings." Pages 39–61 of *Domenico Tiepolo: Master Draughtsman.* Edited by Adelheid M. Gealt and George Knox. Bloomington, IN: Indiana University Press; Milan: Electa.

Knox, John. 1895. *The Works of John Knox.* 6 volumes. Edited by David Laing. Edinburgh: J. Thin.

Knox, John. 1950. *Chapters in the Life of Paul.* Nashville: Abingdon.

Knox, W. L. 1948. *The Acts of the Apostles.* Cambridge: Cambridge University Press.

Konowitz, Ellen. 1984. "Program of Carrand Diptych." *The Art Bulletin* 66: 484–88.

Kovacs, Judith L., and Christopher Rowland. 2004. *Revelation: The Apocalypse of Jesus Christ.* Malden, MA: Blackwell.

Kroegel, A. 2003. "The Figure of Mary in Botticelli's Art." Pages 55–67 in *Botticelli from Lorenzo the Magnificent to Savonarola.* Edited by Doriana Comerlati and Daniel Arasse. Milan: Skira.

Kurita, Hidenori. 1998. "A Visual Source for Poussin's 'Sts Peter and John Healing the Lame Man.'" *The Burlington Magazine* 140: 747–48.

Kydd, Ronald A. N. 1998. *Healing through the Centuries: Models for Understanding.* Peabody: Hendrickson.

Lampe, G. W. H., ed. 1961. *A Patristic Greek Lexicon.* Oxford; New York: Clarendon.

Lanoë, Frédérique. 2009. *Trois maîtres du dessin: Philippe de Champaigne (1602–1674), Jean-Baptiste de Champaigne (1631–1681), Nicolas de Plattemontagne (1631–1706).* Paris: Éditions de la Réunion des musées nationaux.

Lawrence, Henry. 1649. *Some Considerations: A Vindication of the Use of Holy Scriptures and Some Christian Ordinances.* Early English Books Online.

Lawrence, Henry. 1651. *A Plea for the Use of Gospell Ordinances.* Early English Books Online.

Lawrence, Henry. 1659. *Of Baptism. The Heads and Order of Such Things as are Especially Insisted On.* Early English Books Online.

Lefort, L.-T. 1943. *Les Vies coptes de Saint Pachôme et de ses premiers successeurs.* Louvain.

Lefort, L.-T. 1956. *Oeuvres de s. Pachôme et de ses disciples*. CSCO 160. Louvain.

Leo the Great. 1996. *Sermons*. Translated by Jane Freeland et al. Fathers of the Church 93. Washington, D.C.: The Catholic University of America Press.

Levey, Michael. 1985. *Rococo to Revolution: Major Trends in Eighteenth-Century Painting*. New York: Thames and Hudson.

Levey M. 1967. "Introduction." *The Complete Paintings of Botticelli*. Edited by Gabriele Mandel. New York: Abrams.

Levitan, A. 1971. "The Parody of Pentecost in Chaucer's Summoner's Tale." *University of Toronto Quarterly* 40: 236–46.

Lightfoot, John. 1645. *A Commentary upon the Acts of the Apostles*. London: R. C. for Andrew Crooke.

Lightfoot, Joseph Barber. 1865. *The Epistle of Paul to the Galatians: With Introductions, Notes and Dissertations*. London: Macmillan.

Locke, John. 1695. *The Reasonableness of Christianity*. London: Printed for Awnsham and John Churchil. Early English Books Online.

Lombaard, Christo. 2009. "Does Contextual Exegesis Require an Affirming Bible? Lessons from 'Apartheid' and 'Africa' as Narcissistic Hermeneutical Keys." *Scriptura* 100: 274–287.

Lüdemann, Gerd. 1987. *Das frühe Christentum nach den Traditionen der Apostelgeschichte: Ein Kommentar*. Göttingen: Vandenhoeck & Ruprecht. ET: *Early Christianity according to the Traditions in Acts: A Commentary*. Translated by John Bowden. Minneapolis: Fortress, 1989.

Luther, Martin. 1955–86. *Luther's Works*. 55 volumes. Volumes 1–30 edited by Jaroslav Pelikan. Volumes 31–55 edited by Helmut T. Lehmann. Philadelphia: Fortress Press; Saint Louis: Concordia Publishing House. Accessed: Past Masters Online.

Luz, Ulrich. 2001–2008. *A Commentary on the Gospel of Matthew*. 3 volumes. Hermeneia: A Critical and Historical Commentary on the Bible. Minneapolis: Fortress.

MacDonald, Dennis R. 2004. "Lydia and Her Sisters as Lukan Fiction." Pages 105–10 in *A Feminist Companion to the Acts of the Apostles*. Edited by Amy-Jill Levine with Marianne Blickenstaff. Feminist Companion to the New Testament and Early Christian Writings 9. London and New York: T&T Clark.

Machen, J. Gresham. 1921. *The Origin of Paul's Religion*. New York: Macmillan.

Mahon, Denis, ed. 1992. *Guercino: Master Painter of the Baroque*. Washington, D.C.: National Gallery of Art.

Mahon, Denis. 1991. *Giovanni Francesco Barbieri. Il Guercino 1591–1666. Bologna. Museo Civico Archeologico. Cento, Pinacoteca Civica e Chiesa del Rosario 6 September–10 November 1991*. Bologna: Nuova Alfa Editoriale.

Malbon, Elizabeth Struthers. 1990. *The Iconography of the Sarcophagus of Junius Bassus*. Princeton, NJ: Princeton University Press.

Malbon, Elizabeth Struthers. 2012. "Sarcophagus of Junius Bassus." *Grove Art Online*. *Oxford Art Online*. Oxford University Press. Accessed from http://www.oxfordartonline.com/subscriber/article/grove/art/T22204390

Malick, David E. 2007. "The Contribution of Codex Bezae Cantabrigiensis to an Understanding of Women in the Book of Acts." *Journal of Greco-Roman Christianity and Judaism* 4: 158–83.

Mallory, Kathleen. 1949. *Manual of Woman's Missionary Union.* Revised edition. Nashville: Broadman. Originally published by Southern Baptist Convention Woman's Missionary Union, 1917.

Mandel G. (ed.) 1967. *The Complete Paintings of Botticelli.* New York: Abrams.

Mantey, Julius R. 1951. "The Causal Use of *EIS* in the New Testament." *Journal of Biblical Literature* 70: 45–48.

Marcus, Ralph. 1951. "On Causal *EIS.*" *Journal of Biblical Literature* 70: 129–130.

Marcus, Ralph. 1952. "The Elusive Causal *EIS.*" *Journal of Biblical Literature* 71: 43–44.

Moessner, David, Daniel Marguerat, Mikeal Parsons, and Michael Wolter. 2014. *Paul and the Heritage of Israel.* New York: Bloomsbury T &T Clark.

Marshall, I. Howard. 1993. "Acts and the 'Former Treatise.'" Pages 163–82 in *The Book of Acts in its Ancient Literary Setting.* Edited by Bruce W. Winter and Andrew D. Clarke. Grand Rapids: Eerdmans.

Martin, Clarice J. 1989. "A Chamberlain's Journey and the Challenge of Interpretation for Liberation." *Semeia* 47: 105–35.

Martin, Francis. 1972. "Monastic Community and the Summary Statements in Acts." Pages 13–46 in *Contemplative Community: An Interdisciplinary Symposium.* Edited by M. Basil Pennington. Washington, D.C.: Cistercian Publications/Consortium Press.

Martin, Francis, with Evan Smith. 2006. *Acts.* Ancient Christian Commentary on Scripture New Testament 5. Edited by Thomas C. Oden. Downers Grove, IL: IVP Books.

Maston, Thomas Buford. 1959. *The Bible and Race.* Nashville: Broadman.

Maston, Thomas Buford. 1987. *Treasures from Holy Scripture.* Nashville: Broadman.

Matthews, Shelly. 2004. "Elite Women, Public Religion, and Christian Propaganda in Acts 16." Pages 111–33 in *A Feminist Companion to the Acts of the Apostles.* Edited by Amy-Jill Levine with Marianne Blickenstaff. Feminist Companion to the New Testament and Early Christian Writings 9. London; New York: T&T Clark.

McBeth, Leon. 1987. *The Baptist Heritage.* Nashville: Broadman.

Medley, Samuel. 1800. "Preaching Peace by Jesus Christ, he is Lord of all." In *Hymns: the public worship and private devotions of the Christians assisted in some thoughts in verse; principally drawn from select passages of the Word of God.* Eighteenth Century Collection Online.

Metzger, Bruce M. 1968. *Historical and Literary Studies: Pagan, Jewish, and Christian.* Grand Rapids: Eerdmans.

Metzger, Bruce M. 1975. "The Practice of Textual Criticism Among the Church Fathers." Pages 340–49 in *Studia Patristica* 12. Texte und Untersuchungen 115. Berlin: Akademie Verlag.

Metzger, Bruce M. 1994. *A Textual Commentary on the Greek New Testament.* 2nd ed 2002. Stuttgart: Deutsche Bibelgesellschaft; United Bible Societies.

Meyvaert, Paul. 1995. "Bede's Capitula Lectionum for the Old and New Testaments." *Revue Bénédictine* 105: 348–80.

Meyvaert, Paul. 1996. "Bede, Cassiodorus, and the Codex Amiatinus." *Speculum* 71: 827–83.

Mill, John Stuart. 1874. *Three Essays on Religion.* London: Longmans, Green, Reader, and Dyer. Reprint: New York: Greenwood Press, 1969.

Milton, John. 1644. *Areopagitica; a speech of Mr. John Milton for the liberty of unlicenc'd printing, to the Parliament of England*. London.

Mitchell, Ella Pearson. 1985. "Introduction: Women in the Ministry." Pages 11–20 in Volume 1 of *Those Preachin' Women: Sermons by Black Women Preachers*. Edited by Ella Pearson Mitchell. 4 volumes. Valley Forge, PA: Judson Press.

Mitchell, Ella Pearson. 1999. "All Flesh." *African American Pulpit* 2: 50–56.

Monk, Thomas, Joseph Wright, and Frank Stanley. 1661. *Sions Groans for Her Distressed*. Early English Books Online.

Montgomery, Helen Barrett. 1924. *Centenary Translation of the New Testament*. Philadelphia: The American Baptist Publication Society.

Moody, Dale. 1968. *Spirit of the Living God*. Philadelphia: Westminster.

Moon, Charlotte "Lottie." 1876. "Letter to Tupper, March 24, 1876." In *Send the Light: Lottie Moon's Letters and Other Writings*. Edited by Keith Harper. Mercer University Press, 2002.

Moon, Charlotte "Lottie." 1887. "Letter to Tupper, September 15, 1887." In *Send the Light: Lottie Moon's Letters and Other Writings*. Edited by Keith Harper. Mercer University Press, 2002. Originally published in *Foreign Mission Journal* (Dec 1887).

Moore, Joanna Patterson. 1902. *In Christ's Stead*. Chicago: Women's Baptist Missionary Society.

Morikawa, Jitsuo. 2000. *Jitsuo Morikawa: Prophet for the 21st Century*. Council for Pacific Asian Theology.

Müntzer, Thomas. 1968. *Schriften und Briefe: Kritische Gesamtausgabe*. Edited by Paul Kirn and Günther Franz. Gütersloh: Gerd Mohn.

Müntzer, Thomas. 1991. "Sermon to the Princes." Pages 11–32 in *The Radical Reformation*. Edited by Paul Kirn and Günther Franz. Gütersloh: Gerd Mohn.

Musurillo, Herbert. 1972. *The Acts of the Christian Martyrs*. Oxford: Clarendon Press.

Nelson, Joseph A., ed. 1950. *Roman Breviary in English*. New York: Benziger Brothers.

Obama, Barack. 2012. "Lighting of National Christmas Tree." *The American Presidency Project*. Accessed from http://www.presidency.ucsb.edu

O'Day, Gail R. 1998. "Acts." Pages 394–402 in *Women's Bible Commentary*. 2nd edition. Edited by Carol A. Newsom and Sharon H. Ringe. Louisville: Westminster John Knox.

O'Donovan, Oliver. 1986. *Resurrection and Moral Order: An Outline for Evangelical Ethics*. Leicester: Inter-Varsity Press; Grand Rapids: Eerdmans.

Oladipo, Caleb. 1996. *The Development of the Doctrine of the Holy Spirit in the Yoruba (African) Indigenous Christian Movement*. New York: Peter Lang.

Origen. 1887. "Commentary on the Gospel of John." Pages 297–408 in *The Gospel of Peter, The Diatessaron of Tatian, The Apocalypse of Peter, The Vision of Paul, The Apocalypse of the Virgin and Sedrach, The Testament of Abraham, The Acts of Xanthippe and Polyxena, The Narrative of Zosimus, The Apology of Aristides, The Epistles of Clement, Origen's Commentary on John (Books 1–10), and Commentary on Matthew (Books 1, 2, and 10–14)*. Translated by Allan Menzies. ANF 9. Edited by Alexander Roberts and James Donaldson. 10 volumes. Reprint: Peabody, MA: Hendrickson, 1994.

Origen. 1972. *Catena Palestinensis*. In *La chaîne Palestinienne sur le Psaume 118*. Edited by Margurerite Harl with Gilles Dorival. SC 189. Paris: Éditions du Cerf.

Origen. 1990. *Homilies on Leviticus: 1–16.* Translated by Gary Wayne Barkley. Fathers of the Church: A New Translation 83. Washington, D.C.: Catholic University of America Press.

Paley, William. 1790. *The Horae Paulinae.* London: Ward, Lock.

Papias. 2003. *Fragments.* Pages 92–117 in *The Apostolic Fathers, Volume II: Epistle of Barnabas. Papias and Quadratus. Epistle to Diognetus. The Shepherd of Hermas.* Edited and translated by Bart D. Ehrman. Loeb Classical Library 25. Cambridge, MA: Harvard University Press.

Parham, Charles F. 1902. *Kol Kare Bomidbar: A Voice Crying in the Wilderness.* Kansas City, MO: By the author. Reprint Baxter Springs, KS: Robert L. Parham, 1944.

Parham, Charles F. 1926. *Apostolic Faith* (Baxter Springs, KS) 2 (July).

Parham, Sarah E. 1930. *The Life of Charles F. Parham, Founder of the Apostolic Faith Movement.* Baxter Springs, KS: Apostolic Faith Church. Reprint: New York: Garland, 1985.

Parsons, Mikeal C. 2008. *Acts.* Paideia Commentary on the New Testament. Grand Rapids: Baker Academic.

Parsons, Mikeal C. 2011. *Body and Character in Luke and Acts: The Subversion of Physiognomy in Early Christianity.* Waco: Baylor University Press.

Parsons, Mikeal C. 2014. "Luke and the Heritage of Israel." Pages 131–43 in *Interpretation and the Claims of the Text: Resourcing New Testament Theology: Essays in Honor of Charles H. Talbert.* Edited by Jason A. Whitlark, Bruce W. Longenecker, Lidija Novakovic, and Mikeal C. Parsons. Waco, TX: Baylor University Press.

Parsons, Mikeal C., and Richard I. Pervo. 1993. *Rethinking the Unity of Luke and Acts.* Minneapolis: Fortress.

Partoens, G. 2003. "Acts 27–28 in the Preface to Prudentius' first *Liber contra Symmachum.*" *Vigiliae Christianae* 57: 36–61.

Paulson, Graham. 2006. "Toward an Aboriginal Theology." *Pacifica: Australian Theological Studies,* 317.

Pelikan, Jaroslav. 1996. *Mary through the Centuries: Her Place in the History of Culture.* New Haven: Yale University Press.

Pelikan, Jaraslov. 2005. *Acts.* Brazos Theological Commentary on the Bible. Grand Rapids: Brazos Press.

Pelikan, Jaroslav, and Valerie Hotchkiss, eds. 2003. *Creeds and Confessions of Faith in the Christian Tradition.* 5 volumes. New Haven: Yale University Press.

Pendleton, J. M. 1878. *Christian Doctrines: A Compendium of Theology.* Philadelphia: American Baptist Publication Society.

Pendleton, J. M. 1884. *Brief Notes on the New Testament.* Philadelphia: American Baptist Publication Society.

Penny, Nicholas. 2010. "Raphael." *Grove Art Online. Oxford Art Online.* Oxford University Press. Accessed from http://www.oxfordartonline.com/subscriber/article/grove/art/T070770

Perry, John. 2010. "Gentiles and Homosexuals: A Brief History of an Analogy." *Journal of Religious Ethics* 38: 321–47.

Pervo, Richard I. 2006. *Dating Acts: Between the Evangelists and the Apologists.* Sonoma, CA: Polebridge.

Pervo, Richard I. 2009. *Acts: A Commentary.* Hermeneia: A Critical and Historical Commentary on the Bible. Edited by Harold W. Attridge. Minneapolis: Fortress.

Pinnock, Clark H. 1980. *Reason Enough: A Case for the Christian Faith*. Downers Grove, IL: InterVarsity Press.

Pinnock, Clark H. 1984. *The Scripture Principle*. San Francisco: Harper and Row.

Pinnock, Clark H. 1996. *Flame of Love: A Theology of the Holy Spirit*. Downers Grove, IL: InterVarsity Press.

Plesters, Joyce. 1990. "Raphael's Cartoons for the Vatican Tapestries: A Brief Report on the Materials, Technique and Condition." Pages 111–24 in *The Princeton Raphael Symposium*. Edited by John Shearman and Maria B. Hall. Princeton: Princeton University Press.

Polhill, John B. 1992. *Acts*. The New American Commentary 26. Nashville: Broadman.

Polycarp. 2003. "Epistle to the Philippians." Pages 332–56 in *The Apostolic Fathers, Volume I: I Clement. II Clement. Ignatius. Polycarp. Didache*. Edited and translated by Bart D. Ehrman. Loeb Classical Library 24. Cambridge, MA: Harvard University Press.

Pope John Paul II. 1982. "Pentecost Homily, 3 June 1979." In Volume 1 of *The Common Christian Roots of the Nations of Europe: An International Colloquium at the Vatican*. 2 volumes. Edited by Virgilio Levi Rome: Pontifical Lateran University.

Powell, Vavasor. 1649. *Christ Exalted Above all Creatures*. Early English Books Online.

Powell, Vavasor. 1650. *Christ and Moses*. Early English Books Online.

Powell, Vavasor. 1677. *Divine Love: or The Willingness of Jesus Christ to Save Sinners*. Early English Books Online.

Prudentius. 1949. *Preface. Daily Round. Divinity of Christ. Origin of Sin. Fight for Mansoul. Against Symmachus 1*. Translated by H. J. Thomson. LCL 387. Cambridge, MA: Harvard University Press.

Quinn, Jerome D. 1978. Pages 76–98 in *Perspectives on Luke-Acts*. Edited by Charles H. Talbert. Danville, VA: National Association of Baptist Professors of Religion.

Quintilian. 2002. *The Orator's Education, Volume III: Books 6–8*. Edited and translated by Donald A. Russell. LCL 126. Cambridge, MA: Harvard University Press.

Rahner, Hugo. 1992. *Church and State in Early Christianity*. Translated by Leo Donald Davis. San Francisco: Ignatius Press.

Ramsay, William. 1897. *St. Paul the Traveler and the Roman Citizen*. 3rd ed. London: Hodder and Stoughton.

Ramsay, William M. 1915. *The Bearing of Recent Discovery on the Trustworthiness of the New Testament*. 2nd ed. London: Hodder and Stoughton.

Rauschenbusch, Walter. 1907. *Christianity and the Social Crisis*. New York: Macmillan.

Ray, Roger. 1982. "What do We Know about Bede's Commentaries?" *Recherches de théologie ancienne et médiévale* 49: 5–20.

Reimer, Ivoni Richter. 1995. *Women in the Acts of the Apostles: A Feminist Liberation Perspective*. Minneapolis: Fortress.

Richards, John C. 2001. "Giotto di Bondone." *The Oxford Companion to Western Art*. Edited by Hugh Brigstocke. *Oxford Art Online*. Accessed from http://www.oxfordartonline.com/subscriber/article/opr/t118/e1049

Richardson, Samuel. 1645. *Some Brief Considerations on Doctor Featley his Book, entitled the Dipper Dipt*. Early English Books Online.

Richardson, Samuel. 1646. *Certain Questions Propounded to the Assembly*. Early English Books Online.

Richardson, Samuel. 1648. *An Answer to the London Ministers*. Early English Books Online.

Riches, John. 2014. "Reception Exegesis of Lamentations: A Review Article." *The Expository Times* 125: 383–87.

Richmann, Christopher J. 2014. "Living in Bible Times: F. F. Bosworth and the Pentecostal Pursuit of the Supernatural." PhD dissertation, Baylor University.

Riddle, Donald W. 1929. "The Rockefeller-McCormick Manuscript." *Journal of Biblical Literature* 48: 248–56.

Robbins, Vernon. 1991. "The Social Location of the Implied Author of Acts." Pages 305–332 in *The Social World of Luke-Acts*. Edited by Jerome Neyrey. Peabody, MA: Hendrickson.

Roberts, Alexander, James Donaldson, and A. Cleveland Coxe, eds. 1886. "The Gospel of Nicodemus." *Fathers of the Third and Fourth Centuries: The Twelve Patriarchs, Excerpts and Epistles, The Clementina, Apocrypha, Decretals, Memoirs of Edessa and Syriac Documents, Remains of the First Ages*. Translated by Alexander Walker. ANF 8. Buffalo, NY: Christian Literature Company. Reprint: Peabody, MA: Hendrickson, 1994.

Roberts, Alexander, James Donaldson, and A. Cleveland Coxe, eds. 1886. "The Gospel of Pseudo-Matthew." *Fathers of the Third and Fourth Centuries: The Twelve Patriarchs, Excerpts and Epistles, The Clementina, Apocrypha, Decretals, Memoirs of Edessa and Syriac Documents, Remains of the First Ages*. Translated by Alexander Walker. ANF 8. Buffalo, NY: Christian Literature Company. Reprint: Peabody, MA: Hendrickson, 1994.

Roberts, Alexander, James Donaldson, and A. Cleveland Coxe, eds. 1886. "The Gospel of the Nativity of Mary." *Fathers of the Third and Fourth Centuries: The Twelve Patriarchs, Excerpts and Epistles, The Clementina, Apocrypha, Decretals, Memoirs of Edessa and Syriac Documents, Remains of the First Ages*. Translated by Alexander Walker. ANF 8. Buffalo, NY: Christian Literature Company. Reprint: Peabody, MA: Hendrickson, 1994.

Roberts, Perri Lee. 1993. *Masolino da Panicale*. Oxford: Clarendon Press.

Robertson, A. T. 1930. *Word Pictures in the New Testament*. Volume 3: *The Acts of the Apostles*. New York: Harper & Brothers.

Robertson, Jesse E. 2012. *The Death of Judas: The Characterization of Judas Iscariot in Three Early Christian Accounts of his Death*. New Testament Monographs 33. Sheffield: Sheffield Phoenix Press.

Robinson, Bernard. 1994. "The Venerable Bede as Exegete." *Downside Review* 112: 201–26.

Robinson, H. Wheeler. 1942. *Redemption and Revelation in the Actuality of History*. New York: Harper.

Robinson, John A. T. 1956. "The Most Primitive Christology of All?" *Journal of Theological Studies* 7: 177–89.

Robinson, John A. T. 1963. *Honest to God*. Philadelphia: Westminster.

Robson, Janet. 2004. "Judas and the Franciscans: Perfidy Pictured in Lorenzetti's Passion Cycle at Assisi." *The Art Bulletin* 86: 31–57.

Rogers, James Richard, Barton Warren Stone, and William Rogers. 1910. *The Cane Ridge Meeting-House*. 2nd ed. Cincinnati: Standard Publishing Co.

Roper, William. 1909–14. *The Life of Sir Thomas More*. The Harvard Classics 36, Part 2. New York: P. F. Collier & Son.

Ruis-Camps, Josep, and Jenny Read-Heimerdinger. 2004–2009. *The Message of Acts in Codex Bezae: A Comparison with the Alexandrian Tradition*. 4 volumes. London: T&T Clark.

Safarik, Eduard A. 1990. *Fetti*. Milan: Electa.

Salmazo, Alberta De Nicolò, Anna Maria Spiazzi, and Domenico Toniolo, eds. 2006. *Andrea Mantegna e i maestri della Cappella Ovetari: la ricomposizione virtuale e il restauro*. Milan: Skira.

Saxl, Fritz. 1957. *Lectures*. 2 volumes. London: Warberg Institute, University of London.

SBC-Lifeway. 1989. *Native American Bible Studies/Materials (Bridging Cultural Gaps)*. Accessed from http://www.churchplantingvillage.net/site/c.joJMITOxEpH/ b.4667505/k.5D7B/Reaching_Native_People.htm

Schaberg, Jane. 1998. "Luke." Pages 363–80 in *Women's Bible Commentary*. 2nd edition. Edited by Carol A. Newsom and Sharon H. Ringe. Louisville: Westminster John Knox.

Schiller, Gertrud. 1971–72. *Iconography of Christian Art*. 2 volumes. London: Lund Humphries.

Schuckman, Christiaan. 2012. "Vos, Marten de." *Grove Art Online. Oxford Art Online*. Oxford University Press. Accessed from http://www.oxfordartonline.com/ subscriber/article/grove/art/T090181

Segal, Alan. 1986. *Rebecca's Children: Judaism and Christianity in the Roman World*. Cambridge, MA: Harvard University Press.

Shafer, Byron Esely, and United Presbyterian Church in the USA. 1978. *The Church and Homosexuality*. New York: Office of the General Assembly.

Shauf, Scott. 2005. *Theology as History, History as Theology*. Berlin: de Gruyter.

Shearman, John K. G. 1972. *Raphael's Cartoons in the Collection of Her Majesty the Queen, and the Tapestries for the Sistine Chapel*. London: Phaidon.

Shearman, John. 1992. *Only Connect ... Art and the Spectator in the Italian Renaissance*. Princeton: Princeton University Press.

Shelton, Kathleen J. 1986. "Roman Aristocrats, Christian Commissions: The Carrand Diptych." *Jahrbuch für Antike und Christentum* 29: 166–80.

Sherwin-White, A. N. 1963. *Roman Society and Roman Law in the New Testament*. Oxford: Clarendon Press.

Shumway, Charles. 1914. "A Study of 'The Gift of Tongues.'" A.B. thesis, University of Southern California.

Shumway, Charles. 1919. "A Critical History of Glossalalia." Ph.D. dissertation, Boston University.

Siker, Jeffrey S. 1991. *Disinheriting the Jews: Abraham in Early Christian Controversy*. Louisville: Westminster John Knox.

Siker, Jeffrey S. 1994. "How to Decide? Homosexual Christians, the Bible, and Gentile Inclusion as a Model for Contemporary Debate over Gays and Lesbians." *Theology Today* 51: 219–34.

"Site officiel du musée du Louvre." Accessed from http://cartelfr.louvre.fr/cartelfr/ visite?srv=car_not_frame&idNotice=8174

Smith, T. C. 1970. "Acts." Pages 1–152 in *The Broadman Bible Commentary*, Volume 10: *Acts–1 Corinthians*. Edited by Clifton J. Allen. Nashville: Broadman.

Smyth, John. 1607. *Principles and Inferences*. The Baptist Library Online.

Smyth, John. 1608. *The Differences of the Churches of the Separation*. The Baptist Library Online.

Smyth, John. 1609. *The Character of the Beast*. The Baptist Library Online.

Socrates Scholasticus. 1890. "The Ecclesiastical History." Translated by A. C. Zenos. In *Socrates, Sozomenus: Church Histories*. Edited by Philip Schaff and Henry Wace. NPNF 2. Second series. New York: Christian Literature Company.

Spangenberg, Johann. 1545. *Der Apostel Geschichte: Kurtze auslegung Fur die jungen Christen inn Frage verfasset*. Wittenberg: Georg Rhau.

Spencer, F. Scott. 1997. *Acts*. Sheffield: Sheffield Academic Press.

Spencer, F. Scott. 2004. *Journeying Through Acts*. Peabody: Hendrickson.

Spike, John T. 1997. *Fra Angelico*. New York: Abbeville Press.

Sprinson de Jesús, Mary. 2003. "Nicolas Poussin (1594–1665)." In *Heilbrunn Timeline of Art History*. New York: The Metropolitan Museum of Art, 2000–. Accessed from http://www.metmuseum.org/toah/hd/pous/hd_pous.htm (October 2003).

Spurgeon, C. H. 1855. "Paul's First Prayer." Pages 117–24 in Volume 1 of *The New Park Street Pulpit*. 6 volumes. Pasadena, TX: Pilgrim Publications, 1975.

Spurgeon, C. H. 1858. "Paul's Sermon Before Felix." Pages 49–56 in Volume 4 of *The New Park Street Pulpit*. 6 volumes. Pasadena, TX: Pilgrim Publications, 1975.

Spurgeon, C. H. 1858. "The Cry of the Heathen." Pages 193–200 in Volume 4 of *The New Park Street Pulpit*. 6 volumes. Pasadena, TX: Pilgrim Publications, 1975.

Spurgeon, C. H. 1858. "The World Turned Upside Down." Pages 225–32 in Volume 4 of *The New Park Street Pulpit*. 6 volumes. Pasadena, TX: Pilgrim Publications, 1975.

Spurgeon, C. H. 1858. "The Conversion of Saul of Tarsus." Pages 297–304 in Volume 4 of *The New Park Street Pulpit*. 6 volumes. Pasadena, TX: Pilgrim Publications, 1975.

Spurgeon, C. H. 1863. "The Minister's Stock-Taking." Pages 349–60 in Volume 9 of *The Metropolitan Tabernacle Pulpit*. Pasadena, TX: Pilgrim Publications, 1970.

Spurgeon, C. H. 1867. "Grace—The One Way of Salvation." Pages 445–455 in Volume 13 of *The Metropolitan Tabernacle Pulpit*. Pasadena, TX: Pilgrim Publications, 1970.

Spurgeon, C. H. 1869. "To Those Who are 'Almost Persuaded.'" Pages 277–88 in Volume 15 of *The Metropolitan Tabernacle Pulpit*. Pasadena, TX: Pilgrim Publications, 1970.

Spurgeon, C. H. 1916. "The Powerful Truth of God." Pages 301–312 in Volume 62 of *The Metropolitan Tabernacle Pulpit*. Pasadena, TX: Pilgrim Publications, 1980.

Stagg, Frank. 1955. *The Book of Acts: The Struggle for an Unhindered Gospel*. Nashville: Broadman Press.

Staley, Jeffrey L. 2004. "Changing Woman: Toward a Postcolonial Postfeminist Interpretation of Acts 16.6–40." Pages 177–92 in *A Feminist Companion to the Acts of the Apostles*. Edited by Amy-Jill Levine with Marianne Blickenstaff. Feminist Companion to the New Testament and Early Christian Writings 9. London and New York: T&T Clark.

Stayer, James M. 1976. *Anabaptists and the Sword*. 2nd edition. Lawrence, KS: Coronado Press.

Steinmetz, David. 1986. "The Superiority of Pre-critical Exegesis." Pages 65–77 in *A Guide to Contemporary Hermeneutics*. Edited by Donald K. McKim. Grand Rapids: Eerdmans.

Stendahl, Krister. 1962. "Biblical Theology, Contemporary." Pages 418–32 in *The Interpreter's Dictionary of the Bible*, vol. 1. Edited by George Arthur Buttrick et al. New York: Abingdon.

Stendahl, Krister. 1963. "The Apostle Paul and the Introspective Conscience of the West." *Harvard Theological Review* 56: 199–215.

"St. John's Bible." http://saintjohnsbible.org/people/hart.htm

Stone, David M. 1991. *Guercino Catalogo Complete*. Firenze: Cantini.

Stoops, Robert F., and Dennis R. MacDonald, eds. 1997. "The Apocryphal Acts of the Apostles in Intertextual Perspectives." *Semeia* 80.

Strabo. 1924. *Geography, Volume III: Books 6–7*. Translated by Horace Leonard Jones. LCL 182. Cambridge, MA: Harvard University Press.

Strange, William. 1992. *The Problem of the Text of Acts*. Cambridge: Cambridge University Press.

Strauss, D. F. 1835. *The Life of Jesus Critically Examined*. Tübingen: C. F. Osiander.

Strobel, Anna Maria de. 2007. "Raphael's Rooms." *Vatican Museums*. Accessed from http://mv.vatican.va/3_EN/pages/x-Pano/SDR/Visit_SDR_Main.html

Stuehrenberg, Paul F. 1987. "The Study of Acts Before the Reformation: A Bibliographic Introduction." *Novum Testamentum* 29: 100–131.

Stuehrenberg, Paul E. 1989. "The 'God-fearers' in Martin Luther's Translation of Acts." *Sixteenth Century Journal* 20: 407–415.

Sutton, Katherine. 1663. *A Christian Woman's Experiences of the Glorious Working of Gods Free Grace*. Rotterdam: Henry Goddaeus.

Talbert, Charles H. 1974. *Literary Patterns, Theological Themes, and the Genre of Luke-Acts*. Society of Biblical Literature Monograph Series 20. Missoula, MT: Scholars Press.

Talbert, Charles H. 1997. *Reading Acts: A Literary and Theological Commentary on the Acts of the Apostles*. New York: Crossroad.

Taylor, Dan. 1792. *A Compendious View of Nature and Importance of Christian Baptism, for the use of plain Christians*. 3rd ed. Eighteenth Century Collection Online.

Taylor, G. F. 1907. *The Spirit and the Bride: A Scriptural Presentation of the Operations, Manifestations, Gifts and Fruit of The Holy Spirit in his Relation to the Bride with Special Reference to the "Latter Rain" Revival*. Falcon, NC: Falcon Publishing Company.

Tertullian. 1885. *Latin Christianity: Its Founder, Tertullian*. Edited by Alexander Roberts, James Donaldson, and A. Cleveland Coxe. ANF 3. Buffalo, NY: Christian Literature Company, 1885. Reprint: Peabody, MA: Hendrickson, 1994.

Tertullian. 1885. *Fathers of the Third Century: Tertullian, Part Fourth; Minucius Felix; Commodian; Origen, Parts First and Second*. ANF 4. Buffalo, NY: Christian Literature Company. Reprint: Peabody, MA: Hendrickson, 1994.

Tiede, David. 1980. *Promise and History in Luke-Acts*. Philadelphia: Fortress.

Tierney, Brian. 1964. *The Crisis of Church and State, 1050–1300, with Selected Documents*. Toronto: University of Toronto Press.

The Book of Common Prayer. 1844. Pages 9–158 in *The Two Liturgies, AD 1549 and AD 1552*. Edited by Joseph Ketley. Cambridge: Cambridge University Press.

"The Saint John's Bible." 2015. Accessed from http://www.saintjohnsbible.org

Thompson, James. 1992. "Nicolas Poussin." *The Metropolitan Museum of Art Bulletin* 50: 1, 3–56.

Townsend, John T. 1985. "Missionary Journeys in Acts and European Missionary Societies." Pages 433–37 in *SBL Seminar Papers 1985*. SBLSP 24. Atlanta: Scholars Press. Published also as John T. Townsend. 1986. "Missionary Journeys in Acts and European Missionary Societies." *Anglican Theological Review* 68: 99–104.

Trollope, Anothony. 1857. *Barchester Towers*. London: Longman, Brown, Green, Longmans, & Roberts.

Truman, Harry. 1947. "Proclamation 2756 – Thanksgiving Day, 1947." *The American Presidency Project*. Accessed from http://www.presidency.ucsb.edu

Turner, S. J., and Philip Conisbee. "Restout." *Grove Art Online. Oxford Art Online*. Oxford University Press. Accessed from http://www.oxfordartonline.com/subscriber/article/grove/art/T071600

van Unnik, W. C. 1980. "Luke-Acts, a Storm Center in Contemporary Scholarship." Pages 15–32 in *Studies in Luke-Acts*. Edited by L. E. Keck and J. L. Martyn. Philadelphia: Fortress.

Venchi, Innocenzo. 2001. "Il Messaggio teologico della Cappella Niccolina." Pages 63–76 in *Il Beato Angelio e la Cappella Niccolina*. Edited by Francesco Buranelli. Rome: Musei Vaticani and Istituto Geografico de Agostini.

Verdi, Richard. 1995. *Nicolas Poussin 1594–1665*. London: Royal Academy of the Arts.

Vielhauer, Peter. 1980. "On the Paulinism of Acts." Pages 33–50 in *Studies in Luke-Acts*. Edited by L. E. Keck and J. L. Martyn. Philadelphia: Fortress.

von Harnack, Adolf. 1909. *Luke the Physician*. Translated by J. R. Wilkinson. New York: G. P. Putnam.

Wacker, Grant. 2001. *Heaven Below: Early Pentecostals and American Culture*. Cambridge, MA: Harvard University Press.

Wallace, Daniel B. 1996. *Greek Grammar Beyond the Basics: An Exegetical Syntax of the New Testament*. Grand Rapids: Zondervan.

Walton, Steve. 2008. "Primitive Communism in Acts? Does Acts Present the Community of Goods (2:44–45; 4:32–35) as Mistaken?" *The Evangelical Quarterly* 80: 99–111.

Wangerin, Walter. 2001. *Paul: A Novel*. Grand Rapids, MI: Eerdmans.

Warfield, B. B. 1972. "The Cessation of the Charismata." Pages 1–31 in *Counterfeit Miracles*. New York: Charles Scribner's Sons. Reprint Edinburgh and Carlisle, PA: Banner of Truth Trust.

Warren, Rick. 1995. *Purpose Driven Church: Growth without Compromising your Message and Mission*. Grand Rapids: Zondervan.

Warren, Rick. 2002. *The Purpose-Driven Life: What on Earth am I Here for?* Grand Rapids: Zondervan.

Wedderburn, A. J. M. 1981. "Keeping up with Recent Studies, Pt 8: Some Recent Pauline Chronologies." *Expository Times* 92: 103–108.3.

Wesley, John. 1744. "Scriptural Christianity." Accessed from http://www.umcmission.org/Find-Resources/John-Wesley-Sermons/Sermon-4-Scriptural-Christianity#sthash.kTrTOe7H.dpuf

Wesley, John. 1765. "John Wesley's Explanatory Notes on the Whole Bible." Accessed from Christian Classics Ethereal Library (www.ccel.org).

Westcott, B. F., and F. J. A. Hort. 1882. *The New Testament in the Original Greek*. New York: Harper and Brothers.

White, John, and John Shearman. 1958. "Raphael's Tapestries and Their Cartoons." *The Art Bulletin* 40: 193–221, 229–323.

Whitlark, Jason A., Bruce W. Longenecker, Lidija Novakovic, and Mikeal C. Parsons, eds. 2014. *Interpretation and the Claims of the Text: Resourcing New Testament Theology: Essays in Honor of Charles H. Talbert*. Waco, TX: Baylor University Press.

Williams, A. D. n.d. *The Lord's Supper: The Communion of Saints; Not the Communion of Sect.* The Baptist Library Online.

Williams, George Hunston. 1993. "Christology and Church-State Relations in the Fourth Century." Pages 273–328 in *Church and State in the Early Church.* Edited by Everett Ferguson. New York: Garland.

Willoughby, Harold R. 1933. "Codex 2400 and its Miniatures." *The Art Bulletin* 15: 3–74.

Witherington, Ben, III. 1998. *The Acts of the Apostles: A Socio-Rhetorical Commentary.* Grand Rapids: Eerdmans; Carlisle, UK: Paternoster.

Wilson, Stephen G. 1979. *Luke and the Pastoral Epistles.* London: SPCK.

Wood, Ralph C. 2012. "The Lady with the Torn Hair Who Looks on Gladiators in Grapple: G.K. Chesterton's Marian Poems." *Christianity and Literature* 62: 29–55.

Wright, Benjamin G. 2006. "The *Letter of Aristeas* and the Reception History of the Septuagint." *Bulletin of the International Organization of Septuagint and Cognate Studies* 39: 47–67.

Wright, David H. 1973. "The Date and Arrangement of the Illustrations in the Rabbula Gospels." *Dumbarton Oaks Papers* 27: 197, 199–208.

Wright, N. T. 2003. *The Resurrection of the Son of God.* Minneapolis: Fortress.

Wright, N. T. 2008. *Surprised by Hope: Rethinking Heaven, the Resurrection, and the Mission of the Church.* New York: Harper Collins.

Writer, Clement. 1658. *To Mr. Richard Baxter at Kidderminster, an Appendix and Supplement to the foregoing Discourse, by the same Author.* Early English Books Online.

Yoakum, Finis. 1908. "Pentecostal Miracle." *The Pentecost* 1 (Dec): 14.

Yoakum, Finis. 1909. "Men of Different Nationalities Understand Each Other." *Latter Rain Evangel* (Feb): 13.

Yong, Amos. 2007. *Theology and Down Syndrome: Reimagining Disability in Late Modernity.* Waco, TX: Baylor University Press.

York Mystery Plays. http://www.reed.utoronto.ca/yorkplays/York42.html

Zwingli, Huldrych. 1905–1959. *Huldreich Zwinglis Sämtliche Werke.* 14 volumes. Corpus Reformatorum 88–101. Edited by E. Egli et al. Berlin: C. A. Schwetschke. Reprint: Zürich: Theologischer Verlag Zürich, 1983.

Author and Artist Index

Page numbers in *italics* refer to figures.

The Acts of the Apostles Through the Centuries, First Edition. Heidi J. Hornik and Mikeal C. Parsons.
© 2017 Heidi J. Hornik and Mikeal C. Parsons. Published 2017 by John Wiley & Sons, Ltd.

The Acts of the Apostles Through the Centuries, First Edition. Heidi J. Hornik and Mikeal C. Parsons.
© 2017 Heidi J. Hornik and Mikeal C. Parsons. Published 2017 by John Wiley & Sons, Ltd.

Page numbers in *italics* refer to figures.

REPENT AND
BE BAPTIZED
EVERY ONE OF
YOU
IN THE NAME OF
JESUS CHRIST

Figure 10 *Pentecost*, Donald Jackson. Copyright 2002, *The Saint John's Bible*, Order of Saint Benedict, Collegeville, Minnesota, USA. Scripture quotations are from the New Revised Standard Version of the Bible, Catholic Edition, Copyright 1993, 1989 National Council of the Churches of Christ in the United States of America. Used by permission. All rights reserved.

The Acts of the Apostles Through the Centuries, First Edition. Heidi J. Hornik and Mikeal C. Parsons.
© 2017 Heidi J. Hornik and Mikeal C. Parsons. Published 2017 by John Wiley & Sons, Ltd.

FIGURE 13   *Life in Community*, Aidan Hart in collaboration with Donald Jackson, *The Saint John's Bible*, Order of Saint Benedict, Collegeville, Minnesota, USA. Scripture quotations are from the New Revised Standard Version of the Bible, Catholic Edition, Copyright 1993, 1989 National Council of the Churches of Christ in the United States of America. Used by permission. All rights reserved.

FIGURE 31 *Life of Paul*, Aidan Hart in collaboration with Donald Jackson, *The Saint John's Bible*, Order of Saint Benedict, Collegeville, Minnesota, USA. Scripture quotations are from the New Revised Standard Version of the Bible, Catholic Edition, Copyright 1993, 1989 National Council of the Churches of Christ in the United States of America. Used by permission. All rights reserved.